Moscow and the

Italian Communist Party

Moscow and the
Italian Communist Party

From Togliatti to Berlinguer

JOAN BARTH URBAN

Cornell University Press

Ithaca and London

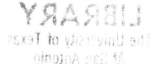

First published 1986 by Cornell University Press.

Library of Congress Cataloging-in-Publication Data

Urban, Joan Barth, 1934–
Moscow and the Italian Communist Party.

Bibliography: p.
Includes index.
1. Partito comunista italiano. 2. Kommunisticheskaia Partiia Sovetskogo Soiuza.
I. Title.
JN5657.C63U73   1986   324.245′075   85-21311
ISBN 0-8014-1832-1 (alk. paper)
ISBN 0-8014-9342-0 (pbk. : alk. paper)

Printed in the United States of America

The paper in this book is acid-free and meets the guidelines for permanence and durability of the Committee on Production Guidelines for Book Longevity of the Council on Library Resources.

To my father

CONTENTS

PREFACE

This book began to take shape in my mind in the mid-1970s when an attempted Communist takeover in Portugal was followed in short order by the emergence of Eurocommunism and a dramatic rise in the electoral strength of the Italian Communist Party. Eurocommunism, the term used to describe the entente that developed among the Italian, Spanish, and French Communist parties during 1975–77, signified a public commitment to the democratic rules of the game. Yet Eurocommunism, no less than Portuguese communism, revived Cold War fears of the expansion of Soviet influence in Europe among many Western statesmen. Henry Kissinger, for one, warned American diplomats and scholars alike that the democratic discourse of the Eurocommunists was no different from the democratic rhetoric of the East European Communists in the mid-1940s: both were ploys to conceal the intent of imposing pro-Soviet totalitarian dictatorships.

Western scholars, in contrast, were intrigued by the evident differences among the four major West European Communist parties. Whereas after the overthrow of Lisbon's decades-old authoritarian regime in 1974 the Portuguese Communists behaved like prototypical Leninists, their Spanish counterparts—who experienced a similar type of authoritarian dictatorship until the death of Francisco Franco in late 1975—were quick to embrace democratic principles and anti-Sovietism. In a parallel vein, the French Communist Party, the only one of the four to have operated in a democratic environment both before and after World War II, was quick to return to the pro-Soviet fold after a brief flirtation with Eurocommunism, defending even the Red Army's invasion of Afghanistan in 1980. But the Italian Communist Party, or PCI, pursued the defense of democracy and national independence—including that of Afghanistan—to the point of a

9

near break with Moscow as a result of the Soviet-backed imposition of martial law in Poland in December 1981.

By the early 1980s, however, the Portuguese Communist threat to Portugal's fledgling democratic institutions had long since been contained. The French Communist Party—because of its rigidity and pro-Sovietism—had been eclipsed by the Socialist Party of François Mitterrand. And the Spanish Communist Party had suffered a precipitous decline in electoral strength and internal cohesion. The PCI alone continued to defy Moscow from a position of domestic strength amounting to 30-odd percent of the Italian electorate. The sources of its conduct remained, therefore, of topical interest.

My own work on the PCI began in the mid-1960s when under the direction of the late Merle Fainsod of Harvard University I wrote my doctoral dissertation on Soviet–PCI tensions during and after the Stalinization of the Comintern. Professor Fainsod, who had himself once contemplated writing a history of the Communist International, encouraged me to pursue an approach that was at the time unorthodox. For it was commonly believed even in academe that under Stalin all Western Communist parties were but unthinking agents of Soviet *diktat,* and that Palmiro Togliatti, head of the PCI from 1927 until his death in 1964, had been a Stalinist par excellence prior to 1956. My doctoral research, based on published sources, pointed instead to the proposition that Togliatti and the PCI elite had in fact been in Stalin's disfavor in the late 1920s and again in the late 1930s. My later reading of the PCI Archives at the Gramsci Institute in Rome in 1974 confirmed those initial findings.

With the onset of the controversy over Eurocommunism in Western political and academic circles, I began to suspect that the more recent political profile of the PCI could be explained with reference to the party elite's troubled relationship with Moscow in the past. I also surmised that the very transformation of the PCI from a tiny clandestine sect during fascism into the largest nonruling Communist party in the West after World War II was likewise related to the fact that the party elite had never been fully Stalinized. Finally, I wondered if the post-1956 differences between the PCI and the French Communist Party could be traced to the divergent character of the two parties' ties with the Soviet Union during the Stalin years. This book is an outgrowth of my effort to verify these hunches.

The PCI lends itself particularly well to a study of this kind. Its archives for the pre-1945 period are largely accessible to independent scholars. Those archives, containing the correspondence of party leaders as well as stenographic accounts of many (not all) Politburo and Central Committee meetings, are an invaluable source for understanding the views of Togliatti and his closest associates during the formative years of their leadership (the second half of the 1920s, in particular). The memoirs of Togliatti's former Communist colleagues such as Ignazio Silone, Jules Humbert-Droz, and Ernst Fischer help to flesh out the portrait conveyed by official proceedings and correspondence. For the wartime years, the letters exchanged between PCI leaders based in Rome (liberated by the Allies in June 1944) and those located in German-occupied northern Italy are also a treasure trove. And they are available in published collections. The postwar years pose more problems. But after 1956 the party press became fairly open and informative. A growing number of memoirs by prominent figures (Gian Carlo Pajetta, for one) have shed light on the attitudes of the PCI leaders toward the Soviet Union since 1964, the year Togliatti died and the Brezhnev era began. Meanwhile, beginning in the late 1960s, PCI analysts started to write in a scholarly vein about the pre-1945 history of their own party, with particular attention to its ties and tensions with the Communist Party of the Soviet Union. At critical junctures, however, their interpretations differ from mine, as mentioned in footnotes throughout the first half of this book. Unlike the PCI historians, moreover, I have consulted the relevant Soviet sources whenever possible.

Because this book was years in the making, the persons who have helped me are many. Foremost among them is William E. Griffith. From the time I worked as his research assistant over two decades ago until the final writing of these pages, Bill Griffith encouraged my interest in the international Communist movement and gave his unflagging support to my efforts to interpret it.

Over the years the following friends and colleagues have also shared my thoughts and aided my understanding of the Communist world and the Italian Communist Party: John Baker, Peter Berton, Donald Blackmer, Giuseppe Boffa, Kevin Devlin, William Friend, Jerry Hough, Peter Lange, Mario Margiocco, Eusebio Mujal-León, Robert Putnam, Michael Sodaro, Angela Stent, Heinz Timmermann, and Erik Willenz. Most of them commented on one or more drafts of this book. To list their names in so perfunctory a fashion does not do justice to the gratitude I feel toward each of them.

At various stages of the manuscript's development, research assistance beyond the call of duty was provided by Brian Corbin, Daniel Sarp, and Angela Ventura. My devotion and thanks to them is unbounded. The need to retype multiple drafts was a constant burden, but one invariably made easier by the imaginative cooperation of Estrella Dizon, the administrative wizard of Catholic University's Department of Politics.

The archives of the Italian Communist Party, located at the Gramsci Institute in Rome, were indispensable to writing the first half of the book. I am grateful to the personnel of the Gramsci Institute for giving me access to the archives and to the National Endowment for the Humanities for funding a sabbatical year in Rome during which I did a large part of the archival research. A generous grant from the Ford Foundation facilitated the final completion of the book. For that grant I owe a special word of thanks to Enid Bok Schoettle.

Parts of the book have been published previously, and I thank the publishers for permission to use those materials here. An early version of chapters 1 and 2 appeared in *Studies in Comparative Communism* 6, no. 4 (1974). A small part of chapter 7 appeared in *The European Left: Italy, France, and Spain* (Lexington Books, 1979), edited by William E. Griffith. Parts of chapters 8 and 9 appeared in *Studies in Comparative Communism* 13, nos. 2/3 (1980), and 15, no. 3 (1982); *Soviet Foreign Policy in the 1980s* (Praeger, 1982), edited by Roger E. Kanet; and *Soviet Policy toward Western Europe* (University of Washington Press, 1983), edited by Herbert J. Ellison. A small part of chapter 8 also appeared in *Orbis* 18, no. 2 (1974), and 19, no. 4 (1976).

This book was made possible above all by the patience and understanding of my family. From start to finish my husband Laszlo gave the project his enthusiastic and good-natured encouragement. Our daughter Rebecca, now almost nine, learned early on to be proud that mommies do other things. My father, Harry Alvin Barth, critiqued and proofed every page of the manuscript. His intellect, wisdom, and love sustain me to this day as they have throughout my life. To him this book is dedicated with gratitude no words can express.

JOAN BARTH URBAN

Chevy Chase, Maryland

ABBREVIATIONS

CCP	Chinese Communist Party
CGIL	Italian General Confederation of Labor
CLN	Committee of National Liberation
CLNAI	Committee of National Liberation for Upper Italy
CPSU	Communist Party of the Soviet Union
DC	Christian Democracy, or Christian Democratic Party
ECCI	Executive Committee of the Communist International
FGCI	Italian Communist Youth Federation
GL	*Giustizia e Libertà*
INF	Intermediate-range nuclear forces
KIM	Communist Youth International
KOR	Workers' Defense Committee
KPD	German Communist Party
LCY	League of Communists of Yugoslavia
MFA	Armed Forces Movement
MPLA	Popular Movement for the Liberation of Angola
PCE	Spanish Communist Party
PCF	French Communist Party
PCI	Italian Communist Party
Pd'A	Party of Action
PSI	Italian Socialist Party
PSIUP	Italian Socialist Party of Proletarian Unity
SFIO	French Section of Socialist International, or French Socialist Party
SPD	German Social Democratic Party
WEB	West European Bureau (of the Communist International)
WTO	Warsaw Treaty Organization

INTRODUCTION

This book traces the relationship between the Soviet Union and the Italian Communist Party (*Partito comunista italiano,* or PCI) over six decades. It is also a political biography of the Italian Communist leadership. The PCI, like the Communist Party of the Soviet Union (CPSU), has been led over the years by oligarchies dominated by a few key personalities: Palmiro Togliatti (1927–64), Luigi Longo (1964–72), and Enrico Berlinguer (1972–84). In recent years numerous works have appeared dealing in one way or another with the political mentality of the successive Soviet leaders and oligarchies. Much less has been done in the way of analyzing the political profiles of nonruling Communist elites, perhaps because they have so often been viewed as unquestioning handmaidens of Soviet interests.

An overview of Soviet–PCI relations offers, at the same time, a slice of the history of the international Communist movement. The interaction between Moscow and the PCI, the Communist party that emerged as the largest in the West after World War II, helps to illuminate the inner workings of the movement as a whole. This aspect is particularly important in the case of the Stalin era. For conventional wisdom still holds that the leaders of nonruling Communist parties were invariably Stalinists at heart until 1956, if not later.

An investigation into any facet of international Communist history is necessarily a study in elite politics because of the Leninist precept of democratic centralism that all Communist parties adopted at their inception. Democratic centralism legitimizes, as it were, the tendencies toward oligarchical rule that characterize every political organization. This is not to say, however, that the political temperaments of Communist leaderships cannot vary dramatically. Indeed, democratic centralism may be said to reinforce, even to reify, differences in mentality.

Viewed from the broader perspective of the history of international communism, the interplay between the CPSU and the PCI provides telling evidence that the movement was never monolithic, even during the heyday of Stalinist centralization. The Comintern bureaucracy was rife with informal coalitions that spanned national party boundaries. Transnational ententes among like-minded cadres of different parties were reduced but not eliminated during the 1930s. This enabled Moscow to link changes in its Comintern line with changes in personnel. As a case in point, Togliatti became second only to Georgii Dimitrov in the Secretariat of the International precisely during the popular front era: for both men had initially opposed the intransigent sectarianism that characterized Comintern policy from 1929 through 1933.

Transnational coalition building emerged from the shadows to become a commonplace feature of the world Communist movement with the outbreak of the Sino-Soviet conflict. In this process the PCI took the lead in forging a Eurocommunist entente with the Spanish and French Communist parties. It likewise took part in an autonomist entente with the Yugoslavians and Romanians. Still, transnational coalition politics were never absent from the international Communist movement in the earlier years, just as factional politics were always present in individual Communist parties.

One of my central arguments is that the PCI leaders from Togliatti to Berlinguer posited reformist alliance policies that, while not breaking with the capitalist order, would—so they hoped—facilitate an eventual transition to socialism. This approach to socialist transformation, which I call the strategy of a democratic transitional stage, characterized PCI policy preferences even when broad alliance tactics were opposed by Moscow. And when the CPSU did favor such a line, the PCI policy makers invariably gave it a more enduring and far-reaching content than their Soviet counterparts had in mind.

The strategy of a democratic transitional stage was conditioned by the circumstances in which the Italian Communists found themselves over the years. Not only did their exposure to Mussolini's rule teach them early on that democracy had its positive side, a conclusion their Stalinist peers reached only after the rise of Hitler, but it also led them to fear that radical social change in postwar Italy might provoke a reactionary backlash. The civil wars in prewar Spain and postwar Greece reinforced this kind of anxiety. Moreover, the Spanish and Greek experiences sensitized PCI policy makers to the danger of foreign intervention on the side of domestic conservatism. These concerns, well ingrained among the PCI elite by the closing phase of World War II, intensified as the political and military presence of the United States in Italy mounted after 1947. Such fears received a shot in the arm, so to speak, from the military overthrow of

Allende's *Unidad Popular* regime in Chile in 1973. Their net effect was to induce in the PCI's postwar leaders a commitment to cautious gradualism, to evolutionary change.

In addition to their reformist approach to social change, the Italian Communist leaders throughout much of their party's history urged tolerance toward dissent in individual Communist parties and the world Communist movement at large. In the late 1920s Togliatti resisted the Stalinists' purge of the Comintern ranks until he found himself under the political gun. During the late 1940s he kept the PCI leadership intact in the face of witchhunts that wracked the other European Communist parties. Beginning in the early 1960s, the Italian party opposed Moscow's organizational maneuvers and polemics against Peking and iconoclastic nonruling Communists such as the Spaniards. The PCI's outspoken condemnation of the Soviet-led invasion of Czechoslovakia in 1968 and the Soviet-sanctioned suppression of Poland's free trade union movement in 1981 were but the most sensational cases of its "opportunism of conciliation," as Stalin had dubbed this tendency decades earlier.

As for the reasons behind the PCI elite's predilections, the greater the diversity among Communist parties, whether during the Stalin or post-Stalin eras, the wider the leeway for PCI policies tailored to Italian conditions. The greater the degree of actual pluralism in the Soviet bloc, the more plausible the PCI's program of socialist pluralism to Italian voters. Calculations of this type, as well as the point at which such *Realpolitik* merges with ideological conviction, are subjects this book also seeks to illuminate.

A final subject I discuss concerns Soviet perspectives on the Communist movement in the developed capitalist world. It is by now a commonplace among Western observers that the CPSU, at least since Stalin's time, has accorded higher priority to Western Communist support for the state interests and revolutionary credentials of the Soviet Union than to local Communist militancy. What remains controversial is the Soviet attitude toward an influential and innovative party such as the PCI. Concretely, would the CPSU oligarchs like to see the PCI win a share of the power in the national government of Italy? Or would they prefer it to be weaker, less legitimate at home, but more intransigently oppositionist? The course of Soviet–PCI relations since the 1970s suggests that the men in the Kremlin see the latter alternative as more advantageous to Soviet *raison d'état*.

At this point, several caveats are in order. The PCI's recent Eurocommunist profile aside, during Stalin's bouts of ultrasectarianism—his historic leftward shifts of 1929 and 1947, not to mention the Great Purge of the late 1930s—the Italian Communist leaders conformed, however reluctantly, to Soviet directives. Their capitulation during the interwar era can be explained in part by their dependence on Moscow, a situation created by their weakness and clandestinity. All the same, their voluntary submission to Stalinist extremism (they had, after all, little reason to fear the Soviet police in their Parisian havens) exposed the limits of their commitment to democratic alliance building and conciliation. Togliatti and his associates were prepared to turn their backs on their preferences in order to avoid being ousted from the PCI leadership. To be sure, their compliance to Stalinist *diktat* after World War II was less than complete. While parroting Moscow's anti-Americanism and extolling Soviet foreign policy, they clung to the strategy of a democratic transitional stage at home and shunned recourse to purges within their own ranks. But when all is said and done, they remained ardent Communists even when that meant working within a movement brutalized by Stalin.

It was only in the post-Stalin era, for reasons I discuss at length in Part Three of this book, that Togliatti and his successors began regularly to resist the imposition of CPSU norms on themselves and other parties. The challenge they mounted at that time to Soviet centralism was, moreover, simply the other side of the coin of their search for a *via italiana,* or Italian path, to socialism. This twofold process ultimately led Longo and Berlinguer to join the radical innovators within the broader European Communist movement (the proponents of the Prague Spring and Eurocommunism). Meanwhile, their Soviet comrades turned out to be unreconstructed sectarians during the long Brezhnev era. Whereas flexibility and innovation became the hallmarks of the PCI elite, intransigence and orthodoxy prevailed in the CPSU—with regard both to revolutionary change in the West and socialism in the Communist world.

I should explain what I mean by the terms "sectarian" and "innovator" inasmuch as they frequently appear in the pages that follow. A given Communist leadership is often labeled moderate or sectarian according to whether it displays flexibility or intransigence in its choice of political strategy. A preference for broad alliance policies (popular fronts, or cooperation with center-left forces) is normally associated with a moderate or innovative profile. An inclination toward narrow alliance policies (united fronts from below, or hostility toward centrists and even socialist elites) is viewed as the mark of intransigent sectarianism. A major drawback to this typology, however, is that it allows little room for politically expedient shifts from broad to narrow alliance policies and back, shifts normally associated with the classical Leninist temperament but not uncommon even among PCI leaders of recent vintage. Here one need only mention Berlinguer's rejection of the *compromesso storico* (historic compromise) in favor of a "left alternative" in the early 1980s.

I find it more fruitful to classify Communist leadership groups on the basis of their attitude toward the fundamental issue of force versus persuasion: to be more precise, their views on the use of force versus persuasion in dealing with "bourgeois" opponents. This is, after all, the issue that lies at the root of Communist divergences over strategy and tactics. For the very notion of an interclass alliance presupposes some limitations on the use of coercion or manipulation against the doctrinal class enemy.

Underlying my analysis of the Soviet–PCI relationship is thus my inclination to divide Communist leaderships into four categories of political mentality based on a force-persuasion continuum: radical sectarian, moderate sectarian, moderate innovator, and radical innovator. The relationship between a given group's political mentality and its approach to alliance policy may be briefly described as follows. The radical sectarians posit the absolute necessity of coercion against the class enemy and therefore reject interclass alliances out of hand, even for expediency's sake. They are doctrinaire and maximalist on all tactical, strategic, and programmatic questions. Amadeo Bordiga, the founder of the PCI, would fit into this group. The moderate sectarians, on the other hand, combine strategic and programmatic intransigence with tactical agility. They admit the possibility of *manipulating* leftist competitors and bourgeois centrists by means of temporary alliances and enticing slogans. But they view alliance policies above all as ploys. The French Communist Party (PCF) has traditionally had this political profile.

The moderate innovators are more flexible. They seek to convert the center left to their views through genuine cooperation, in the medium if not the longer run. For them persuasion is preferable to manipulation and force; and interclass alliances constitute the very fulcrum of revolutionary strategy. The moderate innovators' ultimate vision of socialism, however, is not all that unlike the Soviet bloc model, at least with regard to Communist preeminence. The PCI elite probably belonged to this category in the mid-1940s; the PCF has toyed with it since the mid-1970s.

More than a nuance divides this third group from the fourth, the radical innovators, who view persuasion not simply as preferable but as integral to the struggle for socialism. Their acceptance of interclass cooperation thus bridges the phases of revolutionary struggle and socialist construction. The radical innovators foresee political cooperation *and competition*—according to Western rules of the democratic game—continuing even during the building of socialism. They are actually democratic socialists. This became the predominant position of the PCI in the 1970s. One of my chief objectives in this book is to explain how such a transformation came about.

A Communist elite's political mentality shapes its organizational principles as well. Although Communist parties traditionally hail democratic centralism as their operational rule, their attitudes toward minority dissent within their own ranks vary widely. The sectarians—true to their position on the force-persuasion continuum—favor the purge of internal party dissidents, with the more radical among them urging the expulsion even of those party members who would merely tolerate opposition. The moderate innovators are more conciliatory, arguing that the use of persuasion against opponents within the party is the most effective means of achieving consensus. On this account they prefer dialogue to purge. In contrast, the radical innovators argue that dissent inside the party is not just tolerable: it is legitimate and desirable. They are pluralists in principle.

There are, however, also several caveats with regard to the use of this typology. It is, first of all, highly abstract. No Communist leadership, let alone party, is homogeneous. Approximations of all the above groups probably exist, at least as tendencies, everywhere—even within the CPSU. To classify a given Communist elite as to some degree sectarian or innovative is therefore simply to suggest that its center of political gravity is inclined in that direction. Just as there are clashes between the sectarians and innovators of different Communist parties, there are similar clashes within one and the same party. Second, when it comes to ruling party-states, a given Communist leadership may be innovative in economic policy, as in the case of Hungary, yet fairly sectarian in political matters. Finally, the sectarian-innovator spectrum coexists with a loyalist-autonomist type of cleavage among Communist parties. In the 1970s the Romanian regime took an autonomist position on the structure of the international Communist movement while remaining sectarian on all fronts at home. The PCI developed special ties with both the Hungarians and the Romanians but on different grounds in each case.

This book is organized into four major sections. Part One, "The Political Profile of the PCI Elite," focuses on the late 1920s, when Togliatti became de facto PCI leader after the Mussolini regime's arrest of Antonio Gramsci but prior to Stalin's consolidation of control over the CPSU. Here the central point is that Togliatti was innovative in his approach to PCI strategy under conditions of Fascist repression and conciliatory toward policy differences within the Third Communist International. The first characteristic got him into trouble with a sectarian youth faction in his own party, while the second aroused the ire of Stalin's watchdogs in the Comintern. The latter soon accused the PCI leadership of opportunism and almost hounded Togliatti out of the Communist movement.

Part Two, "The Claims of Iron Discipline, the Crucible of Anti-Fascism," covers the years from late 1929 through early 1944. With the PCI reduced to a clandestine sect in Italy and suspected of deviationism by the Stalinists, Togliatti acquiesced to the ultrasectarian line Moscow imposed in 1929 and withdrew from an active role in Comintern affairs. He re-emerged as a major figure in the Communist International only during the popular front era (probably because of his party's firsthand experience with fascism). The position Togliatti then acquired as a secretary of the Comintern Executive Committee was of cardinal importance for his later prestige in both the European Communist movement and the postwar PCI. Yet it did not suffice to prevent the Italian Politburo (based in Paris at the time) from being once again charged with deviationism by Stalin's emissaries in 1938–39. All the same, during the wartime years, while Togliatti and a number of other PCI leaders were in exile in the Soviet Union or the Americas, Communist militants re-created a center of operations in Italy. And despite their party's browbeating by Moscow on the eve of World War II, they soon joined in a far-reaching organizational alliance with other Italian Resistance groups against the Nazi occupation of Italy—a sharp departure from the Comintern's wartime directives to West European Communist parties.

Part Three, "The *Partito Nuovo* in the Postwar Era," spans an even longer period than Part Two. It begins with Togliatti's return to Italy and his party's entry into the post-Fascist Italian government in the spring of 1944; and it concludes with the PCI's active role in forging an autonomist/Eurocommunist coalition in the pan-European Communist movement in the 1970s. It concentrates on two major themes. The first has to do with the postwar transformation of the PCI into an open mass party of almost two million members and its adoption of a public philosophy of pro-Sovietism and anti-Americanism during the Cold War. It was this public philosophy that thwarted Togliatti's post-Stalin implementation of his famous notion of polycentrism, his conception of a new type of autonomous relationship among Communist parties and a new style of cooperation between Communists and other socialist forces. The second theme deals with the efforts of Togliatti's successors, Longo and Berlinguer, to bring the ideas associated with polycentrism to fruition in the Communist world during the 1960s and early 1970s. They thus found an outlet for activism and innovation precisely during the period of the *centro-sinistra*, the center-left governing formula in Italy that for years narrowed the PCI's domestic space to maneuver.

Part Four, "The Soviet–PCI Rift," deals with the sharp deterioration of Soviet–PCI relations that began in the mid-1970s, when Italian Communist publicists started criticizing the Soviet system of socialism with a fair degree of regularity, and reached a crescendo in the early 1980s when Berlinguer challenged the CPSU's revolutionary credentials across the board. This open rift developed by fits and starts at first, partly because of power political calculations on both sides. The Soviets were concerned with projecting a facade of pan-European Communist unity for the sake of domestic legitimacy and international prestige. The PCI leaders were concerned with preserving a modicum of internal party unity in the face of rank-and-file discontent over their parliamentary support for a Christian Democratic government (the practical crux of the *compromesso storico*). But with the PCI's return to the opposition at home in early 1979 and the Red Army's march into Afghanistan late that same year, Soviet–PCI recriminations rapidly escalated. And CPSU support for martial law in Poland in December 1981 led to a polemical firestorm whose intensity recalled the salad days of the Sino-Soviet conflict. What this "rip" (*strappo*) in interparty relations meant in a nutshell was that the Italian Communists thenceforth sought disengagement from, not autonomy within, the Moscow-centered Communist movement. Despite a return to more muted polemics in mid-1982 and the maintenance of some formal contacts between the two parties, such remained the state of Soviet–PCI relations at the time of Berlinguer's sudden death in June 1984.

A final point about the organization of the book concerns my decision to begin the story of the PCI with the rise of Togliatti rather than Antonio Gramsci. Since the late 1950s the PCI has hailed Gramsci as its most celebrated theorist and founder. Actually, however, Gramsci replaced the party's first leader, Amadeo Bordiga, only in 1923–24 and then at the bidding of the Comintern. Moreover, soon after Gramsci's imprisonment by Mussolini's police in late 1926, he became suspect in the eyes of the Stalinists; and as the PCI conformed to the Comintern's extremism after 1928, Gramsci's policy recommendations and theoretical works were gradually downplayed by party publicists. In other words, his prominence in the post-Stalin era was the result of conscious choice by the Togliatti leadership rather than the outgrowth of Gramsci's uninterrupted intellectual influence among PCI cadres and rank-and-file members. To be sure, that choice reflected political affinity. It was nevertheless Togliatti rather than Gramsci who shaped PCI policy for well over three decades.

One last remark may be useful for the reader before turning to the body of the book. The first two chapters focus on the rather brief timespan of 1926–29 and thus include an abundance of historical detail. It should be kept in mind, however, that the Italian actors in the Soviet–PCI clashes of those years, men who were then only in their twenties and thirties, survived to create the 2-million-member postwar PCI, Togliatti's celebrated *partito nuovo*, less than two decades later. Their youthful experience with the rising Stalinists left an indelible imprint on their mature political mentality, one that influenced the very character of the postwar *partito nuovo*. For this reason the early relationship between Moscow and the Togliatti group warrants more attention than it has hitherto received.

PART ONE

THE POLITICAL PROFILE

OF THE PCI ELITE

In the mid-1920s the Italian Communist leadership backed a number of policies which Stalin and his sectarian supporters in the Third Communist International opposed and ultimately proscribed. During this period, when the struggle for power within the Kremlin hung in the balance, such divergent positions were not unusual. Over the years, however, the views expressed by the PCI in the 1920s acquired greater significance by virtue of the fact that their spokesmen remained in the Communist ranks. They were thus later able to reiterate the same ideas under more favorable circumstances.

The PCI leaders grouped around Antonio Gramsci and Palmiro Togliatti differed from the growing phalanx of Stalinists on two key points. First of all, they perceived—even if dimly—that democracy was a lesser evil than fascism. And second, they took the position that disagreements among Communists should be resolved through dialogue and compromise rather than polemics and purges.

The experience of Fascist repression, especially after the Mussolini regime outlawed the PCI along with other opposition forces in November 1926, played a central role in shaping this political profile. The contrast between clandestinity at home and the relative freedom the Italian Communists enjoyed in their Swiss and French havens gave them an awareness of the advantages of a democratic environment that was not shared by their French and German comrades. The latter could afford to spurn the virtues of Weimar Germany and the Third French Republic precisely because they operated in open societies. The PCI strategists, to be sure, spoke only indirectly of their preference for democracy over fascism, seeking to cloak it in arcane arguments justifying so-called democratic transitional slogans in the Italian context. They did not, moreover, question the basic Leninist assumption that democratic slogans, like democratic institutions, were to be used instrumentally to hasten the proletarian revolution. All the same, their possibilist attitude toward democracy reflected attentiveness to the realities of the situation in which they found themselves. This sense of realism was to become an enduring feature of the party elite's mentality, one that would make its members more susceptible than many other European Communists to the eventual assimilation of pluralist concepts.

The PCI policy makers' conciliatory approach to dissent within the Communist movement predated their clash with the ascendant Stalinists over the pros and cons of using democratic slogans to promote socialist revolution. Indeed, the Italians objected to organizational measures against Trotsky well over a year before their policy disagreements with Moscow began to develop. They likewise sought to avoid disciplinary steps in the struggle against their own sectarian faction led by Amadeo Bordiga. The educational background of Gramsci, Togliatti, and some of their closest associates (for example, Angelo Tasca, Umberto Terracini, and Ignazio Silone) surely contributed to their partiality for reasoned discussion of differing viewpoints. Many had received a high level of university training in the humanities or law. Gramsci had excelled in the former and Togliatti in the latter at the widely respected University of Turin before 1917.[1]

These cultural considerations were reinforced by political calculation, however, once Stalin moved to the left in his showdown with Nikolai Bukharin. As the confrontation in the Soviet party reverberated throughout the ranks of the Comintern, the PCI leaders became ever more outspoken proponents of restraint in handling intraparty altercations. In a word, by urging forbearance toward policy differences in other parties, they hoped to safeguard their own strategic choices.

The first chapter of this book explores the formulation in the 1920s, under Gramsci and then Togliatti, of the PCI's policy of using democratic transitional slogans and its realistic if ambivalent appraisal of the likelihood of a post-Fascist democratic stage in Italy. The second chapter treats the parallel development of the Italian leaders' conciliatory attitude toward policy conflicts in their own party and in the Comintern at large. The evolution of both these facets of the PCI's political profile was conditioned by what was going on at the time in Italy, Moscow, and the Comintern. A few introductory remarks about each are thus in order.

1.Giuseppe Fiori, *Vita di Antonio Gramsci* (Bari: Editori Laterza, 1966), 106–7; and Giorgio Bocca, *Palmiro Togliatti* (Bari: Editori Laterza, 1973), 11–17.

In the 1920s the revolutionary fervor unleashed by the Bolshevik victory of 1917 still shaped the expectations of Communist militants. For them it was an article of faith that the forcible overthrow of the citadels of capitalism and the creation of dictatorships of the proletariat throughout Europe were just around the corner. Nevertheless, the concrete pace and shape of the coming revolution in one or another country remained murky. Endless forums of the Third Communist International—congresses, periodic plenums of its Executive Committee, frequent meetings of commissions dealing with single countries—were devoted to just such questions. Policy controversies abounded as the bolshevization of the Comintern— that is, the imposition of tight organizational discipline—remained a blueprint for the future.

Moreover, individual Communist parties and the Comintern bureaucracy itself comprised shifting coalitions linked by personal loyalty or shared outlook to one or another of the contending factions in the CPSU. It was against this backdrop that the dominant group within the PCI identified first with Stalin and Bukharin against Trotsky and then, briefly, with Bukharin against Stalin prior to the latter's decisive consolidation of power in late 1928. Personal associations were unavoidably affected by these crosscurrents. For example, Togliatti, while PCI representative to Comintern headquarters during 1926, formed an enduring friendship with the erudite and moderate Swiss Communist, Jules Humbert-Droz. In contrast, his relations with the influential German supporters of Stalin, including Ernst Thälmann and Walter Ulbricht, were fraught with tension and distrust early on.

During the last years of the 1920s Stalin, for his part, treated the international Communist movement as little more than an arena for political infighting. With "socialism in one country" as his battle cry, he was unconcerned about Comintern policy except insofar as it affected his domestic struggle for power. The case of China in this regard is well known. In 1927 Stalin insisted on a united front between the Communists and the Kuomintang, preferring to endanger the very existence of the Chinese Communist Party to conceding the validity of Trotsky's arguments against that doomed policy. Following somewhat the same pattern, in 1928 he ordered European Communists to shun transitional slogans. There is no indication that Stalin cared one way or the other about transitional slogans as such. Bukharin, however, was known to be receptive to their use, whereas the reverse was true of Stalin's staunchest supporters in the Comintern, the Thälmann faction in the German Communist leadership. These German sectarians bitterly opposed transitional slogans, deeming them akin to a Trojan horse in the hands of their arch rivals, the German Social Democrats. Stalin thus undertook to champion the policy preferences of his German Communist allies, a step that was all the more expedient given the numerical strength of the German Communist Party (KPD) and its centrality in Comintern decision making.

Meanwhile, back in Italy the PCI suffered staggering setbacks after Mussolini's decision to crush all organized political opposition in late 1926. Within eighteen months the Fascist police had arrested one-third of the 7,500 Italian Communists (the approximate membership at that time); many survivors took refuge abroad, primarily in France. The entire leadership—or at least those of its members who escaped imprisonment— went into exile, shifting the party's headquarters from one city to another in Switzerland and France until 1929 when it was set up on a fairly stable basis in Paris. Most traumatic of all, by the spring of 1928 the leadership in exile lost systematic contact with its domestic base.

Because of these organizational difficulties, the Italian Communist policy makers did not have to concern themselves unduly with incomprehension or adverse reactions among their rank-and-file members as relations with Moscow deteriorated. In effect the elite *was* the PCI during this period and for a long while thereafter. On the other hand, the very weakness of the party made its leaders more vulnerable to criticism. Their position was further undermined by the fact that a sectarian challenge had emerged among the cadres of their own youth federation, giving rise to a controversy over transitional slogans within the leading circles of the PCI itself well before the onset of polemics from the Stalinists. The chief protagonists in this policy clash were Togliatti and Luigi Longo. Yet in the end conciliation prevailed over confrontation, with both men remaining in the PCI leadership for almost four more decades and Longo becoming general secretary in 1964 upon Togliatti's death.

CHAPTER 1

Fascist Rule and the Controversy
over Transitional Slogans

In the 1920s, as in the 1970s, the leadership of the PCI charted a domestic course that ran counter to the CPSU's guiding principles and provoked controversy within the ranks of the Italian party as well. Differences, to be sure, abounded between the PCI's latter-day support for a "historic compromise," that is, some form of accommodation with Italian Christian Democracy, and its advocacy five decades earlier of democratic transitional slogans. The *compromesso storico* was predicated upon acceptance of the democratic rules of the game as they had evolved since the French Revolution. And it was usually described as a kind of way station of indeterminate length between bourgeois democracy and democratic socialism. The party's call for democratic reforms during the mid-1920s was, in contrast, seen as a means of inciting a popular uprising against fascism. And that uprising was expected to lead if not directly to the proletarian revolution against capitalism, then to a democratic transitional stage of only limited duration prior to the historically ordained dictatorship of the proletariat. The two policies had, however, one important feature in common. PCI leaders considered both the democratic transitional stage and the historic compromise as opportunities for garnering mass support, for persuading the middle classes as well as the "toiling masses" of the virtues of socialism.

The PCI's advocacy of transitional democratic reforms became an issue of internal party controversy after the Mussolini regime's November 1926 ban on all opposition groups and arrest of dozens of Communist activists, including Antonio Gramsci, general secretary of the party since 1924. The two years that followed represented a critical juncture in the history of the Italian Communists. In addition to reconstituting the PCI's executive bodies in exile, the party leadership needed to devise a strategy that would take into account the growing repressiveness of Italian fascism. Palmiro Togliatti and Ruggero Grieco, the party's foremost spokesmen during this period, defended not just the advocacy of democratic goals as the revolutionary strategy most appropriate under Fascist rule, but also the possibility of a democratic transitional stage between the downfall of fascism and the coming of socialism. Luigi Longo, the leader of the Italian Communist Youth Federation (FGCI), opposed this line. According to Longo and his associates in the youth organization, support for transitional slogans was equivalent to little less than rank opportunism. In polemics that echoed the intransigence of radical sectarians such as Amadeo Bordiga, they insisted that fascism must be destroyed, not democratized—that democratic slogans could only foster "democratic illusions."

The PCI's debate over transitional slogans was merely one aspect of a more fundamental question that preoccupied all the European Communist parties during the mid-1920s: the question of revolutionary tempo. Broadly stated, would the proletarian revolution in Europe come relatively suddenly, marking a sharp and abrupt break with the capitalist order? Or would there be a more gradual approach to the final collapse of capitalism during which time the industrial workers would acquire the necessary organization for, and commitment to, a revolutionary solution? And, in the event of this more gradualist perspective, was Communist advocacy of reformist objectives (and joint action with non-Communist workers and even middle-class groups on the basis of those objectives) legitimate? Even more controversial was the question of whether the achievement of such interim democratic goals would lead to a transitional stage, concrete in form and delimited in time, between the dictatorship of the bourgeoisie and the dictatorship of the proletariat.

As the postwar revolutionary wave receded in Europe, these issues acquired increasing urgency within the international Communist movement. Among Italian Communists they gained added significance from the specific question of whether Mussolini's Fascist regime would, or could, be superseded by a democratic government rather than a socialist dictatorship. For in the Italian context a democratic regime would represent in effect a transitional stage.

The search for a feasible revolutionary strategy in Europe was also influenced by the fact that Lenin's legacy in this respect was ambiguous. On the one hand, the October Revolution had been the supreme vindication of the strategy of a direct, frontal assault on the old order executed by a minority of political activists. On the other hand, under the less favorable circumstances prevailing in Europe after World War I Lenin himself had adopted a gradualist approach to the proletarian revolution. The consensus reached at the Third Comintern Congress in 1921 was that the postwar revolutionary upsurge was subsiding. Hence the Third Congress resolution on tactics called upon the Communist parties of Europe to increase their following among the working class by supporting demands for an immediate improvement in living conditions—a directive that smacked of the very reformism the Third Communist International had been created to combat. Yet Lenin gave his blanket approval both to the resolution on tactics and to its underlying rationale of winning mass support. He put it this way in his major address to the congress: "An absolute majority is not always essential, but in order to achieve victory, in order to retain power, it is not only necessary to have the majority of the working class—I use the term 'working class' here in the West European sense, meaning the industrial proletariat—but also the majority of the exploited and toiling rural population."[1]

Lenin thus viewed the proletarian revolution from a double perspective. When there was evidence of mass radicalism, as in Russia in the autumn of 1917, he opted for an immediate Communist seizure of power. But when revolutionary ferment was on the decline, as in Europe in 1921–22, he endorsed a more gradualist policy in which piecemeal reforms became acceptable in the short run as the most expedient means of gaining popular support. This was, moreover, the view adopted by the international Communist movement. According to the resolution on tactics approved by the Fifth Comintern Congress in July 1924, shortly after Lenin's death, "two" revolutionary perspectives were possible. "A slow and prolonged development of the proletarian revolution is not to be excluded," the resolution cautioned. "On the other hand, . . . the contradictions of capitalism in general are developing so quickly that the denouement in one country or another can occur in a very short time."[2] The latter perspective, that of a rapidly approaching capitalist crisis, suggested a rather abrupt and sweeping transfer of power from the bourgeoisie to the proletariat, in line with Bolshevik practice. But the first perspective, that of "a slow and prolonged development of the proletarian revolution," conveyed the idea of a more complicated process. It called, implicitly at least, for partial as opposed to maximalist objectives if the Communist ranks were not to be reduced to passive *attentisme*. The nonruling Communist parties were thereby offered what amounted to two alternative approaches to the proletarian revolution: the strategy of frontal assault and the strategy of the transitional stage.

At the end of 1928, however, Stalin denounced the use of transitional slogans except in an "acute revolutionary situation." This move was an

---

1. V. I. Lenin, *Selected Works* (New York: International Publishers, 1934–38), 10:279–88 at 287–88.
2. *V Vsemirnyi Kongress Kommunisticheskogo Internatsionala: tezisy, rezoliutsii i postanovleniia* (Moscow, 1924), 32.

integral part of the Comintern's leftward shift in 1928–29, the essential thrust of which was to reject the strategy of the transitional stage along with temporary alliances with social democracy in favor of the single revolutionary perspective of a frontal assault on the capitalist system. This sectarian shift was prompted in large part by Stalin's struggle against his chief domestic rival and de facto Comintern head, Nikolai Bukharin, whose allies in the international Communist movement tended to support the more gradualist perspective.

At this point the Soviet factional struggle began to impinge directly upon the PCI. In the mid-1920s the Italian Communist leaders had been fairly free to chart their own policies, primarily because of their basic alignment with the Stalin-Bukharin coalition in the struggle against Leon Trotsky. By the winter of 1928–29, however, the bolshevization (read Stalinization) of the Comintern was proceeding in tandem with Stalin's ascendancy over the CPSU. No section of the Third International remained untouched as the Soviet dictator, in his single-minded drive for power, demanded the total subordination of all foreign Communists to Moscow. In the end, therefore, the PCI controversy over transitional slogans was settled not according to the merits of the issue or the political weight of the contending factions in the Italian Communist Party but on the basis of the struggle for power in the CPSU. With Stalin's victory in Moscow, the views of the PCI's youthful sectarians prevailed.

Transitional Slogans under Gramsci

The views on democratic slogans and prospects that brought the Italian Communist leaders into conflict with both the Stalinists and the PCI's youth organization were shaped by Gramsci's approach to these questions. Indeed, the debate that developed among the Italians in 1927–28 revolved around a transitional slogan he had coined in 1925. Conversely, the revolutionary strategy of Gramsci was sharply at variance with that of Bordiga, the party's founder and leader until his replacement by Gramsci in 1923–24.

Bordiga versus Gramsci

Bordiga was the architect of the schism within the Italian Socialist Party (PSI) that led to the creation of the PCI. When two-thirds of the delegates to the PSI's Congress of Livorno in January 1921 refused to accept Lenin's "21 conditions" of admission to the Comintern, the Communist faction led by Bordiga immediately formed a separate party based on the organizational rule of democratic centralism and the programmatic goals of armed revolution and proletarian dictatorship.[3] The newly created PCI joined the Third International forthwith.

However, for Bordiga—whose preeminence within the PCI was not questioned by his Italian comrades in 1921–22[4]—acceptance of Comintern discipline was conditional upon agreement with the policies of the International. And the idea of a united front with social democratic parties, first advanced by the Executive Committee of the Communist International (ECCI) in December 1921, represented in his eyes a betrayal of the founding principle of the PCI: commitment to a revolutionary ideology purged of all reformist or evolutionary illusions. In his policy proposals for the Second PCI Congress, Bordiga thus warned against any Communist cooperation with other political parties.[5] His intransigence provoked a harsh rebuke from the ECCI Presidium, the highest authority in the International.[6] Bordiga nevertheless reaffirmed his opposition to the policy of a united front when the Second PCI Congress took place in late March 1922,[7] and he refused to budge from this position even after the Fourth Comintern Congress ratified the new line the following autumn. From that time until his final defeat at the Third PCI Congress in January 1926, Bordiga did all in his power to oppose the united front.[8]

On the other hand, Gramsci, the leader of the broadly based factory council movement in Turin during the early postwar years, was more receptive to the idea of a united front. As he wrote in February 1924, he had been "in favor of the united front right up to its normal conclusion of a [coalition] workers' government" even prior to the PCI's 1922 Congress.[9] Small wonder that he was the man chosen by Moscow to implement the new line and to replace Bordiga as leader of the PCI.

As in the case of the united front, Bordiga's opposition to transitional slogans was unequivocal. In his opinion democratization of the Italian political system was highly improbable. But even if fascism should be

---

3. Cf. "*Relazione presentata dalla Frazione Comunista al Congresso di Livorno del P.S.I. (15–21 gen. 1921) sull'indirizzo politico del Partito* (Milan: Presso il C. E. Del Partito Comunista d'Italia, 1921), passim.

4. Palmiro Togliatti, *La formazione del gruppo dirigente del Partito comunista italiano* (Rome: Editori Riuniti, 1962), 19.

5. *Tesi del 2 Congresso del PCI (Tesi di Roma)* (Brussels: Les Arts Graphiques, n.d.), 26.

6. "K proektu programmy italianskoi kommunisticheskoi partii," *Kommunisticheskii Internatsional* [henceforth *KI*], no. 23 (November 4, 1922):6214–22.

7. Partito Comunista d'Italia, *Secondo Congresso Nazionale (Roma 20–24 Marzo 1922): relazione del Comitato Centrale* (Rome: Società Anonima Poligrafica Italiana, 1922), 23.

8. For details on the intraparty struggle between Bordiga and the Gramsci group, see Togliatti, *La formazione;* Paolo Spriano, *Da Bordiga a Gramsci*, vol. 1 of *Storia del Partito comunista italiano*, 5 vols. (Turin: Giulio Einaudi Editore, 1967–75); Ernesto Ragionieri's introduction to *Opere 1921–1925*, by Palmiro Togliatti (Rome: Editori Riuniti, 1969); and Giuseppe Berti, "Appunti e ricordi, 1919–1926," in *Annali Feltrinelli* 8 (Milan: Feltrinelli Editore, 1966).

9. "Gramsci a Togliatti, Terracini e C., 9 febbraio 1924," in *La formazione*, by Togliatti, 192.

replaced by some form of democracy, this would signify not a transitional stage on the path to socialism but a strengthening of the capitalist system. Attainment of the goals of the democratic left would lead *not* to an "intermediate step between the capitalist economic and political order and the proletarian one," he protested, but merely to the reinforcement of modern capitalism.[10] Hence the PCI, far from supporting transitional objectives, should strive to expose them as "democratic illusions." Bordiga's view, in short, was that the PCI should gird itself for the time when conditions would be ripe for a frontal assault on the capitalist system.

Once again in contrast to Bordiga, Gramsci conceded the possibility of a post-Fascist democratic stage in Italy and championed the advocacy of non-Communist political goals, including a constitutional assembly (*costituente*). His ideas on this subject evolved gradually, however. At first he was more intent on legitimizing the use of transitional slogans as a maneuver to avoid or cut short an actual transitional stage than on probing and elaborating their political content.

The Evolution of Gramsci's Views

The winter of 1924 offers a convenient point of departure for tracing the development of Gramsci's views on transitional slogans. In November 1923 he left Moscow, where he had represented the PCI at the Comintern since the spring of 1922, to prepare for his return to Italy and assumption of the party leadership. From Vienna he entered into an extensive correspondence with PCI leaders elsewhere in Europe.[11] In a number of these letters he suggested that the overthrow of Mussolini by an anti-Fascist coalition could lead to a transitional stage in the form of a period of active competition between the various democratic anti-Fascist parties and the Communists. "The bourgeois democratic liberals will still have a lot to say," he remarked in a letter to Togliatti and others in February 1924. "I don't doubt . . . that within a given interval of time our party will have the majority [of the working class] with it; but even if this period is not long chronologically, it will undoubtedly be packed with supplementary phases."[12] In another letter written several weeks later, he mentioned that the democratic opposition to fascism might well embrace the goal of a constitutional assembly. Thereupon Gramsci queried pointedly: "Is it possible to think that we will pass from fascism to the dictatorship of the proletariat? What intermediate phases are possible and probable? We must undertake this work of political investigation."[13] Commenting that the

10. *Tesi del 2 Congresso del PCI*, 23–24.
11. Togliatti, *La formazione*, passim.
12. Ibid., 200.
13. "Gramsci a Togliatti, Scoccimarro, Leonetti, ecc., 21 marzo 1924," in ibid., 246.

PCI had done little in this regard, he warned that the party should devise ways of winning over the masses swayed by the democratic left.

Meanwhile, in Italy's parliamentary elections of April 6, 1924, which gave the Fascists an overwhelming three-fourths of the seats in the Chamber of Deputies (374 out of 525), Gramsci was one of nineteen Communists elected. Protected from arrest by parliamentary immunity, he returned to Italy the following month to find that his expectations of renewed democratic resistance to fascism had been warranted. On June 10, 1924, Giacomo Matteotti, a Socialist deputy who had publicly denounced the Fascist electoral tactics of violence and intimidation, was assassinated by *squadristi* reportedly linked to ranking figures in Mussolini's government. In protest the deputies of the non-Fascist parties, ranging from the centrist democratic and Catholic parties to the Communists, withdrew from Parliament. Reassembling as a group in the so-called Aventine secession, they demanded the prosecution of those responsible for Matteotti's murder and the restoration of legality and civil rights. Many hoped that King Vittorio Emanuele would use his constitutional powers to dissolve Parliament and to request the resignation of Mussolini from the premiership, the position to which the king had appointed him in October 1922.[14]

Under these circumstances the task of devising transitional objectives became a practical issue. As Gramsci made clear to the PCI Central Committee in mid-August 1924, the Matteotti crisis heralded not a revolutionary situation but at best a prerevolutionary situation, a "phase of transition" to the direct struggle for proletarian power.[15] Still, Gramsci's directives during this period indicated that he was still groping for the slogans and policies capable of fusing together an interclass anti-Fascist front.[16]

Immediately after Matteotti's death the Communists attempted to persuade the other anti-Fascist parties to launch a nationwide general strike. When neither the moderate deputies not their constituencies proved responsive to such an appeal, the PCI withdrew from the deliberations of the Aventine secession. It subsequently ordered its own militants to intensify their operations in the nonpartisan shop committees still existing in the Italian factories. Yet activism in the factories raised the specter of proletarian revolution, which further divided the ranks of the anti-Fascists. Finally, in October 1924 the PCI appealed to the Aventine secessionists to proclaim themselves the legal parliament of Italy, a so-called anti-Parlia-

14. Luigi Salvatorelli and Giovanni Mira, *Storia d'Italia nel periodo fascista*, 3d ed. (Turin: Giulio Einaudi Editore, 1959), 306–21. See also Charles F. Delzell, *Mussolini's Enemies: The Italian Anti-Fascist Resistance* (Princeton: Princeton University Press, 1961), 8–19 and 26–30.

15. "I documenti d'archivio sui rapporti tra il PC d'Italia e il Comintern," *Rinascita* 19, no. 17 (September 1, 1962):17–18.

16. For a PCI account of Communist policy during this period, see Spriano, *Storia del Partito comunista italiano* 1:381–428. Paolo Spriano was elected to the PCI Central Committee in 1972.

ment opposed to the Fascist-controlled body. As anticipated by the Communists themselves, the proposal was rejected by the non-Communists for fear it might spark a civil war.[17] The PCI used this incident as a pretext for ordering its own deputies to return to Parliament, thus destroying any remaining semblance of anti-Fascist unity.

Meanwhile, on January 3, 1925, Mussolini let it be known in an impassioned speech to the Chamber of Deputies that any further opposition to his regime would be met with repression. From then on violence by the Black Shirts, police harassment, and restrictions on freedom of the press and association steadily increased until all anti-Fascist activity was outlawed in November 1926.[18]

Faced with ever tighter political constraints and negligible popular support, Gramsci and his colleagues began to think seriously about transitional objectives. The principal slogan they coined during this new phase—the slogan that was to become a central bone of contention for the next several years within the PCI and ultimately between the PCI and Moscow—was the "republican assembly on the basis of workers' and peasants' committees." The Italian party first articulated this slogan in May 1925,[19] apparently in response to growing antimonarchist sentiment among the Aventine secessionists. Infuriated by King Vittorio Emanuele's refusal to take any steps against Mussolini, the more militant anti-Fascists began to call for the eventual overthrow of the House of Savoy and the creation of a republic.[20]

There was, however, a great deal of ambiguity in the new Communist slogan. The phrase "republican assembly" conveyed the idea of a constitutional convention representing the sovereign will of the nation. Yet the slogan as a whole indicated that the delegates to such a convention would be selected by "workers' and peasants' committees." In this sense the PCI's notion of a "republican assembly" bore a marked resemblance to the All-Russian Congress of Workers' and Soldiers' Soviets that played so central a role in the October Revolution. Moreover, the "republican assembly" idea was frequently linked with the call for "workers' control of industry" and "land to the peasants," slogans Lenin had used in 1917. This only further recalled the Bolshevik pattern of revolution.[21]

17. Cf. Salvatorelli and Mira, *Storia d'Italia nel periodo fascista*, 325.

18. Delzell, *Mussolini's Enemies*, 23–51.

19. Archivio Partito Comunista, 1927, fol. 545:140. Information from the Archivio Partito Comunista will be cited henceforth as APC, with the relevant year, folio, and page numbers.

20. Delzell, *Mussolini's Enemies*, 42–43.

21. The confusion surrounding the "republican assembly" slogan is not confined to non-Communist students of PCI history. The veteran Italian Communist Giuseppe Berti, in his 1966 account of PCI developments in the 1920s, confessed that it was still unclear to him what Gramsci intended the slogan to mean; see Berti, "Appunti e ricordi, 1919–1926," *Annali Feltrinelli* 8:166. As for Paolo Spriano, in the first volume of his PCI history, he sidestepped any attempt to explain the slogan's meaning by ascribing its origin to the Comintern Presidium. In addition, he

In all probability Gramsci was being intentionally ambiguous. Even as late as the summer of 1926, in his last report to the PCI Central Committee, he spoke of the possibility, albeit remote, of a direct transition to the dictatorship of the proletariat after the collapse of Mussolini's regime. While conceding that a post-Fascist democratic coalition government was the more likely eventuality, he remarked that "we must try to make the democratic *intermezzo* as brief as possible."[22] All the same, later developments suggest that even before his arrest the idea of a "republican assembly" was probably taking the shape of a constitutional assembly in Gramsci's mind.

There is circumstantial evidence to this effect in a letter that Umberto Terracini, one of Gramsci's early associates on the Socialist weekly *Ordine Nuovo,* wrote from prison to the PCI leadership in 1930. Terracini recounted conversations with Gramsci in the spring of 1928, when they occupied the same prison cell in the Roman jail of Regina Coeli, as follows: "Not only was the democratic perspective, that is, the bourgeoisie's return to the democratic method of government, part and parcel of the common ideas of the guests of Regina Coeli, but we also spoke of the tactics which the party would have to adopt during the period between the end of the Fascist 'ministry' and the formation of a parliamentary government; not only that but we also spoke of our electoral tactics for the first democratic assembly."[23]

In 1930, according to another prison companion, Athos Lisa, Gramsci spoke openly of the need for a constitutional assembly.[24] He still referred to the Comintern's double revolutionary perspective. But under Italian conditions the perspective "most probable" was a transitional stage. Lisa recalled Gramsci saying, "it is not possible to speak of the conquest of power without passing through a period of transition, if only of relative duration." And in this context he advocated PCI support for a constitutional assembly. Such a goal, he argued, would appeal to the peasants and rural petty bourgeoisie who were not ready to accept socialism. It would also serve as the basis for a united anti-Fascist front with other opposition parties. The convening of such a body, finally, would provide a platform from which to "discredit all projects for peaceful reform, demonstrating

---

treated its use as a passing and inconsequential episode. See Spriano, *Storia del Partito comunista italiano* 1:463–65. In his second volume, Spriano touched on the slogan only insofar as it developed into a bone of contention within the PCI. See *Gli anni della clandestinità,* 104–7.

22. Antonio Gramsci, "Come si determinano le nostre prospettive e i nostri compiti," *Lo Stato operaio* [henceforth *SO*] 2, no. 3 (March 1928), in *Lo Stato operaio, 1927–1939,* ed. Franco Ferri, 2 vols. (Rome: Editori Riuniti, 1964), 1:144–53 at 151–52. Ferri's anthology will henceforth be cited as *SO 1927–1939.*

23. Quoted from the PCI Archives in Spriano, *Storia del Partito comunista italiano* 2:262–65; cf. ibid., 157.

24. Athos Lisa, *Memorie: In carcere con Gramsci* (Milan: Feltrinelli Editore, 1973), 85–90.

to the Italian laboring class how the only possible solution in Italy lies in the proletarian revolution.''

The Theses of Lyons on "Intermediate Solutions"

The ambiguity of Gramsci's thinking just prior to Mussolini's crackdown in 1926 was reflected in the political resolution he drafted for the Third PCI Congress in January of that year. The document, called the *Theses of Lyons* after the French city where the congress took place,[25] was inconsistent in major respects. Its overall tone was one of revolutionary militancy. Yet its final paragraphs were rather moderate, especially on transitional slogans.

This apparent contradiction may be explained by the fact that Gramsci himself was still in the process of edging his way toward a strategy appropriate for the PCI. And in doing so he was influenced by the mentality common to all Communists in the 1920s: the conviction that the current stability of the capitalist system was merely temporary and that the proletarian revolution was on the horizon in Europe. Then again, prior to the Third Congress Gramsci and his associates were engaged in a final showdown with Bordiga, for whom the very idea of transitional goals was abhorrent.

The theme that dominated the *Theses of Lyons* was thus the need to prepare for the proletarian revolution in Italy. As stated in one of the opening paragraphs: "There does not exist in Italy the possibility of a revolution which is not the socialist revolution."[26] This suggested that the overthrow of fascism would lead directly to the dictatorship of the proletariat.

On the other hand, the use of transitional slogans was endorsed in the closing paragraphs.[27] To be sure, they were rather awkwardly designated as "intermediate solutions of general political problems,"[28] probably in an effort not to antagonize those delegates to the Third Congress still swayed by Bordiga. Furthermore, the document cautioned that such "intermediate" goals should constitute a bridge to the party's ultimate objectives. And it directed Communists to make every effort to transform movements of a democratic nature into socialist revolutionary movements. There was, meanwhile, no concrete description of "intermediate solutions" aside from a parenthetical allusion to the PCI's 1924 call for an anti-Parliament and a

---

25. "La situazione italiana e i compiti del PCI: Tesi del Congresso di Lione," *Trenta anni di vita e lotte del PCI* (Rome: Editore Rinascita, 1952), 93–103.

26. Ibid., par. 4:94.

27. Ibid., pars. 35–44:101–3.

28. Ibid., 103.

reference in passing to the slogans of a "republican assembly" and its companion goals of land reform and workers' control.[29]

Still, the most important aspect of the *Theses of Lyons* in terms of the coming struggle between Gramsci's successors and the Comintern Stalinists was its unequivocal assertion that transitional objectives could include the goals of *democratic* parties during periods of political reaction. This was spelled out in paragraph 43: "The presentation and agitation of these intermediate solutions are the specific form of struggle which should be used against the so-called democratic parties . . . when these so-called democratic parties are connected with important and decisive strata of the laboring population . . . and *when a reactionary danger is imminent and grave.* . . . In these cases *the CP achieves the best results by agitating for the very solutions which ought to be the purview of the so-called democratic parties.*"[30] That a "reactionary danger" was "imminent and grave" during the winter of 1926 in Mussolini's Italy was beyond dispute. According to the *Theses of Lyons,* therefore, the PCI's advocacy of democratic reforms was legitimate.

The PCI Debate: Togliatti versus Longo

During 1927–28 Gramsci's quest for a viable strategy was pursued by the men who, after his arrest, formed the nucleus of the PCI leadership: Togliatti, Ruggero Grieco, Angelo Tasca, and Ignazio Silone. Togliatti—commonly known as Ercoli in those years—was considered *primus inter pares.*[31] However, his preeminence was by no means assured at that time. And on the issue of transitional slogans all four were challenged by the leaders of the party's youth federation, most notably Luigi Longo.[32]

Officially, the party continued to maintain that the proletarian revolution was, objectively speaking, the order of the day. But the leading PCI spokesmen readily acknowledged that the Italian masses were not yet in a

29. Ibid., 102–3.
30. Ibid., 103; my emphasis.
31. "Prefazione di Giorgio Amendola," in *Scritti scelti,* by Ruggero Grieco (Rome: Editori Riuniti, 1966), xli–xlii.
32. Paolo Spriano and Ernesto Ragionieri, the leading PCI historians of this period, were notably reserved in their treatment of the controversies over transitional slogans and the perspective of a "people's revolution," which will be discussed in the following pages. Spriano merely referred to these issues in passing in the second volume of his usually discursive and detailed *Storia del Partito comunista italiano,* while Ragionieri tended to relegate his coverage of the same themes to footnotes in his introduction to *Opere 1926–1929,* by Palmiro Togliatti (Rome: Editori Riuniti, 1972). Since the above volumes were written during Luigi Longo's tenure as PCI general secretary (1964–72), the authors may have felt reluctant to play up the depth of Longo's opposition to Togliatti's policies in the late 1920s. They may, in other words, have exercised a certain degree of self-censorship.

37

revolutionary mood, that they were in fact still under the sway of democratic ideology: hence the need for transitional slogans to prod them into action against the Mussolini regime. The public rationale for this strategy was that the struggle for democratic reforms would ultimately unleash a revolutionary chain reaction. In the course of combating fascism the Italian people would somehow come to see that the realization of democratic goals was impossible without the overthrow of capitalism. Exactly why this should be so was never spelled out. But more to the point, as we shall see, the PCI leaders frankly admitted in inner party councils not just the possibility but even the likelihood of a post-Fascist bourgeois democratic regime. They thus contradicted their formal pronouncements regarding an automatic linkage between democratization and socialist revolution in Italy.

The separate paths by which such individuals as Togliatti, Grieco, and Tasca arrived at this common outlook are beyond the scope of our discussion. Suffice it to say that by the time of the Third PCI Congress Togliatti shared Gramsci's approach, collaborating closely with him in drafting the *Theses of Lyons*.[33] Grieco's conversion was established beyond doubt in 1927 when he became one of the most fervent advocates of democratic transitional slogans. As for Tasca, during the deliberations of the Political Commission that organized the Third Congress, he defended the possibility of an actual coalition "workers' government," a position the Comintern had condemned as right-wing opportunism at its Fifth Congress in 1924.[34]

During 1927, however, opposition to this line emerged within the PCI's ranks. The dissenters were for the most part activists in the FGCI; hence their euphemistic designation as "the youth" (their chief spokesman, Longo, was then twenty-seven years old, Togliatti thirty-four).

The "Republican Assembly" Slogan under Attack

The controversy between the PCI leaders and the youth began soon after the Fascist regime's November 1926 crackdown. Representatives of the youth objected to transitional slogans, the "republican assembly" slogan in particular, at meetings of the Comintern's Italian Commission in January 1927. Moreover, according to Camilla Ravera, then responsible for organizing a clandestine party office near Genoa, the oppositionists

---

33. Alfonso Leonetti, "Siamo nel filo della corrente storica," *Rinascita* 22, no. 34 (August 28, 1965):19; cf. Salvatore Francesco Romano, *Antonio Gramsci* (Turin: Unione Tipografico-Editrice Torinese, 1965), 535–36.

34. "Verbale della Commissione politica per il congresso di Lione," *Critica marxista* 1, nos. 5–6 (September–December 1963):302–26 at 313–18.

communicated their views to members of the PCI base in Italy.[35] Confronted with this challenge, Togliatti and Grieco were initially quite defensive. At party meetings during the spring of 1927 they flatly denied the possibility of an actual post-Fascist "intermediate stage" or "democratic phase."[36]

These disclaimers notwithstanding, the conflict over transitional slogans soon escalated. In October 1927 Longo, writing in behalf of the FGCI to the Politburo,[37] argued that the party should disavow the slogan of a "republican assembly on the basis of workers' and peasants' committees." This slogan, he insisted, was too abstract and ambiguous for the working masses to comprehend. It could serve only to encourage "democratic and Aventinian illusions." Whatever the intentions of those who coined it, its net effect in a revolutionary situation, Longo claimed, would be to promote a post-Fascist democratic stage, not the proletarian revolution.

Longo's views were rebutted at once by Togliatti and Grieco. In a written commentary,[38] Togliatti replied that Longo underestimated the lingering popular appeal of the democratic anti-Fascist parties in the Italian countryside and elsewhere. With regard to a post-Fascist democratic stage, Togliatti now granted that such an eventuality was possible. Indeed, under existing conditions it was probable: "If we can make a prediction, it is that . . . the fall of fascism will not find the working class in a position to carry the revolutionary movement immediately forward to the creation of a Workers' State."[39] In his opinion, however, the reason for this was not the PCI's use of transitional slogans but rather its failure to convince democratic anti-Fascists that their goals could best be achieved in conjunction with the anticapitalist aims of the PCI. And that, he insisted, could only be accomplished with democratic transitional slogans.

Grieco echoed this theme at a Politburo meeting convened to deal with the issues raised by the youth in late October 1927. He, too, conceded that there existed in Italy "the objective conditions for a democratic succession to fascism." Yet he argued that only the defense of democratic goals would enable the PCI to attract the peasant and urban middle-class support necessary for transforming the anti-Fascist movement into the anti-

35. Cf. Camilla Ravera's memoires, *Diario di trent'anni, 1913–1943* (Rome: Editori Riuniti, 1973), 253–96.

36. See their respective remarks in APC, 1927, fol. 557:37, and fol. 560:66.

37. Longo, letter of October 20, 1927, to PCI Politburo, *Annali Feltrinelli* 8, 1927, doc. 5:364–400 at 362–81.

38. Togliatti commentary on Longo's letter of October 20, 1927, ibid., 381–400.

39. Ibid., 390–91.

capitalist revolution.[40] In other words, both Togliatti and Grieco maintained that the use of democratic transitional slogans, far from being conducive to a post-Fascist bourgeois democratic regime as Longo and others contended, was the only way to *avoid* such a turn of events.

The debate resumed at the PCI's Second Conference, which took place in Basel, Switzerland, in late January 1928. The first major gathering since the party was outlawed in late 1926, it was attended by a number of activists from the underground Communist network in Italy. The leadership made Longo promise not to address the conference,[41] hoping to prevent the extension of the policy debate to the middle-level cadres operating clandestinely inside Mussolini's police state. In the course of the three-day meeting a clash of views nevertheless developed. As Grieco pointedly remarked at the close of the conference: "There is among us some dissension regarding the correctness or not of using general political slogans which indicate an intermediate phase in the struggle for workers' power."[42] Clearly, in that broader gathering Grieco felt constrained to revert to the more obscure and presumably less offensive phraseology of the *Theses of Lyons*.

Grieco expressed full agreement with the PCI's use of "intermediate political slogans," even quoting the relevant passages from the *Theses of Lyons*.[43] He placed particular emphasis on the linkage between transitional objectives and the search for middle-class allies. Since the latter were predisposed "toward the reestablishment of democracy in Italy," he argued, the PCI must either mobilize or neutralize them through the use of "partial political slogans."

Togliatti came out squarely on the side of Grieco. Although he dealt with the international situation in his main speech, he championed transitional democratic objectives in his commentary on Grieco's discussion of domestic matters.[44] Most notable was the fact that Togliatti began by describing the current political situation in Italy as "reactionary."[45] What he was actually doing was justifying the PCI's advocacy of "intermediate solutions of general political problems" according to the specific criteria stipulated in the *Theses of Lyons*. Once having established the legitimacy of his position, he proceeded to argue in the same vein as he had the

40. Minutes of October 24, 1927, meeting of PCI Politburo, ibid., 1927, doc. 7:420–36 at 431–36.

41. Berti commentary, ibid., 1928, doc. 1:439. By the same token, the PCI Politburo resolved on January 24, 1928, not to bring any issues to a vote at the conference in order to avoid the formal declaration of reservations the FGCI threatened to make in case of a vote. See APC, 1928, fol. 659:4.

42. *La Seconda Conferenza del Partito Comunista d'Italia (Resoconto stenografico)* (Paris: Edizioni del Partito Comunista d'Italia, June 1928), 148.

43. Ibid., 8–9 and 148–51.

44. Ibid., 72–82.

45. Ibid., 73–74.

previous October: the only way to win control over the "insurrection of the broad masses" was to use "those slogans with a democratic content that can serve to mobilize these masses."[46]

Despite the circumspect manner in which Togliatti and Grieco handled transitional slogans, opposition was nonetheless voiced by delegates from the youth organization. Because of Longo's enforced silence, their views were set forth most articulately by Pietro Secchia. Secchia questioned the leadership's fundamental premise that nonproletarians would be attracted to the side of the PCI by democratic slogans such as a "republican assembly" rather than by orthodox slogans such as a "workers' and peasants' government." In his opinion, the very existence of contact between Communists and middle-class elements presupposed a certain receptivity on the part of the latter and indicated that the more advanced slogans were appropriate.[47] Far from favoring partial democratic goals, he advocated a kind of partial insurrectionism at the local level: "We should not think that we will conquer power through insurrection in one city alone, but such a movement would have enormous repercussions and would find an echo throughout Italy."[48] Secchia was openly backed at the conference by two other dissidents, Battista Santhià and Ottavio Pastore. Santhià repeated the common sectarian view that democratic slogans would only delude the workers.[49] Pastore, on the other hand, took up a position that verged on outright adventurism, declaring that the moment had come for armed insurrection even if unsuccessful: "A crushed insurrection costs more but obviously has greater influence than a strike."[50]

"People's Revolution" or Proletarian Revolution?

The PCI leaders and the youth clearly differed in their assessment of revolutionary prospects in Italy. For the FGCI dissidents, much as for the Bordigan sectarians, only one possibility existed: the anti-Fascist proletarian revolution. For them the revolution against fascism, to succeed, must simultaneously become a revolution against capitalism leading directly to the dictatorship of the proletariat; otherwise it would abort, ending in a return to the *status quo*.[51] The Togliatti circle, on the other hand, viewed the anti-Fascist revolution from a double perspective: it might take the form of a proletarian revolution; but it might also take the

46. Ibid., 77.
47. Ibid., 96.
48. Ibid., 98.
49. Ibid., 29–30.
50. Ibid., 70–72.
51. Secchia confirmed that this was indeed the conviction of the youth at that time in his article, "L'archivio Tasca sul PCI: appunti e ricordi," *Critica marxista* 5, no. 3 (May–June 1967):100–38 at 124.

form of a broadly based democratic movement against fascism in which the PCI would play only a subordinate role. In the latter case, the movement against fascism would fall under the rubric of a "people's revolution" (*rivoluzione popolare*).

The PCI leadership thus gave a novel twist to the Comintern's double revolutionary perspective. The Comintern documents anticipated the strategy of frontal assault in some countries and a more gradual process in others. But the Italian Communists incorporated both perspectives into a single strategy entailing a distinction between the people's revolution and the proletarian revolution. According to this approach, the people's revolution would come first, involving at the outset a vast popular uprising against fascism. If at that stage the PCI was successful in its use of transitional slogans, it would quickly dominate the movement and proceed to the creation of a socialist order as the Bolsheviks had done in 1917. But if not, the people's revolution would lead to the democratic transitional stage that the PCI leaders opposed yet half expected; and the party would then be compelled to maneuver for greater mass support before going on to the proletarian revolution.

The concept of a people's revolution was formulated under circumstances that underscored the close working relationship between the ranking PCI leaders and the supporters of Nikolai Bukharin, at that time head of the Comintern. The people's revolution idea received its official imprimatur in a resolution on Italian affairs approved by the Presidium of the ECCI in late January 1927.[52] While the Presidium was formally the top executive body of the International, its resolutions were usually worked out in national or regional commissions attached to the ECCI's permanent Political Secretariat. And in this case a close reading of the PCI Archives reveals that the Presidium resolution reflected positions taken by Togliatti, Grieco, and Humbert-Droz, one of Bukharin's closest advisers on Comintern matters,[53] at meetings of the Political Secretariat's Italian Commission in early January 1927.[54] According to Humbert-Droz, moreover, Bukharin—who was evidently absent from the January Presidium meeting—personally approved the resolution on Italian developments toward the end of February 1927.[55]

52. "La situazione economica e politica dell'Italia e i compiti del partito comunista" (text of the resolution approved by the Comintern Presidium on January 28, 1927), *SO* 1, no. 1 (March 1927):91–102 at 98–99.

53. Jules Humbert-Droz, *L'Internazionale comunista tra Lenin e Stalin: Memorie di un protagonista, 1891–1941* (Milan: Feltrinelli Editore, 1974), 213 and 223–24.

54. For the remarks of Humbert-Droz and Togliatti, see APC, 1927, fol. 547:11–12 and 24–25. Spriano maintained that the Presidium's resolution was based on a report delivered by Grieco to the Italian Commission; see *Storia del Partito comunista italiano* 2:103–5. Ragionieri, however, merely noted that the document was drafted by a committee that included Togliatti, Grieco, Tasca, and Humbert-Droz, see Togliatti, *Opere 1926–1929*, xc, n. 1. Togliatti, in turn, called Humbert-Droz the "father" of the resolution; ibid.

55. Humbert-Droz to Ercoli, February 26, 1927 (Humbert-Droz Archive, Harvard University).

A heated debate nevertheless erupted over the notion of a people's revolution among those gathered in Moscow to chart the PCI's course under the new conditions of full-blown Fascist dictatorship. To summarize the opposition viewpoint briefly, Solomon Lozovsky, head of the Profintern (Red International of Trade Unions), interpreted Humbert-Droz's comments on the possibility of a democratic transitional stage[56] to mean support for a "peaceful" evolutionary transformation of fascism into a constitutional regime. Lozovsky associated Togliatti with this view as well. He then went on to contend that "there aren't two perspectives in Italy," that the overthrow of fascism by a people's revolution would lead merely to an interlude similar to "the period between February and October," an allusion to the Russian developments of 1917.[57] Dmitry Manuilsky, soon to become Stalin's chief spokesman in the Comintern, also took issue with both Humbert-Droz and Togliatti: "The way in which Comrades Ercoli and Humbert-Droz have posed the question does not seem right to me. . . . If we speak of two stages of this revolution, we can make the error that some comrades committed in Russia during the Kerensky regime, viewing this regime as a historical period. It is absolutely necessary to combat this theory."[58]

As for Longo, in an undated memorandum to the individuals charged with drafting the resolution on Italian affairs, he warned that any halt in the revolutionary momentum would lead to the defeat of the revolution itself inasmuch as "October 1917 also taught something to our enemies."[59] Striking in this context was his insistence on the slogan of a "workers' and peasants' government" in place of the call for a "constitutional assembly," a sure sign that the PCI policy makers were already considering the latter slogan in January 1927. Indeed, Longo's reference lends credence to the supposition that Gramsci's support for a constitutional assembly in talks with fellow prisoners reflected discussions under way before his arrest.

The controversy over the PCI's use of democratic transitional slogans had obviously begun. The record of the Presidium meeting at which the Italian situation was discussed is not available. A letter sent by Togliatti, Grieco, Tasca, and another Italian delegate to the Political Secretariat on January 25 indicates, however, that it was not only the PCI youth who had begun to question such slogans but some Comintern functionaries as well. Indeed, they noted that "the problem which was most discussed at the Presidium" was the Italian party's adoption of the "republican assembly" slogan. They went on to protest that their critics had neglected to read the many documents submitted to the Comintern to explain the Italian

56. See the stenographic account of the Italian Commission in APC, 1927, fol. 547:11.
57. Ibid., 30–32.
58. Ibid., 37–42 at 41.
59. Text in APC, 1927, fol. 545:113–14.

party's policy. Should the International decide to ask the PCI to revise its line, they concluded, surely it would not do so "on the basis of some superficial and banal observations but on the basis of an in-depth study of the questions."[60]

These harbingers of conflict notwithstanding, the PCI's double revolutionary perspective was, as we have seen, endorsed by the Presidium—evidence that the moderates still had the upper hand in that body.

Furthermore, at the PCI's Second Conference a year later, the possibility that Mussolini's regime would be overthrown by a people's revolution rather than by a proletarian revolution was spelled out by both Grieco and Togliatti. As Grieco succinctly put it: "The proletarian revolution is a people's revolution; however, the people's revolution may not yet be the proletarian revolution. . . . *We must give working-class direction to the people's revolution.*"[61] Togliatti was more defensive than Grieco, denying that the PCI in any way favored the democratic perspective. On the other hand, he insisted that a post-Fascist democratic stage could not be precluded out of hand. And he chided "some comrades" for arguing that the anti-Fascist revolution would automatically become the proletarian revolution, declaring this to be "a very grave political error."[62] Clearly Togliatti was polemicizing against the youth.

Indicative of this mounting factional tension was Longo's conduct upon his return to Moscow for the Ninth Plenum of the ECCI in February 1928. On that occasion he challenged his party's views on a much wider range of issues than heretofore, including its assessment of the PCI's base of support in Italy. Togliatti stressed the passivity of the urban workers, the arrest of some 2,500 party members (out of 7,500) since the previous June, and the consequent likelihood of a democratic "transitional period" after the overthrow of fascism.[63] Whereupon Longo retorted that the PCI's position among the Italian masses was actually far more solid than Togliatti indicated.[64] All the same, the ECCI's Latin Secretariat, still dominated by Togliatti's allies, reaffirmed the Presidium's January 1927 resolution on Italy.[65]

By the winter of 1928 the PCI leaders' strategic outlook may thus be said to have coalesced into the following set of perceptions and guidelines. First of all, they assessed the political mood of Italy as reactionary rather than revolutionary. Their immediate task, therefore, was to kindle the anti-Fascist sentiments of the Italian population. Second, they sur-

60. Text in ibid., 140–41.

61. *La Seconda Conferenza del Partito Comunista d'Italia (Resoconto stenografico)*, 148.

62. Ibid., 79.

63. "Rapporto alla commissione italiana dell'Esecutivo dell'Internazionale comunista," in *Opere 1926–1929*, by Togliatti, 338–71 at 355–66.

64. See Togliatti's report on what transpired in Moscow, delivered at the March 1928 PCI Central Committee meeting, in APC, 1928, fol. 653:9.

65. Ibid.

mised that the Fascist regime could not be overthrown without the joint efforts of the middle class and proletariat—without, in short, a people's revolution. Finally, they *hoped* to merge the anti-Fascist revolution with the anticapitalist revolution. But they recognized that if the Communists failed to win hegemony during the struggle against fascism, then a democratic transitional stage would ensue, leading to a halt in the revolutionary process.

Togliatti summed up these alternative perspectives in a statement prepared for delivery to the PCI Central Committee in June 1928: "Much has been said . . . on the problem of the 'people's revolution.' . . . Is it possible that the first wave of an anti-Fascist mass movement will lead at once to the establishment of a dictatorship of the proletariat, or is it conceivable that there will be a period in which, in the open mass struggle against fascism, non-Communist anti-Fascist forces (democracy, social democracy) will succeed in heading the masses or part of them. . . ? We consider the second hypothesis also likely."[66] Togliatti then added, pointedly, that even though the function of the democratic forces would under these circumstances be counterrevolutionary, *"this does not mean they would therefore merge with fascism.* The Aventine was counterrevolution and reaction but not fascism."[67]

Herein lies the real significance of the PCI's double revolutionary perspective: the perception that the victory of the people's revolution, though not the maximum goal of the Communists, would at least represent a step forward. For, as Togliatti plainly stated, a post-Fascist victory by democratic forces would "not mean they would therefore merge with fascism." In other words, confronted with a choice between fascism and a democratic transitional stage, the assumption of the PCI leadership was that the latter was the lesser evil. Democracy was preferable to fascism.

Throughout the Comintern, however, sectarian figures were already arguing that democracy was just as pernicious as fascism—nay, even worse; and they were preparing to champion this position at the Sixth Congress of the International scheduled for the summer of 1928. Little wonder, then, that Togliatti was to declare from the podium of the Sixth Congress that on central issues of Comintern policy honest Communists could disagree.

Stalin's Curb on Transitional Slogans

The strategy of immediate proletarian revolution in advanced industrial countries was unambiguously set forth in the *Program of the Communist*

66. Ercoli, "Osservazioni sulla politica del nostro partito," *SO* 2, no. 6 (June 1928), in *SO 1927–1939*, ed. Ferri, 1:238–55 at 248.
67. Ibid.; my emphasis.

International adopted by the Sixth Comintern Congress. For countries with a "medium" level of capitalist development ("Spain, Portugal, Poland, Hungary, the Balkan countries, etc."), the program endorsed Lenin's 1905 formula of a transitional "democratic dictatorship of the proletariat and the peasantry." But for the highly developed capitalist countries it called for a "direct transition to the dictatorship of the proletariat."[68] And in the eyes of both the Soviets and the PCI, Italy belonged to the category of highly developed capitalist countries.[69]

This sectarian policy was closely related to the factional struggle then developing in the upper reaches of the CPSU as Stalin conspired to undermine Bukharin in his own bailiwick, the Communist International.[70] The public rationale for the new line was that capitalism was becoming increasingly unstable, opening up the prospect of a new wave of proletarian revolutions. According to this assessment, democracy and fascism were but two sides of the same coin. By attempting to preserve the capitalist system, both served the cause of counterrevolution. Even social democracy was—objectively speaking—now no better than fascism. A democratic transitional stage, which in European parliamentary systems implied Communist cooperation with Socialists, was thus precluded even as a contingency objective. Transitional slogans were to be used in a strictly manipulative way, as Lenin had done in 1917, during periods of actual revolutionary upheaval.

A comparison of the draft Comintern program written by Bukharin[71] and the final version of that program worked out in the Program Commission of the Sixth Congress[72] illustrates the differences between the Stalinists and Bukharin on the issue of transitional slogans. In the excerpt quoted below, only the italicized phrases appeared in Bukharin's draft version, while the passage in its entirety appeared in the officially adopted *Program of the Communist International.*

68. "Programma Kommunisticheskogo Internatsionala," *VI Kongress Kominterna: stenograficheskii otchet,* 6 vols. (Moscow, 1929), 6:7-55 at 37.

69. "Osservazioni al 'Progetto di programma della Internazionale comunista' presentate alla commissione del programma del VI Congresso mondiale dalla delegazione del PCI," in *Opere 1926–1929,* by Togliatti, 443–71 at 456–57.

70. Cf. Stephen F. Cohen, *Bukharin and the Bolshevik Revolution* (New York: Oxford University Press, 1980), 291–95.

71. Bukharin had been entrusted with drafting a Comintern program since 1922. For an account of his activity in this regard prior to the Sixth Congress, see Ernesto Ragionieri, "Il programma dell'Internazionale comunista," *Studi storici* 13, no. 4 (October–December 1972):671–725.

72. Ragionieri argued that the final program did not differ substantially from Bukharin's draft version, that changes took the form of additions rather than deletions; see the second installment of Ragionieri's article in *Studi storici* 14, no. 1 (January–March 1973):114–39 at 131–32. This interpretation does not really hold up under scrutiny, however, as evidenced by the discussion in the following pages as well as by Bukharin's own remark to Lev Kamenev that "Stalin had spoiled the program for me in many places"; quoted in *Bukharin and the Bolshevik Revolution,* by Cohen, 292.

In the absence of a revolutionary upsurge the Communist parties ought to advance partial slogans and demands arising from the everyday needs of the toilers, combining them with the fundamental tasks of the Communist International. At the same time, however, the Communist parties must not advance those transitional slogans which are designed especially for a revolutionary situation and in its absence are transformed into slogans denoting a merging with the capitalist system of organization (for example, the slogan of workers' control, etc.). Partial demands and slogans are an indispensable part of correct tactics in general, whereas a number of transitional slogans are indissolubly tied to the presence of a revolutionary situation. On the other hand, the *rejection "on principle" of partial demands and transitional slogans is incompatible with the tactical principles of Communism for it in fact condemns the party to passivity and isolates it from the masses.*[73]

The revised version distorted almost beyond recognition the original intent of the passage. Whereas Bukharin had approved the use of transitional slogans even "in the absence of a revolutionary upsurge," the amended program said just about the opposite, declaring that "a number of transitional slogans are indissolubly tied to the presence of a revolutionary situation." In fact, the relevant passage as formulated in the final version intimated that the advocacy of transitional slogans was an opportunist deviation *except* in a revolutionary situation.

Unfortunately, the minutes of the Program Commission—according to Humbert-Droz who chaired it—were never published, although almost all the congress delegates attended its sessions, suggesting over six hundred amendments.[74] However, in the late winter of 1929 during a heated exchange over transitional slogans, Longo made the following cryptic reference to the debate that led to the above revisions: "We know that the paragraph in the program on transitional slogans did not come to light easily. It was discussed a great deal."[75] Togliatti, we might note, had made no objections to the original version of that paragraph in his July 1928 critique of the draft program.[76]

Several months after the Sixth Congress, at a meeting of the Comintern Presidium on December 19, 1928, Stalin went even further with regard to transitional slogans, personally restricting their use to an "acute revolu-

---

73. The italicized phrases are taken from the draft program, "Proekt programmy Kominterna," *VI Kongress Kominterna* 3:156–92 at 190. The passage in its entirety appears in "Programma Kommunisticheskogo Internatsionala," ibid., 4:52.

74. Humbert-Droz, *L'Internazionale comunista tra Lenin e Stalin,* 222–23.

75. See minutes of March 2, 1929, PCI Central Committee meeting, *Annali Feltrinelli* 8, 1929, doc. 15:803–89 at 869–70. Ragionieri, on the basis of the Program Commission materials selected for publication in *International Press Correspondence,* did not mention transitional slogans as one of the issues discussed; "Il programma," *Studi storici* 14, no. 1 (January–March 1973):114–39.

76. "Osservazioni al 'Progetto di programma,' " in *Opere 1926–1929,* by Togliatti, 457–60.

tionary situation.'' The issue at hand involved the question of how to deal with the moderates in the German Communist Party (KPD), many of whom still looked for political guidance to their former leader, Heinrich Brandler. (Brandler had been denounced as a right-wing opportunist in 1924 for viewing a coalition "workers' government" as a concrete transitional stage.)[77] So central was this group to the political infight in the Comintern that the Presidium meeting had been convened in order to approve an "Open Letter" directing the KPD to take disciplinary measures against them; and in his formal address Stalin bluntly called for their expulsion.[78] The details of this confrontation will be discussed in chapter 2. Of relevance here is that Stalin also struck out at the German dissidents' defense of democratic transitional slogans. According to Angelo Tasca, who attended the Presidium meeting as a PCI representative, Stalin insisted that the use of such slogans be limited not simply to a revolutionary situation but to an "acute" revolutionary situation.[79]

Stalin's remarks to this effect were evidently made in the course of drafting the "Open Letter." His views were then incorporated into its text. Specifically, the document denounced as opportunism the advocacy of workers' control of production (a transitional slogan then favored by the German moderates) except in an "acute revolutionary situation" (*situation révolutionnaire immédiate*).[80] Even more to the point, the "Open Letter" stipulated that the dissidents, in order to remain in the KPD, would have to "accept without reservation" not only the *Program of the Communist International* as a whole but precisely that passage on transitional slogans which had been inserted into Bukharin's draft program during the Sixth Congress. Indeed, quoting verbatim from the program, the "Open Letter" reiterated that "Communist parties must not advance those transitional slogans which are designed especially for a revolutionary situation and in its absence are transformed into slogans denoting a merging with the capitalist system of organization."[81] The key role of transitional slogans in the rapidly escalating Comintern infighting could not have been more clearly underscored.

77. For details, see Werner T. Angress, *Stillborn Revolution: The Communist Bid for Power in Germany, 1921–1923* (Princeton: Princeton University Press, 1963), 258ff.

78. J. Stalin, "O pravoi opasnosti v Germanskoi kompartii," *KI*, no. 52 (December 28, 1928):14–20 at 20.

79. See Tasca letter of December 26, 1928, to PCI Secretariat, *Annali Feltrinelli* 8, 1928, doc. 28:610–13 at 612.

80. "Lettre ouverte du C.E. de l'I.C. au P.C.A. sur les dangers de droite dans le P.C.A.," *La Correspondance Internationale* 8, no. 155 (December 29, 1928):1825–28 at 1826. Tasca maintained that the adjectives "acute" and "immediate" were in this context identical in meaning; see his report of February 28, 1929, to PCI Central Committee, *Annali Feltrinelli* 8, 1929, doc. 14:671–803 at 698.

81. "Lettre ouverte," *La Correspondance Internationale* 8, no. 155 (December 29, 1928):1827.

In the light of the foregoing, Togliatti's unqualified support for the double revolutionary perspective at the PCI's June 1928 Central Committee meeting acquires added significance. For in actuality he was polemicizing both with his own party's youth faction and with the upcoming Stalinist *apparatchiki* in the Comintern. At that same Central Committee session, moreover, the dispute between Togliatti and the PCI opposition, represented primarily by Longo, reached a new level of intensity.

Probably because Togliatti felt on the defensive toward both the Stalinists and the youth, he sharply differentiated his own position from that of the Comintern moderates, who were by then commonly stigmatized as "right-wing opportunists." For one thing, he stressed that the notion of a people's revolution in no way indicated the *necessity* of a post-Fascist bourgeois democratic phase. For another, he reiterated a point that had also been made in the theses of the PCI's Second Conference, namely, that the term "republican assembly" in no way signified an intermediate *form of government* between fascism and the dictatorship of the proletariat. "That is, in substance, the path of Brandlerism," Togliatti protested,[82] thereby hedging his bets in the coming showdown between Stalin and the KPD moderates.

Yet in this same document Togliatti defended the PCI's advocacy of democratic goals in a more direct, resolute, and polemical fashion then he had in either his late 1927 correspondence with the youth or his January 1928 address to the Second Conference. He denounced as entirely mistaken "the comrades who oppose the Party's agitation for partial political demands or—which is the same thing—who have doubts regarding the advisability of agitating for slogans with a democratic content."[83] Moreover, he alluded to widespread popular support for a constitutional assembly in a manner that resembled the view Gramsci spelled out in his prison conversations: "The mobilization of the masses who aren't yet part of the worker-peasant bloc comes about instead on the basis of a struggle for the republic and for a constitutional assembly. . . . It is from this point of view that the slogan of a republican assembly on the basis of workers' and peasants' committees . . . is justified."[84]

From the viewpoint of the wider Comintern controversy, however, the real bite in Togliatti's June 1928 position was his pointed defense of the use of transitional slogans under prerevolutionary rather than revolutionary conditions. He conceded that the political situation in Italy was different from that confronting Lenin in 1917 when he (Lenin) had included radical democratic demands in the Bolshevik program—the difference in

82. Ercoli, "Osservazioni sulla politica del nostro partito," in *SO 1927–1939*, ed. Ferri, 1:249.
83. Ibid., 251.
84. Ibid., 254.

question being the presence of reaction in Italy and revolution in Russia. But he maintained all the same that precisely because of the reactionary nature of fascism democratic slogans would be likely to precipitate a general revolutionary upheaval. For under such conditions, he argued, "it is easier to get across to the consciousness of the masses . . . that none of these demands can be satisfied without a successful struggle for the over-throw of the regime."[85]

In other words, Togliatti defended the use of democratic transitional slogans in a nonrevolutionary situation as opposed to an acute revolution-ary situation—in direct contrast to the Stalinist line then evolving in Moscow. As will be recalled, on this same occasion Togliatti also sug-gested that a post-Fascist democratic interlude after a people's revolution would not be tantamount to a return to fascism. Yet the distinction be-tween democracy and fascism, already blurred in Comintern pronounce-ments, was soon to be obliterated by the Stalinists' indiscriminate onslaught against social democracy qua social fascism. In June 1928, therefore, the man who was to lead the PCI for the duration of the Stalin era and beyond expressed views that would shortly thereafter be castigated as right-wing opportunism.

Meanwhile, in a written speech delivered to the same June 1928 Central Committee session, Longo attacked Togliatti's position with a verbal ferocity that suggested he was receiving encouragement from the growing band of extremists in Moscow. His assessment of political conditions in Italy as approaching "an immediately revolutionary situation" not only contradicted Togliatti's appraisal but also echoed the jargon of the Sta-linists.[86] More important, he insinuated that the PCI leaders were guilty of "tailism," of trailing behind the spontaneous anti-Fascist outbursts of the Italian masses.[87] Most provocative of all, he accused them of "econo-mism," explicitly equating the party's advocacy of democratic slogans and "theory of stages" with that most serious of Leninist heresies.[88] He thereupon flatly condemned Togliatti's suggestion of rallying mass sup-port on the basis of a constitutional assembly and took instead the ultrasec-tarian position that the workers and peasants should be shielded from any bourgeois alliance or influence.[89]

During the Central Committee debate that followed, Longo's argu-ments were rebutted by one after another speaker, with Grieco going so far as to accuse him of reviving "*Bordighismo.*"[90] And only Secchia

---

85. Ibid., 251–52.
86. Text in APC, 1928, fol. 653:66–93 at 69–70.
87. Ibid., 78.
88. Ibid., 84.
89. Ibid., 87.
90. Ibid., 109.

joined him in abstaining on the meeting's concluding resolution.[91] As for Togliatti, he chided Longo for a lack of "political seriousness" in charging the leadership with "economism" and for verging on anarchism with all his talk of terrorism.[92] He nevertheless opposed any sanctions against Longo: "We don't want to reject Gallo (Longo), we will never reject his critical collaboration provided that he backs the general line of the party, but we have attacked him in order that he might reflect" upon what he was doing to the unity of the party.[93] In the face of Longo's challenge Togliatti thus displayed a remarkably conciliatory attitude, a characteristic that was, as we shall see in the next chapter, becoming a hallmark of his political personality.

From the vantage point of democratic principles, the parties to the controversy over transitional slogans were all sectarians at heart. While the members of the Gramsci–Togliatti circle rejected the extreme intransigence of Bordiga and the youth, they nonetheless viewed reformist objectives not as ends in themselves even in the short run but as a means of mobilizing the middle classes (in addition to the workers) against fascism. They sought in the process to transform this anti-Fascist movement into a struggle against capitalism. Their use of democratic slogans to win middle-class allies was thus manipulative in intent. Only because of their party's weakness did the PCI leaders acquiesce to the alternative prospect of a democratic stage between fascism and socialism during which they would have to compete with centrist parties to gain mass support. At this stage of their development they were more adaptive than innovative on questions of revolutionary strategy.

Still, the readiness of the men around Togliatti to assess realistically the possibilities for action in the Italian context marked them as moderates compared to the radical sectarians in the PCI and the Comintern at large. Furthermore, unlike individuals from proletarian backgrounds such as Longo and Ernst Thälmann, they knew from their own life experience that it was indeed possible to persuade middle-class people of the virtues of communism.

One final remark is in order. Even the PCI's chief dissidents, Longo and Secchia, differed from someone like Thälmann in that their radical sectarianism was not infused with political ambition. Their purpose was to change their party's policies, not to replace its leaders. Once that objective was achieved, they were quite prepared to continue party work alongside their erstwhile opponents.

---

91. Ibid., 129.
92. Ibid., 127–29.
93. Ibid., 127.

CHAPTER 2

Stalin's Ascendancy and the PCI's "Opportunism of Conciliation"

Stalin and his agents gained control over the bureaucracy of the Third International during the period between the Sixth Comintern Congress (July–August 1928) and the Tenth Plenum of the ECCI (July 1929). The preceding two years had seen the political defeat of the Soviet left-wing opposition led by Leon Trotsky and its foreign Communist supporters. Stalin was thus free to turn against his more moderate opponents, those who backed Nikolai Bukharin and opposed the forcible collectivization of the Soviet countryside. Indicative of what was to come was the conduct of the pro-Stalin delegates to the Sixth Congress. At their prodding, Bukharin's draft version of the conclave's political resolution was amended to include not just the denunciation of right-wing opportunism but also the command to combat "the conciliatory attitude" toward right-ist views.[1] In other words, forbearance toward dissent within the Communist movement was no longer to be brooked.

Yet a purge of Soviet and foreign Communist moderates could not be undertaken at once. Stalin first had to consolidate his support and discredit his opponents. He did not dare directly challenge the leaders of the CPSU right wing until he had disarmed them ideologically and organizationally both at home and in the Comintern, where Bukharin still enjoyed wide-spread prestige. Therefore, the political resolution finally adopted by the Sixth Congress equivocated on the *methods* to be used against the right-

---

1. J. Stalin, "The Right Deviation in the CPSU(B): (Excerpt from a Speech Delivered at the Plenum of the Central Committee of the CPSU(B), April 1929)," *Problems of Leninism* (Moscow, 1941), 240–93 at 248–49.

ists. On the one hand, the resolution ordered, at Stalin's instigation, "a general tightening up of iron internal party discipline."[2] On the other hand, while it called right opportunism the main threat, it also warned against the continuing danger of leftist deviations. And it instructed the Communist parties to fight both tendencies "*above all by means of persuasion.*"[3] Not until almost a year later, at the Tenth Plenum of the ECCI, did the Stalinists become strong enough to issue a blanket order for the use of "organizational measures"—the Comintern's euphemism for purge—against both the right-wing oppositionists and the conciliators.

Until the Tenth Plenum the PCI leaders opposed, openly or indirectly, the organizational methods of the Stalinists. They advocated political persuasion rather than the threat of expulsion as the most effective way of overcoming intraparty dissent, whether of the left or right. By 1928 this conciliatory posture had become linked to their own policy preferences. Because a number of Stalin's most outspoken opponents, especially in the KPD, were advocates of transitional slogans, the PCI elite's pleas for organizational restraint toward the deviationists was a way of warding off criticism of the Italian line.

At the same time, the views of the PCI leaders grouped around Togliatti and Grieco were not all that divergent from those of the Stalinists. During the period of the Trotskyite opposition they had backed the New Economic Policy and the united front line. But even when Stalin shifted to the left, many affinities remained between the Italian and Soviet parties. For instance, the documents of the Sixth Congress proclaimed the beginning of the end of "the partial stabilization of capitalism" that had prevailed during the 1920s, and announced the onset of a "third" postwar period[4] of imperialist aggressiveness, class conflict, and revolutionary upheavals.[5] From the vantage point of the PCI's clandestine struggle in Fascist Italy, the Italian Communists could hardly take issue with this global outlook. On a more controversial note, the final resolution of the Sixth Congress named social democracy the Communists' worst enemy, accusing Socialists everywhere of supporting the imperialist war preparations and blunting the revolutionary activism of the masses. But here again the PCI leaders did not take undue exception, doubtless because of their deep-seated distrust of the PSI's pre-Fascist tradition of accommodating the status quo.

2. Ibid.

3. Sixth Congress theses, "O mezhdunarodnom polozhenii i zadachakh kommunisticheskogo internatsionala (Tezisy po dokladu t. N. I. Bukharina)," in *VI Kongress Kominterna*, 6 vols. (Moscow, 1929), 6:56–80 at 80; my emphasis.

4. In the Comintern lexicon, the revolutionary wave after World War I constituted the "first" postwar period; the slackening revolutionary tempo in the mid-1920s constituted the "second" postwar period.

5. Sixth Congress theses, in *VI Kongress Kominterna* 6:56–80.

53

Togliatti, for example, spoke in his major address to the Sixth Congress of the "inevitability" of an imperialist war against the Soviet Union and warned of the intensification of class conflict in Western Europe as war drew near.[6] He also supported the call for a more relentless struggle against social democracy, citing its reactionary role in binding the workers to the bourgeois state. For the same reason he endorsed the struggle against rightists in the Communist ranks.[7] Similarly, in October 1928 the PCI Central Committee approved the decisions of the Sixth Congress regarding the dangers of war and social democracy, even expelling a well-known reformist economist, Antonio Graziadei, from the party.[8]

Still, several of Togliatti's remarks to the Sixth Congress differed significantly from the content of the final resolution. Like Bukharin in his opening report,[9] Togliatti was rather cautious in his appraisal of the current capitalist crisis. He discerned on the whole "a certain development of capitalism," a result in part of its technological advances (a view also expressed by Bukharin), while he noted that the economic crisis in Italy had somewhat abated.[10] It was precisely this sort of restraint that was later to become a cardinal tenet in Stalin's indictment of Bukharin.[11] Furthermore, Togliatti repeatedly warned against undue generalizations and insisted instead upon objective, concrete analyses of the international scene, including those aspects that appeared unfavorable to the Communists. He cited in this context Lenin's last admonition to the Fourth Comintern Congress in 1922 "to study and learn."

Togliatti also appealed for a "differentiated analysis" of such questions as the nature of fascism, the linkage between fascism and social democracy (was their mass base one and the same?), and the actual degree of radicalization of the working masses.[12] For example, while the resolution of the Sixth Congress called Italian fascism "the classical type of Fascist system,"[13] he cautioned: "With respect to the possibility of generalizing the experience of fascism as it has developed in Italy, we cannot go too

6. Ercoli, "L'orientamento del nostro partito nelle questioni internazionali (Esposizione fatta a nome della delegazione del PCI al VI Congresso mondiale)," *Lo Stato operaio* [henceforth *SO*] 2, no. 7 (July 1928), in *Lo Stato operaio, 1927–1939*, ed. Franco Ferri, 2 vols. [henceforth *SO 1927–1939*] (Rome: Editori Riuniti, 1964), 1:271–94 at 278–80. Togliatti's speech to the Sixth Congress was published, with some omissions, in the Soviet stenographic report of the Congress; *VI Kongress Kominterna* 1:496–509.

7. Ercoli, "L'orientamento del nostro partito," in *SO 1927–1939*, ed. Ferri, 1:285.

8. "Risoluzione del CC sul VI Congresso mondiale," *SO* 2, no. 9 (October 1928):668; see also "Riunione del Comitato Centrale (October 1928)," ibid., 665–67.

9. Bukharin, in *VI Kongress Kominterna* 1:26–40.

10. Ercoli, "L'orientamento del nostro partito," in *SO 1927–1939*, ed. Ferri, 1:275–76; the reference to technological progress was omitted from the Russian version of the speech.

11. Stalin, "The Right Deviation in the CPSU(B)," *Problems of Leninism*, 247–48.

12. Ercoli, "L'orientamento del nostro partito," in *SO 1927–1939*, ed. Ferri, 1:281–84.

13. Sixth Congress theses, in *VI Kongress Kominterna* 6.65.

fast nor too far and we must make a differentiated analysis."[14] Implicit in the idea of a "differentiated analysis" was Togliatti's concern with specific national conditions, his respect for national particularities, as well as his intellectualism, his preoccupation with detail and nuances.

The issue on which Togliatti actually clashed with the Stalinists was, however, the organizational one. In contrast to the equivocation of documents from the Sixth Congress on this question, Togliatti explicitly warned against the use of "organizational measures" to quell dissent.[15] Not only that, but he, like Bukharin, declined even to mention the danger of "conciliation" toward right opportunism. Indeed, in his major address Togliatti was openly conciliatory toward the moderates in the KPD.

What Togliatti and his associates failed to anticipate was the Stalinists' insistence on total compliance. The PCI leaders calculated that by questioning only their organizational methods, not their general political line, they would be able to preserve freedom of action on purely Italian questions: namely, the use of democratic transitional slogans to incite and hopefully dominate a people's revolution against fascism. They did not realize that for Stalin and his cohorts the true measure of loyalty was organizational conformity. Political power, not revolutionary strategy, lay at the core of the Soviet leader's concerns.

At the Tenth Plenum of the ECCI in mid-1929 the Stalinists thus latched onto the issue of transitional slogans as a way of retaliating against the PCI leadership for its defiance on organizational matters. As we have seen, limitations on transitional slogans were imposed at the Sixth Congress and made even more stringent the following autumn in response to developments in the KPD. However, Stalin's ready support for the use of transitional slogans during the popular front years and after World War II suggests that in 1928 he was (as always) moved by calculation rather than conviction. He and his men simply used the Togliatti group's position on transitional slogans as an excuse to impugn its ideological rectitude and thereby subdue it. This maneuver was made all the easier by the cleavages on this question within the Italian party.

In the end Togliatti and Grieco capitulated to Stalin. In September 1929, following the Tenth Plenum, the PCI Central Committee repudiated its support for transitional slogans and expelled Angelo Tasca, the most outspoken Italian supporter of Bukharin, in a process that will be detailed in chapter 3. Yet their reluctance to do so, their tenacious defense of dialogue rather than purge, were precursors of the PCI's organizational principles in the post-Stalin era. Even under the full weight of Stalinization, supporters of opposing views continued to coexist in the PCI lead-

14. Ercoli, "L'orientamento del nostro partito," in *SO 1927–1939*, ed. Ferri, 1:281.
15. Ibid., 290–94.

ership: Togliatti and Grieco alongside Longo and Secchia. Thereafter the party, led by Togliatti until his death in 1964 and then by Longo until 1972, countenanced internal party differences on numerous issues while Togliatti privately urged the freer circulation of ideas in the CPSU. And in the international Communist arena the PCI also championed the organizational norms of dialogue and conciliation in handling disputes among Communist parties. On few other issues are the pre-Stalin and post-Stalin continuities in PCI conduct so evident.

Togliatti and the Tendency toward Conciliation

The significance of the PCI elite's conciliatory approach toward Comintern rightists in 1928–29 can be fully understood only in the light of its similar conduct toward the CPSU's left-wing oppositionists in 1926–27.

The PCI leadership first clashed with the CPSU over organizational measures in October 1926. At that time the Italian Politburo asked Gramsci to draft a letter to the CPSU Central Committee expressing its alarm over the direction the factional struggle between Stalin and Trotsky was taking.[16] The letter was delivered for transmittal to Togliatti,[17] PCI delegate to the Executive Committee of the Comintern since February 1926. Gramsci warned that the growing schism between the Stalin–Bukharin majority and the left-wing opposition might endanger the hard-won unity of the individual non-Soviet parties (especially the PCI, in view of its recent struggle against Bordiga) by crystalizing latent leftist and rightist tendencies. He took care to endorse the New Economic Policy of the Stalin–Bukharin leadership and conceded that party discipline was essential to its success. But he insisted that "unity and discipline in this case cannot be mechanical and forced."[18]

Gramsci concluded on a bold note, given the atmosphere of suspicion prevailing in the upper echelons of the CPSU. On the one hand, he paid tribute to the past revolutionary leadership of Trotsky, Grigorii Zinoviev, and Lev Kamenev, citing them as having been "among our masters." On the other hand, he implied that responsibility for the bitterness of the current intra-CPSU struggle rested not only with the left-wing minority but also with the Stalin–Bukharin majority. He then came to the heart of the matter: "We wish to be sure that the majority of the C.C. of the CPSU does not intend to abuse its victory in the struggle and is disposed to avoid

16. See the testimony of both Togliatti and Grieco in *Annali Feltrinelli* 8 (Milan: Feltrinelli Editore, 1966), 1926, doc. 11:299–320 at 299 and 319–20.

17. Text of Gramsci's letter in ibid., 312–16.

18. Ibid., 316.

excessive measures."[19] In short, Gramsci pleaded for restraint in the treatment of the Trotskyite opposition.

Within a month Gramsci was arrested by the Fascist police. However, during the next two years his successors voiced similar warnings against disciplinary measures in closed and public meetings of the Comintern, with one exception: Togliatti's reply to Gramsci's above-mentioned letter.[20] Togliatti argued that the defense of the Stalin–Bukharin line was more important than the possible impact of a split in the Soviet leadership. He sidestepped the question of "excessive measures" against the opposition, rebuking Gramsci for even conceiving of such an eventuality, and dwelt instead on Gramsci's appeal for CPSU unity. Togliatti pointed out that "the unity of the Leninist old guard" would probably never again exist: "the party line will [henceforth] be fixed through discussions and debates."[21] That being the case, he urged the foreign comrades to familiarize themselves with the issues rather than criticize the debate itself.

But the most significant aspect of Togliatti's reply was his reaction to Gramsci's allusion to shared responsibility for the crisis atmosphere that had developed. He took Gramsci to task for intimating that the Stalin–Bukharin group was even partially accountable for the impasse. Not only were they in no way responsible, wrote Togliatti, but any criticism by the PCI on this score could only add grist to the opposition's mill: "When one is in agreement with the line of the Central Committee [of the CPSU], the best contribution to overcoming the crisis is to express one's own adherence to this line without reservation."[22]

Togliatti's letter to Gramsci was dictated partly by circumstances. As PCI representative to the Comintern, he was subject to the direct influence of the Soviet faction in power. Upon receiving Gramsci's letter he immediately consulted Bukharin. Bukharin was evidently not responsible for the exact wording of Togliatti's reply. He nevertheless suggested that the PCI Central Committee reject the views expressed by Gramsci and support without reservation the conduct of the CPSU majority.[23] Similarly, the ECCI's Political Secretariat (headed by Bukharin) ordered the Swiss Communist Jules Humbert-Droz—then chief of its Latin Secretariat—to travel to Italy to persuade the PCI Central Committee to take an unequivocal stand against the CPSU's left-wing opposition.[24] Bukharin may have feared that the PCI would be suspected of harboring pro-Trotsky sympa-

19. Ibid.
20. Text of Togliatti's letter in ibid., 316–19.
21. Ibid., 317.
22. Ibid., 318.
23. Ibid., Togliatti's and Berti's commentary, 300–301 and 304.
24. Ibid., 300ff.

thies if it persisted in its criticisms of the Stalinists' methods of struggle. As Humbert-Droz recalled years later, Gramsci's 1926 letter provoked precisely such suspicions among certain circles in Moscow.[25] Suspicions of this type would explain Togliatti's disregard for the issue of disciplinary measures and emphasis on the need for a united front against Trotsky: it was the only way of allaying budding distrust of the PCI.

It is also possible that Togliatti did not yet believe the Stalin–Bukharin majority would actually "abuse its victory" over the opposition or resort to "excessive measures" against it, as Gramsci feared. Given the political temperaments of Bukharin and Humbert-Droz, he had no compelling reason to anticipate such an eventuality. For if Bukharin was later to vacillate on organizational questions, Humbert-Droz was to be an outspoken "conciliator."

Whatever the case, according to Humbert-Droz's later recollection of his encounter with PCI leaders at a rump meeting of the Central Committee in Italy during the first days of November 1926 (just before the party was banned), they reiterated their objections to the Soviet methods of handling intraparty dissent, despite their withdrawal of Gramsci's letter.[26] Thereafter Togliatti, too, began to object to disciplinary action against opponents of the official Soviet–Comintern line.

The first such instance occurred at the Seventh Plenum of the ECCI in the autumn of 1926, when the PCI delegation defended the right of the leaders of the left-wing opposition to participate and voice their views. At the opening session Zinoviev, whom the CPSU Central Committee had already deposed as chairman of the ECCI the previous month, formally resigned from that post "and in general from work in the Comintern."[27] Evidently it was the intention of the Soviet leadership to exclude Trotsky as well as Zinoviev from the plenum, for the PCI representatives sent a letter of protest on this account to the CPSU delegation. They insisted that since Trotsky and Zinoviev had been elected to the ECCI by the vote of all the member parties, they could not be removed by the decision of the Russian delegation alone.[28] The Soviet leaders conceded the point and commissioned Togliatti to convey this fact to the plenum. Togliatti did so on December 4, reporting that Zinoviev and Kamenev as members of the ECCI and Trotsky and Grigorii Sokolnikov as candidate members had

25. See his note to Giuseppe Berti in 1964 in ibid., 302, n. 2.

26. See ibid. and Berti's commentary, in ibid., p. 305; cf. Paolo Spriano, *Storia del Partito comunista italiano*, 5 vols. (Turin: Giulio Einaudi Editore, 1967–75), 2:59–60.

27. Seventh Plenum, *Puti mirovoi revoliutsii: stenograficheskii otchet* (Moscow, 1927), 1:14–15.

28. See Berti's commentary in *Annali Feltrinelli* 8, 1926, doc. 11:309; cf. Camilla Ravera, *Diario di trent'anni, 1913–1943* (Rome: Editori Riuniti, 1973), 284.

"the right to participate in all our debates and to speak on all questions which are discussed at the plenum."[29]

On this occasion, in other words, Togliatti acted with the reluctant consent of the Soviet leadership. The latter apparently hoped to thwart an attempt by supporters of the CPSU oppositionists to provoke an incident over the right to speak.[30] Even Stalin's protégé, Ernst Thälmann—presiding officer at the December 4 session—backed Togliatti. Though soon to become a vocal proponent of organizational measures against both left and right, Thälmann stated that "Comrades Zinoviev and Trotsky, as members of the Executive Committee, have the right to come here at any hour and at any moment to take the floor if they wish."[31] And four days later the CPSU delegation officially declared that it could not "forbid Comrade Zinoviev to appear before the plenum" even though it considered such an appearance "inadvisable."[32]

For his part, Togliatti likewise supported the Soviet and German delegations to the plenum on key issues. On behalf of the PCI, he drafted a declaration (read by Carlo Reggiani)[33] that not only endorsed the domestic policies of the Stalin–Bukharin majority and denounced the factionalism of the Soviet leftists, but also hailed the leading role, or *"funzione dirigente,"* of the CPSU in the Communist International.[34] Moreover, he and Longo both agreed, during private meetings of the Italian delegation, with a step that was widely contested at that time: namely, the decision to expel the left-wing oppositionists, Ruth Fischer and Arkadi Maslow, from the KPD.[35] Even on the initial question of the CPSU leftists' right to speak, Togliatti qualified his earlier position after the ringing denunciations of "socialism in one country" made by both Zinoviev and Trotsky. As he put it in his major address on December 10: "This right [to speak] is one thing and the use that they have made of this right is quite another; . . . [it represents] an attempt to disorganize the leading role which the Russian party holds in the International."[36]

29. Seventh Plenum, *Puti mirovoi revoliutsii* 1:512.

30. Cf. ibid., 512–13.

31. *La Correspondance Internationale* 6, no. 144 (December 30, 1926):1876.

32. *International Press Correspondence* 7, no. 2 (January 6, 1927):17–18 [henceforth cited as *Inprecor*].

33. See the minutes of the meetings of the PCI delegation to the Seventh Plenum in APC, 1926, fol. 377:40.

34. For the text of the declaration, see ibid., 41–44.

35. Ibid., 19–20. Interestingly, Humbert-Droz also agreed with them on this point; cf. ibid., 22–23.

36. *Inprecor* 7, no. 4 (January 12, 1927):62–63.

The Eighth Plenum: PCI Conciliation toward Trotsky

Togliatti's bearing at the Eighth Plenum of the ECCI in May 1927 nevertheless suggested that his defense of the left-wing opposition's right to speak at the Seventh Plenum had not been merely a minor divergence from the CPSU but a harbinger of more profound differences to come. During the intervening months, the balance in the Russian factional struggle had shifted to the point where the Stalinists felt strong enough to silence Trotsky and prevent the attendance of Zinoviev at the Eighth Plenum. Yet even under such conditions of open confrontation Togliatti again defended the opposition's right to be heard. Not only that, but he also opposed the Stalinists' unprincipled methods of factional infighting.

Togliatti's first run-in with the Stalinists occurred at a restricted pre-plenum meeting of top-ranking Communist leaders convoked by Stalin himself to build up a case for the expulsion of Trotsky from the ECCI. The primary source of information on this episode is the postwar autobiographical essay of Ignazio Silone, who as a member of the PCI delegation attended the meeting with Togliatti.[37] (Togliatti confirmed the accuracy of Silone's account.)[38] In brief, Thälmann, as presiding officer, proposed that the plenum pass a resolution condemning Trotsky's document, "The Chinese Revolution and the Theses of Comrade Stalin," which attacked the CPSU's then faltering China policy. (The Kuomintang's slaughter of Communist workers in Shanghai had just taken place.) However, the document itself had not at that time been circulated outside the Soviet Politburo. Hence Silone and Togliatti refused to condemn it sight unseen, to the undisguised indignation of Stalin's supporters. One wonders to what extent Togliatti's reaction may have been influenced by his own experience the previous January when sectarians on the Comintern Presidium criticized the PCI's policy on transitional slogans without having read the relevant documents. In any event, when a Comintern emissary, Vasil Kolarov, tried to persuade them in private to side with the Soviet majority regardless of the contents of Trotsky's critique, Togliatti replied that they could not declare themselves for the majority or minority in advance.[39]

The friction between the Italian delegation and the Comintern leadership continued during the full plenary sessions. At the opening meeting, again according to Silone's account,[40] Zinoviev was barred from entering

---

37. Silone's fullest account appears in the second edition of *Uscita di sicurezza* (Rome: Associazione italiana per la libertà della cultura, 1955), 46–52. Cf. Berti's commentary, *Annali Feltrinelli* 8, 1927, doc. 2:332–49 at 334–35. An abbreviated version appears in *The God That Failed*, ed. Richard Crossman (New York: Harper and Row, 1963).

38. Silone, *Uscita di sicurezza*, 52, n. 1; cf. *l'Unità*, January 6, 1950.

39. Paraphrased in Silone, *Uscita di sicurezza*, 51.

40. Ibid., 53–54.

the ECCI assembly hall by two uniformed policemen. When Trotsky rose to protest, Osip Piatnitsky retorted that Zinoviev had voluntarily resigned both as Comintern president and as member of the ECCI at the preceding plenum. Whereupon Togliatti objected that he had been entrusted precisely by the Russian delegation to communicate to the Seventh Plenum that Zinoviev was indeed abandoning the post of president, but that he nevertheless remained a duly elected member of the ECCI. His objection was overruled by none other than Thälmann, once again the presiding officer. At the Seventh Plenum Thälmann had taken a position identical to Togliatti's with respect to the opposition leader's right to speak. However, his remarks to this effect had meanwhile been expunged from the Russian stenographic account of the plenum in a striking example of the growing collusion between the leadership of the German party and the Russian Stalinists in the Comintern hierarchy.[41] Thus he was now able to reverse himself with impunity.

But the act that had the most lasting impact on Soviet–PCI relations was the Italian delegation's refusal to go along with a move to expel Trotsky then and there from the ECCI. From the available documentation it is unclear whether this happened at the preplenum meeting or at the full plenary sessions. According to Togliatti's later report to the PCI Politburo, however, the push for expulsion—led by the German delegation—was opposed by seven of fifteen parties present.[42] The PCI delegation objected, he explained, partly because Trotsky was still revered by the masses as one of the leaders of the October Revolution (an echo of Gramsci's 1926 letter to the CPSU) and partly because one could not rule out the possibility that "in some important party one might have to fight a factional struggle [lotta di tendenza] in order to rectify its line." The implication was that under some circumstances a struggle by a minority against the majority might be justified. Togliatti probably had in mind the PCI's own battle with Bordiga. Because of the reluctance of a number of other delegates as well to accept the Germans' proposal, the CPSU delegation finally made a compromise motion authorizing the ECCI Presidium to expel Trotsky at a later date if he persisted in his factional activity.[43] In Togliatti's words, "a first count gave seven votes in favor [the moderates] and eight against. Stalin's intervention was necessary in order to convince

41. Compare the stenographic account of the December 4 session of the Seventh Plenum which appeared in *La Correspondance Internationale* 6, no. 144 (December 30, 1926):1875–80, to *Puti mirovoi revoliutsii* 1:511–27.

42. See Togliatti's report to a plenary meeting of the PCI Politburo which took place in Paris June 10–14, 1927, in APC, 1927, fol. 560:43–47 at 46.

43. For the final text, see "Resolution on the Statements of Comrades Trotsky and Vuyovitch at the Plenary Session of the ECCI," *Inprecor* 7, no. 35 (June 16, 1927):735–37.

all the comrades to vote for the compromise resolution. The attitude of our delegation on this question was crucial [*determinante*]."[44]

Stalin's conciliatory conduct notwithstanding, there can be little doubt but that the CPSU delegation was behind the German party's initiatives against Trotsky. The Soviet compromise motion was plainly a ruse to ensure that the extremists would get their way through the manipulation of the smaller Presidium, an eventuality that all too quickly came to pass. As Bukharin (whose role in all this remains unclear) remarked shortly afterward to a meeting of the Moscow CPSU organization, among the delegates to the Eighth Plenum "the *great majority* [*sic*] were for much harsher sanctions against the opposition."[45] In point of fact, the delegations (if not the delegates per se) who favored the expulsion of Trotsky constituted a majority of one.

Such careful documentation is essential since the Stalinists, in an effort to conceal the dissension that had developed over how to treat the CPSU leftists, did not see fit to publish a stenographic account of the Eighth Plenum in any language.[46]

Togliatti evidently felt uneasy in his new role of oppositionist. He was, after all, a firm supporter of the domestic Soviet line. Moreover, in his speech to the Eighth Plenum he had spoken at length on the correctness of the Comintern's strategy in China.[47] Indeed, as a member (along with Bukharin and the French leftist, Albert Treint) of the plenum's three-man Chinese Commission, he had supported Stalin against the attacks of Trotsky and his allies on that score.[48] Thus before leaving Moscow Togliatti decided (according to Silone) that it would be expedient to send a letter to the Soviet leaders explaining his delegation's conduct.

The letter actually dealt only with the PCI delegates' objections to the exclusion of Zinoviev from the plenum's proceedings,[49] an indication that

---

44. See note 42 to this chapter.

45. *La Correspondance Internationale* 7, no. 71 (July 2, 1927):957–62 at 962; my emphasis.

46. Witold S. Sworakowski, *The Communist International and Its Front Organizations* (Stanford: The Hoover Institution, 1965), 238. Ragionieri's account of Togliatti's conduct at the Eighth Plenum is misleading. He questioned the accuracy of Silone's version, while he nowhere mentioned Togliatti's report on these developments to the PCI Politburo, cited above and readily available in the PCI Archives. See his introduction to *Opere 1926–1929*, by Palmiro Togliatti (Rome: Editori Riuniti, 1972), lvi–lviii. Spriano, on the other hand, accepted Silone's account and also quoted extensively from Togliatti's Politburo report (for which, however, he gave the wrong citation). See Spriano, *Storia del Partito comunista italiano* 2:127–30.

47. "Sulla tattica comunista nella rivoluzione cinese," *SO* 1, no. 5 (July 1927):533–44. That this was Togliatti's speech to the Eighth Plenum was confirmed by Giorgio Caforno in his article, "Il dibattito al X Plenum della Terza Internazionale sulla socialdemocrazia, il fascismo e il socialfascismo," *Critica marxista* 3, no. 4 (July–August 1965):117–73 at 141–42, n. 33.

48. Robert C. North, *Moscow and Chinese Communists*, 2d ed. (Stanford: Stanford University Press, 1963), 104–5.

49. For the text, see APC, 1926, fol. 377:77–78. Cf. Togliatti's report on the Eighth Plenum in APC, 1927, fol. 560:46. Curiously, the letter—which carried no date—appears among the

they still thought themselves in the clear on the question of Trotsky. In it they maintained that they opposed not the barring of Zinoviev but the legalistic grounds upon which it was done. Instead of citing his resignation from the ECCI chairmanship at the Seventh Plenum, they argued, the plenum organizers should have frankly stated that Zinoviev was being excluded on disciplinary grounds, that is, because he broke a pledge to refrain from further factional activity. At the same time, the Italians expressed full support for the CPSU and the *"direction russe"* of the Comintern. All the same, this letter met with the same fate as Gramsci's letter six months earlier. According to Silone's account, it was intercepted by Bukharin "who sent for us at once and advised us in a friendly way to withdraw it so as not to worsen our already precarious personal situation."[50]

The position of the PCI leadership was indeed precarious. At the Eighth Plenum Silone and Togliatti had provoked the ire of the Stalinists, both Russian and non-Russian, who were rapidly rising in the Comintern hierarchy and soon to reduce that organization to a personal instrument of the Soviet dictator. They had in particular antagonized the plebeian Thälmann, who was doubtless aware that on personal grounds he was no match for the urbane and articulate Italian leaders. This was so much the case that Thälmann, insinuating that it was the fault of the Italian Communists that fascism was still in power in Italy, requested an investigation into all domestic PCI policy. Silone reports that "due to the known political ties between Bukharin and Togliatti" this punitive review had to be postponed until after the defeat of the Soviet rightists in 1929.[51] However, as we shall see, German encroachments upon Togliatti's position within the Italian party began considerably earlier.

Presumably alarmed by this turn of events, the PCI leadership was quick to denounce the Trotskyites during the remainder of 1927. In editorials and formal resolutions it roundly condemned them for ideological deviations and factionalism, deploring what it described as their verbal violence toward the Russian leaders, unconstructive criticism of Soviet policy, and persistent attempts to undermine the unity of the CPSU and the Comintern.[52] In a formal report to the PCI Politburo on August 27, 1927, Togliatti repudiated the leftists on these same grounds, all the while expressing reservations about taking disciplinary action against them.[53]

---

documents of the Seventh Plenum even though its contents clearly identify it as a response to developments at the Eighth Plenum.

50. Silone, *Uscita di sicurezza*, 56.
51. Ibid., 65; cf. ibid., 53.
52. See "L'opposizione 'russa' e l'Internazionale," *SO* 1, no. 5 (July 1927):564–70; and PCI Central Committee resolution of August 27, 1927, in *Annali Feltrinelli* 8, 1927, doc. 2:347–49. This resolution was actually approved by the Politburo, not the Central Committee.
53. Ibid., 337–47.

His restraint in this regard, however, was no different than that publicly voiced at the time by Bukharin.[54] And the PCI proceeded to back the expulsions of Trotsky and Zinoviev from both the CPSU and the ECCI when they finally did occur in the fall of 1927, even though the Italian resolution to this effect was perceptibly softer than the uniformly pejorative statement of the ECCI Presidium.[55]

Efforts to Remove Togliatti from the PCI Secretariat

This compliance notwithstanding, in the spring of 1928 Togliatti's enemies in the Comintern hierarchy, probably encouraged by the divisions that had meanwhile developed within the Italian party itself, attempted to remove him from the leadership of the PCI by assigning him to work in the West European Bureau (WEB) of the International. Significantly, the WEB was located in Berlin and hence subject to the direct influence of the German Communist leadership. Indeed, the scheme to transfer Togliatti apparently originated among the growing circle of German and Soviet Stalinists and failed only as a result of the determined opposition of Humbert-Droz and Togliatti's own companions in the PCI.

The Stalinists' distrust of Togliatti, already aroused at the Eighth Plenum, apparently intensified as a result of two developments at the Ninth Plenum of the ECCI in February 1928. First of all, the Latin Secretariat— still headed by Humbert-Droz—reaffirmed the Presidium's January 1927 resolution on the PCI even after hearing in person Longo's spirited criticism of the policies sanctioned by that document.[56] Second, despite a prior Comintern directive (the origins of which are not clear) to shift Togliatti to the recently formed WEB, the Italian leader worked out a compromise with the International's chief organizational *apparatchik,* Osip Piatnitsky, and Humbert-Droz whereby he would help out in the WEB when necessary but remain active in the PCI leadership.[57]

It was against this backdrop that Richard and Willi Münzenberg, German partisans of Thälmann who had been entrusted with overseeing the WEB organization, sent a letter to the PCI Politburo on March 16, 1928, virtually commanding Togliatti to report "immediately" to the post to

54. Cf. "La lotta contro l'opposizione nella riunione plenaria del CC del Partito russo," *SO* 1, no. 7 (September 1927):806–10 at 810.

55. "Resolution of the Presidium of the ECCI on the Question of the Opposition," *Inprecor* 7, no. 68 (December 1, 1927):1532–33; cf. the PCI's resolution in *Inprecor* 7, no. 73 (December 29, 1927):1668–69.

56. See Ercoli's report on this to the March 1928 PCI Central Committee meeting in APC, 1928, fol. 653:9.

57. See Togliatti's March 19, 1928, letter to the PCI Politburo in APC, 1928, fol. 675:114–19 at 114.

which the Comintern had purportedly assigned him "months and months" ago.[58]

Togliatti's riposte came in a formal letter to the PCI Politburo dated March 19 and a personal note to Humbert-Droz dated March 17. To the PCI he protested that the summons to Berlin contradicted a decision by the Comintern's Political Secretariat in January 1927 that he leave the ECCI for full-time work in his party as well as a decision by that same body in November 1927 that he assume direction of the PCI Secretariat (of which Gramsci remained, of course, the titular head). The Münzenbergs' order also ran counter to the agreement he had reached with Piatnitsky and Humbert-Droz at the Ninth Plenum. In short, it was—in Togliatti's words—an example of the "bureaucratic brutality" that had begun to characterize the organizational style of the International.[59] In addition to these procedural objections, he went on to argue that his presence in the day-to-day work of the PCI was essential because of the many Italian cadres arrested by the Mussolini regime and the enormous organizational problems facing the party.

Finally, to both his party comrades and Humbert-Droz, Togliatti made what can only be called an impassioned defense of his right to serve the Communist movement as a PCI activist rather than Comintern functionary. Particularly in the March 17, 1928, note to his long-time friend, Humbert-Droz, he deplored the heavy-handed attempt to remove him from the party leadership without prior consultation with the PCI Central Committee: "One can't consider the leading organs of a party as a doll from which one detaches an arm or leg at pleasure," he protested. But even more telling was his insistence that he himself was unfit for the life and duties of a Comintern *apparatchik*. Only as an activist in the Italian party, he contended, would he be able to work "with all the energy and all the passion that are necessary." Not only that, but to uproot him from the PCI at this time would mean to uproot him permanently and completely: "It is much better—for me at least—to see these things now than to have to recognize a little later that I have become one of the numerous demoralized, lost, superficial, empty elements that one can only let fall by the wayside."[60]

The upshot of these appeals was a vote of confidence in Togliatti by the PCI Central Committee and a draw in the Political Secretariat of the ECCI. At a late March 1928 PCI Central Committee meeting, from which Longo was notably absent, the Münzenbergs' letter and Togliatti's reply

58. Text in APC, 1928, fol. 671:2 and reverse side.
59. Text in APC, 1928, fol. 675:114–19, esp. 114–15.
60. Togliatti's letter of March 17, 1928, in Jules Humbert-Droz, *Il contrasto tra l'Internazionale e il PCI 1922–28* (Milan: Feltrinelli Editore, 1969), 251–52. Cf. APC, 1928, fol. 675:118.

were read by everyone present. It was then agreed that the party's objections to Togliatti's transfer to the WEB would be expressed by the Politburo in a letter to the Comintern offices concerned. It was also decided (at Togliatti's suggestion) that Grieco would temporarily replace him as head of the party Secretariat—the Secretariat, however, would still include Togliatti along with Silone and a youth representative.[61] Grieco was, accordingly, responsible for drafting the PCI's reply to the Comintern. In that document he tactfully avoided Togliatti's heated criticisms of the organizational practices of the International, noting that the Politburo did not wholly agree with him on this matter. Instead Grieco concentrated on procedural details and on the needs of the PCI in the wake of the Fascist crackdown.[62]

At this point, according to Humbert-Droz's later correspondence with Togliatti,[63] the lineup in the Political Secretariat of the ECCI was as follows. Togliatti's transfer to Berlin was supported not only by Piatnitsky and the discredited and hence powerless Czechoslovakian moderate, Bohumír Šmeral,[64] but also by Hermann Remmele, a German who was to play a key role in the PCI's later capitulation to the Stalinists. Only Humbert-Droz and Egidio Gennari, the new Italian delegate,[65] favored Togliatti's retention in the PCI leadership. Bukharin was absent from the meetings in question. Perhaps it was the unflinching support of his own party that won the day for Togliatti. In any event, on April 18 Humbert-Droz officially informed the PCI in behalf of the ECCI Secretariat that the compromise solution arranged at the Ninth Plenum would remain in effect.[66] The Stalinists in the Comintern hierarchy were as yet not powerful enough to defy the will of a cohesive party leadership.[67]

61. See the minutes of the meeting in APC, 1928, fol. 653:1–42 at 41.

62. The text of Grieco's letter, "Al Segretariato dell'I.C. al W.E.B.," dated March 30, 1928, is in APC, 1928, fol. 671:7–9.

63. See Humbert-Droz's letter of May 2, 1928, to Ercoli (as well as Ercoli's reply of May 11) in *Il contrasto tra l'Internazionale e il PCI 1922–28*, by Humbert-Droz, 252–55.

64. Zdeněk Eliáš and Jaromír Netík, "Czechoslovakia," in *Communism in Europe*, ed. William E. Griffith, 2 vols. (Cambridge, Mass.: MIT Press, 1966), 2:155–276 at 170; in the late 1920s Šmeral was assigned to work in the WEB offices in Berlin.

65. In his spring 1928 correspondence with Togliatti, Humbert-Droz refers to a certain "Maggi," whom he identifies as Egidio Gennari in his *"L'Oeil de Moscou" à Paris* (Paris: Julliard, 1964), 243 and 255.

66. Text in APC, 1928, fol. 671:32.

67. Spriano mentioned this incident in passing and stressed the PCI's opposition to Togliatti's transfer, but he did not touch on the motives or persons who proposed it in the first place; see *Storia del Partito comunista italiano* 2:184 and n. 1. Ragionieri devoted a number of pages to the WEB affair, but he failed to mention Togliatti's reference to the "bureaucratic brutality" of the Münzenbergs, let alone the probable motives underlying the demand to transfer him to Berlin. Instead Ragionieri treated the matter as a fairly routine organizational disagreement over how Togliatti could best serve the International. See Togliatti, *Opere 1926–1929*, cxxi–cxxvi.

The PCI and the "Opportunism of Conciliation"

By the late spring of 1928, on the eve of the Sixth Comintern Congress, the Stalinists' resentment over the PCI's conciliatory attitude toward the Soviet left-wing oppositionists, both at the Eighth Plenum and before, had been compounded by their inability to remove Togliatti from an active role in the Italian party leadership. Meanwhile, among PCI cadres the controversy over transitional slogans had intensified to the point where Longo, provoked by developments at the party's Second Conference in January 1928, had aired the arguments of "the youth" at the Ninth Plenum of the ECCI in Moscow the following month. It is only logical to assume that contacts between the Italian youth faction and Togliatti's opponents in the Comintern bureaucracy were established then, if not earlier. The very virulence of the polemics at the PCI Central Committee meeting of June 1928, discussed in the previous chapter, suggests that the FGCI leaders were receiving influential outside support. Indeed, one may surmise that the individuals behind the campaign against transitional slogans that began during the Sixth Congress were sympathizers of the PCI dissidents. It was, however, over the issue of organizational measures— this time against Comintern moderates, or rightists—that Togliatti and the Stalinists locked horns.

Togliatti's Plea for Restraint at the Sixth Congress

By the time the Sixth Congress convened in July 1928, the struggle not just against the rightists but against those who opposed disciplinary steps against them, the so-called conciliators, was already well under way in the KPD. As early as the Ninth Plenum in February 1928, a joint postplenum session of the Russian and German delegations had secretly resolved that "*tolerance* toward the representatives of right deviations" was inadmissible.[68] And the following summer the majority of the German delegates to the Sixth Congress, meeting in closed caucus, had further agreed that the main danger in the KPD was represented not by rightists but "by comrades who exhibit tolerance" toward the rightists.[69]

An open dispute erupted on the very floor of the congress among the German delegates over the question of whether rightists should be combated by organizational or ideological means, that is, by purge or political persuasion. On July 26 Thälmann took the offensive in favor of disciplin-

68. See references to this session in Ewert's speech to the Sixth Congress, in *VI Kongress Kominterna* 1:379–90 at 388; my emphasis.
69. Ibid.

ary action.[70] The next day Artur Ewert, KPD Politburo member and moderate, took issue with Thälmann, arguing that "the repudiation of tolerance toward these [right-wing] deviations does not mean the application of organizational measures alone in the struggle against them. . . . Organizational measures are the last resort."[71] But the crux of the dispute was whether disciplinary steps should be taken not merely against the rightists but against conciliators like himself. Ewert expressly warned of this danger in his speech.[72] And his fears were confirmed by Walter Ulbricht in his rebuttal to Ewert on July 28. Quoting an earlier statement by Thälmann, Ulbricht threw down the gauntlet: "*Against the supporters of the conciliatory tendency,* who prevent the party from conducting an appropriate struggle against the rightists, *we must conduct a struggle by* both ideological and *organizational means.*"[73]

At this point Togliatti attempted to come to Ewert's support. In the prepared text of his major address to the congress, which he delivered shortly after Ulbricht's speech, he cautioned against the adoption of organizational measures against the minority in the KPD Politburo, namely, Ewert: "With regard to the . . . Politburo of the [German] party, it seems to us that the diversity of opinions which exist among them on different questions are differences which can normally exist in a leading center without unleashing a struggle of groups and factions."[74] Purportedly because of a lack of time, Togliatti was not permitted to read these comments,[75] which appeared in the last two paragraphs of his speech. They were, however, included in the Russian stenographic report of the congress.[76]

Furthermore, before being cut off Togliatti managed to voice a general warning against the use of organizational measures in Comintern affairs,[77] especially at the level of the party leaderships: "With regard to our activity in the formation of the leading centers of our parties, we might take as our slogan the last words of the dying Goethe: 'More light!' *The vanguard of the proletariat cannot fight in the shadows. The chief of staff of the revolution cannot be formed in an unprincipled factional struggle.* For this reason we think one must be careful about transferring the politi-

70. Thälmann, in ibid., 333–46 at 344–45.

71. Ewert, in ibid., 389.

72. This warning appeared in the Russian stenographic account of the congress but not the Comintern press version of the same; see ibid. Cf. *La Correspondance Internationale* 8, no. 86 (August 18, 1928):905–8.

73. Ulbricht, in *VI Kongress Kominterna* 1:454–60 at 459; my emphasis.

74. Ercoli, "L'orientamento del nostro partito," in *SO 1927–1939,* ed. Ferri, 1:293.

75. Ibid., 294, n. 1; cf. *Rinascita* 21, no. 28 (July 11, 1964):15.

76. Ercoli, in *VI Kongress Kominterna* 1:509.

77. For the timing of the cut-off, see the editorial note appended to Ercoli, "L'orientamento del nostro partito," in *SO 1927–1939,* ed. Ferri, 1:294, n. 1.

cal struggle among different currents which can exist inside a party and its leading organs onto the plane of organizational measures."[78] If disciplinary steps had to be taken against those guilty of extreme factionalism, Togliatti asked that they be taken on the basis of an open struggle for a specific political line rather than an unprincipled struggle involving compromises among diverse groups. And he boasted that observance of this guideline was the reason for the PCI's unique position as the only Communist party whose leadership had remained intact since the Fifth Comintern Congress in 1924.[79]

Togliatti thus echoed from the podium of the Sixth Congress the appeal for restraint made by Gramsci in his October 1926 letter to the CPSU Central Committee.[80] Also notable was his oblique criticism of the behind-the-scene maneuvers that were becoming the standard practice of the Stalinists (was he thinking of the attempt to remove him from the PCI leadership several months earlier?). It is in this sense that his plea for "more light" and his allusion to fighting "in the shadows" must be understood. And the Stalinists' sensitivity on this score was revealed by their use of yet another underhanded maneuver to blunt the impact of Togliatti's criticism. They altered the text of his speech in the Russian stenographic account, substituting for the above italicized passages the following sentence: "One must avoid at all costs an unprincipled factional struggle."[81] Even this watered-down version appeared only because of the insistence of Angelo Tasca, then PCI representative in Moscow.[82]

Bukharin's response to the above debate on the factional struggle in the German party foreshadowed the equivocal position on organizational measures that was to be incorporated into the political resolution (theses) of the Sixth Congress. On the one hand, he insisted that discipline was essential and stated that the ECCI fully supported Thälmann's leadership of the KPD. On the other hand, he appealed for "a kind of internal-party *tact*" in dealing with the right-wing danger and announced that the CPSU was opposed to any attempt "to oust Comrade Ewert from the party leadership."[83] He concluded with the following quotation from an unpublished letter of Lenin: "If you are going to drive out all the not

78. Ibid., 292–93; my emphasis.

79. Ibid., 291–92.

80. According to the summary of Togliatti's report on the Sixth Congress to the PCI Central Committee in October 1928, he also criticized the organizational practices of the Comintern bureaucracy in the "Senior-Convent," a restricted meeting of senior party delegates. Unfortunately, no further details are available on this incident. See APC, 1928, fol. 653:250.

81. Cf. Ercoli, "L'orientamento del nostro partito," in SO 1927–1939, ed. Ferri, 1:292–93, to Ercoli, in VI Kongress Kominterna 1:508.

82. See Tasca's letter of October 18, 1928, to the PCI Secretariat, Annali Feltrinelli 8, 1928, doc. 8:520–22 at 522.

83. Bukharin, in VI Kongress Kominterna 1:587–615 at 612–13.

particularly obedient but clever people and retain only the obedient fools, you will ruin the party *for sure*."[84]

By the same token, despite Togliatti's outspokenness the PCI was treated relatively gently at the Sixth Congress. To be sure, the conclave's final resolution cautioned that right-wing tendencies "under present conditions . . . represent a very serious danger to the party."[85] This warning was, however, rather moderate compared to the accusations of rightism leveled at the French, Czechoslovakian, Polish, and German parties during the congress. As a case in point, when Thälmann reported on the various amendments to the resolution, he alluded only to tactical errors on the part of the PCI, whereas he sharply castigated the French Communist Party for right-wing deviations.[86] Moreover, shortly after the congress the ECCI Political Secretariat endorsed a resolution on the PCI stating that "notable manifestations of [right-wing] deviations have not been recently observed."[87]

Still, discordant voices were raised during the formulation of the ECCI's resolution on the Italian party. Hermann Remmele, for one, argued that the PCI's use of transitional slogans for agitational purposes was inadmissible, and even Bukharin asked tentatively whether the party's position on such slogans "wasn't in contradiction with the Program of the C.I." Remmele's objections may well have been inspired by Longo's reiteration of his criticisms of PCI policy in the Comintern's Latin Secretariat following the Sixth Congress.[88] And they surely underscored the key role of the German Stalinists in the escalating campaign against transitional slogans. For after the debate in the Political Secretariat, the draft resolution on the PCI was amended to limit the Italian party's advocacy of transitional slogans to propaganda rather than agitation.[89]

Stalin's Offensive against the "Opportunism of Conciliation"

This process of carping and minor concessions was a portent of things to come. For within a matter of months the Stalinists gained the upper hand, first within the KPD and then throughout the Comintern bureaucracy. On September 26, 1928, a coalition of German rightists and conciliators persuaded the KPD Central Committee to oust Thälmann from the

84. Ibid., 614.
85. Sixth Congress theses, in *VI Kongress Kominterna* 6:74–75.
86. Thälmann, in ibid. 5:123.
87. "Risoluzione sulla politica del PCI," *SO* 2, no. 9 (October 1928):662–64 at 662.
88. See Togliatti's allusions to Longo's criticisms in his two speeches delivered at that meeting, in *Opere 1926–1929*, by Togliatti, 506–41 at 525 and 539–40.
89. For a description of what transpired at the ECCI Political Secretariat's meeting on the PCI, see Tasca's letter of September 7, 1928, to the PCI Secretariat in APC, 1928, fol. 673:118–19 and reverse sides of handwritten letter.

leadership on the grounds of complicity in a financial scandal perpetrated by one of his backers in the German party apparatus. That decision was promptly reversed by Thälmann's supporters in Moscow in a flagrant misuse of the authority accorded by the Comintern's statutes to its executive organs. On October 6 Stalin, Thälmann, Vyacheslav Molotov, and Otto Kuusinen convoked a meeting of the ECCI Presidium without notifying the many Presidium members (including Bukharin and Humbert-Droz) who were away from Moscow on vacation following the six-and-a-half-week long Comintern congress.[90] In a resolution of the same date, the rump body proceeded not only to reinstate Thälmann as head of the KPD but also to give him its unqualified support, naming him "one of the chief representatives of the line of the Sixth World Congress."[91]

The brashness of this move polarized both the German party and the Comintern hierarchy. The German rightists, largely followers of the former KPD leader, Heinrich Brandler, and his associate August Thalheimer (both of whom had been admitted to the CPSU and given minor posts in Moscow after being made the scapegoats for their role in the abortive German Communist uprising of October 1923) now began actively to develop a factional platform and organization. Whereupon the Stalinists undertook the disciplinary measures they had so long advocated. They expelled the most outspoken rightists, Brandler and Thalheimer included, while they reassigned conciliators such as Ewert to work in Moscow as a way of removing them from active participation in KPD affairs.[92]

Meanwhile, the maneuvers of the Stalinists, both in Moscow and Berlin, provoked an angry outcry from Humbert-Droz and Tasca (see below) as well as a more muted sense of outrage on the part of others. Thereupon the Stalinists again took the offensive. As discussed in the previous chapter, on December 19, 1928, the Comintern Presidium approved an "Open Letter" to the KPD which demanded that the German rightists accept unconditionally the Comintern line, including even harsher restrictions on transitional slogans than had been imposed at the Sixth Congress. Equally important, the document bluntly asserted that conciliation toward the rightists was henceforth inadmissible: "The time has come when each member must choose between the party and the right wing. A conciliatory attitude toward the latter would now mean . . . a support of the said wing against the party."[93]

90. For details see Humbert-Droz, "L'Oeil de Moscou" à Paris, 256–59; Tasca's diary, in Annali Feltrinelli 8, 1928, doc. 7:515–20 at 518–20; and Tasca's letter of October 21, 1928, to the PCI Secretariat, ibid., 1928, doc. 9:523–24.

91. "Decision of the Presidium of the ECCI on the Happenings in the Hamburg Party Organization," Inprecor 8, no. 71 (October 12, 1928):1293–94.

92. For details see Tasca's letters to the PCI Secretariat of November 4 and December 18, 1928, Annali Feltrinelli 8, 1928, doc. 12:531–34 at 532, and doc. 24:593–96 at 594.

93. "Open Letter from the ECCI to the CP of Germany in Regard to the Right Danger in the Latter," Inprecor 8, no. 91 (December 27, 1928):1725–28 at 1727.

This amounted to a call for a purge of conciliators throughout the Communist International. Indeed, the attitude of the individual parties toward both the "Open Letter" and the expulsion of the German rightists was soon to become a measure of the degree to which they had been bolshevized (read Stalinized). As Dmitry Manuilsky—one of Stalin's rising spokesmen in the Comintern—announced some two months later: "No single section of the Communist International may remain indifferent to the discussions in the German C.P."[94]

According to this yardstick the Italian Communists were out of line. The PCI Central Committee had endorsed the Presidium's October 1928 decision to reinstate Thälmann as leader of the KPD only in December 1928 under circumstances that recalled the Italian party's withdrawal of Gramsci's 1926 letter to the CPSU Central Committee.[95] Just as Humbert-Droz had been sent to Italy to secure the retraction of Gramsci's statement, Manuilsky was dispatched from Moscow to persuade the PCI Central Committee of the Stalinists' view of the Thälmann incident.[96] By the same token, on the cardinal issue of the "Open Letter" the PCI's approval was, relatively speaking, both late in coming and reserved in content. In contrast to earlier resolutions by the German, French, Austrian, Czechoslovakian, and Norwegian parties devoted specifically to the "Open Letter,"[97] the PCI Central Committee dealt with it only cursorily in a March 1929 resolution on Comintern problems in general. Unlike the above parties, moreover, it did not explicitly endorse either "organizational measures" as such or the actual expulsion of the German rightists. Instead it limited itself to a rather perfunctory one-sentence endorsement of the "Open Letter" as "an act of capital importance in the struggle against the rightist danger and the currents of conciliation toward it."[98]

More significant, the PCI leadership failed to purge its own ranks of one of the most outspoken oppositionists in the Comintern at that time, Angelo Tasca. Throughout the escalation of the KPD crisis during the autumn of 1928, Tasca, PCI representative to the ECCI since mid-October, had boldly opposed the trend toward organizational measures in

94. D. Manuilsky, "The Discussion in the German Communist Party," *Inprecor* 9, no. 9 (February 22, 1929):139–44 at 140.

95. "Resolution of the CC of the CP of Italy on the Happenings in the CP of Germany," *Inprecor* 9, no. 1 (January 3, 1929):11–12.

96. Berti's commentary in *Annali Feltrinelli* 8, 1928, doc. 23:584–93 at 584 and 588. The records of the December 1928 meeting of the PCI Central Committee are missing from the PCI Archives at the Gramsci Institute. Cf. Ragionieri's introduction to *Opere 1926–1929*, by Togliatti, cxcv.

97. Their respective resolutions appear in *Inprecor* 9, nos. 1, 2, 4, 5, and 7 (January 3, 10, 18, 25, and February 8, 1929):9–10, 34, 68, 85, and 115, respectively.

98. "Risoluzione sui problemi della Internazionale," *SO* 3, no. 2 (February 1929):167–70 at 167; also in *Inprecor* 9, no. 14 (March 15, 1929):267–68.

both his private utterances and official statements.[99] Twice he abstained on measures backed by the Stalinists, first when called upon to endorse the expulsions and personnel shifts in the KPD,[100] and then when called upon to approve a resolution censuring Humbert-Droz (who voted *against* the KPD purge) for opportunism.[101] Even more provocatively, during the heated discussion of the draft version of the "Open Letter" at the Presidium's December 19 meeting, he denounced the document for its "glaring political weakness."[102] And his speech on that occasion ended on the following audacious note: "In our Italian party we adopted this method which you call 'conciliatory' *vis-à-vis* the left, which permitted us to draw into the work of the party the great majority of those who previously followed Comrade Bordiga."[103]

As a result of his persistent opposition, and especially his refusal to endorse the "Open Letter" to the KPD, Tasca drew upon himself the personal wrath of Stalin at the December 19 meeting. Tasca and Humbert-Droz, in arguing against the expulsion of the German rightists, referred to the passage on "persuasion" in the political resolution of the Sixth Congress. Stalin derisively countered their arguments with a reference to the same resolution's simultaneous call for "iron internal party discipline."[104] And, in what under the circumstances could only be considered a very grave threat, he denounced them both for falling into "the mire of cowardly opportunism, . . . the opportunism of conciliation toward the right deviation."[105]

Meanwhile, Tasca gradually broadened the scope of his criticism to include the entire range of policies adopted by the Stalinists. On February 28, 1929, he presented to the PCI Central Committee a lengthy report in which he attacked Stalin's domestic economic policy as well as his characterization of the international scene.[106] On the latter the crux of Tasca's argument was that the gap between the objective contradictions of capitalism and the low level of mass militancy was even greater in 1928 than

99. *Annali Feltrinelli* 8, 1928, docs. 7–17 and 20–26:515–50 and 568–607, passim.

100. Tasca's letter of November 4, 1928, to PCI Secretariat, ibid., 1928, doc. 12:531–34 at 532–33.

101. Tasca's letter of December 20, 1928, to PCI Secretariat, ibid., 1928, doc. 25:596–98 at 598.

102. Tasca's speech to December 19, 1928, meeting of the ECCI Presidium, ibid., 1928, doc. 26:598–607 at 601. The speech is found at 601–7.

103. Ibid., 607.

104. Stalin, "O pravoi opasnosti v Germanskoi kompartii," *KI*, no. 52 (December 28, 1929):14–20 at 17.

105. Ibid., 14; cf. the description of this same meeting in the memoirs of a participant, Henri Barbé, "Stalin and the 'Rebellion' of Tasca and Humbert-Droz," in *The Comintern: Historical Highlights*, ed. Milorad M. Drachkovitch and Branko Lazitch (New York: Praeger, 1966), 217–33.

106. Text in *Annali Feltrinelli* 8, 1929, Doc. 14:671–803.

it had been in 1921, and that the political line of the Third and Fourth Comintern Congresses (favoring transitional slogans and the united front with social democracy) should therefore remain in force.[107] He also opposed the collectivization of Soviet agriculture.[108]

The personal reactions of Togliatti and the other Italian leaders to Tasca's conduct will be dealt with in chapter 3. What is important here is that, despite Tasca's open defiance of Moscow, they refrained from taking disciplinary action against him. The PCI Central Committee categorically repudiated his views in its March 1929 resolution,[109] the same one that approved the "Open Letter" to the KPD. Nevertheless, it permitted him to remain a member of both the Politburo and the Central Committee. Thus, just as Tasca assumed a conciliatory attitude toward the German rightists, the Italian Communist leadership assumed a conciliatory attitude toward Tasca. Yet, as we have seen, it was precisely the "opportunism of conciliation toward the right deviation" that had become the Stalinists' number one target.

The Tenth Plenum: Togliatti under Attack

By the time the Tenth Plenum of the ECCI convened in July 1929, the rout of the Soviet rightists throughout the Comintern was far advanced. During the preceding months, Bukharin had been progressively isolated within the ranks of the CPSU and openly attacked by Stalin in top party councils.[110] Within the Comintern bureaucracy Stalin's supporters had also taken the offensive against Bukharin. As Humbert-Droz reported to the Politburo of the Swiss Communist Party in early December 1928: "In the corridors of the apparatus a campaign against Bukharin is developing which makes his further work very difficult."[111] Bukharin thus stopped participating in the activities of the Comintern for fear that he would be bound by CPSU discipline to support a line he opposed,[112] failing even to attend the critical December 19 meeting of the ECCI Presidium.[113] And in April 1929 the CPSU Central Committee recommended his removal from the leadership of the International. Meanwhile, in addition to the KPD, the Communist parties of Czechoslovakia, France, Poland, and the United

107. Ibid., 688–702.
108. Ibid., 743.
109. "Risoluzione sui problemi della Internazionale," *SO* 3, no. 2 (February 1929):167–70.
110. Robert Vincent Daniels, *The Conscience of the Revolution* (Cambridge, Mass.: Harvard University Press, 1960), 363–69.
111. Humbert-Droz to the Politburo of the Swiss Communist Party, December 3, 1928 (Humbert-Droz Archive, Harvard University).
112. Tasca's letter of November 4, 1928, to PCI Secretariat, *Annali Feltrinelli* 8, 1928, doc. 14:540.
113. Humbert-Droz to the Politburo of the Swiss Communist Party, January 9, 1929 (Humbert-Droz Archive, Harvard University).

States were widely purged of rightists. And at the Tenth Plenum, Bukharin as well as Tasca, Humbert-Droz, and the American Benjamin Gitlow were formally excluded from the Presidium of the ECCI.[114]

The Stalinists were now in a position to turn the brunt of their fury against the conciliators. During the course of the Tenth Plenum, which met throughout most of July, the Communist parties of Great Britain, Sweden, and Italy were all sharply criticized. However, Molotov, the chief Russian delegate to the Comintern between Bukharin's fall and his own assumption of the Soviet premiership in 1930,[115] concentrated his fire almost exclusively on the PCI. By attacking the Italian leadership for its toleration of Tasca (alias Serra), he in effect accused it of "the opportunism of conciliation." Given Molotov's stature and the harshness of his judgment, his comments warrant quotation at some length:

> In March the C.C. [of the PCI] emphatically condemned Serra's line as hostile to the VI Congress. In regard to this, the Italian comrades say now that *already* in March the C.C. condemned Serra's stand, but there is of course more justification to say that, unfortunately, the C.C. condemned Serra's line *only* in March. In any case, no matter how belated this decision, it was absolutely necessary. Although Serra showed himself to be an outright opportunist and rightist, the C.C. continued *even* in March an utterly unaccountable, in the given case, flirtation with him. (Hear, hear!). . . The C.C. . . . even decided to retain him in the Politburo. . . . In regard to Serra who is openly hostile to the line of the Comintern, such a decision on the part of the C.C. was, of course, a gross error. . . . One cannot help saying that it was [also] a mistake on the part of the Italian Communist Party to have proposed at the VI Congress Serra as its representative in the Executive Committee of the Comintern. In any case, . . . a *determined struggle* against right elements such as Serra is absolutely necessary.[116]

Molotov then proceeded to rebut Tasca's views on Soviet economic policy, charging that he stated openly what the rightists in the CPSU were thinking.[117]

Kuusinen was less discursive but even more uncompromising on the Tasca question. After exhorting "the Italian comrades Ercoli and Garlandi" (alias Togliatti and Grieco) to take a further step down the path of bolshevization, he stated: "Comrade Serra must declare clearly and unequivocally whether he submits unconditionally to all the decisions of the

---

114. "Statement by the Political Secretariat of the ECCI," *Inprecor* 9, no. 35 (July 24, 1929):745; this document was dated July 20, 1929.

115. Lazitch, "Two Instruments of Control by the Comintern," in *The Comintern*, ed. Drachkovitch and Lazitch, 59 and 385, n. 25.

116. *Inprecor* 9, no. 49 (September 12, 1929):1049–50.

117. Ibid., 1051.

Comintern . . . ; if not, he shall be thrown out of the Communist Party.''[118]

In view of the fact that positions such as those of Tasca had been under attack for the past year, his individual fate was already sealed. The target of the above slurs was thus really Togliatti, who was held responsible for the PCI's bearing toward Tasca. While he was at no point accused literally of conciliation, he was successively denounced by Stalinist spokesmen for displaying what was in actuality a conciliatory attitude toward Tasca, Ewert, and Trotsky.

Manuilsky took the offensive at the second session of the plenum, the evening of July 3. After reeling off the ideological deviations of Tasca, he stated equivocally: ''We do not doubt that the Italian comrades, and particularly Comrade Ercoli, hold in unison with the plenum that the public defense of such views is incompatible with affiliation with the Comintern.''[119] Togliatti took this as Manuilsky's way of asking why the PCI had not taken disciplinary steps against Tasca. And on July 8, after denouncing Tasca for his many ''revisionist'' deviations,[120] he replied that the party leadership had not done so first of all because Tasca agreed to its demand ''that he not propagate his ideas either in the party or in the Central Committee.'' The second reason Togliatti gave was that it was necessary to carry the struggle against Tasca beyond the Politburo and Central Committee to the party rank and file. But this had not yet been possible (presumably because of the continuing tenuousness of contacts with the domestic base). Nevertheless, Togliatti said, the PCI would in due time apply ''all the necessary measures'' against Tasca. Not only that, but he hailed the ''struggle to the bitter end'' that the International was conducting against ''opportunism and conciliators.''[121]

Clearly Togliatti's explanation did not suffice; for a full-scale verbal attack with the Germans in the lead was launched against him forthwith. The next day Heinz Neumann declared that the reply to Manuilsky's question regarding Tasca was ''thoroughly unsatisfactory.''[122] He then made what can only be called a loaded remark: ''Serra has overstepped Hercules' pillars of opportunism; or as expressed in Italian, Serra ha oltrepassato le colonne d'*Ercole* dell 'opportunismo! (Hilarity).''[123] Since the names of Communist leaders were normally italicized in Comintern

118. *Inprecor* 9, no. 53 (September 25, 1929):1151.
119. *Inprecor* 9, no. 40 (August 20, 1929):862.
120. Togliatti, *Opere 1926–1929*, 726–47 at 738–42.
121. Ibid., 742–43.
122. *Inprecor* 9, no. 51 (September 17, 1929):1080.
123. Cf. text of Neumann's speech in Caforno, ''Il dibattito al X Plenum,'' *Critica marxista* 3, no. 4 (1965):166. This comment was omitted from the English version in *Inprecor;* the original speech was presumably in German.

protocols and Togliatti's party alias was Ercole Ercoli, Neumann's play on words was an unmistakable slur against the PCI leader.

Thälmann continued in the same vein, questioning whether Togliatti had been entirely accurate when he said that Tasca promised to refrain from making propaganda for his ideas.[124] Thälmann also subjected Togliatti to a relentless browbeating for his defense of Ewert at the Sixth Congress, quoting verbatim the relevant passage from the stenographic account of Togliatti's speech. Significantly, it was exactly the passage that Togliatti had been prevented from reading at the Sixth Congress. The KPD leader then added, menacingly: "Comrade Ercoli will no doubt have to admit at this plenum that he took then an entirely wrong view of the development of the Communist International and of the German party. (Hear, hear.)"[125] At that point, Kuusinen, rubbing salt in the wound and associating Togliatti with Bukharin by implication, advised the PCI leader to relinquish his "non-political 'sense of tact' " toward Tasca: "The same sense of tact," he recalled, "was shown by Ercoli toward Trotsky at the Eighth Plenum, which was also a mistake." Whereupon Ulbricht interjected: "Perhaps this is something more than a sense of tact."[126]

The Comintern hierarchy did not limit itself to denouncing the PCI's temporizing toward Tasca. Piatnitsky also complained that "we workers of the ECCI are badly informed on what is going on in the Communist Party of Italy at home,"[127] and spoke of a Chinese wall separating the Comintern bureaucracy from the Italian party. More important, the Stalinists accused the PCI leaders of a number of theoretical deviations behind the closed doors of the ECCI's Italian Commission. Nowhere in the public record of the plenum's proceedings was the question of the PCI's political line raised. All the same, at a closed meeting of the Italian Commission (a partial stenogram of which was released by the Soviet Institute of Marxism-Leninism four decades later), the party's double revolutionary perspective and position on transitional slogans were denounced as right opportunism.[128]

The reaction of Togliatti and his colleagues to these latter charges was a curious amalgam of protest and compliance: protest at the substance and mode of the Stalinists' criticism; yet acceptance of the need for disciplined

---

124. *Inprecor* 9, no. 51 (September 17, 1929):1105.
125. Ibid., 1104.
126. *Inprecor* 9, no. 53 (September 25, 1929):1151.
127. *Inprecor* 9, no. 44 (August 30, 1929):939.
128. Ernesto Ragionieri, ed., "Togliatti, Grieco e Di Vittorio alla commissione italiana del X Plenum della Internazionale comunista," *Studi storici* 12, no. 1 (January–March 1971):108–70. Since the texts of the Stalinists' speeches are not included, the precise wording of their accusations is not known. However, the substance is clear from Ragionieri's summary as well as from the rebuttals of the Italian delegates. See esp. 112–114, 145–70.

adherence to the new Comintern line, regardless of one's personal views. To Piatnitsky, Togliatti retorted that all the documentation on the PCI was available in the Comintern's archives. "The Chinese wall of which Piatnitsky spoke" was hence "not a wall which separates our party from the International but rather one which separates the archives of the International from Comrade Piatnitsky's office."[129] Before the restricted Italian Commission Togliatti also deplored the surprise attack on the Tasca question at the open plenary sessions, an attack that left—in his words—"the impression that you wanted to challenge us and to make us recant."[130] Grieco then joined in chiding Moscow's spokesmen for denouncing a line that the Comintern itself had endorsed and even encouraged in years past.[131] And a third Italian, Giuseppe Di Vittorio, flatly denied that the Stalinists knew what they were talking about when it came to the PCI.[132] But the most striking was Togliatti's stand regarding the party's double revolutionary perspective: "If the Comintern says it isn't right, we will no longer posit it," he conceded, adding equivocally, "each of us will think these things and will no longer say them."[133] He made the same point more forcefully a bit later: "Since one can't prevent us from thinking, we will keep these things to ourselves and stick to making some general statements."[134]

Over a period of three years the PCI leaders did indeed, as the Stalinists so cuttingly charged, display a conciliatory bent toward dissent in the Comintern's ranks. While Togliatti and his colleagues unabashedly acknowledged the "leading function" of the Soviet Communists in the International, they were also quite prepared to criticize the actual performance of that function. Of critical importance in this regard was Togliatti's shift to Gramsci's position on the need to avoid "excessive measures" in handling internal party disagreements. It is also noteworthy that the PCI Politburo practiced what Gramsci preached in dealing with Bordiga, who remained a member of the Central Committee even after the party's Third Congress.

Togliatti's conduct at the Eighth Plenum of the ECCI in May 1927 signaled his alignment with the views expressed by Gramsci in his October 1926 letter to the CPSU. Several considerations help to explain his change of mind. For one thing, it could hardly have escaped Togliatti's attention that his Italian comrades had been correct in anticipating that the

129. Togliatti, *Opere 1926–29*, 744.
130. Ragionieri, "Togliatti, Grieco e Di Vittorio," *Studi storici* 12, no. 1 (1971):139–40.
131. Ibid., 145–46, 154.
132. Ibid., 165–66, 170.
133. Ibid., 148–49.
134. Ibid., 151.

CPSU majority might ''abuse its victory'' over the left-wing oppositionists. For another, his concern with procedural proprieties, first voiced
at the Seventh Plenum in late 1926, was reinforced by the irregularities
that came to light during the deliberations over PCI policy in the executive
bodies of the Comintern in January 1927. As Togliatti, Grieco, and Tasca
protested in writing at the time, their critics had not even bothered to read
the available documents explaining the Italian party's line. No wonder
Togliatti and Silone refused to condemn sight unseen Trotsky's critique of
Stalin's China policy.

By the summer of 1928 political calculation began to play a role in
Togliatti's conciliatory posture. The abortive attempt to reassign him from
the PCI Politburo to the Comintern's West European Bureau in Berlin
brought home to him the deviousness of which the Stalinists were capable.
The concerted campaign against the moderates in the KPD also pointed to
the vulnerability of the PCI leaders, all the more so in view of their
deteriorating relations with the youth and the latter's growing outspokenness in Moscow. There were, to be sure, substantial differences between
the KPD rightists and the PCI leaders. Both advocated transitional slogans, but the Germans considered them as a basis for cooperation with
social democracy, whereas the Togliatti group—ever disdainful of the
Italian Socialists—viewed them as a way of prodding the many Italians
influenced by center-left parties into an uprising against fascism. Such
nuances were, however, beyond the ken of the Stalinists. In short, the
interests of the PCI itself were at stake in Togliatti's eloquent appeal to the
Sixth Congress for tolerance of dissent and the avoidance of underhanded
organizational maneuvers throughout the Communist movement.

Still, the pleas made by Gramsci and Togliatti for restraint toward the
Trotskyite left suggest that the PCI elite's later conciliatory posture—
toward Tasca as well as the German moderates—was not dictated by
expediency alone. The Italian leaders preferred forbearance toward internal party dissent provided the minority did not initiate an undisciplined
power struggle. With regard to the organizational norms to be observed by
Communists, they were moderates, not sectarians.

PART TWO

THE CLAIMS OF IRON DISCIPLINE, THE CRUCIBLE OF ANTI-FASCISM

For the international Communist movement the 1930s were years of unparalleled trauma and testing. The popular front interlude notwithstanding, there was a chilling continuity between the radical sectarianism that ushered in the decade and the Stalinist purges of 1936–38. If the first entailed political fratricide between Communists and socialists, the second resulted in internecine bloodletting throughout the Comintern itself. According to the memoirs of former Communists and the later findings of scholars alike, Stalin's obsessive drive for power was responsible for the first of these extremist phases; the mounting opposition within the Bolshevik ranks to his conception of party and state was responsible for the second.

Less generally understood are the reasons why tens of thousands of European Communists, instead of cutting their ties with a movement gone mad, gave into Stalin's will or even bowed to his supposed wisdom. Much has been written about the betrayal of liberal principles, the "escape from freedom" on the part of the interwar intellectuals of the left. Less attention has been given to the historical context in which their capitulation to Stalinism occurred: the Great Depression and the Fascist surge across Europe. At a time when Marx's predictions regarding the self-destruction of capitalism seemed on the verge of coming true, extremism on the right virtually invited extremism on the left. Justified or not, for many honest men and women the Soviet Union appeared to promise both economic salvation and a bulwark against Fascist expansionism.

The Italian Communists, engaged since 1926 in an underground struggle against Mussolini, were more attuned than some other Europeans to the realities of fascism. At the same time, the years of clandestinity had taken their toll not just in the number of cadres imprisoned but in the loss of political self-confidence. From 1930 onward the Italian party's leadership in exile made repeated attempts to reconstruct the domestic apparatus that had been destroyed after the onset of full-scale Fascist repression. Yet the efforts to build a solid structure in Italy foundered in the face of Mussolini's consolidation of power.

For a good ten years the *Duce,* by bringing about a reconciliation between church and state through the Lateran Pacts of 1929 (which accorded legal status to the Vatican and recognized Catholicism as the state religion of Italy) neutralized much grassroots opposition. His conquest of Ethiopia in 1936 and evocations of imperial grandeur likewise elicited a degree of positive support. The symbiotic relationship that developed between Italian business interests and the Fascist hierarchy further contributed to the staying power of the regime until its impending defeat in World War II.[1] Over the years, therefore, all the Communists accomplished was the creation of a fragile network of activists that crumbled time and again under police blows, leaving only pockets of isolated loyalists. In short, political ineffectuality made the PCI elite more vulnerable to criticism from Moscow than, for example, the KPD before 1933 or the PCF during the popular front era.

Following the browbeating Togliatti received at the Tenth Plenum of the ECCI, he had no choice but to heed in practice what he had previously acknowledged only in principle: the leading role of the CPSU in Comintern affairs. Observance of iron discipline had become the price of remaining in the Communist movement. Thenceforth the PCI, like all other Communist parties, had to demonstrate an outward show of total subservience to the frequently shifting line of the Stalinized Comintern bureaucracy.

Such compliance was all the more difficult because twice in rather quick succession the Comintern fluctuated between radical sectarianism and relative moderation, between treating as enemies or courting as allies the parties of the center left. The sectarian extremism initiated after the Sixth Comintern Congress was soon superseded by the popular front directives to form alliances with socialists and even bourgeois democrats in a joint struggle against fascism. With the signing of the German–Soviet Non-Aggression Pact on August 23, 1939, and the ensuing outbreak of World War II, the European Communists again retreated into isolationism, spurning cooperation with democratic parties in what was dubbed an interimperialist conflict. Only after the German invasion of the Soviet Union on June 22, 1941, did the International revert to a policy of united action with all forces opposed to Nazi aggression.

1. H. Stuart Hughes, *The United States and Italy,* 3d ed. (Cambridge, Mass.: Harvard University Press, 1979), chaps. 4 and 5.

Viewed from Moscow, these shifts were undertaken not to advance the cause of European communism but to secure the vital interests of the Soviet state and its leader. On both these accounts Stalin actively opposed social democracy, not fascism, prior to Hitler's rise to power. Many rightists in the nonruling Communist parties not only opposed Stalin but also viewed the socialists as potential allies. By denouncing socialists as social fascists, Stalin was thus able to discredit his moderate critics in the Comintern. Social democratic parties were, moreover, largely anti-Soviet and pro-Western in their international orientation. This was especially true with regard to Germany, the focus of Bolshevik diplomatic overtures since the Treaty of Rapallo in 1922. There the German Social Democratic Party (SPD) championed the reintegration of the Weimar Republic into Western Europe in the late 1920s.[2] Fascism, in contrast, posed no threat to Stalin's ascendancy over the CPSU or Comintern. Nor did fascism-in-power appear adversely to affect Soviet state interests. For relations between the Soviet and Italian governments developed normally even while Mussolini tightened his domestic grip.[3]

By 1934, on the other hand, the Nazi threat to Soviet security had overshadowed all other considerations in shaping Stalin's foreign policy, including his attitude toward Communist cooperation with social democrats. In December of that year he thus agreed to the popular front line as a maneuver to buttress his quest for collective security with the Western democracies against German expansionism. There is, however, no reason to suppose that Stalin's suspicion of democratic socialism ever abated or that he much cared about the gains in prestige and strength that accrued, say, to the French and Spanish Communist parties as a result of the popular front policy. Indeed, his instrumental approach to the Communist International was blatantly revealed during the period of the German–Soviet Non-Aggression Pact.

The European Communists faced their most searing loyalty test from September 1939 through June 1941 when Moscow directed them to renounce the struggle against fascism just as Hitler began his onslaught against Europe. This radical *volte-face* gave rise to massive defections, recriminations, and confusion in the Communist ranks. Only after Hitler's invasion of the Soviet Union were the Western Communist parties able to recoup those losses through armed resistance to the Nazi occupation forces. But even then Comintern–Kremlin circles encouraged them to resist in order to tie down German divisions in Hitler's rear rather than to promote Communist power in Western Europe.

2. For a comprehensive treatment of the impact of German conditions on Comintern policy during the post-1928 radical sectarian phase, see E. H. Carr, *Twilight of the Comintern, 1930–1935* (New York: Pantheon Books, 1982), pt. 1.

3. Alan Cassels, *Mussolini's Early Diplomacy* (Princeton: Princeton University Press, 1970), passim.

The PCI elite's perspective on the Comintern's policy fluctuations differed dramatically from that of Moscow. The Italian leaders were preoccupied above all with establishing a Communist presence in Italy and triggering a people's revolution against Mussolini's regime. If they conformed to the radical sectarian shifts for reasons of political survival, they displayed considerably greater initiative during the more flexible periods of the popular front and wartime Resistance. In a sense it was their good fortune that their clandestine domestic network was so moribund in both 1929 and 1939. For rather than having to justify and manage on a day-to-day basis the sectarian twists and turns of the Comintern line, they could devote their energies to reviving their domestic base. With Moscow's shift to the popular front, on the other hand, the Togliatti–Grieco team's earlier ideas regarding transitional slogans and stages reentered the mainstream of Communist strategic thinking as Ercoli himself became second only to Georgii Dimitrov in the formal structure of the International.

During the popular front years the PCI Politburo went so far as to devise slogans aimed at mobilizing dissident Fascists against Mussolini. And Togliatti came up with the concept of "new democracy" as an intermediate form of government between bourgeois democracy and socialism. Formulated with specific reference to Spain at war, the term was also laden with implications for a future post-Fascist Italy. Inasmuch, however, as the PCI's domestic ranks were even weaker during the popular front era than earlier (membership dropped to about twenty-four hundred by mid-1934), these innovations were confined for the time being to the realm of rhetoric and conjecture. Only during the last years of World War II did the Communists' long-time expectation of a post-Fascist democratic transitional stage become realistic. At that point the PCI elite, in contrast to French Communist practice and Soviet directives, agreed to cooperate organizationally as well as militarily with all other anti-Fascist parties in the Italian committees of national liberation (CLNs).

As we shall see in chapter 5, the PCI leaders' decision to join the interclass CLNs predated Moscow's command to both the Italian and French Communists to participate in postwar coalition governments. It reflected in part the realities of the Italian political scene where, after Mussolini's overthrow in July 1943, revulsion at the conduct of his successors elicited genuine solidarity among all anti-Fascist groups. But it also suggested the readiness of the Italian party's cadres to escape the domestic isolation and ineffectuality they had experienced throughout the 1930s. The prospect of an actual post-Fascist democratic stage proved enormously appealing to militants who had spent almost two decades in exile or in prison.

There is, finally, reason to believe that the Comintern's harsh and frequent attacks on the PCI, which reached a high-water mark in 1938–

39, enhanced the eagerness of Togliatti and others to acquire a domestic base of support whatever the terms. They hoped thereby to lessen the party's psychic dependence on Moscow and vulnerability to Stalinist pressure. Their longing for such autonomy was all the greater since the PCI elite had never been fully bolshevized. Togliatti was, by the early 1930s, the only European Communist leader whom the Stalinists had not placed in power. His associates in the party's Paris center for the most part made only brief trips to Moscow. Even Ercoli, contrary to widespread misconceptions, spent only 1926, the mid-1930s, and the four wartime years in the Soviet Union. Although cut off from the PCI's new internal center of direction during its formative stage in 1943–44, he was thus quick to acclaim the party's participation in the Italian CLN's.

The story of Togliatti's return to Italy after almost two decades abroad to head the PCI during its emergence as a mass-based party and cabinet partner belongs to Part Three of this book. Chapter 3, to which we now turn, covers the Italian Communist's capitulation to the Stalinization of the Comintern. Chapter 4 deals with the contradictory era of the popular front and the Stalinist purges. Chapter 5 explores the transformation of the PCI from an émigré sect to a major domestic political force during the early period of the wartime Resistance.

The Price of Commitment

The eleven months between the Sixth Comintern Congress and the Tenth Plenum of the ECCI saw not just the consolidation of Stalin's power over the bureaucracy of the International but the imposition of a radical sectarian line to boot. In contrast to the equivocal formulations of the Sixth Congress, the official documents of the Tenth Plenum described the world scene as one of uniformly disintegrating capitalism and accelerating revolutionary momentum.[1] Incitement to revolution thus became the blanket order of the day, and collaboration with reformist elements of any kind was proscribed. Democracy was equated at best with fascism; and social democracy was branded as no less than a Fascist front. Both served only to blunt the militancy of the masses. Transitional slogans were now banned under any circumstances, even including an "acute" revolutionary crisis. And Communist parties were directed to gear their everyday conduct to the perspective of immediate proletarian revolution, to mobilize and lead the mounting popular struggle against capitalism.

In the end those individuals or groups who opposed this extremist wave were compelled either to shut up or get out of the International. They were given the choice of unconditional submission to the rulings of the Comintern or rupture with the Communist movement.

Even at the Tenth Plenum, however, Togliatti did not wholly conform. His protests against the Stalinists' heavy-handed methods have already been mentioned. In addition, while toeing Moscow's general line on the crisis of capitalism and the imminence of revolution, he still showed glimmers of independent thinking in his major address to the plenum. Most notably, he echoed his Sixth Congress call for a "differentiated analysis of objective reality," that is, of concrete national conditions. As

---

1. See Tenth Plenum theses, in *Inprecor* 9, no. 46 (September 4, 1929):973–78.

a case in point, he persisted in denying that Italian fascism was a prototype of fascism in general. "Of *which* Italian fascism do you speak?" he asked, claiming that there had been at least three different phases of fascism in Italy alone since 1919.[2] Moreover, he urged respect for national particularities during the discussion of trade-union tactics, polemicizing in particular with Thälmann.[3] Togliatti also avoided the question of social fascism, leaving this sensitive topic to his less beleaguered comrade, Grieco. Grieco, in turn, denied the identity of either democracy or social democracy with fascism, though conceding the growing fascistization of both.[4] Echoing one of Togliatti's frequent arguments, he maintained that social democracy and fascism differed in their historically formed class base and ideology.

Even more important than these theoretical nuances, Togliatti and Grieco tried in the aftermath of the Tenth Plenum to avoid the wholesale repudiation of their earlier policies by going along with Moscow's order to discipline Tasca. For reasons that will be elaborated below, they were not in fact adverse to that step. But it soon became evident that only the renunciation of the "republican assembly" slogan and the idea of a people's revolution would satisfy the ascendant Stalinists. Even these steps did not suffice. Throughout the early 1930s, Comintern spokesmen repeatedly subjected the PCI leadership to criticism and snide innuendoes.

Meanwhile, the PCI's capitulation to Stalinism was accompanied by a reconciliation between Togliatti and Grieco, on the one hand, and their erstwhile opponents in the youth federation on the other. The basis of this new alignment was their shared perception of the need to transfer the PCI's center of direction and operations back to Italian soil, a move that soon became known as the organizational *svolta* (shift) of 1930. The available evidence suggests, however, that in order to achieve a rapprochement with Longo and Secchia, Togliatti and Grieco were obliged not simply to renounce the "republican assembly" slogan and the double revolutionary perspective, as the Stalinists demanded, but also to admit that the advocacy of these policies during 1927–28 had been mistaken.

Togliatti and the Tasca Affair

Togliatti's readiness to accommodate Moscow on the Tasca question, despite his reluctance to reverse the PCI's policies with regard to Italy,

---

2. *Inprecor* 9, no. 48 (September 11, 1929):1031–37 at 1034.

3. *Inprecor* 9, no. 59 (October 15, 1929):1259–62 at 1259.

4. *Inprecor* 9, no. 51 (September 17, 1929):1090–93. Grieco's—but not Togliatti's—speech was published in the PCI monthly, *Lo Stato operaio* [henceforth *SO*]: Garlandi, "Fascismo e socialfascismo," *SO* 3, no. 6 (July–August 1929):476–87.

was evident at the Tenth Plenum. It reflected a growing estrangement between the Togliatti circle and Tasca which requires some elaboration because of the insight it offers into the thinking of Togliatti and the men around him at this critical juncture of PCI history.

During the closing months of 1928 Tasca, as PCI delegate to the ECCI, was in frequent communication with Togliatti, who was then overseeing the party's Secretariat in Basel. On the basis of their correspondence we can trace Togliatti's reaction to Tasca's growing opposition to the Stalinists. In brief, that reaction may be described as one of initial agreement with Tasca's objections to organizational measures, followed by consternation over his ever more outspoken sympathy for the German rightists under attack, and culminating in shock and personal pique when Tasca denounced the CPSU's policies across the board. The Tasca–Togliatti letters of October–December 1928 are particularly valuable because of the limited materials available on this period in the PCI Archives. For example, the report on the Sixth Congress and related matters that Togliatti delivered to the party's October 1928 Central Committee meeting appears as a schematic summary of some six pages. What is more serious, there is no record whatsoever of the decisive Central Committee meeting of December 1928, about which more will be said below.

The Parting of the Roads

Togliatti's first letter to Tasca on the German question came from Moscow, where he remained for several weeks following the Sixth Congress, and was dated October 6, 1928—the same date as the Comintern Presidium's controversial decision to reinstate Thälmann as head of the KPD. (Tasca was then in Berlin in transit to the Soviet Union to assume his new post as PCI representative.) Togliatti made no reference in the letter to the Presidium meeting, which suggests that he was not yet informed of it. He did, however, make it plain that he was upset over what was transpiring in the KPD. After urging Tasca to sound out some of their German friends on the Thälmann case, he expressed alarm over the KPD's drift toward factional infighting in much the same vein as he had at the Sixth Congress: "What I fear is that a process of disintegration is also beginning in the German party. . . . Until now we had to fear sectarianism with all its dangers, but not this other thing which is always the most serious." More important, Togliatti warned Tasca to remain neutral on policy questions. He advised him, specifically, to stick to the issue of organizational methods and to avoid siding with one faction against the other in order "to exercise *at least a minimum of influence, for today or for tomorrow.*"[5]

5. Text in *Annali Feltrinelli* 8 (Milan: Feltrinelli Editore, 1966), 1928, doc. 6:512–15 at 514–15; my emphasis.

This effort to strike a balance between political realism and conviction, to resist the drift toward Stalinist regimentation without taking the side of the anti-Stalinists, was the path that Togliatti and the PCI leadership as a whole were to follow throughout the autumn of 1928. Though alarmed by the direction events were taking within the Comintern *apparat,* they refrained from doing anything that might be construed as support for the rightists. In this way they hoped to retain their own autonomy with regard to PCI affairs and a modicum of influence in Moscow.

As Tasca's opposition intensified during October and November, Togliatti remained for the most part silent. But in a letter dated December 17 he finally replied to Tasca's many communications on KPD developments.[6] He began by describing two documents approved at a recently concluded Central Committee meeting, the one held in early December 1928 for which there is no archival record. The first was a formal resolution in which the party endorsed the Comintern Presidium's reinstatement of Thälmann as a necessary measure against right opportunism. As we have already seen, this resolution was approved under the prodding of Manuilsky. By way of contrast, the second document, intended for internal circulation only, criticized the methods of the Comintern bureaucrats. To quote Togliatti directly: "In the confidential document there is instead the opinion that one ought to criticize very frankly the manner in which the International intervened after September 26 and the manner in which it tends to control the internal affairs of the KPD, and that from this criticism one ought to proceed to a criticism of the bad internal regime of the parties and the Communist International in general."[7]

Togliatti also commented on the political errors of the German rightists. His overall tone, however, was one of apprehension over the worsening organizational climate of the International. As Togliatti put it, "the struggle of groups and factions is spreading to all the parties."[8] Of utmost significance for his thinking at the time, he concluded by assuring Tasca that the PCI leadership was behind him: "As for your attitude, we are broadly in agreement with it."[9]

Togliatti promised to mail Tasca the party's confidential critique of the Comintern's administrative methods. But there is no evidence that it ever arrived or was even officially recorded.[10] Instead Togliatti penned a second letter to Tasca ten days later which contrasted sharply with his mid-December note.[11] Not only did he protest that Tasca was beginning to side

6. Text in ibid., 1928, doc. 23:584–93 at 588–93.
7. Ibid., 589.
8. Ibid., 590.
9. Ibid., 592.
10. Berti's commentary, in ibid., 1928, doc. 30:619–20.
11. Togliatti's letter of December 27, 1928, to Tasca, in ibid., 1928, doc. 29:613–18 at 616–18.

with the German rightists and deviate from the line of the Sixth Congress, but he also chided him for his tendency to stress only the negative side of Comintern and Soviet developments. He contended that if all Tasca said was true there would be no alternative but to reconstruct the International from below. "I had occasion to say this to Nikolai [Bukharin] during the Congress when he . . . hinted at taking the same path you have taken in these 'outbursts' you have sent us," Togliatti pointedly remarked. "But . . . this perspective . . . is profoundly mistaken. The German right has fallen headlong, with eyes shut, into this abyss."[12]

Togliatti's own "outburst" was provoked in part by a letter from Tasca to the PCI Secretariat, dated December 14, 1928,[13] which crossed the path of Togliatti's supportive letter of December 17. In it Tasca, increasingly angered by developments in Moscow, began to broaden the scope of his criticism from organizational matters to policy issues. As an opener, he declared that on such questions as transitional slogans the KPD leadership was more in error than the German rightists: "*On that the right remains less far removed from Leninism than the present majority.*"[14] But the crux of his argument was that conditions in the capitalist world were not yet ripe for revolution and that the International should therefore return to the more flexible line of the Third Comintern Congress. Tasca concluded by requesting his transfer from the ECCI: "As long as I am in this post I will never refrain from saying what I think. And that will end by bringing about a crisis in relations between the Party and the C.I."[15]

At first glance there was not all that much in Tasca's assessment with which Togliatti and Grieco might disagree. The key issue, however, was not the validity of Tasca's views but the fact that he openly aligned himself with the German moderates. He thus not only failed to heed Togliatti's October 6 advice not to side with one faction against another; but he also threatened to upset the delicate balancing act the Italian leaders were pursuing vis-à-vis Moscow. Though harboring a number of reservations about the Stalinists' conduct, their aim was to mitigate its long-term impact by resisting expulsions and thereby preserving intact the human corpus of the International. For this reason they endorsed Tasca's stand against the KPD purge of rightists. Indeed, as Togliatti reiterated in his December 27 letter to Tasca, "I have already communicated to you that the two declarations of vote you communicated to us did not find us in basic disagreement."[16] But by opposing the Stalinists' policies as well as their methods, Tasca jeopardized this whole approach. As Giuseppe

12. Ibid., 617.
13. Text in ibid., 1928, doc. 22:577–84 at 578–84.
14. Ibid., 579.
15. Ibid., 583–84.
16. Ibid., 1928, doc. 29:616.

Dozza, a leader of the FGCI, remarked in a letter he sent to a colleague in Moscow with the approval of the PCI Secretariat: "An attitude such as his [Tasca's] would surely make it impossible for us to have any influence whatsoever in correcting the errors he criticizes, and would lead to the opposite result from what he proposes."[17]

To make matters worse, about this time word reached Togliatti of the December 19, 1928, meeting of the Comintern Presidium. The import of Stalin's depiction of Tasca as wallowing in the "mire of cowardly opportunism" was not lost on Togliatti. On January 2, 1929, he derisively scolded Tasca for neglecting to inform the party Secretariat of precisely what transpired at that "historic session."[18] And the very next day he summoned all members of the PCI Central Committee to a meeting with Tasca, informing them that "the attitude taken by Comrade Serra in the Presidium meeting . . . has exacerbated his relations with the majority of the leading organs of the C.I."[19]

For Togliatti an open break with Moscow was evidently out of the question. He was prepared to press his viewpoint to the brink of defiance but no further. He thus took up the cudgels against Tasca in order to clear the record of the PCI before the party as a whole came under attack.

The PCI Central Committee Meeting of March 1929: Tasca under Attack

The showdown with Tasca took place on the last day (March 2) of a PCI Central Committee session held in Paris in late February and early March 1929. As it turned out, tensions were by then even further exacerbated as a result of the sweeping critique of Stalin's policy that Tasca presented to the party leadership on February 28 (noted in chapter 2). In addition to eleven Italians, including Tasca, the meeting was also attended by a delegate from the KPD, Hermann Remmele.[20] Remmele, at that time second only to Thälmann in the KPD,[21] served the dual function of German Communist apologist and Stalinist watchdog.

Togliatti opened the meeting by rebutting Tasca's views and toeing Moscow's line on capitalist instability, working-class radicalization, Soviet economic policy, right opportunism, and even transitional slogans.[22]

17. Giuseppe Dozza's letter of December 27, 1928, to Gino Amadesi, in ibid., 1928, doc. 30:618–23 at 623.

18. Text of letter in ibid., 1929, doc. 1:626–29 at 628–29.

19. Text in ibid., 1929, doc. 2:629–37 at 636–37.

20. Minutes of March 2, 1929, PCI Central Committee session, in ibid., 1929, doc. 15:803–89 at 805.

21. Tasca's letter of November 4, 1928, to PCI Secretariat, in ibid., 1928, doc. 12:532.

22. Minutes of March 2, 1929, PCI Central Committee session, in ibid., 1929, doc. 15:805–28, passim.

Regarding the last point, he tried to justify the PCI's past conduct by arguing, in what was a patent distortion of the facts, that the Italian Communists had used transitional slogans only in connection with "an acute revolutionary situation."[23] But his speech was most notable in two respects: his unqualified backing of the current KPD leadership and his bitter condemnation of Tasca. With regard to the KPD, he declared that "we must approve without reservation the Presidium's open letter to the German party." With regard to Tasca, he agreed, abjectly, with Stalin's definition of him as a "hypocritical opportunist": "The image of Serra that emerges from the documents he has presented to us is really that of an opportunist who doesn't have the courage to show himself openly and seeks, in vain, to mask and conceal his own thought."[24] Tasca's agitation over the German question, Togliatti continued, was simply a smokescreen to hide his attempt at a "radical revision of the political line of the International."[25]

Togliatti's positions on Tasca and the KPD were, of course, but two sides of the same coin. As he stated at the outset of his speech, the time had come for the PCI to pass judgment on both the Presidium's "Open Letter" to the KPD and Tasca's opposition to the "Open Letter."[26] He had evidently resolved to take the side of Moscow on both issues ever since it became clear that Tasca was steering a collision course with the Stalinists. Nevertheless, the presence of Stalin's emissary Remmele must have had some bearing on the tone of his address. This is all the more likely since, according to Giuseppe Berti, Togliatti's private contacts with Tasca during the first weeks of 1929 were rather conciliatory in nature.[27]

At the same time, Togliatti's vehemence toward Tasca cannot be explained solely in terms of *Realpolitik*. An element of personal bitterness must have also entered the picture. Tasca had acted contrary to Togliatti's advice of the previous fall. But more to the point, by becoming openly defiant Tasca tended to vindicate the youth who had been accusing the PCI leaders of opportunist leanings for at least two years. He thus endangered not only his own standing in Moscow's eyes but that of Togliatti and Grieco as well. Togliatti reportedly warned Tasca of just such an eventuality in their personal conversations during the early winter of 1929

23. Ibid., 822.
24. Ibid., 806–7.
25. Ibid., 807.
26. Ibid., 806.
27. Berti's commentary, in ibid., 1929, doc. 1:626–28. One gets a similar impression from the following remarks in Tasca's diary: "During the first or second conversation I had with Ercoli upon my return from Moscow for the meeting of the Central Committee, he reproached Bukharin . . . for his refusal to fight. He recalled having already made the same reproof to Bukharin himself during the Sixth Congress"; Tasca's diary, in ibid., 1929, doc. 16:889–920 at 895.

and urged him on this account to desist from his collision course with Moscow.[28] His apprehension turned out to be all too well founded. For Longo did in fact implicate Togliatti in Tasca's "opportunist deviation" on transitional slogans during the March 2 confrontation. As he bluntly put it, "Comrade Serra does nothing but repeat the position which the party, the C.C. in its majority, and again this morning Comrade Ercoli in a more prudent manner, has repeated on the question, for example, of the slogan of a 'republican assembly.' "[29] Longo thereupon called for the immediate repudiation of everything that had been said on the subject of transitional slogans in previous party resolutions.[30]

Here it is important to note that the views expressed by the other Central Committee members differed little from those of Togliatti.[31] Even Ignazio Silone, whose ethical revulsion against the Stalinists had been triggered at the Eighth Plenum and was soon to carry him from the Communist ranks, joined in the chorus of recriminations. Inquiring rhetorically exactly when the PCI had become suspect in Moscow's eyes, he replied: "When our attitude seemed to be connected with the political position of Comrade Serra, who did not share our platform but attacked across the board the political line of the Comintern."[32] Such unanimity suggested that Togliatti's resentment toward Tasca was widely shared. Not only that, but the other participants were no doubt also influenced by the presence of Remmele. Whatever lingering reservations there may have been regarding the Tasca affair, group loyalty took precedence when confronted with a Stalinist informer.

The end result of the March 2 clash was the PCI's official denunciation of Tasca's views and approval of the "Open Letter" to the KPD in a resolution agreed to by all except Tasca.[33] The cursory endorsement of the "Open Letter" has already been mentioned. More pointed was the condemnation of Tasca. He was charged with attempting a "radical revision of the line of the Sixth Congress" and with favoring a series of "grave opportunist deviations."[34] As for the Comintern line in general, the resolution supported both Stalin's economic policies and his characterization of contemporary capitalism. More relevant from the viewpoint of internal PCI politics, it renounced the advocacy of transitional slogans in a nonrevolutionary situation in the following oblique but unmistakable manner:

28. See Berti's commentary, in ibid., 1929, doc. 1:627.
29. Minutes of March 2, 1929, PCI Central Committee session, ibid., 1929, doc. 15:870.
30. Ibid., 871.
31. In addition to Tasca and Togliatti, the following members attended the meeting: Grieco, Ravazzoli, Silone, Leonetti, Longo, Ravera, Giovetti, Seechia, and Dozza; ibid., 805.
32. Ibid., 862.
33. Ibid., 888.
34. "Risoluzione sui problemi della Internazionale," *SO* 3, no. 2 (February 1929):167–70.

"The opportunist currents propose to modify the tactical principles which the Comintern has established in its Program (*the use of transitional slogans only in periods of acute [sic] revolutionary crisis*)."[35] Meanwhile, party commentaries began to concentrate on the single perspective of proletarian revolution in Italy, neglecting even to mention an anti-Fascist people's revolution.

All the same, the PCI Central Committee refrained from any direct criticism of its earlier policies and slogans, despite Longo's demands. More to the point, it also declined to take disciplinary action against Tasca. With the exception of his post on the ECCI, from which he had asked to be relieved and which was now assigned to Grieco,[36] he remained a member of the executive bodies of the Italian party. Togliatti in fact limited his recommendations to the following: "The Central Committee ought now to disavow and condemn, without any hesitation or reservation whatsoever, Comrade Serra. And this is all."[37] Tasca's own request to resign from the Politburo was turned down by the Central Committee. Only Pietro Tresso, a member of the youth faction who was absent from the meeting because of illness, recommended in a letter appended to the minutes "eventual organizational measures against Comrade Serra (for example his exclusion from the P.B.)."[38]

Capitulation and Purge

The PCI leaders' estrangement from Tasca made it easier for them to comply with the Stalinists' insistence at the Tenth Plenum that he recant or be purged. More difficult to accept, as well as unexpected—judging by their remarks before the ECCI's Italian Commission—was the suggestion that they disavow their strategic perspectives. For Togliatti and Grieco two key questions remained after the Tenth Plenum: to what extent would they have to repudiate their policies of the past three years? and would they be able to retain their positions within the PCI despite their "opportunism of conciliation"? In the end the second question was contingent on the first. Only by rejecting their policies would they be able to remain at the head of the party. This became clear at a Politburo session of August 28–29, 1929, which—like the March 1929 Central Committee meeting—was attended by a key Comintern functionary.

35. Ibid., 169; my emphasis.
36. Minutes of March 2, 1929, PCI Central Committee session, in *Annali Feltrinelli* 8, 1929, doc. 15:888.
37. Ibid., 827.
38. Ibid., 888–89.

Mutual Recriminations

At the Tenth Plenum Tasca's fate was already sealed. As we saw in the previous chapter, Molotov, Manuilsky, and others repeatedly attacked Tasca as an unqualified rightist while rebuking the PCI leaders, especially Togliatti, for their conciliatory attitude toward him. In the face of this orchestrated polemic, Grieco finally conceded on behalf of his colleagues that "the PCI committed an error, after having condemned Comrade Serra on ideological and political grounds, by not taking organizational measures . . . and keeping Comrade Serra in the Political Bureau." He then went on to say: "The Italian delegation, *in agreement with the comrades of the ECCI,* promises to propose and support in the C.C. of the PCI the removal of Comrade Serra from the Political Bureau and from the C.C."[39] Grieco also stipulated the conditions to which Tasca would have to agree or be expelled from the party itself. These included the public recantation of his February 1929 memorandum and the severing of all ties with rightist elements, particularly those within the CPSU.[40]

This set of conditions was unacceptable to Tasca. He was prepared to bow to Communist discipline but not to submit to "ideological capitulation," as he put it in a letter to a Polish friend, Fanny Jezierska.[41] Thereafter the denouement was not long in coming. At a meeting of the PCI Secretariat on August 24, 1929, Tasca was formally presented with the conditions enumerated by Grieco.[42] In a letter to the PCI Central Committee dated August 30, he rejected those conditions on the ground that his opinions had not substantially changed since the previous winter.[43] And during the first week of September, in the face of Tasca's tearful but resolute refusal to recant,[44] the Central Committee voted unanimously to expel him from the PCI.[45]

Far more significant than the September Central Committee meeting, however, was the PCI's Politburo session of August 28–29, 1929. The keeping of a verbatim account of the proceedings—in contrast to the abbreviated minutes of earlier Politburo meetings—was in itself indicative of its importance. Even more so was the presence of a Comintern emis-

39. Declaration of Grieco to Tenth Plenum of ECCI, July 19, 1929, in ibid., 1929, doc. 26:941–42; my emphasis.

40. Ibid., 942.

41. Tasca's letter of August 12, 1929, to Fanny Jezierska, in ibid., 1929, doc. 30:960–61 at 960.

42. See Tasca's letter of August 28, 1929, to Fanny Jezierska, in ibid., 1929, doc. 33:964–65 at 964.

43. He had, however, somewhat modified his views on domestic Russian questions; see text in ibid., 1929, doc. 34:965–68 at 966.

44. Berti's commentary, in ibid., 1929, doc. 37:972.

45. "Via gli opportunisti dalle file del Partito Comunista d'Italia (Risoluzione del Comitato Centrale per l'espulsione di Serra)," *SO* 3, no. 7 (September–October 1929):630–34.

sary, a Bulgarian by the name of Stepan Minev who went by the alias of Stepanov and was responsible for overseeing the Latin European parties after 1928.[46] Comintern advisers had already begun to make appearances at Central Committee meetings: Manuilsky in December 1928, Remmele in March 1929, perhaps Stepanov as early as June 1928.[47] But this was the first time since the emergence of the post-Bordiga leadership that a Politburo session had been so graced. Most unprecedented, however, was the mood of the meeting. The atmosphere was laden with tension as the participants aimed recriminations and slurs at one another and above all at Togliatti. As surprising as it was puzzling, one of the few voices of conciliation—in the sense of urging mutual forbearance and restraint— was Stepanov's. Another was that of Secchia, Longo's ally in the youth federation.

A brief account of the highlights of the debate is therefore in order. By way of introduction, the Politburo at that time included Togliatti, Grieco, Silone (who was absent), Camilla Ravera, Paolo Ravazzoli, Pietro Tresso, Alfonso Leonetti, and Longo (a candidate member). Tasca was formally still a member but his expulsion was, of course, pending. Present, in addition, were Secchia as the FGCI delegate with a deliberative vote and Giuseppe Dozza.[48]

To start off, Grieco gave a report on the Tenth Plenum in which he urged organizational measures against Tasca.[49] Togliatti then gave a report on PCI activity in which he renounced the "republican assembly" slogan as simply no longer appropriate because of the worsening socioeconomic situation and approaching revolutionary crisis, in Italy and elsewhere.[50] Both men were responding to the ECCI's complaints but only in a limited manner, apparently in line with a prior decision to that effect reached by the PCI Secretariat[51] (composed of Togliatti, Grieco, Silone, Ravera, and Secchia from the FGCI). As Togliatti put it in his report, "it would be wrong to say that our party line has been mistaken these past three years."[52] Whereupon Leonetti and Tresso berated Togliatti for his failure to condemn both the people's revolution concept and

46. See Palmiro Togliatti, *Opere 1935–1944,* 2 vols., ed. Franco Andreucci and Paolo Spriano (Rome: Editori Riuniti, 1979), 1:272.

47. Another alias used by Minev, in addition to Stepanov, was Mario, a name that appeared on the list of those present at the June 1928 Central Committee meeting but whose identity is not clear beyond the fact that he sided with the youth in their opposition to transitional slogans; APC, 1928, fol. 653:122.

48. Additional individuals may have attended the meeting but only those mentioned above spoke up for the record. For the composition of the Politburo as of October 1928, see APC, 1928, fol. 653:291.

49. APC, 1929, fol. 745:96–111 at 108–9.

50. Ibid., 112–25.

51. This was intimated during the Politburo debate by Togliatti, in ibid., 161.

52. Ibid., 116.

the "republican assembly" slogan as erroneous from the start (i.e., January 1927).[53] Secchia then accused Tresso and Leonetti of opportunism for waiting so long to express their opposition to these ideas, if opposed they really were.[54] Whereupon Ravera rebuked Secchia, arguing that everyone had a right to change his mind.[55]

Meanwhile, Longo, like Tresso and Leonetti, found Togliatti's partial self-criticism wholly unsatisfactory and called for "corrections" across the board, explicitly accusing him of "conciliation" for his persistent defense of transitional slogans.[56] To Togliatti's refusal to recant the party's policies of earlier years, Longo retorted: "One must say to the whole party, 'Yes, we have made mistakes,' not 'We are right.' "[57] He also maintained that only a new PCI congress could give an air of legitimacy to the Politburo, a veiled call for a change of leadership.

The second day of the meeting Stepanov stepped forward to voice what was at first glance the position of Togliatti and Grieco: namely, the party line needed clarification rather than a total overhaul, *precisazioni* rather than *correzioni*. The Comintern, he insisted, did not "condemn" the PCI, nor did it think that it had erred "profoundly," as several of the Italian comrades contended the day before. Unlike the case of other parties to which the ECCI had dispatched "open letters" and detailed directives, the Comintern executive bodies had no intention of telling the PCI exactly what to do. Instead they asked that the Italian party undertake self-criticism and decide upon its own course. Only afterwards would the Political Secretariat of the International evaluate the situation.[58] Yet, this show of restraint notwithstanding, he added pointedly: "I wouldn't say that the tone of self-criticism which Ercoli made yesterday is right; I would say rather that it is a bit insufficient."[59] He proceeded to ask that the Italians correct "only two" aspects of their policy: the "republican assembly" slogan and the double revolutionary perspective!

Stepanov's message seemed clear enough. Togliatti did in fact have to disavow the policies so long criticized by the youth; but, once having done so, no further disciplinary action would be taken. What remains unclear is the reason for such forbearance after the cutting remarks against Togliatti at the Tenth Plenum. Were the Stalinists of two minds, with the Germans, for example, calling for his political head as the price of his conciliationist past and the Russians and others preferring merely to cow him, to force

53. Ibid., 126–32 and 133–39, respectively.
54. Ibid., 144–45.
55. Ibid., 146–49 at 146.
56. Ibid., 140–43.
57. Ibid., 141.
58. Ibid., 166–76.
59. Ibid., 171.

him into total conformity? Or had the Comintern bureaucrats simply concluded that—unlike the situation in so many other Communist parties—there was no alternative leadership waiting in the wings?

We may surmise that at least some of the Stalinists were eager to replace the Togliatti–Grieco team. According to a later account by Tasca, when he returned from Moscow in early 1929, a member of the PCI Secretariat (probably Silone) had explained Togliatti's abrupt, if still partial, submission to the Comintern line in the following way: "We had to give in on the Russian and international questions in order to save the Italian policy of our party. Otherwise Moscow would have had no scruples in arranging a leftist leadership with some lads from the Lenin School."[60] The Togliatti circle may have feared that Longo was a likely candidate for such a maneuver. Already at the June 1928 PCI Central Committee meeting Longo had articulated the sectarian view regarding the rapid approach of a revolutionary crisis.[61] And his airing of his disagreements with the party leadership at various Comintern forums had evidently won him friends. For after the Sixth Congress the Communist Youth International (KIM) invited him to represent the PCI in Moscow. Longo was receptive but the PCI Politburo refused to permit it.[62] Even so, during the winter of 1928–29 two members of the youth faction remained in Moscow, Giovanni Germanetto and Luigi Amadesi, the Italian delegates to the Profintern and KIM.[63]

On balance, however, the arguments against replacing Togliatti and Grieco apparently outweighed the advantages. For one thing, Secchia, FGCI representative on the PCI Secretariat and Politburo, would not have supported such a maneuver. At the August 1929 Politburo meeting he was quite critical of the Comintern hierarchy for waiting so long to back the positions of the youth. Collaboration in the formulation of policy was one thing; ex post facto intervention quite another, he protested.[64] And at a KIM meeting in the fall of 1929, he withstood pressures to denounce Togliatti on the ground that the PCI was then in the process of correcting its errors.[65] There is, moreover, no way of knowing whether Longo

60. Tasca's November 18, 1929, declaration to the anti-Fascist press, *Annali Feltrinelli 8*, 1929, doc. 45:981–83 at 982. Spriano, who includes this same quotation in his history of the PCI, refers to it as "slander which perhaps is not only that"; cf. Paolo Spriano, *Storia del Partito comunista italiano*, 5 vols. (Turin: Giulio Einaudi Editore, 1967–75), 2:228.

61. APC, 1928, fol. 653, see esp. 69–71.

62. See Grieco's remarks on this during the debate at the October 1928 Central Committee meeting in APC, 1928, fol. 653:261.

63. Both Germanetto and Amadesi behaved deplorably toward Tasca during his stay in Moscow; see Tasca's diary, in *Annali Feltrinelli 8*, 1929, doc. 5:643–44, and his letter of January 16, 1929, to the PCI Secretariat, ibid., 1929, doc. 9:659–65 at 661–63.

64. APC, 1929, fol 745:144.

65. Pietro Secchia, *L'azione svolta dal partito comunista in Italia durante il fascismo, 1926–1932; Ricordi, documenti inediti e testimonianze—Annali Feltrinelli 14* (Milan: Feltrinelli Editore, 1970), 233 and 272–273.

himself would have been receptive to such a move. His conduct in later years certainly did not suggest any personal disloyalty to Togliatti.

In addition, the majority of the participants at the August 1929 Politburo meeting still supported Togliatti to some degree. Grieco endorsed him without reservations; Ravera and Ravazzoli (also Dozza) continued to favor the former party line, although Ravazzoli had a personal grudge against Ercoli;[66] Secchia at least backed Togliatti personally. Only Longo, Tresso, and Leonetti expressed unqualified opposition. On top of all this, the PCI's cadres had already been dangerously depleted by Fascist arrests.

The upshot was that the Stalinists chose to subdue rather than purge Ercoli. What this meant in actuality was that he remained head of the PCI Secretariat at the sufferance, not at the behest, of Moscow. Viewed from a broader perspective, as the 1930s began he was the only European Communist leader to enjoy that ambiguous distinction.[67]

Here some speculation is in order as to just what was going on in Togliatti's mind during this time. According to the memoirs of Camilla Ravera, both he and Grieco were quite prepared at one point to withdraw from an active role in the PCI leadership because of the opposition coming from the Comintern and their own comrades. Togliatti in particular thought of returning to more scholarly pursuits, where he would be "freed from petty intrigues, rancors, suspicions."[68] Ravera maintained that he rejected that idea only because of loyalty to Gramsci and reluctance to let all their efforts to form a new party leadership in the mid-1920s come to naught.[69]

However that may be, Togliatti's eventual decision to compromise with Stalinism was surely also conditioned by the character of the Italian political scene. The Fascist presence in Italy gave a black-and-white coloring to political choices. Those who elected a legal existence at home were compelled in a sense to collaborate with the Mussolini regime. Those who chose to combat that regime could likewise not be too fastidious about the means used to do so. It is in this light that Togliatti's often cited remarks to Silone around this same time can best be understood: "The present state of the International . . . is certainly neither satisfactory nor agreeable. But our good will is powerless to change it. Objective historical conditions are involved and must be taken into account. The forms of the proletarian revolution are not arbitrary. If they don't correspond to our preferences, so much the worse for us."[70]

66. Camilla Ravera, *Diario di trent' anni, 1913–1943* (Rome: Editori Riuniti, 1973), 449–51.
67. E. H. Carr, *Twilight of the Comintern, 1930–35* (New York: Pantheon Books, 1982), 248.
68. Ravera, *Diario di trent' anni*, 449.
69. Ibid., 449ff.
70. Paraphrased by Ignazio Silone, *Uscita di sicurezza* (Rome: Associazione italiana per la libertà della cultura, 1955), 71.

Still, in the summer of 1929 Togliatti—and apparently Grieco as well—were ready to give in to the Stalinists only within limits. They were willing to go along with the new Comintern line but not to repudiate their entire political past, to subject themselves to what Tasca had termed "ideological capitulation." At the PCI's late August Politburo meeting, therefore, neither Togliatti nor Grieco flinched in the face of their comrades' sharp criticisms. They stuck for the most part to a defense of the policies they had championed since January 1927 even while conceding that these were no longer valid under current conditions.[71] Grieco made their position absolutely clear: if the majority sought a condemnation of the party's directives since the Third Congress, they should name somebody other than Ercoli to deliver the keynote report to the forthcoming Central Committee meeting. As for a change in the party leadership, Grieco remarked a bit later, "the representative of the International will say what he thinks."[72] Stepanov, as we have seen, called for a change in PCI policy, not personnel. Ravazzoli's subsequent proposal that Ercoli deliver the Central Committee report was unanimously approved.[73]

Repudiation of the Past

For several months following the August 1929 Politburo meeting, Togliatti and Grieco managed to avoid a full recantation of their directives of the previous three years. In his report to the Central Committee session of September 3–5, 1929, Togliatti continued to suggest the earlier validity of the party's discredited slogans.[74] The formal communiqué on the proceedings also echoed Stepanov's words: it "recognized the necessity of defining *precisely*" the party line, of undertaking "a careful, severe and profound *self-criticism*" of all its activity in order "to correct and to overcome existing *deficiencies*," not errors.[75] To be sure, party documents began to criticize the "republican assembly" slogan for its ambiguity and to demand that it be dropped.[76] Nevertheless, the PCI's use of this slogan in the past was not raised, nor was the perspective of a people's revolution broached.

By the end of 1929, however, Togliatti and Grieco gave in and attacked

71. See their remarks during the debate on August 28 in APC, 1929, fol. 745:155–62; and Togliatti's second speech to the meeting, delivered after Stepanov's, in ibid., 203–21.

72. APC, 1929, fol. 745:155 and 160.

73. Ibid., 219.

74. Palmiro Togliatti, *Opere 1929–1935*, ed. Ernesto Ragionieri, 2 vols. (Rome: Editori Riuniti, 1973), 1:29–77.

75. "Riunione del Comitato Centrale del PCI," *SO* 3, no. 7 (September–October 1929):629; my emphasis.

76. "Lettera aperta del CC del PCI a tutte le organizzazioni di Partito, A tutti compagni,"*SO* 3, no. 7 (September–October 1929):551–68.

the earlier advocacy of both notions. The Wall Street Crash may have been partly responsible for their turnabout. From October 1929 onward a convincing note of reality was injected into Moscow's assessment of the world scene. Facts could now be garnered to support the predictions of both the Stalinists and the PCI youth regarding the imminent collapse of capitalism. As Togliatti announced editorially in the PCI monthly, *Lo Stato operaio*, during the closing weeks of 1929, an "acute revolutionary situation" was just around the corner in Italy as elsewhere.[77] On the other hand, at about this same time Togliatti also reached a meeting of minds with Longo on the need to transfer the bulk of the party's activities back to Italy. This initiative once again split the Politburo's ranks, thereby requiring the utmost solidarity between Togliatti and Longo. It may be, in other words, that the "ideological capitulation" so long resisted by Togliatti and Grieco was also part of a deal they struck with Longo as opposition to their organizational proposals developed in the upper ranks of the party.

Whatever the case, in the same issue of *Lo Stato operaio* in which Togliatti announced the approach of an "acute revolutionary situation" in Italy, he also wrote a sweeping critique of the "republican assembly" slogan. Ironically, just when the use of transitional slogans should have become legitimate according to the guidelines of the International, he rejected the one that had constituted the main bone of contention with the youth. After declaring that the PCI had erred in not openly discarding and criticizing the slogan earlier, he censured it on two accounts.[78] First of all, it was too complex to serve as a slogan of mass agitation. Second, it was equivocal, that is, susceptible to opportunist interpretations regarding a transitional stage between the bourgeois and proletarian dictatorships. On the other hand, to Togliatti's credit he sought to minimize Gramsci's responsibility for these errors by specifying that the "negative elements of the slogan" did not have a decisive influence during the years 1925–26.

Soon the perspective of a people's revolution was also denounced. An article by Grieco in 1930 and the Central Committee report to the Fourth PCI Congress in 1931 explicitly criticized this notion as formulated in the January 1927 resolution of the Comintern Presidium and the resolution of the PCI's Second Conference in January 1928. Grieco equivocated somewhat, arguing that the PCI had always maintained that the anti-Fascist revolution would be socialist and proletarian regardless of the pace of its development.[79] But the Central Committee's report to the party's Fourth

77. Unsigned editorial, "Andiamo noi, in Italia, verso una situazione rivoluzionaria acuta?" *SO* 3, no. 8 (November 1929): 696–701; cf. Togliatti, *Opere 1929–1935* 1:113–20.

78. Ercoli, "A proposito di una parola d'ordine (Critica della parola d'ordine dell' 'Assemblea repubblicana sulla base dei Comitati operai e contadini, ecc . . .')," *SO* 3, no. 8 (November 1929), in *Trenta anni di vita e lotte del PCI* (Rome: Editore Rinascita, 1952), 138–41.

79. Ruggero Grieco, "I nostri errori," *SO* 4, no. 9 (September 1930):570–72.

Congress was harsher and more accurate. It admitted that both the Comintern's 1927 document and the PCI's 1928 resolution did in fact convey the idea that a post-Fascist bourgeois democratic phase was possible; and it roundly condemned this perspective.[80] The PCI leaders' ideological capitulation was thus complete.

The *Svolta* of 1930 and Its Aftermath

If Togliatti wavered in his resolve to remain a member of the PCI leadership in mid-1929, his subsequent conduct bespoke his determination to put an end to the émigré and passive character of the party and to move its center of operations back into Italy. He was likewise bent upon avoiding involvement in Comintern affairs. With the exception of excerpts from some of his speeches, he contributed no pieces to the Comintern's biweekly newssheet during 1929–31 nor did any articles by him appear in *Kommunisticheskii Internatsional* for over three years (from the end of May 1929 through the end of September 1932). He also declined to attend the Eleventh Plenum of the ECCI in the early spring of 1931, ostensibly because of the forthcoming PCI Congress. In April 1932 Giuseppe Dozza, PCI representative in Moscow at that time, sent a letter to the party Secretariat conveying the Comintern bureaucracy's displeasure over the PCI's "isolation" from the work of the International.[81] Togliatti retorted that such isolation at the party base was only natural and that he himself had no time to contribute to the Comintern press.[82] But his avoidance of contact with his recent detractors was clearly the dictate of prudence.

At the same time, Togliatti had to pay a high price for both his preoccupation with the *svolta* and his detachment from the Comintern. The decision to rebuild the party's domestic network led to a virtual split in the Politburo and the eventual expulsion of four of its members. And Togliatti had to compensate for his aloofness from the International by obsequiously kowtowing to its functionaries on those few occasions when he visited Moscow in the early 1930s. By the same token, his references to Soviet affairs in his articles in *Lo Stato operaio* and private correspondence alike (for instance, a letter that reached Terracini in prison in May 1932) were filled with adulation of Stalin and all his undertakings.[83]

---

80. "L'attività del PCI dal III al IV Congresso (Rapporto del CC al IV Congresso)," *Il IV Congresso del Partito Comunista d'Italia (Aprile 1931): Tesi e Risoluzioni* (Paris: Edizioni di coltura sociale, 1931), 162–93 at 169–70.

81. See the excerpts in Togliatti, *Opere 1929–1935* I:lxxxiii, n. 1.

82. Text in APC, 1932, fol. 1033:11–15 at 15.

83. Cf. Ragionieri's comments in Togliatti, *Opere 1929–1935* I:lxxxv–xcii.

The Organizational Svolta

In the spring of 1928 the PCI leadership in exile had lost contact with its domestic base, and its internal network was all but destroyed.[84] Thereafter arrests by the Fascists continued to pulverize the remaining Communist cells in Italy. It was thus clear that the Tenth Plenum's call for the revolutionary mobilization of the masses would require the return of the party's émigré cadres to Italian soil at great personal risk.

On December 28, 1929, Longo presented a proposal to the PCI Politburo for the immediate revival of a domestic leadership center as well as the transfer to Italy of most cadres. This initiative, which was to go down in party history as the *svolta* of 1930, precipitated a major crisis.[85] In a vote taken on January 10, 1930, Togliatti, Secchia, and Ravera supported Longo's plan while Tresso, Leonetti, and Ravazzoli—who were from this time forward branded in party polemics as "the three"—rejected it. And in a declaration dated January 15, 1930, Silone indicated his opposition as well. (Grieco was in Moscow at the time as PCI representative to the ECCI.) The central argument of the three was that conditions in Italy were not yet ripe for the wholesale resumption of clandestine activity. On the basis of their personal experience in the Italian underground, in which they had all been active after 1926, they emphasized the efficiency of the Fascist police in destroying the original PCI apparatus during 1927–28 and protested that the situation had not substantially changed since then.

The question was brought before the Comintern Presidium in the second half of February 1930. As if to curry support for his side in the controversy, Togliatti applauded the Comintern's criticisms of the PCI at the Tenth Plenum and boasted of his party's subsequent compliance with its directives. He then pleaded the case of the organizational *svolta*, accusing its opponents within the Italian Politburo of being open or covert

---

84. As Grieco bluntly put it in his report to the PCI Central Committee in October 1928, "You know our conditions at the end of May. We lost contact with the Party at the end of May"; APC, 1928, fol. 653:233.

85. PCI historians have dealt at length with the course and impact of the *svolta*, including the purge of the three and Silone. While the significance of the *svolta* for the Italian party's morale and later anti-Fascist profile remains a topic of controversy (see the Longo–Terracini debate in *l'Unità*, December 10, 11, and 23, 1975, 3), regret over the personal recriminations and unprecedented expulsions to which it gave rise is evident, at least on the part of Amendola and Ragionieri. See Amendola, *Storia del Partito comunista italiano, 1921–1943* (Rome: Editori Riuniti, 1978), 158–62 and 178–81; Spriano, *Storia del Partito comunista italiano* 2:230–61; and Ragionieri's introduction to Togliatti, *Opere 1929–1935* 1:xlix–lxxxi. Indicative of this attitude was the readmission to the PCI in the late 1950s of Alfonso Leonetti, one of the two surviving members of the three (Tresso perished during World War II); see "Una lettera di Leonetti," *l'Unità*, December 23, 1977, 3. For an exhaustively documented account sympathetic to Silone and the three (and dedicated to Leonetti), see Ferdinando Ormea, *Le origini dello stalinismo nel PCI: Storia della "svolta" comunista degli anni Trenta* (Milan: Feltrinelli Editore, 1978), esp. chaps. 7, 8, 10, and 11.

opportunists.[86] In a closing statement he was even more obsequious toward the authorities in Moscow. While remarking that the International should not interfere "in all the details" of internal PCI affairs, he affirmed its right to express its opinion on policy matters. And while denying an insinuation evidently made at the meeting that a majority of the PCI Central Committee members were against the Comintern's policy, he declared that even if it were, "the majority is the line of the Communist International and of all its sections, [and] it would be created."[87]

On this occasion Togliatti received the full backing of the Stalinists. As *Kommunisticheskii Internatsional* stated in a lead editorial in early March 1930, "the enlarged plenum together with the majority of the Italian comrades rejected and subjected to sharp criticism the viewpoint of those who don't see the . . . *new* tasks of the Party, . . . [particularly the task of transferring the whole weight of work from activity among the refugees abroad to activity in the country itself]."[88] The end result was a Comintern-approved resolution based on the recommendations made by the pro-*svolta* faction during the February meeting of the Presidium. This document endorsed the *svolta* and denounced its opponents within the Italian Politburo.[89]

The showdown within the PCI leadership was not long in coming. At a meeting of the Politburo in France right after the Presidium session, Longo, backed by Togliatti, made a formal motion to reestablish the internal center. On this concrete issue the Politburo split in two. But Longo's motion carried with the support of Secchia who, as representative of the youth federation, was entitled to a deliberative vote. The decision of the majority was upheld at a Central Committee meeting held in March 1930, despite the insistent objections of the three and perhaps partly because of their diatribes against Togliatti. In a nutshell, they accused him of "opportunism" for purportedly backing Longo out of expediency rather than conviction. In the end it was they who were condemned for opportunism; and all four dissidents were removed from the Politburo. The defeated three soon made overtures to Trotsky, as a result of which they were expelled from the party in June 1930.[90] Silone, whose participation in the inner circles of the PCI had been more intense and of longer duration than the three, arrived at the point of rupture inde-

86. Text in Togliatti, *Opere 1929–1935* 1:159–87, esp. 182–87.

87. Text in ibid., 188–93 at 192–93.

88. "Na Vyshuiu stupen," *KI*, no. 7 (March 10, 1930):3–8 at 3; the bracketed phrase appears only in the later English edition, *Communist International* 7, no. 4 (April 15, 1930):103–9 at 104.

89. "Risoluzione del CC del PCI, approvata dal Presidium allargato del CE dell'IC," *Bollettino del PCI-1930* (n.p.: clandestine PCI publication, n.d.), 2–13.

90. See their letter to Trotsky of April–May 1930 in *Annali Feltrinelli* 8, 1930–1931–1932, doc. 7:1032–57.

pendently—and with greater personal anguish—in the spring of 1931.[91]

Between 1929 and 1931 five out of nine members of the PCI Politburo were thus purged—amid bitter acrimony and contrary to the organizational principles Togliatti had hitherto championed. Indeed, the ouster of the three was carried out at Togliatti's insistence and despite the doubts of both Grieco (still PCI delegate to the ECCI) and the Comintern hierarchy. Grieco favored the reassignment of the opponents of the *svolta* to work in Moscow, the same kind of treatment that had been accorded the German moderates in the mid-1920s. But as Togliatti explained to him, the *public* challenge mounted by the three—coming as it did on the heels of the "brutality" of the Stalinists' criticisms at the Tenth Plenum—necessitated their expulsion if Togliatti and Grieco were to retain any authority whatsoever.[92] As in the case of Tasca, their preference for conciliation had to be sacrificed to *Realpolitik*.

A new PCI Politburo thus emerged that included not only Togliatti, Grieco, and Ravera but also their long-time critics, Longo and Secchia.

The Implacable Guardians of Comintern Orthodoxy

Despite the compliance of the PCI in 1929–30, the Comintern overseers remained unconvinced of the Italian party's political reliability. This became clear during the proceedings of the ECCI's Italian Commission in July 1930. At that time Togliatti presented a rather favorable picture of PCI affairs, in terms of organizational advances and the rout of the right. Among other things, he claimed that the *svolta* had been "in large part achieved." And he went on to explain why it had been necessary to move without the Comintern's prior approval against the anti-*svolta* group, namely, because of their ties to Trotsky, their "bloc without principles" with the ultraleft.[93]

Togliatti's report elicited a cutting rebuttal from Manuilsky. Indeed, his comments on the PCI contrasted sharply with his reaction several weeks earlier to a report by Maurice Thorez on conditions in the PCF. While Manuilsky criticized the PCF for its sectarian methods and "poor implementation" of Comintern directives, he also affirmed that its political line was absolutely correct and specifically commended Thorez.[94] Yet he was unbending and derisive toward the PCI and Togliatti in particular.

91. Silone, *Uscita di sicurezza,* 106ff.; and Spriano, *Storia del Partito comunista italiano* 2:322–24.

92. For excerpts from the correspondence of Togliatti and Grieco on this subject, see Togliatti, *Opere 1929–1935* 1:lxix–lxxi.

93. Text in ibid., 248–80 at 264–80.

94. "Rech tov. Manuilskogo vo frantsuzskoi komissii IKKI," *KI,* no. 18 (June 30, 1930):42–53. On the other hand, Thorez began his report with the self-effacing admission that "the work of

Manuilsky charged that Togliatti had exaggerated the PCI's organizational achievements. After asking rhetorically, "Where are the party organizations about which Comrade Ercoli spoke to us?",[95] he declared that he could not "share the optimism of Comrade Ercoli" regarding the total defeat of the rightists within the PCI. Pursuing this theme, he warned his Italian comrades of the continuing need "to break many political backbones" in the course of implementing the Comintern line.[96]

Manuilsky also reproached the PCI for its "cliquishness"—despite the recent wave of unprecedented purges. He argued that the party's domestic militants were but "closed circles of friends, evidently old comrades," and that "the whole party organization from top to bottom bears a cliquish character."[97] To top it off, he applied to the PCI leadership the distinctively Soviet epithet of "intimate family circle," with it connotation of personal interests taking precedence over loyalty to the party line.

The PCI leadership nevertheless rallied behind Togliatti during the discussion of party policy in *Lo Stato operaio* prior to the Fourth PCI Congress scheduled for April 1931. Only Mario Montagnana—Togliatti's brother-in-law—felt impelled, perhaps because of the family connection, to question the past conduct of the Togliatti–Grieco team. He argued that the "three opportunists" ought never to have been permitted to attain positions of authority in the first place and blamed this error on the foremost elements of the "party center." He went so far as to deprecate the tendency to consider as "irreplaceable" certain "luminaries," an unmistakable allusion to Togliatti and Grieco.[98] Their defense was thereupon taken up by none other than Secchia, who pointed out that the three had been properly elected to the Central Committee in 1926.[99] To this Montagnana retorted that Secchia had still not explained how the three had risen to their appointed posts in the PCI Politburo and Secretariat. And he insisted that the party leadership must never again slip into "that character of a closed, limited group that Comrade Manuilsky justly pointed out and criticized" the previous summer.[100]

Meanwhile, Grieco had a run-in with the Comintern hierarchy at the

---

our party suffers from great weaknesses and defects, of which the primary one is the continuous weakening of organizational work." Maurice Thorez, "Polozhenie vo frantsuzskoi Kompartii," KI, no. 18 (June 30, 1930):37–42 at 37.

95. "Iz rechi tov. Manuilskogo v italianskoi komissii IKKI," *Kommunisticheskii Internatsional* [henceforth *KI*], *KI*, no. 22 (August 10, 1930):38–49 at 40.

96. Ibid., 43.

97. Ibid., 42.

98. Mario Montagnana "La scelta degli elementi," *SO* 4, no. 9 (September 1930):577–84.

99. Botte [Pietro Secchia], "La causa di una crisi e la formazione del Centro del Partito," *SO* 4, no. 9 (September 1930):584–92 at 591.

100. Mario Montagnana, "Ancora della scelta degli elementi," *SO* 5, nos. 3–4 (March–April 1931):175–79 at 179.

Eleventh Plenum of the ECCI, held in late March–early April 1931. When he attempted to defend the idea that an anti-Fascist political crisis might precede a fully developed anticapitalist revolution,[101] he was coldly rebuked by Manuilsky: "The setting up of the political crisis as some sort of special stage preceding the 'real' revolutionary crisis suggests that there is thereby sanctioned so-called 'transitional periods' in the Brandler sense of the word."[102] Grieco's show of independence at the Eleventh Plenum appears to have been the last of its kind for some time on the part of the PCI leaders.

Shortly after the Eleventh Plenum the Fourth PCI Congress met clandestinely in Germany (April 14–21, 1931). The sessions of the congress were held with the assistance of the KPD at two successive locations between Cologne and Düsseldorf and were attended by fifty-six delegates, over half of whom came directly from Italy. Secchia, who was largely responsible for the domestic preparations for the congress, was arrested in Italy shortly before it opened. Although there is no stenogram of the proceedings,[103] the official documents and available speeches indicate that it marked the apogee of the PCI's radical sectarian phase. Held in the wake of the Comintern's wide-ranging criticisms of the PCI leaders and under the auspices of their chief faultfinders, the prevailing tone was set by the call "for the destruction of fascism and capitalism, . . . for a Soviet Italy, for the dictatorship of the proletariat."[104]

The only significant result of this otherwise unremarkable conclave was the designation of a new Politburo consisting of Togliatti, Grieco, Longo, Di Vittorio, Dozza, and Battista Santhià.[105] Neither in the published record nor in the accounts by Ernesto Ragionieri and Paolo Spriano is there any indication that Togliatti was officially singled out as the preeminent leader (the imprisonment of Gramsci evidently precluded the formal appointment of a general secretary). Giorgio Bocca suggests that on this occasion the Comintern authorities actually wanted Longo to replace Togliatti as chief of the PCI Secretariat.[106] However, according to the memoirs of one of the participants, Gian Carlo Pajetta, Ercoli's position as de facto *capo* (head) was unquestioned: "He was still young, 39 years old, but knew he was the *capo* of the Party and carried on his shoulders the

101. Text of Grieco's speech in *Inprecor* 11, no. 36 (July 6, 1931):661–63 at 661.

102. D. Manuilsky, "Problemy revoliutsionnogo krizisa i zadachi sektsii Kommunisticheskogo Internatsionala," *KI*, nos. 13–14 (May 20, 1931):51–69 at 57.

103. Togliatti, *Opere 1929–1935* I:cxxiii–cxxvi and 341.

104. "Il manifesto del IV Congresso al popolo italiano," *Trenta anni di vita e lotte del PCI*, 141–50 at 141; cf. Spriano, *Storia del Partito comunista italiano* 2:312–22.

105. Ibid., 322.

106. Giorgio Bocca, *Palmiro Togliatti* (Bari: Editori Laterza, 1973), 216–18. To support his argument, Bocca quotes extensively from personal interviews with Longo, Santhià, and others. Unfortunately, his occasional tendentious use of written documents reduces the credibility of his interpretations based on oral history.

responsibility of what Gramsci had left behind. . . . Everyone perceived in him . . . the comrade who could represent the party.''[107]

About this same time, the tactic of infiltrating Fascist mass organizations in order to take advantage of any legal possibilities for action was pressed upon the PCI by Comintern spokesmen. This was not a new theme. The International had recommended the legal possibilities tactic with specific reference to the PCI in its Sixth Congress resolution.[108] Piatnitsky returned to the same subject in a more critical vein at the Tenth Plenum: ''As far as I know, the Italian comrades have not yet done and are not doing one very important piece of work; they do not work in the Fascist unions.''[109] In his July 1930 speech to the ECCI's Italian Commission, Manuilsky also remarked upon the absence of PCI initiatives in this respect.[110] In response to Moscow's reproaches, the Central Committee report to the Fourth PCI Congress deplored the party's failure to transfer a part of its activity inside the Fascist organizations.[111] All the same, the infiltration of Fascist unions and youth groups remained merely a secondary aspect of the policies enunciated in the congress resolutions.[112] For the Comintern bureaucracy, however, it represented part of a general rivival of the tactic of a united front ''from below'' with non-Communist workers as the Great Depression intensified amid few signs of actual revolutionary ferment.[113]

Probably because of this more flexible line as well as Togliatti's greater sense of security as party *capo*, he appeared once again as chief spokesman for the PCI at the Twelfth Plenum of the ECCI (August 27–September 15, 1932).[114] While Togliatti now began to take a more active part in Comintern matters, Longo was transferred to Moscow as PCI representative.

This latter step was related to the Central Committee's condemnation in the autumn of 1932 of the party's organizational work in Italy for over-centralization, conspiratorial ''primitivism,'' and failure to consolidate the clandestine network.[115] In point of fact, the *svolta* had been a fiasco. During its initial stages party membership had risen from a low of somewhat over 2,000 in early 1930[116] to a variously estimated figure of from

107. Gian Carlo Pajetta, *Il ragazzo rosso* (Milan: Arnoldo Mondadori Editore, 1983), 104–5.
108. Sixth Congress theses, *VI Kongress Kominterna* 6:75.
109. *Inprecor* 9, no. 44 (August 30, 1929):931–39 at 939.
110. ''Iz rechi tov. Manuilskogo,'' *KI*, no. 22 (August 10, 1930):46–49.
111. ''L'attività del PCI dal III al IV Congresso,'' *Il IV Congresso*, 174.
112. See ''Tesi sulla situazione italiana e sui compiti del PCI'' and ''Risoluzione sui problemi di organizzazione,'' in *Il IV Congresso*, 51–91 and 141–50.
113. Carr, *Twilight of the Comintern*, 29ff.
114. Togliatti, *Opere 1929–1935* 2:104–28.
115. ''La situazione del partito e i suoi compiti,'' *SO* 6, no. 12 (December 1932):782–89.
116. See Togliatti's report to ECCI Presidium, February 1930, in Togliatti, *Opere 1929–1935* 1:162.

7,000[117] to 10,000[118] in mid-1932 (the latter also included members of the youth organization). However, during the course of 1931–32 the Fascist police had repeatedly tracked down the whereabouts of the internal center and arrested many of the PCI's most able cadres,[119] including Politburo members Secchia, Ravera, and Santhià. And in the summer of 1932, according to the later testimony of Giorgio Amendola, "the entire network of illegal functionaries was destroyed."[120]

Longo was apparently made the scapegoat for the failure of the *svolta* that had taken place under his direction.[121] At the meeting of the Central Committee criticism of Longo was instigated by Togliatti, although actually voiced by Montagnana and Giuseppe Berti.[122] In other words, the earlier friction between the two men had not been entirely overcome.

Meanwhile, despite the PCI leadership's admission of its shortcomings in late 1932, it was unable to rectify them to Moscow's satisfaction. The deficiencies of the Italian Communists were again publicly deplored at the Thirteenth ECCI Plenum in December 1933. Kuusinen, for example, remarked that he was "astonished" to hear that the Italian party "now has an extraordinary number of passive members."[123] Shortly thereafter, at the Seventeenth Congress of the CPSU in January 1934, Manuilsky remarked: "For years the Comintern has been battling with the Italian Communist Party in order to break down the resistance of the Italian comrades to work in the Fascist trade unions, and it has not attained a complete change in this respect even now."[124]

In sum, the relationship between the PCI and the guardians of Comintern orthodoxy continued to be uneasy. The Italian Communist leadership—contrary to the organizational principles it had defended in 1927–28—had purged itself of everyone unwilling to capitulate to Moscow. It had disavowed all slogans signifying the possibility of a post-Fascist transitional stage. Yet it proved incapable of reviving its domestic appa-

117. Manuilsky's estimate, reported in May 1934; APC, 1934, fol. 1180:2–3.

118. Spriano, *Storia del Partito comunista italiano* 2:352, n. 4.

119. Ibid., 339–54.

120. "Prefazione di Giorgio Amendola," in *Scritti scelti,* by Ruggero Grieco, 2 vols. (Rome: Editori Riuniti, 1966), 1:li.

121. That Longo's transfer was a form of censure is implied in "Introduzione di Giorgio Amendola," *Il comunismo italiano nella seconda guerra mondiale* (Rome: Editori Riuniti, 1963), xviii. Following an allusion to the organizational criticisms of 1932, Amendola stated: "After this critical examination, Longo left the direction of the organizational work to assume the task of PCI representative to the C.I." Cf. his cryptic comments on this same question in his *Storia del Partito comunista italiano, 1921–1943,* 198–202. Spriano refers only in passing to Longo's assignment to Moscow in *Storia del Partito comunista italiano* 2:398, as does Ragionieri in Togliatti, *Opere 1929–1935* 1:xciii.

122. Berti's commentary, *Annali Feltrinelli* 8, 1929, doc. 14:671–803 at 780 and doc. 15:803–89 at 805; cf. Bocca, *Palmiro Togliatti,* 231–32.

123. Otto Kuusinen, *XIII Plenum IKKI: stenograficheskii otchet* (Moscow, 1934), 578.

124. *Inprecor* 14, no. 12 (February 26, 1934):309–20 at 316.

ratus on a permanent basis, let alone mobilizing resistance to Mussolini's regime through the legal possibilities tactic. As Pajetta aptly explained it some five decades later, this weakness was tied to the party's "refusal to acknowledge what was for us most bitter: the almost listless acceptance of fascism by ever more extended circles of people."[125]

If Manuilsky was dissatisfied with the accomplishments of the PCI, how much more so must have been Togliatti and his colleagues! Not only had the *svolta* been a disaster in human as well as organizational terms, but the revolutionary crisis that was to justify it had not materialized. This twofold disappointment could only have exacerbated the moral and psychological costs of the PCI leaders' earlier capitulation to Moscow and purge of their own ranks. As for the impact of this whole sectarian period upon Togliatti, after 1930 he became, according to his perceptive biographer, Ernesto Ragionieri, severe and aloof in his working style and personal associations; and his natural reserve intensified to the point of cantankerousness.[126]

On the eve of the popular front era, moreover, the Italian political scene hardly vindicated the double revolutionary perspective favored by Togliatti and Grieco a half decade earlier. If the proletarian revolution was not on the horizon, neither was there any sign of a popular revolt against fascism. Mussolini's consolidation of power engendered resignation rather than rebelliousness even on the part of wage earners and sharecroppers who had nothing to gain from the regime. Among the middle classes it was becoming a popular dictatorship. Under these circumstances one may conjecture that the PCI leaders experienced not simply a loss of confidence but a lack of any political perspective.

125. Pajetta, *Il ragazzo rosso,* 112.
126. See Ragionieri's introduction to *Opere 1929–1935,* by Togliatti, 1:lxxxi.

CHAPTER 4

Popular Front Initiatives,
the Great Purge, and the PCI

I f the Great Depression lent a certain *ex post facto* rationale to the Stalinists' turn to the left of 1928–29, Hitler's consolidation of power in Germany was the catalyst for Moscow's popular front initiatives of the mid-1930s. No longer was the capitalist world portrayed as a hostile monolith. Instead the Western democracies were singled out as potential allies of the Soviet Union against Nazi aggression. By the same token, socialists were no longer stigmatized as "social fascists." Instead European Communists were directed to cooperate with all center-left groups in defending bourgeois democracy against fascism. Under these circumstances the PCI's discredited notion of an anti-Fascist people's revolution and its corollary of a post-Fascist democratic stage reemerged as valid Communist objectives. In a radical reversal of their earlier stance, the Comintern authorities now endorsed the use of democratic transitional slogans. As Georgii Dimitrov declared from the podium of the Seventh Comintern Congress in the summer of 1935, the International had erred in stating "that there will be *no intermediary stages* in the Fascist countries and that Fascist dictatorship is *certain to be immediately* superseded by proletarian dictatorship."[1]

While this abrupt turnabout in the international Communist line suited Soviet *raison d'état*, it ran counter to Stalin's perception of his personal security interests. For his thirst for power was matched only by his distrust of the innovative, conciliatory impulses still extant in the Bolshevik and European Communist ranks, impulses that were given new life by the popular front policies. The quest for interclass allies in the struggle against

1. See Dimitrov's speech in reply to discussion at the Seventh Congress in Georgi Dimitrov, *The United Front against Fascism and War* (New York: Workers Library Publishers, 1935), 105.

Fascist subversion and expansionism was thus accompanied by Stalinist insistence on ever greater ideological vigilance. Indeed, just when the Comintern began to endorse the gradualist approach to revolution backed by Bukharin's supporters in the 1920s, Bukharin himself was denounced as a traitor to the Soviet party and state. His arrest in February 1937 coincided with the International's call to arms on the side of the Republican forces in the Spanish Civil War. And as the International Brigades were being formed with Soviet material support, the European Communist parties were subjected to unprecedented regimentation—even by post-1928 standards. Not only that, but the Third International as an organizational entity suffered the same fate as the Communist Party of the Soviet Union: both became hollow structures appended to Stalin's personal bureaucracy.

The PCI, like all other Communist parties, could not escape this paradoxical combination of popular front initiatives and carping, punctilious surveillance from Moscow. During 1936 a debate developed among the Italian leaders over how best to apply the Comintern's popular front line in Italy. One proposal called for replacing the Mussolini regime with bourgeois democracy through a united struggle of anti-Fascist forces, that is, a variation on the theme of people's revolution. A second posited as the PCI's immediate goal the democratization of the Fascist state itself through a policy of "national reconciliation." No sooner did the latter, more daring, initiative win the upper hand in party councils, however, than it was criticized as verging on "Fascist reformism" by the Comintern overseers. The PCI Politburo duly retracted the slogan of "national reconciliation," only to have the Stalinists use it in 1938 as a handle with which to impugn the reliability of the entire PCI elite. These accusations were all the more ominous in that they followed on the heels of Bukharin's execution and coincided with the dissolution of the Polish Communist Party.

Togliatti had meanwhile been elevated to the newly created seven-man Secretariat of the International and become a key Comintern adviser in Spain. Yet even his prominence in the Comintern hierarchy could not prevent the shadow of Bukharin from hanging over the PCI. Only because the party center was located in democratic France rather than Moscow did its leaders suffer public humiliation and not worse as the 1930s drew to a close.

The Popular Front and the Revival of Transitional Slogans

The popular front line differed in its concrete implementation from one country to another. The revival of transitional slogans, indeed the outright advocacy of a democratic transitional stage in the form of a "people's democracy" or a "new democracy," had specific application only to the Fascist regimes and the Spanish scene. Still, this doctrinal readjustment was to have important ramifications a decade later. If in Eastern Europe it was to become window dressing for the imposition of Soviet-style regimes, in Italy it was to provide a theoretical framework for PCI conduct in the closing phase of World War II. And in the formulation of the transitional slogan of a "new democracy," Togliatti played a central role.

Origins and Spokesmen

The bureaucratic genesis of the popular front line was as important as its policy thrust. Personal memoirs and archival materials point to the following reconstruction of this process. Among the early proponents of unity of action with social democratic forces were Manuilsky (somewhat surprisingly), Kuusinen, and above all Dimitrov. Opposed to the shift were such sectarian stalwarts as Piatnitsky, Solomon Lozovsky, and the Hungarian, Bela Kun.[2] While Stalin acceded to the initiative, he never gave it his personal imprimatur and admitted as late as July 1934 his hesitations in this regard. Meanwhile, Maniulsky served the dual role of chief Soviet spokesman for the change in policy and devil's advocate regarding the potential dangers of cooperation with social democracy.

Soviet and Bulgarian documents attest to the key role of Dimitrov in Moscow's bid for a rapprochement with the socialists. Immediately upon his release from prison in Germany in late February 1934, the hero of the *Reichstag* fire trial became a ranking figure in the Comintern hierarchy. In early April of that year he presented the case for a united proletarian front to Stalin, encountering the latter's skepticism but also winning his consent to Dimitrov's de facto leadership of the International.[3] On May 11 he informed a reluctant Thorez of his enthusiasm for Communist–Socialist cooperation in the struggle against fascism.[4] Then in a letter dated July 1, 1934, addressed to Stalin and the ECCI's preparatory commission on tactics for the Seventh Comintern Congress, Dimitrov asked pointedly: "Is the indiscriminate qualification of social democracy as social fascism correct? . . . Is the indiscriminate treatment of all leading cadres of the [socialist] parties and reformist unions as conscious traitors of the working class correct?" His answer was no, whereupon he proposed a genuine united front untrammeled by "petty tutoring" and hegemonic claims on the

---

2. E. H. Carr, *Twilight of the Comintern, 1930–1935* (New York: Pantheon Books, 1982), 124–30.
3. Ibid., 126.
4. Ibid., 191.

part of the Communists. He reiterated these views—in more temperate language—the next day in his speech before the preparatory commission.[5]

Stalin's reaction to Dimitrov's letter was indicative of his continuing hesitation and uncertainty. At a meeting of the CPSU Central Committee several days after receiving it, he said to Dimitrov: "I haven't answered you, I haven't had time. In my head there is still nothing on this problem. We must prepare something."[6]

Meanwhile, Togliatti also became a prominent supporter of the popular front initiatives. According to Ragionieri, this did not happen until the summer of 1934, however, when Ercoli began collaborating with Dimitrov in the preparations for the Seventh Congress.[7] Only then did he overcome a perplexing "moment of inertia" with regard to the need for cooperation with social democracy.[8] Such inertia may have stemmed from a loss of confidence induced by the PCI's defeats of recent years. No longer persuaded of the correctness of either the *svolta* or the double revolutionary perspective, he had lapsed into reflexive conformity to the Comintern's sectarian clichés. Still, by June 1934 it was decided that Togliatti would be one of the four main speakers at the Seventh Congress along with Dimitrov, Manuilsky and the German Communist Wilhelm Pieck.[9] A major reason for the selection of Togliatti, we may assume, was his long-time familiarity with fascism.

In this whole decision-making process Manuilsky's position remained somewhat ambivalent, presumably reflecting Stalin's attitude. To be sure, Soviet historians with access to the Comintern's archives depict him as backing Dimitrov from the spring of 1934 and also lobbying for a change in French Communist policy toward social democracy.[10] At one point he is reported to have exclaimed to the PCF representative in Moscow, Albert Vassart (who also supported the emerging line), "I am risking my neck for the sake of your affairs."[11] On the other hand, according to a Peruvian ex-Communist, Manuilsky "piled up objections, pointed up

5. "Dokumenty G. M. Dimitrova k VII kongressu Kommunisticheskogo Internatsionala," *Voprosy istorii KPSS*, no. 7 (July 1965; to press June 23, 1965):83–88; for an extensive English translation of these key documents as well as further information on the circumstances of their origin and destination, see Jonathan Haslam, "The Comintern and the Origins of the Popular Front, 1934–1935," *Historical Journal* 22, no. 3 (September 1979):673–91.

6. Quoted from Bulgarian archives in Fausto Ibba, "E allora perché l'Europa ci è contro compagno Stalin?" *l'Unità*, June 18, 1982, 3.

7. Palmiro Togliatti, *Opere 1929–1935*, ed. Ernesto Ragionieri, 2 vols. (Rome: Editori Riuniti, 1973), I:clxxxvii–clxxxviii.

8. Ibid., clxxxii–clxxxiv.

9. "O poriadke dnia VII kongressa Kominterna," *Kommunisticheskii Internatsional* [henceforth *KI*], no. 16 (June 1, 1934; to press June 15):64.

10. See the citations in Carr, *Twilight of the Comintern*, 126–30.

11. Célie Vassart and Albert Vassart, "The Moscow Origin of the French 'Popular Front,'" in *The Comintern: Historical Highlights*, ed. Milorad M. Drachkovitch and Branko Lazitch (New York: Praeger, 1966), 234–52 at 246.

dangers and weighed the magnitude of the obstacles'' involved in the new orientation, with particular reference to the possible emergence of rightist deviations.[12] This testimony gains credibility from the fact that as late as September 1935 Manuilsky stressed the tactical nature of the popular front in a commentary in *Kommunisticheskii Internatsional*. Explaining that the directives of the Seventh Congress corresponded to the correlation of forces between the Communists and other political parties ''at the present time,'' he went on to say: ''But this relationship of forces will change. Tomorrow the Communist parties may have greater opportunities for direct influence over the masses without the existing old, outdated organization and parties. *And this may again demand a sharp change* of tactics.''[13] Significantly, the English version of the same article, not published until December 1935, substituted for the above quotation the following brief sentence: ''These tactics are being operated in earnest and for a long time.''[14] And the Comintern journal did not carry another article with Manuilsky's byline for more than two years.

In view of Manuilsky's prominent role in Comintern affairs in 1938–39, it is unlikely that this temporary withdrawal from the limelight indicated any kind of official disfavor. Rather, Stalin's inner circle probably decided to let the non-Soviet Communist leaders take the lead in playing the popular front card, without investing any more of the Kremlin's prestige than necessary in such a risky venture.[15]

At the Seventh Congress in mid-1935 Dimitrov and Togliatti thus took center stage in advancing the popular front initiatives. There was a commensurate improvement in their official status. Dimitrov was designated general secretary of the International while Togliatti was elevated to membership in a new seven-man Secretariat of the ECCI. He shared this honor with Manuilsky, Pieck, Kuusinen, André Marty, and Klement Gottwald. However, Togliatti's alias, Ercoli, consistently followed Dimitrov in the formal listings of the Secretariat (despite the fact that such an ordering of names was not called for by the Cyrillic alphabet).[16]

The reasons for Moscow's choice of Dimitrov and Togliatti as major spokesmen for the popular front are not difficult to fathom. Both men were committed to the new line, of course. But far more important was the

---

12. Eudocio Ravines, *The Yenan Way* (New York: Scribner's, 1951), 116 and 145.

13. D. Z. Manuilsky, ''Itogi VII Kongressa Kommunisticheskogo Internatsionala,'' *KI*, no. 27 (September 20, 1935; to press October 16):3–41 at 33–34; my emphasis.

14. D. Z. Manuilsky, ''Results of the Seventh Congress of the Communist International,'' pt. 2, *Communist International* 12, nos. 23–24 (December 20, 1935):1580–1602 at 1593.

15. The standard Soviet source on this period, which cites only a few of the Soviet archival materials on which it draws, gives no hint of such an interpretation, arguing that Stalin expressed doubts only until October 1934; see B. M. Leibzon and K. K. Shirinia, *Povorot v politike Kominterna*, 2d ed. (Moscow: Mysl, 1975), 90ff.

16. See ''Sostav rukovodiashchikh organov Kommunisticheskogo Internatsionala,'' *KI*, nos. 23–24 (August 20, 1935; to press September 10):159–60 at 160.

message their selection conveyed to the European Communist movement. Criticism of the Comintern's previous sectarianism was conspicuous by its absence at the Seventh Congress, if only because all the leading Comintern functionaries were implicated in the earlier policy. In this respect, Dimitrov and Togliatti differed markedly from the norm. Both men had resisted the extremist trend of the late 1920s. Whereas Togliatti was subjected only to public rebuke, Dimitrov was actually shunted from the leadership of the Bulgarian party in May 1929 by a group of young sectarians backed by Stalinists in the ECCI apparatus.[17] Moreover, about this same time both men were assigned to the Comintern's West European Bureau in Berlin. While Togliatti successfully thwarted this maneuver, Dimitrov took over the direction of the WEB in April 1929, only to request release from that post—to no avail—in late 1930.[18] That the formal leadership of the International was now in the hands of individuals who had earlier been in disfavor for conciliation, if not unqualified right-wing opportunism, could not be openly vaunted. But the point was surely not lost on the European Communist cadres. It lent an aura of authenticity to the new international Communist line.

Togliatti's reasons for agreeing to relinquish day-to-day direction of the PCI for full-time work in the Comintern are less readily apparent, not least because of the absence of any record of his views on the subject. In contrast to the extensive materials available on his fight against transferral to the WEB in 1928, both the PCI Archives and the memoirs of protagonists shed little light on his 1934 shift. Authoritative Italian Communist sources do not even agree on the date of his assignment to the Comintern apparatus, with one citing October, another November,[19] and yet another late summer 1934.[20] This is probably because he divided his time between Paris and the Soviet capital during those months—and even earlier. We do know, on the other hand, that he attended meetings of the PCI Politburo through early November but was listed as not present beginning with a meeting of that body on November 23, 1934.[21] As for Togliatti's own reticence on this matter, it was probably a result in part of continuing uncertainty about becoming a Comintern *apparatchik* and in part of some embarrassment over his willingness in 1934 to take a step he

17. Joseph Rothschild, *The Communist Party of Bulgaria: Origins and Development, 1883–1936* (New York: Columbia University Press, 1959), 287–99.

18. Fausto Ibba, "E allora perché," *l'Unità*, June 18, 1982, 3.

19. For the conflicting views of Paolo Robotti and Franco Ferri, see Giorgio Bocca, *Palmiro Togliatti* (Bari: Editori Laterza, 1973), 237–38.

20. See Ragionieri's introduction to *Opere 1929–1935*, by Togliatti, 1:clxxxiv–clxxxv, n. 2. He cites as evidence in this regard the following excerpt from a September 19, 1934, letter from Togliatti to Dozza: "The decision regarding me isn't even related to the [Seventh Congress] report . . . but to more general problems of extreme interest to me. For this reason the decision cannot but be accepted."

21. APC, 1934, fol. 1194, 177.

had heatedly opposed six years earlier. Given the dismal plight of the PCI, his departure could be construed as deserting a sinking ship.

On balance, however, Togliatti's reservations must have been more than offset by the prestigious position he was to occupy as well as the opportunity it would afford him to avenge his earlier humiliation at the hands of the Soviet and German sectarians. Moreover, the new line plainly entailed approval of the strategic views he had advocated in the late 1920s. This was underscored by Togliatti's reaffirmation in *Kommunisticheskii Internatsional* on the eve of the Seventh Congress of both the legitimacy of transitional objectives and the need for a "differentiated analysis" of concrete national conditions. "Partial economic and political demands are no longer enough," he asserted. Rather, "it is necessary to set forth more advanced demands. . . . In each country these demands will have a different content, depending on the conditions . . . , but everywhere they must be *demands of a transitional character,* opening the path to struggle for power."[22]

At the same time, Togliatti was entrusted by Dimitrov with the supervision of the Communist parties of Central Europe.[23] And in this capacity he was at last able to retaliate against the German Communists for their earlier vindictiveness toward the PCI. As Comintern delegate to the Fourth KPD Conference, held in October 1935 in Moscow, Togliatti called for a "profound and precise self-criticism" of the sectarian errors committed by the German party after the rise of Hitler.[24] This occasion represented the culmination of the Comintern Secretariat's efforts since late 1934 to replace the surviving German left-wing extremists with individuals more receptive to the popular front line, notably Pieck (who became acting leader of the KPD) and Ulbricht.[25] In a different vein, Togliatti was also able to propose, at a meeting of the ECCI Presidium on December 1, 1935, that his long-time friend Humbert-Droz resume the leadership of the Swiss Communist Party (a position he had lost three years earlier).[26] The proposal was accepted. And thereafter Togliatti was unstinting in his praise and encouragement of the erstwhile Swiss "conciliator."[27]

22. Ercoli, "Problemy edinogo fronta," *KI*, nos. 20–21 (July 20, 1935; to press July 20):49–57 at 56; my emphasis.

23. Marcella Ferrara and Maurizio Ferrara, *Conversando con Togliatti* (Rome: Edizioni di Cultura Sociale, 1953):249.

24. Ercoli, "Edinyi antifashistskii front i ocherednye zadachi K.P. Germanii," *KI*, no. 30 (October 20, 1935; to press November 23):14–24.

25. Ibid., 15; cf. Haslam, "The Comintern and the Origins of the Popular Front," 687–88; Togliatti, *Opere 1929–1935* 1:cxcviii–cciv; Palmiro Togliatti, *Opere 1935–1944,* ed. Franco Andreucci and Paolo Spriano, 2 vols. (Rome: Editori Riuniti, 1979), 1:3–22; and *Inprecor* 16, no. 1 (January 4, 1936):17.

26. Jules Humbert-Droz, *Dix ans de lutte anti-fasciste: 1931–1941* (Neuchatel, Switzerland: Éditions de la Baconnière, 1972), 138–39.

27. Ibid., 164, 185, 192.

The implementation of the popular front line developed gradually, beginning with the PCF in 1934 and reaching a high-water mark in 1936 when popular front coalitions in Spain and France won electoral victories. At the instigation of the Comintern authorities, the French Communists entered into negotiations with the leaders of the SFIO (the French Section of the Socialist International, or French Socialist Party) and finally reached agreement on a formal Unity of Action Pact on July 27, 1934. The pact pledged joint PCF–SFIO defense of the Third French Republic against Fascist subversion and an end to the bitter polemics between the two parties that continued to bedevil relations through mid-1934. The following October, this time upon the initiative of PCF leader Thorez, an offer was made to broaden this alliance strategy to include the centrist Radical Party. Thus was born the idea of the interclass popular front.[28]

The Seventh Comintern Congress (July 25–August 21, 1935) formally promulgated the popular front policy for all Communist parties. According to the congress resolutions, the following changes in the world situation justified the new line: the intensification of the Fascist threat and Nazi aggressiveness;[29] and the differentiation of the capitalist states into those striving for a new partition of the world and those favoring the status quo.[30] As Togliatti spelled out in his major address, the status quo group consisted of "capitalist countries which for the most part have preserved a parliamentary regime."[31] Dimitrov discerned a corresponding differentiation of social democracy into "revolutionary" and "reactionary" elements.[32] In the principal ECCI report to the congress, he thus endorsed a united front with members of the Second International and even Catholic, anarchist, and unorganized workers.[33] He also spoke of a popular front between the proletariat and the peasantry, urban petty bourgeoisie, and intelligentsia, going so far as to suggest Communist willingness to support a popular front government.[34] In line with this shift, he called for the defense of democratic liberties.[35]

A parallel theme running through the congress speeches and resolutions was that the Comintern bureaucracy should relax discipline and respect

28. For an exhaustive treatment of the French sources on this subject, see Daniel R. Brower, *The New Jacobins: The French Communist Party and the Popular Front* (Ithaca, N.Y.: Cornell University Press, 1968), esp. 47–67. For studies using more recent Soviet and Bulgarian sources, see Haslam, "The Comintern and the Origins of the Popular Front," 673–91, and Carr, *Twilight of the Comintern,* 184–203.

29. Seventh Congress theses on Dimitrov's report, in *Inprecor* 15, no. 43 (September 7, 1935):1121–26 at 1121.

30. Seventh Congress theses on Ercoli's report, in ibid., 1126–28 at 1127.

31. Ercoli, *The Fight against War and Fascism* (Moscow: Co-operative Publishing Society of Foreign Workers in the USSR, 1935), 32.

32. Dimitrov, *The United Front,* 26.

33. Ibid., 27.

34. Ibid., 66–73.

35. Ibid., passim.

national differences among Communist parties, should avoid "the mechanical application of the experience of one country to another."[36] In Dimitrov's famous words that have been periodically recalled by Communist innovators ever since, "*national forms* of the proletarian class struggle are in no contradiction to proletarian internationalism; on the contrary, it is precisely in these forms that the *international interests* of the proletariat can be successfully defended."[37] The resolution on organization thus instructed the ECCI "as a rule to avoid direct intervention in the internal organizational matters of the Communist parties."[38]

These directives proved all too soon to be wishful thinking. They were already violated in spirit by the uniformity of views, the absence of debate, and the pervasive obsequiousness toward Stalin that were hallmarks of the Seventh (and last) Comintern Congress. Still, Togliatti was plainly committed to greater freedom of initiative for individual Communist parties. Dimitrov's letter of July 1, 1934, to Stalin and the ECCI also urged more autonomy for the Comintern's member parties.[39] The incorporation of such views into the documents of the Seventh Congress reflected the extent to which the operational control of the International was at that time in the hands not simply of non-Soviets but of moderates rather than sectarians. Yet on the eve of Stalin's Great Purge what was actually in store was ever greater centralization, for the Comintern as for the CPSU. The Seventh Congress was in fact to be the swan song of the International as an organizational entity, with even the ECCI never again holding a plenum.

Meanwhile, militant undertones could still be detected at the Seventh Congress. Even while the resolution based on Dimitrov's report approved the new line, it hailed it as "*the decisive link in the preparation of the toilers for the forthcoming great battles of the second round of the proletarian revolutions.*"[40] There was similar equivocation regarding the prospects for peace. Togliatti, during the discussion of his speech, asserted that it was possible to avoid war altogether.[41] By way of contrast, the resolution based on Togliatti's address indicated that war was still inevitable, declaring that when it came every effort should be made to convert it into a civil war against capitalism.[42]

36. Seventh Congress theses on Pieck's report, in *Inprecor* 15, no. 46 (September 19, 1935):1175–76 at 1176.

37. Dimitrov, *The United Front*, 76–77.

38. Seventh Congress theses on Pieck's report, in *Inprecor* 15, no. 46 (September 19, 1935):1176.

39. "Dokumenty G. M. Dimitrova," *Voprosy istorii KPSS*, no. 7 (1965):83–86.

40. Seventh Congress theses on Dimitrov's report, in *Inprecor* 15, no. 43 (September 7, 1935):1126.

41. Ercoli, *The Fight against War*, 113.

42. Seventh Congress theses on Ercoli's report, in *Inprecor* 15, no. 43 (September 7, 1935):1127–28.

During 1936, however, emphasis was increasingly placed upon the defense of peace and democracy rather than the promotion of revolution. In a step that underscored Moscow's security concerns, Stalin flatly denied in an interview with the American journalist, Roy Howard, on March 1, 1936—a few days prior to the Nazi reoccupation of the Rhineland—that the Soviet Union wanted to promote world revolution.[43] Shortly thereafter, the ECCI May Day appeal called the creation of a popular front for peace *"the central task of the international proletariat,"* mentioning only that *by struggling for peace* the workers of the world would "bring nearer the victory of *socialism*."[44] Dimitrov wrote commentarires in the same vein in the Comintern journal.[45] The open profession of revolutionary goals thus gave way to vague correlations of the preservation of peace with the coming of socialism in a shift that served both the interests of Soviet foreign policy and the political advance of the European left. Nowhere was the latter more evident than in the formation of popular front governments in Spain and France (during February and May 1936, respectively).

"Democracy of a New Type"

If Togliatti was inconspicuous during the formulation of the popular front line, he was bold and assertive in the initiatives he proposed for the PCI and Spain in 1935–36. For both he returned to the approach he had favored in the mid-1920s. He suggested intermediate objectives that might mobilize broad strata of the population against fascism and result in a democratic transitional stage prior to the coming of socialism. The only difference was that he now hailed democracy as a value in itself and not merely a lesser evil.

His search for effective modes of political action was abetted by his newly gained prominence in the Comintern hierarchy. The political environment with which he had to contend in the mid-1930s was also a far cry from the one in which he operated a decade earlier. His advocacy of transitional slogans during the mid-1920s had actually been a kind of political shadow play, with his target, the Italian masses, cowed by Fascist repression and the domestic PCI network close to extinction. By 1935, in contrast, there was a groundswell of anti-Fascist sentiment among center-left forces in the European democracies, and the Communists' call for unity of action with these groups had greatly improved their public image. At the same time, socialist leaders had begun to ask what objectives their

43. Text in *KI*, nos. 5–6 (March 25, 1936; to press March 21): 5–12 at 7.
44. "Proletarii vsekh stran mira!" *KI*, no. 8 (April 25, 1936; to press April 25):3–7.
45. See, for example, G. Dimitrov, "Edinyi front borby za mir," *KI*, no. 9 (May 10, 1936; to press May 9):3–11 at 11.

would-be Communist allies had in mind beyond the defeat of fascism: if not the dictatorship of the proletariat (read Communist parties), then bourgeois democracy? Neither, of course, was acceptable to the social democratic parties. Already aware of this dilemma in late 1934, Togliatti mentioned in a letter to Manuilsky the need to devise a "program of a *revolutionary workers' government*, but of a government that cannot be from the start a pure Soviet government."[46] In other words, conditions were ripe for a political formula that would flesh out the hitherto nebulous strategy of a transitional stage on the path to socialism.

At the Seventh Comintern Congress Dimitrov tentatively advanced such a formula under the name of a "united front" or "popular front" government. But he cautioned that such a government would be only a temporary expedient during the interval between the anti-Fascist people's revolution and the anti-capitalist proletarian revolution. Dimitrov rejected the "rightist" demand for a simple parliamentary coalition during a period of normalcy. Neither did he define the new governing formula except to say that it should be anti-Fascist in origin and intent. In line with the radical tone that still pervaded Comintern rhetoric, he was explicit on only one point. This transitional government would constitute *not* a peaceful parliamentary transition to the dictatorship of the proletariat but merely an approach to armed proletarian revolution.[47]

Yet the outbreak of the Spanish Civil War in July 1936—after revolutionary talk had been silenced in the interests of Soviet *raison d'état* and Western Communist electoral gains—confronted the Comintern decision makers with a genuinely revolutionary situation. With Moscow's decision several weeks later to intervene on the side of the Republican forces, the need for a clarification of the International's short-run political objectives became pressing. Now if ever in the West the question was: *chto delat* (what is to be done)? Accordingly, at a meeting of the ECCI Secretariat in September 1936, Dimitrov postulated the transitional goal of a "people's democracy" for Spain. This "people's democracy" would not yet be a "Soviet democracy" but rather "a democratic state where the popular front has decisive influence yet where the bourgeois system still exists. . . . Theoretically it might be correct to define this as a special form of the democratic dictatorship of the workers and peasantry."[48] Soon thereafter the lead editorial in the October 1936 issue of *Kommunisticheskii Internatsional*, echoing Dimitrov's words and most likely written by him, defined the immediate goal of the Spanish people's revolution as a noncapitalist and nonsocialist "people's democracy" in which the

46. Quoted in Togliatti, *Opere 1929–1935* 1:cxcvi–cxcvii.
47. Dimitrov, *The United Front*, 66–73.
48. "Dokumenty Ispolkoma Kominterna o borbe za edinyi rabochii i narodnyi front, protiv fashizma i voinu," *Voprosy istorii KPSS*, no. 3 (March 1969):12–13.

working classes would "smash once and for all the backbone of fascism and open up the road to the building of new political and social forms."[49]

A companion piece by Togliatti in the same issue of the Comintern journal went even further than Dimitrov. In an essay entitled "On the Particularities of the Spanish Revolution," he depicted the goal to which the Spanish revolutionaries aspired as a "democracy of a new type" which would have a *broader class base* than the orthodox Leninist "democratic dictatorship of the workers and peasants": namely, it would include numerous segments of the urban bourgeoisie who had been alienated by the Spanish Fascists. It would, moreover, undertake a series of radical measures that would "go substantially beyond the program of a government of the revolutionary democratic dictatorship." Specifically, it would purge all Fascists, destroy the material basis of fascism through agrarian reform and confiscation of rebel property, and offer "a guarantee for all further economic and political conquests of the Spanish toilers."[50] The last point went, of course, to the heart of the matter. What Togliatti implied was that the "new democracy" would actually open the path to socialist transformation, that it would obviate the very need for a violent proletarian revolution.

In this latter respect, his line of argument recalled Lenin's occasional use of the term "new democracy" in 1917 to describe a possible coalition government of Bolsheviks, Mensheviks, and Socialist Revolutionaries (responsible only to the Soviets) that would permit "the peaceful development of the revolution."[51] Togliatti's "democracy of a new type" differed from Lenin's formulation, however, both in its interclass composition and in the much slower pace of anticipated revolutionary development. While Lenin contemplated a brief interlude in which the Bolsheviks would maneuver for hegemony, the crux of the 1936 concept was its connotation of a concrete transitional stage between bourgeois democracy and socialism. Its underlying purpose was, indeed, to hold out the promise of social reform while allaying fears of Communist revolution.

There is reason to believe, moreover, that Togliatti had in mind a form of genuine participatory democracy. For when he arrived in Spain the following summer as Comintern adviser to the Spanish Communist Party (PCE), he deplored the absence of authentic democratic structures. His complaints on this score in a confidential report to the ECCI warrant quotation at length:

49. "Deviatnadtsataia godovshchina," *KI*, no. 16 (October 1936; to press November 5):8–14 at 13.

50. Ercoli, "Ob osobennostiakh ispanskoi revoliutsii," ibid., 15–23; cf. "Sulle particolarità della rivoluzione spagnola," *SO* 10, no. 11 (November 1936), in *SO 1927–1939*, ed. Ferri, 2:496–512. Citations are taken from the Ferri version of the Italian text, 503–10.

51. V. I. Lenin, *Sochineniia*, 2d ed. (Moscow-Leningrad, 1926–32), 21:132–36 and 227–28.

The thing that above all strikes the eyes is the absence of those democratic forms which permit the vast masses to participate in the life of the country and in politics. In present-day Spain Parliament represents almost no one. . . . The municipal councils . . . and provincial councils have been formed from above. . . . The committees of the popular front have ceased in fact to exist. . . . There are factory committees, but it is very difficult to establish whether they have been elected or nominated from above by the leadership of the trade unions: it seems to me that for the most part they have been nominated from above. In the trade unions, which have become a powerful economic organization, there is very little democracy. . . . The life of the country develops beyond the control of the masses.[52]

The irony of sending such a dispatch to Stalin's Russia of 1937 was evidently lost on Togliatti. Yet this only heightens the light it sheds on his own vision of the ideal society as well as his illusions regarding Soviet reality.

Already in the autumn of 1936 there was apparently some controversy behind the scenes over the meaning of "people's democracy" and "democracy of a new type." Both were, as we have seen, postulated in the October issue of *Kommunisticheskii Internatsional*. Yet in the very next issue of the journal (which, however, took six weeks rather than the usual two to four to come out), an unsigned commentary insisted that only Soviet democracy represented "authentic people's democracy."[53] All the same, Togliatti's essay on the Spanish revolution was translated into numerous languages and widely disseminated by Moscow. As a result, it influenced the thinking of Communists from Yugoslavia, where the Yugoslavian Communists managed to have its essence published legally in the largest prewar daily, *Politika*,[54] to China, where Mao Tse-tung adapted Togliatti's term to Chinese conditions in his celebrated tract, *On New Democracy*, first published in 1940.

The PCI's Bid for "National Reconciliation"

The impact of the Comintern's popular front policy upon the PCI was ultimately quite dramatic. Not only did the PCI leaders proclaim bourgeois democracy, not proletarian revolution, their general goal after the Seventh Comintern Congress, but in the summer of 1936 they began to

52. "Relazione del 30 agosto 1937," in Togliatti, *Opere 1935–1944* 1:258–72 at 264–65; cf. Paolo Spriano, *I comunisti europei e Stalin* (Turin: Giulio Einaudi editore, 1983), 21.

53. "Konstitutsiia sotsialisticheskoi demokratii," *KI*, no. 17 (November 1936; to press Dec. 16):40–44 at 44.

54. Ivan Avakumović, *History of the Communist Party of Yugoslavia* (Aberdeen: Aberdeen University Press, 1964), 1:105, n. 63.

call for reform of the Fascist regime itself as a first step in the return to a democratic order in Italy. This initiative culminated in an appeal for the implementation of Mussolini's original Fascist Program of 1919, with its democratic and even leftist strains. By calling for limited reforms within the very ambit of the Fascist regime, the Italian party aimed to create a basis for unity of action between anti-Fascists and dissident Fascists, a platform for "national reconciliation."

If the Italian Communists were motivated by the desire to weaken a detested regime, foreign policy considerations were uppermost in the minds of the Soviets. No longer did the PCI occupy a secondary place in Moscow's strategic calculations. Its political effectiveness became a top priority as the prospect of a German-Italian military alliance against the Soviet Union became ever more threatening. From the Soviet perspective the PCI's chief task was thus to agitate against the formation of the Rome–Berlin Axis. To this end it was encouraged to play upon the almost universal Italian fear of the *Anschluss,* the union of Austria with Germany, which would extend the Third Reich to the Brenner Pass. That, in turn, would pose a threat to the Italian borderlands of the South Tyrol and Trieste, the ethnically mixed territories that had been Italy's reward for entry into World War I on the side of the Entente.

Mussolini was fully aware of the Nazi aspirations to both Trieste and the South Tyrol, with its Austro-German population of over two hundred thousand, and early recognized that Austrian independence was in the national interest of Italy.[55] After the assassination of Austrian Chancellor Dollfuss in July 1934, he ordered Italian mobilization at the Brenner Pass.[56] Following Hitler's remilitarization of the Rhineland, the *Duce* again reinforced the Austro-Italian frontier. Nevertheless, from mid-1936 on, as a result of Hitler's acclaim for Italy's conquest of Ethiopia and intervention in Spain, Mussolini gradually acquiesced in the Nazi subversion of Austria.

All the while the PCI sought to portray the *Anschluss* as a threat to Italian territorial integrity. Togliatti said in his speech to the Seventh Comintern Congress that the German annexation of Austria would mean a "direct menace to the frontiers of Italian imperialism."[57] He likewise suggested in a letter to the PCI leadership in late October 1935 that it exploit "certain 'national' themes," citing by way of example the idea that "Mussolini's policy incurs the risk that Italy will be attacked at the Brenner Pass by the [Nazis]."[58] Longo subsequently voiced this argument

55. Elizabeth Wiskemann, *The Rome-Berlin Axis* (London: Oxford University Press, 1949), 22ff.

56. Ibid., 40.

57. Ercoli, *The Fight against War*, 33.

58. APC, 1935, fol. 1261:25–28.

in the July 1936 issue of *Lo Stato operaio.* "What interest does our people have," he warned, "in having Hitler at its own frontiers? (The *Anschluss* would create such a situation.) What interest does our country have in favoring indirectly the Hitlerite thrust toward Trieste, toward the Adriatic? None."[59] Such a line could hardly be expected to influence the Mussolini regime directly, of course. It was of practical value only insofar as it stimulated pressure among Fascist dissidents for a realignment in Italian foreign policy.

From Sectarianism to Innovation

The shift in PCI policy was initiated at a restricted meeting of the ECCI Political Secretariat in May 1934. As so often before, Manuilsky and Piatnitsky were scathing in their criticisms of the Italian Communists, especially for their "sectarian" error of failing to carry out the legal possibilities tactic. Manuilsky began by pointing out that PCI membership had fallen from 7,000 members in 1932 to some 5,200 members in 1934. Of those, 2,800 were either imprisoned or deported, leaving an effective membership of 2,400. He attributed this weakness to "sectarian isolation from the masses." In his words, the PCI resembled not a Bolshevik organization but rather "the old Russian *Narodnaia Volia* except without bombs." Whereupon Piatnitsky interjected that it was "an organization of the terrorist type without terrorism. It doesn't even know how to create a commotion." Manuilsky concluded that the Italian section was one of the weakest in the Comintern "*at a time when the international situation makes the action of the PCI much more important.*"[60]

The sorry state of the PCI was again taken up at an enlarged meeting of the ECCI Latin Secretariat on June 10–11, 1934. On that occasion Manuilsky was much less harsh, perhaps because the Italians present, including Montagnana, Dozza, and Berti, dutifully seconded the Soviet officials' reproaches and directives.[61] In return Manuilsky went so far as to engage in self-criticism, chiding the Comintern for not having "occupied itself seriously with the problem of Italy." He then spelled out that "the way to apply the united front" was to "work in the factories and in the mass organizations of fascism."[62]

In the meantime there had been some changes in the composition of the PCI Politburo since the Fourth Congress, when Togliatti, Grieco, Longo, Dozza, Di Vittorio, and Santhià were elected to that body. Santhià was now in prison, Togliatti in Moscow, and Longo (who had returned from

59. Luigi Gallo, "Il popolo italiano vuole la pace," *SO* 10, no. 7 (July 1936):478–82 at 482.
60. Text in APC, 1934, fol. 1180:2–3; my emphasis.
61. "Interventi di membri del C.C. al Segretariato Romano (10 e 11 guigno 1934)," APC, 1934, fol. 1180:10–12.
62. Text in APC, 1934, fol. 1180:5–7.

Moscow in early 1934) assigned to work among the Italian émigrés in Paris.[63] Montagnana had therefore been coopted into the Politburo despite his criticism several years earlier of the PCI inner circle's excessive concern with "unity." Indicative of his new rapport with this same group, he now praised Togliatti and Grieco for having "maintained intact in these difficult years . . . the unity of our party."[64] And during the mid-1930s he became one of the four top figures in the Paris center of the PCI along with Grieco, Dozza, and Di Vittorio.[65]

As the first step in the development of a new line, the PCI followed the PCF pattern of overtures toward social democracy in the summer of 1934. This was evidently a result of the fact that the party's operational center was in Paris. For on July 15, the day on which the French Socialists voted to conclude a pact with the PCF, the PCI proposed a united front with the PSI.[66] And on July 27, the day the French Unity of Action Pact was formally signed, the two Italian parties started negotiations.[67] Shortly thereafter, on August 17, 1934, they signed a pact endorsing joint action against war and for the improvement of domestic Italian conditions.[68]

Polemics between the two parties nevertheless continued. In declarations published simultaneously with the pact, the PSI charged that the PCI, unlike the PCF, had not relinquished the "theory of social fascism" nor pledged itself to defend democratic liberties. The PCI retorted that it would continue to denounce the "deception and illusions" of bourgeois democracy and to struggle for a Soviet government.[69] The airing of such reservations toward democratic principles was accompanied by veiled polemics among the Italian Communists themselves over whether sectarianism was now the main danger in their ranks.[70] Both phenomena indicated how the mindset of the PCI cadres—like that of Communists everywhere—had been shaped by the Comintern's post-1928 extremism.[71]

63. "Introduzione di Giorgio Amendola," *Il comunismo italiano nella seconda guerra mondiale* (Rome: Editori Riuniti, 1963), xvii.

64. C. Roncoli, "Dieci anni di lotte (Nel decimo anniversario delle Leggi eccezionali)," *Lo Stato operaio* [henceforth *SO*] 10, no. 12 (December 1936):836–45 at 844.

65. "Introduzione di Giorgio Amendola," *Il comunismo italiano*, xviii.

66. "Per l'unità d'azione del proletariato," *SO* 8, no. 7 (July 1934), in *SO 1927–1939*, ed. Ferri, 2:205–10 at 208–10.

67. "Il fronte unico," *SO* 8, no. 8 (August 1934): 571–80 at 578.

68. Text in ibid., 571–78.

69. Ibid., 578–80.

70. See, *inter alia*, Erc., "Postilla," *SO* 8, no. 7 (July 1934):554–56 at 554; L., "Settarismo e deficienze nel lavoro di massa," *SO* 8, no. 9 (September 1934): 693–97 at 694; C. Roncoli, "Osnovnye uroki borby kompartii Italii protiv fashizma v usloviiakh 'totalitarnogo' rezhima," *KI*, nos. 26–27 (September 20, 1934; to press October 10):22–30 at 25 and 28; and Tinelli, "O kharaktere i istochnikakh sektantstva v kompartii Italii," *KI*, nos. 32–33 (November 20, 1934; to press December 2):48–52. The identity of the polemicists is not always clear from the pseudonyms they used.

71. For a comparative study, see Carr, *Twilight of the Comintern*, passim.

Under the prodding of Togliatti, however, the PCI's position was soon transformed. In a letter to the Paris center on March 25, 1935, he urged that the party stress not Soviets but "political liberty." He went on to emphasize the need for "partial political demands," for "*agitation with a democratic content.*" And he voiced skepticism over the idea that "*every* expansion of the mass movement . . . will create at once a revolutionary situation in which the masses will struggle for the Soviets."[72] Soon after the Seventh Comintern Congress, at the October 1935 session of the PCI Central Committee, Grieco thus declared that the Italian masses had to choose not "between proletarian dictatorship and fascism but between fascism and bourgeois democratic liberties."[73] Not only that, but even Longo referred several times to the need for an anti-Fascist "people's revolution,"[74] a major *volte-face* from his position in the late 1920s.

If during 1935 the PCI Politburo merely responded to signals from the Comintern, in 1936 it struck out on its own. In an August 1936 manifesto, "For the Salvation of Italy, for the Reconciliation of the Italian People," it appealed for the reconciliation of all Italians, Fascists and non-Fascists alike, in a joint struggle against the "handful of capitalist parasites" who were threatening the country with war for the sake of their own enrichment. In the Italian party's most extreme formulation of the legal possibilities tactic, it flatly stated: "Today . . . we Communists take as our own the Fascist Program of 1919." It went on to describe the contents of that program as a minimum wage, land reform, the nationalization of weapons factories, progressive taxation, a tax of 85 percent on war profits, universal suffrage, and "a foreign policy which undertakes to enhance everywhere, in the works of peace, the Italian Nation."[75]

By playing on leftist and pacifist impulses within the Fascist ranks, the Italian Communists apparently hoped to create pressure within the inner councils of the regime itself not only for the reform of fascism but also for its realignment in the international sphere. The actual Italian-German agreement that led to Mussolini's coining of the term, "Rome–Berlin Axis," was not reached until Foreign Minister Gaetano Ciano's trip to Germany in October 1936.[76] The August 1936 manifesto thus called upon the Italian government to sign mutual assistance pacts with France and the Little Entente (Czechoslovakia, Yugoslavia, and Romania), to renounce

72. Text in APC, 1935, fol. 1261:1–4.

73. Report by M. Garlandi, "Il nostro partito di fronte ai compiti attuali," *SO* 9, nos. 11–12 (November–December 1935):683–98 at 692.

74. Report by Luigi Gallo, "I primi risultati verso la costituzione del fronte popolare," in ibid., 699–706.

75. "Per la salvezza dell'Italia riconciliazione del popolo italiano!" *SO* 10, no. 8 (August 1936):513–36.

76. Wiskemann, *The Rome-Berlin Axis*, 65–68.

its "present foreign policy which . . . has opened to Hitlerism the path toward the Brenner and Trieste."[77]

In September 1936 the PCI Central Committee, convening for the first time since October 1935, confirmed the August reconciliation initiative. It promulgated as the party's central slogan the *"reconciliation and union of the Italian people for bread, peace and liberty."*[78] The major reason for this step, according to the speeches later published in *Lo Stato operaio*, was that the anticapitalist connotations of Fascist corporatist doctrine had imbued many Italian youth[79] as well as Fascist functionaries of working class origin[80] with a real urge for social justice. This radical sentiment formed the basis for joint action between Fascists and anti-Fascists. Indeed, the formal resolution of the September meeting went so far as to argue that *"the Fascist unions can be an instrument of struggle against management and, . . . therefore, they ought to be considered as the workers' unions in the present Italian situation."*[81]

Moreover, speaker after speaker, while describing democracy as the PCI's general objective "during the present period," reiterated the August 1936 manifesto's support for Mussolini's original Fascist program. As Egidio Gennari stated in his report on the current tasks of the PCI, "In the present situation we are ready to uphold any democratic political reform whatsoever . . . even if it *doesn't go beyond the framework of the present regime*—like the program of 1919."[82] The official Central Committee resolution likewise declared that the party was prepared to struggle for *"the Fascist Program of 1919, which is a program of liberty."*[83]

The Origins of the Reconciliation Initiative

Both mystery and controversy surround the PCI's mid-1936 bid for national reconciliation. The mystery is related to the fact that there is no available record of who drafted the August 1936 manifesto.[84] The docu-

77. "Per la salvezza dell'Italia," *SO* 10, no. 8 (August 1936):523.

78. See "Unire!" lead editorial in *SO* 10, no. 10 (October 1936):645–48 at 645; the slogan of "reconciliation and union of the Italian people" was frequently reiterated in the speeches and reports of the September 1936 PCI Central Committee meeting. Cf. "Riconciliazione e unione del popolo italiano per la conquista del pane, della pace e della libertà (Risoluzione del CC del PCI)," in ibid., 729–32.

79. Ruggero Grieco, "Per la salvezza delle nuove generazioni," in ibid., 668–86; cf. "Problemi di un movimento della gioventù italiana (Dichiarazione del CC del PCI)," in ibid., 733–35. See also speech by Celeste Negarville, "Per un movimento giovanile italiano," in ibid., 687–93.

80. Mario Montagnana, "Quadri operai fascisti," in ibid., 711–16.

81. "Riconciliazione e unione del popolo italiano," in ibid., 730.

82. Egidio Gennari, "Le agitazioni operaie e la lotta per la libertà," in ibid., 649–62 at 661.

83. "Riconciliazione e unione del popolo italiano," in ibid., 731.

84. Both Paolo Spriano and Giorgio Amendola skirted the question of the origins of the August 1936 manifesto. See Paolo Spriano, *Storia del Partito comunista italiano*, 5 vols. (Turin: Giulio

ment had the distinction of bearing the legal names (not aliases) of most leading figures of Italian communism—those in Moscow (e.g., Togliatti) and those in Fascist confinement (e.g., Secchia and Umberto Terracini) as well as the members of the party center in Paris. Togliatti's name headed the list of signatories. He was surely not the author, however, for he later objected to the lack of consultation in drafting the August 1936 manifesto and, indeed, reproached the Paris leaders for not giving him enough advance notice of the September Central Committee meeting to enable him to attend it.[85]

The reconciliation initiative nevertheless bore the imprint of Togliatti's mode of political analysis, both in its attentiveness to reality and its concentration on the mass base of fascism. During the winter of 1935 the new Comintern secretary had delivered a series of lectures to Italian students at the Lenin School in Moscow in which he summed up, revised, and elaborated his many previous commentaries on fascism.[86] Two points stood out: Togliatti's characteristic concern with nuance and his preoccupation with weaning away the mass of Fascist followers—lower-middle-class elements and misguided workers—from their reactionary leaders. If only the proletariat would staunchly defend democracy, he insisted, fascism need never come about.[87] Yet once it had, one could nevertheless combat it by exploiting every possible divergence between the Fascist base and oligarchs: "Every time the Communist party manages to find a crack, a fissure in fascism, it must introduce a wedge so as . . . to reopen the possibilities of struggle."[88] The PCI's 1936 reconciliation initiative was based on the assumption that Mussolini's foreign policy and corporatist rhetoric were creating just such "fissures."

Togliatti's communications to the Paris center during late 1935 and early 1936 emphasized above all the cracks emerging between the regime's cadres and leaders as a result of Mussolini's military campaign against Ethiopia. In his October 1935 letter to the PCI leadership, Togliatti anticipated (erroneously) the emergence of antiwar opposition among Fascist activists. And he enjoined the party to devise *"a policy that favors the formation of this opposition,"* to draw a clear-cut distinction between those Fascist cadres in favor of the Ethiopian War and those opposed to it. He then suggested the specific slogan, "down with those responsible for

---

Einaudi Editore, 1967–75), 3:64–67; and Giorgio Amendola, *Storia del Partito comunista italiano, 1921–1943* (Rome: Editori Riuniti, 1978), 260–61.

85. See Aladino Bibolotti's report to the PCI Politburo on his conversations with Ercoli during January and early February 1937 in APC, 1937, fol. 1432:19–43 at 27 and 29.

86. Togliatti, *Opere 1929–1935* 1:ccx–ccxv.

87. "Corso sugli avversari," ibid., 2:531–671 at 536.

88. Ibid., 550.

the war.'' Togliatti indicated, however, that these were only suggestions, not directives: ''Naturally the things I say are only advice.''[89]

During the next few months Togliatti could not have been more outspoken about the need to focus attention on the Fascist establishment. In a letter addressed to Dozza on January 1, 1936, he wrote that if in a given factory ''80 percent are passive Fascists and 15 percent convinced Fascists,'' the PCI should ''aim at the 15 percent and create a breach'' in their ranks.[90] At the same time, both then and in an earlier letter to Grieco on November 17, 1935, he lambasted the ''types who live in Paris''—of whom he identified only Longo—for their schematic and mistaken fixation on the formula of a ''popular front government.'' Togliatti denied the applicability of the French Communist policy of a ''popular front government'' to the Italian setting. Instead he urged a more flexible approach to the question of the post-Fascist succession, raising in his November letter even the idea of a ''constitutional assembly.''[91] He also discounted the utility of a united front with the Italian Socialists: ''The problem of the united front poses itself differently [in Italy] than in all the other countries. *Not with the Socialists but with the Fascists. . . .* With the malcontents who don't want war.''[92]

These themes were reiterated, albeit in more reserved language, in a resolution approved by the Presidium of the ECCI in February 1936.[93] Togliatti's role in its formulation was underscored by a laudatory reference in that document to one of his recent letters to the PCI leadership.[94]

If Toglatti's thinking appears to have inspired the August 1936 manifesto, the record of the debate provoked by that document within the PCI Politburo reveals that Montagnana and Di Vittorio were its chief supporters and suggests, furthermore, that Montagnana may have been its author. At a mid-August 1936 Politburo meeting attended by a dozen or so persons, Grieco and Dozza both criticized the manifesto, thus ruling out their involvement in its drafting. They as well as Longo and several participants of lesser stature urged that the PCI's immediate goal should be the overthrow of fascism and creation of a bourgeois democracy. Support for the Fascist Program of 1919 was all right but only as a means of spurring joint action between anti-Fascists and Fascist dissidents against the Mussolini regime. By way of contrast, Montagnana and Di Vittorio argued that the party's short-term aim should be the *democratization of the Fascist system.* Indeed, they warned against advocating a bourgeois democracy when

89. APC, 1935, fol. 1261:25–28.
90. APC, 1936, fol. 1352:1–2.
91. APC, 1935, fol. 1261:31–32.
92. APC, 1936, fol. 1352:1–2; my emphasis.
93. APC, 1936, fol. 1349:5–7.
94. Ibid., 5.

many Italians were suspicious of democracy and, after Mussolini's spring 1936 victory in Ethiopia, sympathetic toward fascism.[95]

At times the contention between these two groups became quite intense, reflecting a cleavage that had characterized Politburo discussions since early 1935.[96] As a case in point, Dozza protested that if the Politburo accepted Montagnana's views, it would "commit an error of an opportunist nature." "The policy of the party," he insisted, "cannot be summed up in the reform of fascism."[97] Still, the overall tone was one of reasoned dialogue. Montagnana went to great lengths to clarify his position. As he explained it, the PCI's current slogan was not the overthrow of fascism because "after the military victory in Abyssinia, people in Italy no longer believe in the immediate overthrow of fascism. Our present objective, which we will certainly modify tomorrow, is [to win] democratic liberties in the Fascist regime. Today we want to improve fascism because *we cannot* do more."[98] Di Vittorio wholeheartedly seconded Montagnana's arguments.[99]

In the end the PCI leaders arrived at a compromise position whereby, in the public documents of their September 1936 Central Committee meeting, they embraced the goals of democracy and of national reconciliation at one and the same time. And in the January 1937 issue of *Kommunisticheskii Internatsional* Grieco explained that an appeal to overthrow Mussolini would scarcely evoke broad support among the masses who had so recently—and even willingly—borne arms in his behalf. At present, he argued, the Italian people should instead be rallied to a struggle against the "handful of parasites" who were directly exploiting them.[100] He affirmed that the goal of democracy was more desirable, yet wondered aloud whether it would be "possible to reconcile and unite the Italian people for this aim." "An everyday united struggle," he continued, "ought to have a more general political aim of a programmatic character. Therefore, our party has declared that it will take as a starting point the Fascist Program of 1919 which is a democratic program, and will struggle for it."[101] He concluded by saying that the PCI was prepared to begin this struggle *"within the framework of the Fascist regime."*[102]

---

95. Politburo minutes, August 10–11, 1936, in APC, 1936, fol. 1358:100–116.

96. See, for example, the Politburo meeting of January 28, 1935, where Dozza accused Di Vittorio of "opportunism" for his stress on work in the Fascist unions. APC, 1935, fol. 1269:24–30.

97. APC, 1936, fol. 1358:109–10.

98. Ibid., 104.

99. Ibid., 105–13.

100. M. Garlandi, "Za edinenie Italianskogo naroda," *KI*, no. 1 (January 1937; to press February 7):17–25 at 18.

101. Ibid., 21.

102. Ibid., 24.

Reproaches, Reprimands, Recriminations

Judging from the Comintern journal's publication of Grieco's article, one would hardly suspect that the PCI's mid-1936 initiatives were already provoking criticism among the Comintern authorities in early 1937 and would in 1938 be targeted for denunciation by Manuilsky in a wide-ranging attack on the PCI. These two waves of reprimands differed significantly from one another, however. The first was related to the rapid internationalization of the Spanish Civil War; and its prime mover was Dimitrov. In other words, it was prompted by considerations of Comintern policy which, though aligned with Soviet foreign policy, still had a separate identity and matrix.[103] At that time, moreover, the PCI's quiet retraction of the slogan "national reconciliation" sufficed to still the criticism. By way of contrast, the second, much sharper, wave of rebukes emanated from Stalin's political designs, from his final showdown with Bukharin and, quite possibly, from his wish to reach an accommodation with Hitler. Above all, it reflected Stalin's drive to break the political backbone of the European Communist movement along with that of the CPSU.

Whereas Togliatti was a participant in the 1937 reproaches, he was a target, if only by implication, in the 1938 attack spearheaded by Manuilsky. Togliatti shared some of the Comintern hierarchy's winter 1937 doubts about the PCI's national reconciliation line even though he was not as opposed to it as Dimitrov, given his own insistence on reaching out to dissident Fascist cadres. On the other hand, the second wave of reprimands occurred long after he had been sent to Spain as an adviser to the PCE (in July 1937). And it coincided with the public trial and execution of Bukharin.

One can neither document nor dismiss lightly the suspicion that the PCI and Togliatti himself were incriminated in Stalin's campaign against the right wing of the Old Bolsheviks. For, as we shall see, Manuilsky's castigation of the PCI in 1938 included references to the Italian party's deviations in *1927–28*. At the same time, Manuilsky tried to turn the Italian Communist leaders against one another by hinting to Togliatti— who briefly returned to Moscow in August 1938—that his comrades in Paris were hatching a plot against him. News of this insinuation prompted a flood of recriminations within the PCI's inner circle that was halted only by Togliatti's warnings against further quarreling.

In the end Togliatti's conciliatory approach, combined with the felicitous location of the party center in Paris rather than the Soviet capital,

103. For the period up till mid-1935, see Carr, *Twilight of the Comintern*, 3–155. That this was still the case in early 1937 is clear from the materials in the PCI Archives cited in the following pages.

saved the PCI from factional disintegration or worse. The Italian Communist elite thus survived the Great Purge physically intact, only to be singled out for unparalleled denunciation at the Eighteenth Congress of the CPSU in March 1939.

1937: Revolutionary Vigilance and Popular Front Orthodoxy

The first indications of Moscow's dissatisfaction with the PCI's mid-1936 policies surfaced at a Politburo meeting in early November 1936. On that occasion Domenico Ciufoli, who had just returned from Moscow, reported on the Comintern leaders' single-minded preoccupation with developments in Spain. Because of this they objected to the PCI's bid for reconciliation with Fascist dissidents, fearing that it might undermine efforts to promote antiwar sentiments among young Italians recruited to fight on Franco's side. Mentioning only Manuilsky by name, Ciufoli summed up their assessment in the following words: "Not reconciliation with the Fascist regime but reconciliation of the [Italian] people in order to overthrow the Fascist dictatorship."[104]

Ciufoli's report provoked a debate that echoed the arguments exchanged among Politburo members the previous August, except for the fact that Dozza now seemed more receptive to Montagnana's position. He cautioned, for example, that only a small part of the Italian people were presently against fascism and warned that the PCI's domestic organization might be destroyed—and with no positive results, at that—if it openly attacked the regime. In a telling show of independence, he remarked: "We have the duty to do what the 'International' tells us to do but we should also be very prudent."[105]

The record of the discussion reveals that the criticisms conveyed by Ciufoli were also expressed in a letter from Togliatti—a letter that is missing from the PCI Archives but that had been read by everyone present. What is striking is not so much Togliatti's reservations as the reaction of his comrades. Although they were respectful toward him, they were by no means wholly receptive to his suggestions. Just as Dozza advised caution in implementing the directives of the International, Grieco and others voiced disappointment at the tone of Ercoli's letter and Montagnana objected to its substance as well.[106] Moreover, one Aladino Bibolotti—who had just completed eight years in Fascist jails and was soon to be sent to Comintern headquarters for an extended briefing—speculated that the comrades "over there" (in Moscow) would surely agree with the Italian party once they had seen all the materials from the

---

104. Politburo minutes of November 6, 1936, in APC, 1936, fol. 1358:230–37 at 230–31.
105. Ibid., 232.
106. For their views see ibid., 232–37.

September 1936 Central Committee meeting. In short, supine kowtowing to the men in Moscow was not yet characteristic of the PCI's Paris center.

For the rest of 1936 there was little word from Togliatti or the Comintern, causing Montagnana to protest in a mid-December letter to Ercoli that "we don't understand your silence on many questions about which we have written you for some time."[107] This silence ended during Bibolotti's stay in Moscow from early January through mid-February 1937. His subsequent report to the PCI Politburo on his many talks with Togliatti provides vital insight into Ercoli's thinking during what was a historic moment in Soviet history.[108] The public trial of seventeen Old Bolsheviks including several friends of Bukharin began on January 23, 1937, and Bukharin himself was implicated in the crimes of the defendants and finally arrested on February 27.[109] Bibolotti's meetings with Togliatti were decisively influenced by that trial. Beforehand Togliatti appeared sympathetic albeit anxious regarding the PCI's activities. Afterwards his comments took on a sharp and critical edge.

Togliatti's lack of communication with the Paris leaders toward the end of 1936 was probably a result of his preoccupation with the intensifying campaign against the Old Bolsheviks. Indeed, one of his main points during his initial conversations with Bibolotti was the need for greater PCI vigilance: "Fill in the gap of 1936 and initiate a vigorous campaign against Trotskyism in general and against Trotskyism in Italy," he advised on January 12.[110] His other major concern had to do with the operating style of the Paris center. Specifically, he recommended fewer meetings and less talk at the Politburo level.[111] Returning again and again to this theme, he asked that both meetings and discussion be kept to a minimum. Evidently Togliatti wanted to put a damper on the kind of debates which had been taking place. He spoke of the need for more study and thought. But given the conspiratorial and paranoid atmosphere that was enveloping the upper reaches of the CPSU and Comintern, we may surmise that he was also trying to impress upon his comrades the wisdom of keeping one's mouth shut.

Bibolotti did not meet with Togliatti from January 16 through the first week of February, the period during which the trial of CPSU rightists was held. Thereafter there were four encounters within six days, culminating

---

107. APC, 1936, fol. 1352:16–18.

108. For the text of Bibolotti's report, see APC, 1937, fol. 1432:19–43. Curiously, Bibolotti's twenty-five-page single-spaced report is mentioned only in passing by both Amendola in *Storia del Partito comunista italiano, 1921–1943*, 347, and Spriano in *Storia del Partito comunista italiano* 3:170.

109. Stephen F. Cohen, *Bukharin and the Bolshevik Revolution* (New York: Oxford University Press, 1980), 368–72.

110. APC, 1937, fol. 1432:26.

111. Ibid., 25–27.

in a session on February 12 attended by other Italians present in Moscow—and presumably Comintern officials as well. There was an unmistakable change in Togliatti's tone at this group session.[112] He repeated, far more emphatically than earlier, his recommendations on operating procedures as well as his call for an uncompromising struggle against *Trotskisti–Bordighisti*. But in addition, the party line as a whole now came under scrutiny. On two issues Togliatti was adamant: the need to foment opposition to the Rome-Berlin Axis, to stress the threat it posed to Italian independence; and the need for the PCI to uphold ''at the present stage'' the goal of a ''democratic republic.'' With regard to the second point, he reprimanded Montagnana by name for suggesting the intermediate step of reforming fascism.[113] And he chided the PCI Politburo as a whole for downplaying his own autumn 1936 reproaches on this score.[114] He also echoed Manuilsky's by now standard criticism, made once again after Bibolotti's arrival in Moscow,[115] regarding the PCI's inability to carry any political weight in Italy.[116]

Equally important, however, Togliatti did *not* oppose either his party's propagandistic use of the Fascist Program of 1919 or the slogan of ''national reconciliation.'' His comments on the latter warrant quotation at some length. ''The slogan of *reconciliation* should be used with caution,'' he warned. ''It *can* lead one to think that we are reconciling with the enemy, with the Fascist Party, with the Fascist regime. . . . Therefore, take care that it not be understood as reconciliation with the Fascist regime.''[117]

It was Dimitrov, not Togliatti, who two days later ordered the PCI to drop the reconciliation initiative. ''Do away absolutely with the slogan *reconciliation*,'' he enjoined Bibolotti at a meeting also attended by Ercoli.[118] He granted that it was more appropriate to extend a hand to dissident Fascists in Italy than in Germany. Still, ''the political concept of reconciliation with elements belonging to the Fascist Party'' was mistaken because it gave the Fascists themselves the false idea of struggling ''*to reform*'' the regime.[119] Immediately afterward Togliatti jotted down some brief notes for Bibolotti to take back with him to Paris.[120] Foremost among them was the directive to get rid of the reconciliation slogan because, as Dimitrov had insisted, it could be misunderstood as suggest-

112. Ibid., 29–38.
113. Ibid., 33.
114. Ibid., 32.
115. Ibid., 24.
116. Ibid., 32.
117. Ibid., 36.
118. Ibid., 39.
119. Ibid., 42.
120. Ibid., 19.

ing that "the aim of the PCI was that of reforming fascism and not overthrowing it."[121]

Dimitrov's rejection of the reconciliation slogan was plainly related to his push for greater solidarity between the Comintern and European social democracy. Indeed, in the case of Italy the PCI's initiatives of mid-1936 had presented the most serious stumbling block to a renewal of the 1934 Unity of Action Pact with the PSI.[122] The Italian Socialists had rejected from the start the PCI's bid for national reconciliation and especially its tactical backing of the Fascist Program of 1919. PSI letters of protest to this effect had been published (with rebuttals) even in the pages of *Lo Stato operaio* in the fall of 1936.[123] As Socialist leader Pietro Nenni recalled in mid-1937, "if the method of preventive discussion had been applied, we wouldn't have lost a year in the polemic over the so-called reconciliation of all Italians."[124]

As for Togliatti, his growing involvement in the Spanish Republican cause brought home to him as never before the importance of Communist–Socialist unity in general. Still, the particularities of the Italian scene persuaded him of the need to incite dissent among Fascist cadres if there was to be any prospect of overthrowing Mussolini's regime. When confronted with Dimitrov's directive, however, he agreed. At a time when Stalin's purges were intensifying, the defense of departures from orthodox popular front formulations was hardly advisable.

Discipline prevailed in the PCI's Paris center as well. Togliatti's notes to his comrades and Bibolotti's exhaustive report were discussed at a Politburo meeting on March 4. The very next day that body—amid ingratiating tributes to the International and Ercoli—retracted the reconciliation slogan, endorsed the goal of a democratic republic, and called for a verification of party cadres to combat Trotskyism and "every form of conciliation toward it."[125] No doubt the insistent demand for revolutionary vigilance that had begun to emanate from Moscow prompted this new air of submissiveness—which contrasted so sharply with the demeanor of the Italian leaders the previous autumn.

The March–April 1937 issue of *Lo Stato operaio* conveyed the news of the shift to the party base. Whereas the appeal for the "reconciliation and union of the Italian people" had appeared frequently in the January and

---

121. Text in APC, 1937, fol. 1440:20–24 at 20. Spriano quoted this document at length in *Storia del Partito comunista italiano* 3:171–73.

122. Cf. Franco Ferri, "Programma 'diciannovista,'" *Rinascita* 23, no. 11 (March 12, 1966):26.

123. Cf. "Problemi e discussioni: Due lettere di compagni socialisti dall' Italia," *SO* 10, no. 11 (November 1936):788–800.

124. "Una lettera del Partito socialista italiano," *SO* 11, nos. 7–8 (July–August 1937):416–18 at 417.

125. APC, 1937, fol. 1432:46–54 at 46.

February issues, the combined (and delayed) March–April issue neglected to mention it at all. More to the point, Egidio Gennari, in an obviously distorted remark in the "Problems and Discussions" section, declared: "The political line fixed by the Party Central Committee in September was synthesized in the formula, *union of the Italian people.*"[126] Then on June 10, 1937, Grieco—in an address urging the Italian Socialists to update the PCI–PSI Unity of Action Pact—not only omitted any reference to the reconciliation slogan but also conceded that the Communists had probably been wrong "in having sometimes assumed political positions without consulting the Socialist comrades."[127] The details of the subsequent negotiations between the two parties need not concern us here.[128] Suffice it to say that by July 26, 1937, the Italian Communists and Socialists had arrived at a compromise agreement on short-term goals that resulted in a new Unity of Action Pact against fascism.[129]

1938: The Lengthening Shadow of Bukharin

The PCI's quiet retraction of the reconciliation initiative notwithstanding, in 1938 Moscow launched a wholesale campaign to discredit, split, and even disband the leading organs of the Italian party. The rationale for these moves, according to Manuilsky, was the PCI's continuing inability to mobilize mass action against the Fascist regime. The overt targets were Grieco, head of the Secretariat in Togliatti's absence, and Dozza, then responsible for organizational work and cadres. Yet Togliatti was also implicated in his comrades' malfeasance. And over all of them hung the shadow of Bukharin, whose public trial and execution immediately preceded the onset of this latest PCI ordeal.

At the end of 1937 there was already a hint of things to come when Giuseppe Berti, PCI representative to the Comintern in the mid-1930s, accused Dozza of insufficient revolutionary vigilance.[130] Berti followed this up with objections to the policy adopted by the PCI Central Committee at a meeting in mid-March 1938. At that time, in response to the long anticipated *Anschluss* on March 12, the Italian Communists appealed to their countrymen to defend Italy's territorial unity and national independence against the threat of Nazi invasion across the former Austro-Italian

126. E. G., "Problemi e discussioni," *SO* 11, nos. 3–4 (March–April 1937):251–58 at 252.
127. Ruggero Grieco, "I doveri dell'antifascismo italiano nell'ora presente," *SO* 11, nos. 5–6 (May–June 1937):324.
128. For an overview, see Joan Barth Urban, "Moscow and the Italian Communist Party: 1926–1945" (Ph.D. diss., Harvard University, 1967), 230–36.
129. "Nuova carta di unità d'azione tra il Partito comunista e il Partito socialista," *Trenta anni di vita e lotte del PCI* (Rome: Editore Rinascita, 1952), 147–48.
130. Spriano, *Storia del Partito comunista italiano* 3:232–35.

frontier.[131] Berti protested that the Soviet Union was instead threatened by aggression from the Rome–Berlin Axis.[132] Thereafter Grieco and Dozza were summoned to Comintern headquarters for official talks. In contrast to the high visibility of Togliatti and Dimitrov during Bibolotti's briefing the previous year, the main interlocutor was now Manuilsky.[133] Meanwhile Berti was ordered to set the party's Paris center in order, replacing Dozza as head of cadres and apparently also Grieco as head of the Secretariat.[134]

From late April through June 1938 Grieco and Dozza, as well as Ciufoli and other PCI functionaries present in Moscow, were subjected to a political browbeating, the gist of which may be gleaned from three statements: a speech by Manuilsky to the ECCI's Italian Commission on June 14[135] and two resolutions formulated shortly thereafter—one by the Comintern Presidium[136] and the other by the ECCI's Political Secretariat, based on a draft prepared by the PCI delegation.[137] The immediate target was the PCI's recent call for the defense of Italian territorial unity and national independence. Mussolini's Italy, thundered all three documents, was allied with—not threatened by—Hitler's Germany. But the Communists' failure to instigate popular resistance to the wars in Ethiopia and Spain was also decried. And this weakness was blamed on their inability—dubbed sectarian and opportunist by turns—to penetrate the Fascist mass organizations. The resolution drafted by the PCI delegation itself castigated the party for advocating only a short while earlier the "reform of fascism" and the "reconciliation" slogan.[138] From Grieco's later report to the PCI Secretariat on what transpired in Moscow,[139] it is clear that these allusions echoed criticism made from on high during the spring 1938 talks.

The reprimands were accompanied by unprecedented organizational sanctions. As Manuilsky put it in his June 14 speech, there was a need to "remake" (*peredelat*) the leadership of the PCI.[140] The upshot was a decision, conveyed by Grieco to his colleagues upon his return to Paris,[141] to dissolve the PCI's existing leadership organs and to create in their place a four-man "center of reorganization" along with a carefully selected

---

131. For details, see the report by Grieco and Dozza to the Comintern authorities dated April 28, 1938, in APC, fol. 1488:1–33 at 16–17.
132. Spriano, *Storia del Partito comunista italiano* 3:248.
133. See Grieco's remarks to this effect in APC, 1938, fol. 1494:120.
134. Spriano, *Storia del Partito comunista italiano* 3:249 and 252.
135. Text in APC, 1938, fol. 1488:34–37.
136. Text in ibid., 69.
137. Text in ibid., 70–75.
138. Ibid., 70.
139. APC, 1938, fol. 1494A:30–36.
140. APC, 1938, fol. 1488:36.
141. APC, 1938, fol. 1494A:35 and 38.

Central Committee of only eight persons. The function of these new bodies would be to convoke a party conference to review all PCI policies and to revamp its organizational structure.

The most destructive step on Moscow's part, however, was to insinuate that there was a move afoot against Togliatti within the inner circles of the PCI elite. The bitter recriminations unleashed within the party Secretariat by this allegation pointed to Manuilsky as its source. According to the minutes of a mid-September 1938 Secretariat meeting attended by Togliatti, for the first time in years, Ercoli—or Alfredo, to use his Spanish *nom de guerre*—reported only that the comrades "over there" had spoken of "something like a group struggle without principles and also of some elements of a struggle against Ercoli."[142] During the heat of the ensuing debate, however, both Dozza and Berti disclosed that this allegation originated with Manuilsky.[143]

The available evidence suggests that Manuilsky's innuendoes were intended to sow distrust and rancor among the PCI elite—as indeed they did—rather than to protect or alert Togliatti. For during the fateful spring of 1938 this tested Stalinist also implicated Ercoli in the PCI's deviationism. In his above noted speech to the Comintern's Italian Commission in June, Manuilsky traced the Italian party's "vacillations" right back to the Eighth ECCI Plenum of May 1927.[144] His allusion in 1938 to Togliatti's efforts to avert the Stalinists' showdown with Trotsky eleven years earlier was ominous, to say the least. Similarly, during Manuilsky's talks with the Grieco-Dozza delegation, shortly after Bukharin's execution, he rebuked the Italian comrades for their "vacillations" of 1926, 1928, and 1929 in "the struggle against Trotskyism and *Bukharinism*."[145] These cutting remarks coincided with the interrogation and torture by Stalin's police of one of Togliatti's in-laws, Paolo Robotti, in what the latter claimed was an attempt to incriminate the top PCI leadership.[146] (Robotti, arrested on March 9, 1938, and freed only in September 1939, was married to a sister of Rita Montagnana, Togliatti's wife at that time.) There were, to be sure, contradictory signals, not the least of which was Togliatti's safe return from an August 1938 visit to Moscow and continuing representation of the Comintern in Spain.[147] But this may merely have indicated that Manuilsky's word was not law in the Comintern, over which Dimitrov still presided.

On balance, Moscow's inquisitorial approach toward the PCI during the

---

142. APC, 1938, fol. 1494:117–22 at 117.
143. Ibid., 121.
144. APC, 1938, fol. 1488:36.
145. Disclosed by Grieco in his August 12 report; APC, 1938, fol. 1494A:35; my emphasis.
146. Amendola, *Storia del Partito comunista italiano, 1921–1943*, 344.
147. Spriano's introduction to *Opere 1935–1944*, by Togliatti, 1:cxvi–cxix.

spring and summer of 1938 appears to have been shaped by two considerations: the party's ineffectuality; and the Italian Communist leaders' past deviationism and guilt by association with the now condemned CPSU right wing. There is no doubt but that the PCI's clandestine network in Italy was in disarray. According to Montagnana, ties between the party's Paris center and domestic operatives in mid-1938 were even weaker than in mid-1932, when the organizational *svolta* had led to the virtual decimation of cadres working in Italy.[148] But if so, such weakness was certainly largely a result of objective difficulties, namely, the efficiency of the regime's police combined with Mussolini's adroit manipulation of nationalist sentiments and Italy's partial recovery from the Great Depression. The unbending condemnation of the PCI can thus be understood only in terms of the atmosphere of fear, suspicion, and betrayal which pervaded the International at the height of Stalin's purges.

One other explanation may also be advanced. The Comintern's organizational overhaul of the PCI coincided with its outright dissolution of the Polish Communist Party.[149] Some observers attribute that step to Stalin's anticipation of a deal with Hitler at Poland's expense (as was to occur one year later with the signing of the German–Soviet Non-Aggression Pact) and his wish to eliminate beforehand any embarrassing opposition from the only pro-Russians among the Polish people.[150] Pursuing such reasoning to its logical conclusion, a Soviet agreement with Berlin would also entail some kind of understanding with Rome, to which a self-confident PCI might rightly be expected to object. Stalin and his henchmen may thus have set out to frighten the Italian Communists into total submission with an eye to Moscow's eventual accommodation to fascism.

The Stalinists' 1938 assault on the PCI and insinuations of a "struggle against Ercoli" did in fact provoke a paroxysm of recriminations among individuals whose relations had until then been characterized by mutual support and cohesion—or, to use the Soviet epithet, by *semeistvennost* (familylike solidarity). Charges and countercharges abounded during meetings of the PCI Secretariat in mid-August and mid-September 1938.[151] The Secretariat—composed of essentially the same persons as the Politburo in 1936—met during August 10–18 to hear Grieco's report on his and Dozza's trip to the Soviet Union. The tenor of the subsequent discussion was one of sycophancy toward the Comintern authorities (Togliatti included), backstabbing among themselves, and an abject search

148. APC, 1938, fol. 1494A:38.

149. This step was taken in August 1938. See Spriano's introduction to *Opere 1935–1944*, by Togliatti, 1:cxvii–cxviii.

150. M. K. Dziewanowski, *The Communist Party of Poland* (Cambridge, Mass.: Harvard University Press, 1959), 154.

151. For the minutes of these meetings, see APC, 1938, fol. 1494A:26–62, and APC, 1938, fol. 1494:117–22.

for scapegoats. Each sought to shift responsibility for the party's purported deviations to others in the group. A number of participants—Di Vittorio, Bibolotti, and Berti—also blamed the party's recent shortcomings on Togliatti's absence from the Paris center, hence on their inability to profit from his guidance. Others accused Grieco and Dozza of trying to gloss over the PCI's defects in Moscow. Grieco himself insisted that the fundamental party line remained the one laid out "in the letters of Er[coli] of 1935–1936 and in the Resolution of the C.I. of 1936."[152] While this assertion was certainly accurate, the wisdom of trying to use Togliatti's prestige to shield the Paris leadership from Moscow's retribution was by then open to question.

There was, in addition to the tension generated by Moscow's criticism, a substantive issue dividing the Paris group, namely, the question of who would belong to the PCI's new "center of reorganization." Grieco initially selected not only himself and Ciufoli but also Dozza[153]—despite the latter's self-confessed responsibility for the domestic weakness of the party. The designation of Ciufoli and Dozza was rejected in Moscow and also by Togliatti at a rather mysterious meeting with Grieco and Montagnana (presumably in Spain) sometime in July.[154] Even more open to question, in the eyes of the Italians at least, was Grieco's exclusion of Montagnana from the projected eight-man Central Committee, an omission he attributed to "forgetfulness" at a stormy meeting of the Secretariat on August 10.[155] With the entire PCI leadership under attack for the popular front initiatives originally championed by Montagnana, Grieco probably calculated that his removal from the inner circles of the party would be in the common interest. This view was, needless to say, not shared by either Montagnana or his long-time supporter, Di Vittorio. They thereupon tried to discredit Grieco for an alleged cover-up of Dozza the previous spring in Moscow, arguing that the PCI's organization had fared far better under Montagnana's direction in 1935–36 than under Dozza's more recent tutelage.[156]

At this point Berti intervened, calling for self-criticism on the part of everyone. Whereupon Grieco conceded that he had erred in supporting Dozza, and Di Vittorio challenged Montagnana to admit his own organizational shortcomings. The disintegration of the PCI's inner core had reached the point where the closest of comrades were turning on one another.

152. APC, 1938, fol. 1494A:32.
153. Disclosed by Di Vittorio at the September 1938 Secretariat meeting; APC, 1938, fol. 1494:119.
154. Disclosed by Grieco at the September meeting; ibid., 120.
155. Minutes in APC, 1938, fol. 1494A:26–30.
156. Ibid., 38 and 45.

Meanwhile, under Berti's prodding the Secretariat passed a resolution that formally removed Dozza from his organizational responsibilities and, more important, appointed Grieco, Berti, Di Vittorio, and Antonio Roasio (a worker trained in Moscow and recently returned from Spain) to the "center of reorganization." It also criticized Grieco and Dozza by name for insufficient self-criticism during their spring 1938 talks in Moscow.[157]

The personnel issues raised in August were nevertheless again heatedly debated at a meeting of the PCI Secretariat on September 16–17, 1938. Perhaps because of Togliatti's presence—along with the insinuations of a cabal against him which surfaced on that occasion—a greater degree of candor informed the exchanges. The alignment of Montagnana and Di Vittorio against Grieco and Dozza also reemerged. Grieco, backed by Dozza and Ciufoli, indignantly rejected the allegation that he was somehow responsible for a "subterranean action" against Ercoli. Montagnana and Di Vittorio, in contrast, were more than receptive to the idea.[158] Not only that, but Montagnana argued that Grieco was most at fault for the party's recent shortcomings and should himself be excluded from the projected "center of reorganization,"[159] while Di Vittorio called for Montagnana's inclusion in that body.[160]

The make-up of the opposing groups recalled the policy cleavage of late 1936. Although nobody spelled it out, this similarity doubtless fanned the suspicions of an anti-Togliatti plot. One could plausibly surmise that Grieco was not simply edging Montagnana out of the party's inner circle because of his earlier dalliance with "Fascist reformism" but was also trying to implicate Togliatti. Not only were the two related by marriage, but as we have seen, Ercoli's entire approach to the analysis of fascism in his letters of 1935–36 probably inspired Montagnana's positions. Whether Grieco really intended to cast a shadow on Togliatti seems unlikely, given their past ties. But Montagnana and his supporters, once informed of Manuilsky's innuendoes regarding a "struggle against Ercoli," latched on to this theme in order to salvage their own positions.

At this point Togliatti intervened. Simply stated, he advised his comrades to stop fighting one another, to make no further changes in the leadership center decided upon in August, and above all not to rock the boat any further by pursuing their arguments (as Montagnana proposed) in a letter to Manuilsky. He urged, in short, conciliation—all the while refraining from passing judgment on either Moscow's criticisms or the substance of his colleagues' recriminations.[161] Furthermore, he enjoined

157. Text in APC, 1938, fol. 1494:112.
158. Minutes in ibid., 117–22.
159. Ibid., 119.
160. Ibid.
161. Ibid., 122.

the party "to concentrate all its efforts" in the direction of Italy.[162] This directive pervaded all the Comintern documents of the previous spring, but it also recalled Togliatti's recommendations of early 1930, a time of comparable tension between Moscow and the PCI.

If Togliatti's conciliatory approach helped to halt the disintegration of the PCI's inner core, much less is known about his role in overall Comintern affairs during 1937–38, the height of Stalin's Great Purge. For from the spring of 1937 onward a shroud of contradiction obscured Ercoli's actions and even whereabouts, a shroud he was reluctant to lift during his lifetime. Indeed, until the 1970s official Communist sources maintained that Togliatti was in Spain uninterruptedly from July 1937 through March 1939 and that he returned to Moscow only in the spring of 1940.[163] Paolo Spriano, however, in his introduction to Togliatti's collected works for the years 1935–44, acknowledged that Ercoli traveled to Moscow in August 1938 and again in March 1939, after the defeat of the Spanish Republic.[164] Spriano also effectively discredited a widely cited account of Togliatti's activities during 1936–39 by the Spanish ex-Communist, Jesús Hernández.[165] At the same time, a PCI insider insisted to Giorgio Bocca that Togliatti had already visited Spain by 1936,[166] which is plausible in view of his knowledgeable commentaries on the Spanish political scene.

Similar obfuscation surrounds the question of Ercoli's involvement in the arrest of numerous Central European Communists (who came under his titular jurisdiction) as well as in the actual dissolution of the Polish Communist Party. Bocca, in his biography of Togliatti, set forth the many conflicting interpretations of Ercoli's behavior in this regard as well as later in Spain—without, however, answering the question of whether he abetted or simply acquiesced in Stalin's purge of the International.[167]

Whatever Togliatti's motives—whether he was caught up in the siege mentality fomented by Stalin or simply paying the price of his commitment to the cause—there can be little doubt that he was an accessory to the crimes of Stalin, as was Nikita Khrushchev and every other high-ranking member of the CPSU and Comintern hierarchies. For this very reason, a more fruitful approach to understanding the political profile of the PCI and its later development is to focus on the distinctiveness of Togliatti's conduct during the late 1930s.

162. Ibid., 117.

163. Cf. Marcella Ferrara and Maurizio Ferrara, *Conversando con Togliatti,* 249–50 and 269–93; Paolo Robotti and Giovanni Germanetto, *Trent'anni di lotte dei comunisti italiani* (Rome: Edizioni di Cultura Sociale, 1952), 191; *l'Unità,* August 22, 1964, 6; and "Dirigente dell'Internazionale," *Rinascita* 21, no. 34 (August 29, 1964):22–24.

164. Togliatti, *Opere 1935–1944* 1:xcviii, cxvi, and cxix.

165. Jesús Hernández, *La Grande Trahison* (Paris: Fasquelle Editeurs, 1953); see Spriano, *Storia del Partito comunista italiano* 3:215, n. 1.

166. See Mauro Scoccimarro's testimony in *Palmiro Togliatti,* by Bocca, 283 and 286.

167. Ibid., 259–315.

Here three considerations come to the fore. The first is that he chose to escape the cutthroat machinations of the Comintern bureaucracy for work in the field. Once in Spain, he asked to remain there as long as possible.[168] And he shunned participation in the broader activities of the International. As during the early 1930s, between July 1937 and December 1940 he published not a single article in *Kommunisticheskii Internatsional*. He alone among the Comintern's seven secretaries remained silent for such a prolonged period. That this was a matter of preference rather than circumstances is suggested by the fact that the arduousness of duty in Spain did not prevent André Marty, political overseer of the International Brigades, from contributing half a dozen articles to the Comintern journal during that same period.[169] Second, in his reports to Moscow during 1937–38 Togliatti repeatedly recommended that the Spanish Communist leaders be given greater autonomy and that the Comintern "advisers" (he always put the word in quotation marks) stop acting like the bosses (*padroni*) of the PCE.[170] His insistence on this point not only recalled the organizational directives of the Seventh Comintern Congress but also explained his own unobtrusive style,[171] which led some to label him the eminence grise of the PCE.[172] Finally, those same reports exuded a profound commitment to genuine cooperation with other political forces rather than an attempt to gather all the levers of power in the hands of the Communists, as some of his Spanish comrades wished.[173]

The Ambiguous Balance Sheet

By late summer 1938 the time had come for the members of the PCI's Paris center to convey to the party base the criticism and self-criticism they had been undergoing since the previous spring. In the October 1 issue of *Lo Stato operaio* a "Letter to a Base Organization," signed by the "Secretariat of the Party," bluntly stated that "in party documents you will receive, you will read the most frank and open self-criticism."[174] Those documents began appearing in the journal forthwith. And in 1939

168. "Relazione del 30 agosto 1937," in *Opere 1935–1944*, by Togliatti, 1:258–72 at 272.
169. Urban, "Moscow and the Italian Communist Party: 1926–1945," 211.
170. "Relazione del 30 agosto 1937," in *Opere 1935–1944*, by Togliatti, 1:271–72; "Ai compagni D. e M.," in ibid., 273–79 at 274; "Sui problemi del Comitato centrale del PCE," in ibid., 280–92 at 291–92; and "Relazione del 28 gennaio 1938," in ibid., 293–308 at 300.
171. See the comments by Santiago Carrillo quoted in ibid., civ.
172. Bocca, *Palmiro Togliatti*, 289.
173. See, for example, "Relazione del 28 gennaio 1938," in *Opere 1935–1944*, by Togliatti, 1:299 and 306; and "Relazione del 21–22 aprile 1938," in ibid., 309–24 at 319–20.
174. "Su alcune gravi deviazioni dalla linea del partito: lettera ad una organizzazione di base," *SO* 12, nos. 16–17 (October 1, 1938):275–77. Not surprisingly, *Lo Stato operaio*, then a semimonthly journal, skipped four issues between June 15 and October 1 and published no issue whatsoever between August 15 and October 1, 1938.

they were reprinted in a single volume, *Unione del popolo italiano per il pane, la pace e la libertà.*[175]

Grieco launched the campaign with a lead article in the October 1 issue in which he described the slogan of the defense of the territorial unity and national independence of Italy as both "mistaken and false." It was false because Italy was allied with—not threatened by—Hitler. It was mistaken because the Italian people and proletariat, instead of defending Italy, "ought to *want* her defeat, and to *cooperate* in her defeat," in order "*to transform the war of fascism into a struggle for the liberation of the Italian people.*"[176] At the same time, he recanted the party's "error of launching, in 1936, the slogan of the *reconciliation of the Italian people.*"[177] Evidently the PCI's inconspicuous retraction of that slogan in early 1937 was not enough. Only public groveling would satisfy Moscow's current standards of ideological rectitude.

In the very next issue of the party journal, Di Vittorio dwelt on the PCI's repeated error of limiting itself to slogans appropriate to a Fascist mass opposition and of concealing its Communist character and objectives.[178] Indeed, he went so far as to declare that the PCI had erred in the direction of "Fascist *revisionism,*" citing as one example of "this error, in a *revisionist* sense," the PCI's September 1936 definition of the Fascist unions as "the workers' unions in the present situation in Italy."[179]

The Italian Communist leaders' abject self-criticism notwithstanding, they came under public attack at the Eighteenth Congress of the CPSU. In Manuilsky's report on the international Communist movement, one party alone received no word of praise, one party alone was subjected to unmitigated censure: the PCI. With the exception of references to "Fascist-Trotskyite agents" in the already defunct Polish party and an allusion to earlier factionalism in the Hungarian and Yugoslavian parties, Manuilsky generally acclaimed the activities of the foreign Communists. The French were applauded for their popular front successes. The Germans were praised for supposedly maintaining their illegal organization intact. Even the British Communist Party, albeit "one of the backward sections of the Comintern," was commended for its numerical growth and expanding

175. *Unione del popolo italiano per il pane, la pace e la libertà: Documenti e direttive del PCI* (Paris: Edizioni di Cultura Sociale, 1939); henceforth this volume will be cited as *UPI*. Not one of the articles in this 1939 anthology appeared in Franco Ferri's two-volume collection of materials from *Lo Stato operaio* published in 1964.

176. Ruggero Grieco, "La lotta per la democrazia," *SO* 12, nos. 16–17, in *UPI*, 63–85 at 82–83.

177. Ibid., 80.

178. Giuseppe Di Vittorio, "La lotta delle masse contro la guerra e la miseria in Italia," *SO* 12, no. 18 (October 15, 1938), in *UPI*, 87–110 at 96.

179. Ibid., 97–98.

influence in the trade unions.[180] His denunciation of the PCI was thus an isolated phenomenon. As such it deserves to be quoted at length:

> We must note the serious weakness of the Italian Communist Party. In all the long years of the Fascist dictatorship it has not been able to weld together a strong illegal organization, to carry on serious work in the Fascist trade unions and other Fascist mass organizations, or to wean any considerable section of the younger generation from the influence of Fascism. The theory of certain Italian Communists that only defeat in war can bring about the collapse of Fascism is in reality but a mask for *opportunist passivity*.[181]

The implications of Manuilsky's attack become apparent if one considers that the Yugoslavian Communist Party—according to Tito—had been privately threatened with dissolution in 1938 for the very reason for which the PCI was now publicly castigated: ineffectuality.[182]

In the light of Manuilsky's unremitting denunciations of 1938–39, a fundamental question remains to be explored: the extraordinary fact that the PCI elite survived the Great Purge. Whereas countless Polish, Yugoslavian, Hungarian, and German Communists were never heard from again, none of the Italian leaders perished at the hands of the Stalinists. According to an Italian study sponsored by a group in no way sympathetic to communism, the two hundred or so PCI victims of the purges were almost all "simple militants of the base" who worked in the Soviet Union as ordinary laborers.[183] The most obvious explanation for this anomaly lies in the fact that the PCI's operational headquarters were in France, and to France returned the veterans of the Spanish Civil War.

Members of Communist parties from the European democracies were by and large immune from the Stalinist blood bath even during their sojourns in Moscow;[184] and the PCI's Paris center evidently fell into this category. Individual PCI leaders resided for periods of time in the Soviet capital or briefly journeyed to Moscow during the purges. Yet the few who were arrested were subsequently released.[185] Given the survival of the PCI leadership, moreover, Moscow's criticisms had to be within the limits of plausibility. Dead men could not refute false charges. But the Italian Communists at large in Western Europe could hardly be denounced as Fascist spies and traitors. They were thus berated for the line they had

180. See Manuilsky's report to the Eighteenth Congress of the CPSU in *World News and Views* [formerly *Inprecor*] 19, no. 19 (April 6, 1939):373–84 at 380–82.

181. Ibid., 381; my emphasis.

182. Vladimir Dedijer, *Tito* (New York: Simon and Schuster, 1953), 378; cf. Avakumović, *History of the Communist Party of Yugoslavia* 1:125–26.

183. Guelfo Zaccaria, *200 comunisti italiani tra le vittime dello stalinismo* (Milan: Edizioni Azione Comune, 1964), 21.

184. Cf. Lazitch, "Stalin's Massacre," in *The Comintern*, ed. Drachkovitch and Lazitch, 141–42.

185. Zaccaria notes, for instance, the arrest and subsequent release of Paolo Robotti and Emilio Sereni in *200 comunisti italiani*, 22–24 and 85–87.

in fact endorsed and for deficiencies they could do little to surmount—indeed, deficiencies that were hardly the purview of the PCI alone in that era of Fascist repression.

In the short run the Stalinists' criticisms of the PCI doubtless had the desired effect of undermining the cohesion, confidence, and stature of the Italian Communist leaders—in a word, of breaking them and making them more amenable to Soviet *diktat*. In the longer run, however, the 1938–39 confrontation boomeranged. Several of the members of the 1938 PCI Politburo were later relegated to secondary positions. But others—for example, Grieco and Di Vittorio—remained in the party's postwar Politburo (renamed the *Direzione*), while Dozza became the long-time mayor of the Communist stronghold, Bologna. And none of them was likely to forget the humiliation he had suffered in the late 1930s. As Togliatti was bluntly to state in June 1956, "the judgment that was passed at the Eighteenth Congress of the Bolshevik Party concerning our party . . . was a profoundly mistaken and even foul judgment."[186]

In retrospect one of the striking features of the PCI elite during the popular front era is the extent to which its members conducted themselves according to the norms of what would one day be called collective leadership. Collegiality and dialogue characterized Politburo discussions until early 1937. Grieco, who took over the direction of the Secretariat when Togliatti left for full-time work in Moscow in November 1934, showed no signs of arrogating to himself undue authority. Indeed, Grieco, Di Vittorio, Montagnana, and Dozza, among others, seemed to participate equally in the decision-making process. This organizational mode may be attributed in part to Togliatti's own leadership style. Although he sent numerous letters to the Paris center during 1935–36, they were more advisory than admonitory in tone. In effect, he left his comrades considerable leeway in the formulation of concrete directives. To be sure, the collegiality of the party leadership was severely strained as a result of the 1938 crisis. But here again Togliatti's conciliatory demeanor helped to smooth over the difficulties and avert "a struggle without principles." As for Togliatti himself, the task of implementing the popular front line in the Comintern Secretariat and in Spain reinforced his earlier receptivity to a post-Fascist democratic stage in Italy. Beyond that, the years of isolation abroad, ineffectuality in Italy, and low esteem in Moscow had left their mark on all these men. They longed for contact with the Italian masses, for visibility and clout, for political space at home—if only as one of many parties competing in a democratic system.

186. "La via italiana al socialismo: Rapporto tenuto il 24 giugno 1956 al Comitato centrale del PCI," in *Problemi del movimento operaio internazionale (1956–1961)*, by Palmiro Togliatti (Rome: Editori Riuniti, 1962), 121–69 at 143.

CHAPTER 5

The Wartime Resistance: Togliatti, Moscow, and the PCI

From the onset of the German–Russian conflict in 1941 Communist parties throughout Europe were notable for their activism in local resistance struggles against Nazi domination. During the final two years of World War II the PCI was no exception. Indeed, in the course of the Italian Resistance movement against the German occupation of northern and central Italy (September 1943–April 1945) the PCI was dramatically transformed. From a prewar figure of some several thousand exiled or imprisoned militants, its membership surged to well over one and a half million by the end of 1945. From an opposition party proscribed for almost two decades, it became a partner in the first post-Fascist coalition cabinet to govern Italy. And from a Comintern section subjected to public censure by the International in 1939 because of its ineffectuality, it emerged from the war as the largest Communist party in Western Europe.

From mid-1943 onward the Italian Communists spearheaded the partisan movement in northern Italy and proved themselves an able political force in the south. Nevertheless, their role in the Italian Resistance differed significantly from that dictated by the Comintern prior to its dissolution in May–June 1943. As will be detailed shortly, *Kommunisticheskii Internatsional* instructed the West European Communist parties to resist German occupation through the formation of national fronts open to all anti-Nazis, monarchists included, and receptive to any anti-Fascist government, whether republican or monarchist in form. These disparate forces were to be welded into a monolithic organization controlled by the Communists. Non-Communist figureheads in the national front hierarchy of a given country and cooperation in the *maquis* with other Resistance forces were permissible, in fact desirable. But Communist hegemony within the national front and autonomy vis-à-vis other groups were to be strictly observed.

While the Italian Communist cadres who gradually made their way back to Italy initially sought to comply with this line, their conduct after the German occupation in September 1943 was distinguished by republican intransigence, on the one hand, and participation in a genuine coalition of anti-Fascist parties on the other. In a word, just as the Italian Resistance gathered momentum, the PCI deviated from Moscow's policy. Rather than assuming the vanguard role in an Italian national front, it became a joint leader of the Italian Committee of National Liberation (CLN) along with five other parties: the resurgent Socialists and Liberals, the emergent Christian Democratic Party (DC) and Party of Action (Pd'A), and the Rome-centered Party of Democratic Labor. Most important, the members of the CLN observed the procedural rule of *unanimity*. No major decision could be made without the approval of all parties. Thus the Italian Liberal Party (PLI)—conservative and monarchist in the Italian context—was in a position to veto proposals by the parties of the left, and vice versa.

Meanwhile, as the Allies overran Sicily and prepared to invade the Italian mainland, Mussolini was overthrown on July 25, 1943, by a palace coup of dissident Fascists and monarchists. The king then appointed a government of technicians headed by Marshal Pietro Badoglio. A period of political temporization followed. As the Badoglio government sparred with the Allies over armistice terms, German reinforcements to the tune of eight militarized divisions rolled unopposed into northern Italy. The anti-Fascist parties, agonizingly aware of the menace from the north, refrained from overt resistance preparations so as not to provoke German retaliation before an agreement was reached with the Allies. On September 8, 1943, Italy's unconditional surrender was announced and the major Allied landing at Salerno, south of Naples, began. Thereupon the royal family and Premier Badoglio, without any warning or instructions to the civilian and military authorities, fled southward behind Allied lines.

This betrayal provided the emotional impetus for the creation of the unified CLN movement in German-occupied northern and central Italy. Communists and Liberals as well as traditional republicans were caught up in a wave of antimonarchist revulsion. The abdication of the king became their precondition for joining the government. It was only in April 1944 that the PCI, at Togliatti's direction upon his return from Moscow, broke with the united republican front and agreed to accept cabinet positions prior to the abdication of King Vittorio Emanuele III. Yet by then the unified structure of the Italian resistance movement was well enough established to survive what was thenceforth to be called the *svolta* of Salerno.

The *svolta* of Salerno and the transformation of the PCI in the mid-1940s into a party of government with a mass base will be examined in chapter 6. The present chapter deals with Moscow's early wartime instructions to the West European Communist movement and the Italian party's initial efforts to implement them. It then examines the formative period of the Italian resistance movement and the way in which the PCI diverged from the Soviet line. It explores, finally, Togliatti's role during the early 1940s and the intraparty cleavages that he sparked in 1943–44.

Togliatti and the PCI Diaspora

The transformation of the PCI into a mass-based party in 1944–45 was all the more remarkable in that the years 1939 through 1942 represented the nadir of the party's organizational existence. The disarray provoked by Moscow's criticisms in 1938 was compounded by the shock of the German–Soviet Non-Aggression Pact in August 1939. The German invasion of Poland triggered an official French backlash against the PCF and the PCI émigré network alike, with the Paris authorities arresting numerous prominent Italian Communists including Togliatti, Longo, and eventually Di Vittorio. Togliatti managed to conceal his identity and gain his freedom after six months. Many others were transferred to Italian jurisdiction after the German defeat of France, thus swelling the roster of PCI notables imprisoned by the Mussolini regime. Meanwhile, those who escaped arrest fled to widely scattered sanctuaries—for example, the United States (Berti), Mexico (Montagnana), or Moscow (Grieco)—with only a handful remaining underground in France.

The tentative restructuring of the party's executive organs under Berti's guidance thus came to an abrupt halt, while *Lo Stato operaio*, which he continued to edit from New York City,[1] ceased to have any direct influence in the party. And in July 1940 the Comintern appointed Togliatti head of a new PCI leadership committee located—for the first time in the party's history—in Moscow. Systematic contact between Togliatti and the tiny circle of militants who continued to direct the party's "foreign bureau" in Marseilles after the Nazi occupation of Paris was, however, precluded by the Vichy regime. And although an internal center was finally established in Milan by Umberto Massola in late 1941, it func-

---

1. See, for example, "Ai compagni italiani delle due Americhe," lead editorial in *SO* [published from this date onward in New York City] 14, no. 1 (March 15, 1940):1–2.

tioned in virtual isolation from the PCI cadres in both Moscow and France.

Prior to the German–Soviet pact, the PCI's relations with Moscow as well as its organizational structure remained unsettled.[2] During the winter of 1939, as a result of the Comintern's criticisms and directives of the previous year, the party attempted to reestablish internal centers in Milan and Genoa. Yet these efforts were immediately foiled by the Fascist police.[3] In mid-August 1939 the reorganization conference called for a year earlier was held in Paris and attended by about twenty leaders, including Togliatti and Longo. The minutes of that meeting are missing from the PCI Archives. According to Giorgio Amendola, however, its results were indecisive, with the cleavages and recriminations of the preceding summer apparently continuing.[4] Berti, still acting head of the Secretariat, delivered the opening report. Togliatti's status at that time was (and remains) unclear—even though he had spent the spring and early summer of 1939 in Moscow.[5] This circumstance lends a certain credibility to the allegations later made by Secchia's long-time private secretary, Giulio Seniga, to the effect that there was an attempt by Manuilsky, Stepanov, and others to make Togliatti a scapegoat for the final collapse of the Spanish Republic in March 1939.[6]

The political turmoil at the apex of the PCI was exacerbated by the "confusion" and "bewilderment" (terms repeatedly used by Amendola in his history of this period) induced by the German–Soviet Non-Aggression Pact. Dissension erupted among Italian cadres, as among all European Communists, over the Soviet Union's accommodation to Hitler. The dismay was particularly acute over Moscow's designation of France and England as the prime instigators of the second great "imperialist" war and its consequent defeatist guidelines. Opposition, especially on this account, was voiced by Di Vittorio, Montagnana, and Grieco in France, and Terracini and Ravera in confinement, as well as by others of lesser stature.[7] Leo Valiani, a future key Resistance leader, broke with the PCI at this time.

2. From 1939 throughout the wartime years the paucity of archival materials or regular party publications compels the analyst to rely largely on memoirs. One of the figures close to the events of 1939–43 who contributed the most to our knowledge of them was Giorgio Amendola; see his *Storia del Partito comunista italiano, 1921–1943* (Rome: Editori Riuniti, 1978).

3. Umberto Massola, "Parigi, agosto 1939: L'organizzazione del PCI nella clandestinità," *Rinascita* 23, no. 48 (December 3, 1966):17–20 at 17.

4. Amendola, *Storia del Partito comunista italiano, 1921–1943,* 398–400.

5. Togliatti, *Opere 1935–1944,* ed. Franco Andreucci and Paolo Spriano, 2 vols. (Rome: Editori Riuniti, 1979), I:cxxvi–cxxviii; cf. Berti's later remarks in Giorgio Bocca, *Palmiro Togliatti* (Bari: Editori Laterza, 1973), 331–32.

6. Giulio Seniga, *Togliatti e Stalin* (Milan: Sugar editore, 1961), 27–28.

7. Amendola, *Storia del Partito comunista italiano, 1921–1943,* 450. Although Amendola suggested that Grieco backed the Soviet line all along, Berti disclosed that he initially opposed the

The impact of the 1939 pact on the PCI was, however, far less damaging than it was on the PCF. For one thing, the Italian Communists had no organized mass base to which they had to explain the 180-degree shift, no network of party cells to be reoriented from antifascism to "revolutionary defeatism." For another thing, the very notion of revolutionary defeatism had a very different connotation in the Italian context: there it meant the downfall of fascism and thus had been part of the PCI line since mid-1938. Finally, the absence of any clearly recognized leadership organs contributed to a kind of conciliation by default toward those who opposed the pact. It was, ironically, the party groups in Fascist confinement that undertook sanctions against outspoken dissidents. For example, Terracini and Ravera were actually expelled from the PCI by the Communist organization on the island of Ventotene (only to be reinstated by the new national *Direzione* in 1945).[8] But Di Vittorio was spared such treatment by his fellow émigrés in France prior to his arrest in March 1941.[9]

This, then, was the general situation when Togliatti, who had been arrested by the French authorities on September 1, 1939, under an assumed name, was released in late February 1940. At that point he took charge of what remained of the PCI network in France, evidently on his own initiative.[10] At a meeting in Paris in early March he not only reaffirmed the 1938 decisions to dissolve the then existing Central Committee, Politburo, and Secretariat, but he also disbanded the new "center of reorganization" created at Berti's prodding in August–September 1938. Of the four persons appointed to that body, Berti was now in New York, Grieco in Moscow, and Di Vittorio in disfavor for his opposition to the German–Soviet pact. Only Antonio Roasio, a working-class activist who had returned from Spain in 1938, was still deemed suitable. Togliatti thus named a new leadership group comprising Roasio, Umberto Massola, Agostino Novella, and later Celeste Negarville and Giorgio Amendola; and he instructed them to transfer their center of operations to Italy at the

---

German–Soviet pact within the inner circles of the PCI; see Giuseppe Berti, "Negli scritti di Grieco," *Rinascita* 23, no. 25 (June 18, 1966):21–23 at 23.

8. Adriano Guerra, *Gli anni del Cominform* (Milan: Gabriele Mazzotta editore, 1977), 38; cf. Alessandro Coletti, *Il governo di Ventotene* (Milan: La Pietra, 1978), 90–110.

9. Indeed, in a letter dated January 15, 1941, the foreign bureau requested authorization from Moscow to assign Di Vittorio to responsible party work despite his ongoing doubts about the pact; see excerpts quoted in Paolo Spriano, *La fine del fascismo: Dalla riscossa operaia alla lotta armata*, vol 4 of *Storia del Partito comunista italiano* (Turin: Giulio Einaudi editore, 1973), 31. One exception to this conciliatory pattern was the expulsion of the PCI head of the Italian émigré popular front organization, Romano Cocchi. It is, however, unclear which party organization did this; see Amendola, *Storia del Partito comunista italiano, 1921–1943*, 402.

10. During the brief period between his release from prison and departure for Moscow, Togliatti stayed at the apartment of Umberto Massola; see Massola's *Memorie 1939–1941* (Rome: Editori Riuniti, 1972), 9–62.

earliest opportunity.[11] As in 1929–30, he reacted to the Comintern's sectarian reversal of 1939–40 by seeking to redirect the Italian party's activities back to Italy.

Meanwhile, neither in his official statements nor, according to Amendola,[12] in his private utterances did Togliatti display any reservations regarding Moscow's diplomatic *volte-face*. In articles for a projected party journal penned while hiding out in Massola's Paris apartment in March 1940, he echoed the Comintern line enunciated by Dimitrov in *Kommunisticheskii Internatsional*. In a word, the Hitler regime was less responsible than the Western democracies for the outbreak and prolongation of this second imperialist conflict. These commentaries, however, had little likelihood of being circulated in France. It is thus possible, as Paolo Spriano suggests,[13] that they were written more with an eye to a readership in the Kremlin than for PCI militants. This is all the more plausible since Togliatti, once back in Moscow, privately insisted on the instrumental and temporary nature of the German–Soviet pact.[14]

In any event, Togliatti's compliance won him the support of the Soviets. In the spring of 1940, just before the German *blitzkrieg* into Belgium and France, he managed to return to Moscow. That summer the Comintern Secretariat and Presidium (the latter during a rump meeting attended only by Togliatti, Grieco, Dimitrov, Manuilsky, and a certain otherwise unidentified Zkhakaya) endorsed the actions Togliatti had taken. They also confirmed him as the overseer of a new "center of ideological and political direction" to which Rigoletto Martini and Vincenzo Bianco, two hitherto minor party functionaries, were also appointed. Henceforth all PCI groups operating in France or Italy were to serve as the "delegates" of this new triumvirate in Moscow, while the Paris center appointed by Togliatti the previous March was renamed the foreign bureau.[15]

By mid-1940, therefore, the enigmatic character of Togliatti's relations with Moscow in 1938–39 had dissipated. In contrast to his ambiguous status at the PCI conference the previous summer, he resumed the leadership of his party while also continuing as a secretary of the International. Several considerations may explain this. As Stalin's massive purge of the Soviet bureaucracies subsided, so too did its reverberations within the

---

11. Amendola, *Storia del Partito comunista italiano, 1921–1943*, 452–53; cf. Massola, *Memorie,* 61–62.

12. Amendola, *Storia del Partito comunista italiano, 1921–1943*, 452; cf. Massola, *Memorie,* passim.

13. Togliatti, *Opere 1935–1944* 1:cxli–cxliii.

14. Ernst Fischer, *Ricordi e riflessioni* (Rome: Editori Riuniti, 1973), 508–11.

15. Amendola, *Storia del Partito comunista italiano, 1921–1943*, 454–56. Paolo Spriano quoted at some length the relevant Comintern documents, copies of which are filed as "uncatalogued" materials in the PCI Archives; see his *Storia del Partito comunista italiano* 4:22–24.

Comintern. There were, as far as we know, no further snide allusions to Ercoli's past deviations such as those made by Manuilsky in 1938. In addition, there was a rough parallel between the international environment confronting Moscow in the summer of 1940 after the victorious Nazi sweep to the English Channel and the one confronting it in 1934. In a word, the Soviet Union faced a hostile Germany isolated and alone, the diplomatic formalities of the German–Soviet pact notwithstanding. As in 1934, there was a need to rethink the requirements of Soviet national security and the corresponding role of the Communist movement, if only in anticipation of an eventual German invasion.[16] For this reason the talents of all leading Communist functionaries were once again in demand. In the case of the PCI, moreover, the Soviet authorities had few alternatives. Given the party's organizational disarray, only Togliatti, by virtue of the prestige accruing from his Comintern post and past party positions, had the personal authority to direct—if only through shortwave radio broadcasts—the scattered and disoriented Italian cadres.

Moscow's National Front Strategy

Soviet historians have disclosed far more about the bureaucratic genesis of the Comintern's popular front policy than about the origins of Moscow's wartime national front strategy. The reasons for the paucity of details regarding the formulation of the national front line are not difficult to fathom. The popular front directives were announced only after extensive consultations within the still fully operational executive bodies of the International. They were, moreover, based on the judgment of Dimitrov and others as to what would best serve the interests of the European Communist movement as well as the Soviet state. In contrast, by 1941 the Comintern organization had become a hollow shell, resembling in this respect the CPSU. The ECCI—like the CPSU Central Committee—had ceased to function, while the Presidium—like the CPSU Politburo—met only occasionally and then in rump sessions attended by representatives with similar responsibilities, in the case of the Presidium those from the same geographical region.[17] The national front strategy was thus devised by a small group of Comintern officials working closely with Stalin's foreign policy advisers. The new line was, in short, an integral part of the

16. The memoirs of Ernst Fischer, then the Austrian delegate to the Comintern, are revealing in this regard; see *Ricordi e riflessioni*, 506–8.

17. See the references to such meetings in ibid., 508–11, and in Spriano, *Storia del Partito comunista italiano* 4:24 and 60.

Soviet Union's national security policy.[18] The Soviet authorities have evidently been loathe to admit this even in retrospect.

Nothing more clearly underscored the dependent character of the International by the end of the 1930s than the way in which its members were compelled to echo the CPSU's interpretation of the 1939 German–Soviet pact as a "pact for peace" and a blow against (Anglo-French) imperialism. But it was the dissolution of the Comintern in May 1943 that signaled, from Moscow's viewpoint, the final subordination of the international Communist movement to Soviet interests. The public rationale set forth by Stalin in an interview with Harold King of Reuters News Service on May 28, 1943, and reiterated in a Presidium announcement was, to be sure, quite the opposite. Both argued that the Communist parties of Europe required more autonomy to better resist the Nazi occupation and adapt to their national environments.[19] European Communists such as Togliatti and Tito could have had no quarrel with this assessment. In actuality, however, Stalin probably viewed the elimination of the Comintern as a way of facilitating his control over Communist parties that were growing in stature in Western Europe and likely to be placed in power in Eastern Europe (the Soviet-sponsored Union of Polish Patriots had been formed shortly before, in April 1943). However hollow the bureaucratic structure of the International had become by 1943, its postwar revival under such circumstances could not be precluded. Yet everything we know about Stalin's temperament suggests that the last thing he wanted was an organizational framework in any way conducive to genuine multilateral consultations among Communist leaderships that might come to power or enjoy a substantial local base of support after the war. It was his fear of such an eventuality, in short, which led him to dissolve the Comintern.[20]

The very process through which the International was disbanded epitomized Stalin's preferred—and future—manner of dealing with any and all Communist parties. As related by Vincenzo Bianco,[21] then the official

18. Cf. Giuseppe Boffa, *Storia dell'Unione Sovietica*, 2 vols. (Milan: Arnoldo Mondadori Editore, 1979), 2:175; and the memoirs of Giulio Cerreti, *Con Togliatti e Thorez* (Milan: Feltrinelli Editore, 1973), 250 and 261–62.

19. "Postanovlenie Prezidiuma Ispolnitelnogo Komiteta Kommunisticheskogo Internatsionala," *Kommunisticheskii Internatsional* [henceforth *KI*], nos. 5–6 (1943; to press June 23, 1943):8–10 at 9; and "Otvet tov. I. V. Stalina na vopros glavnogo korrespondenta angliiskogo agenstva Reuter," ibid., 11.

20. Many analysts, Communist and non-Communist alike, have attributed the dissolution of the Comintern to Stalin's desire to curry favor with the Anglo-American Allies in order to hasten the launching of the second front. Such reasoning misses the mark. If foreign policy considerations had been at the root of the decision, it would have been made still earlier in the war. Stalin sought to gain a propaganda windfall from the disbandment of the International, to be sure, but it was undertaken for quite different reasons.

21. His unpublished report on what transpired is quoted at length in Guerra, *Gli anni del Cominform*, 30–31.

PCI delegate to the ECCI, he was summoned to Dimitrov's Moscow office in April 1943 and exhorted on a one-to-one basis to agree to a draft Presidium proposal calling for the dissolution of the Comintern. He pleaded that he be allowed time at least to consult with Togliatti before signing the document in behalf of the PCI—to no avail. From Bianco's account we may infer that Dimitrov consulted in a similar fashion with the delegates of other parties. The proposal was then jointly approved at a mid-May Presidium meeting that was convened with little notice and conducted with minimal discussion.[22] Shortly afterward Stalin told the Reuters correspondent about the imminent demise of the Third International, without waiting to consult the dozen or more Communist parties not represented in Moscow during the war.[23] This method of imposing Soviet policies on the Communist movement—by fiat and through the intimidation of individual Communist leaders behind closed doors—was to become commonplace during the period of postwar Stalinism.

During the first two years of the German–Soviet conflict, however, the exigencies of national survival took precedence over such long-range calculations. The Comintern remained valuable as a symbol of international support for the Soviet war effort at the time of the Soviet Union's greatest need. Indeed, it became a ready-made department of psychological warfare,[24] with its foreign Communist functionaries beaming radio broadcasts throughout German-occupied Europe. According to a Soviet history of the International, after the German invasion Ercoli along with Dimitrov and Manuilsky "were made responsible for the immediate everyday direction of all the work" of the Comintern.[25] But in fact the latter two worked in the Soviet government bureaucracy in Kuibyshev and Moscow, leaving Togliatti to oversee the foreign programs transmitted from the Comintern offices in Ufa.[26] *Kommunisticheskii Internatsional* remained the authoritative source of directives in this endeavor. Edited by Ernst Fischer from mid-1938 until the outbreak of the war when Dimitrov transferred him to Togliatti's operation,[27] the Comintern journal became for all practical purposes a Soviet agitprop organ.

The national front strategy spelled out in *Kommunisticheskii Internatsional* embraced three components: partisan warfare in occupied Europe to tie down German divisions; the widest possible social and political mobilization in support of such armed resistance; and the organization of all anti-Nazi forces in a national front movement directed by the Commu-

22. Ibid.; cf. Cerreti, *Con Togliatti e Thorez,* 279.
23. Paolo Spriano, *I comunisti europei e Stalin* (Turin: Giulio Einaudi Editore, 1983), 185.
24. Cf. ibid., 164.
25. *Kommunisticheskii Internatsional: kratkii istoricheskii ocherk* (Moscow, 1969), 505.
26. Cerreti, *Con Togliatti e Thorez,* 276.
27. Fischer, *Ricordi e riflessioni,* 483–567, passim.

nists. In doctrinal terms, this policy was highly innovative. It called for open-ended interclass cooperation to defeat fascism and establish democracy. The Comintern journal eventually dropped even the guarded allusions to socialist revolution that it had printed at the height of the popular front era. Yet its organizational guidelines were entirely orthodox. In fact the national fronts actually set up during World War II were prototypes of the Communist front movements that proliferated after the war, serving as Soviet propaganda instruments in the West and a cover for Communist domination in Eastern Europe.

This national front policy was elaborated gradually, receiving its fullest exposition only toward the end of 1942. The first reaction of *Kommunisticheskii Internatsional* to the Nazi invasion of Russia was to call for partisan resistance in Western Europe to alleviate the military pressures upon the Soviet Union. From early 1942 on (when it resumed publication after a hiatus of several months) the journal carried appeals for strikes, sabotage, and guerrilla warfare—whether in occupied Yugoslavia, divided France, or Fascist Italy—in order to deflect enemy forces from the Eastern front.[28] It argued, of course, that such resistance activism was in the national interest of the various European peoples. But during the battle of Stalingrad, it conceded that this strategy also served Soviet interests, describing partisan warfare in France, Belgium, Holland, and Norway as "the path of lightening the Red Army's task of defeating the enemy."[29]

The Comintern journal went to extraordinary lengths to instigate such armed resistance. Despite Moscow's wartime reservations toward Tito, it upheld the Yugoslavian partisan struggle as the example to be followed everywhere in Western Europe. An article in April 1942 declared that Yugoslavia caused the invaders "immeasurably greater trouble . . . than any other [*sic*] of the occupied West European countries."[30] The idea that the Yugoslavian pattern was not feasible further west was brusquely rejected: "Some people think that in the densely populated countries of Western Europe a partisan movement is impossible, but this is not true," protested the lead editorials in March 1942[31] and again in August.[32]

The Communist parties throughout Europe were also instructed early on to form broad-based national fronts. Already on June 22, 1941, the Yugoslavian Communists received a cable from the Comintern leadership

28. Cf. "Velikii primer Krasnoi Armii," *KI*, nos. 1–2 (1942; to press March 13, 1942):18–24; "Bit zakhvatchikov vo vsekh okkupirovannykh stranakh," *KI*, no. 7 (1942; to press August 24, 1942):2–6.

29. "Borba narodov Evropy protiv okkupantov," *KI*, nos. 10–11 (1942; to press November 20, 1942):68–75 at 69–70.

30. B. Voinich, "Boevoi primer Yugoslavii," *KI*, nos. 3–4 (1942; to press April 27, 1942):25–35 at 25.

31. "Velikii primer Krasnoi Armii," *KI*, nos. 1–2 (1942):23.

32. "Bit zakhvatchikov," *KI*, no. 7 (1942):4.

instructing them "to develop a movement under the slogan of a united national front."[33] A similar directive was apparently received by the PCF, for in July 1941 a leaflet appeared in occupied France bearing the ponderous title, *The National Front of Struggle for the Independence of France Has Been Created.*[34] The creation of national fronts was subsequently urged in the Comintern journal. For example, in March 1942 Togliatti described conditions in Italy as extremely propitious for creating a "broad national front" to overthrow the Fascist regime.[35] And immediately after the reemergence of the Polish Communist movement under the name Polish Workers' Party, *Kommunisticheskii Internatsional* called for the formation of a Polish national front.[36]

By autumn 1942 the national front strategy appears to have been decisively formulated. The keynote was sounded in the October 1942 issue of *Kommunisticheskii Internatsional* by an article entitled "From the Popular Front to the All-National Front." Written by Ernst Fischer, it signaled the emergence of a clearly delineated policy for Western Europe. "In our day . . . the popular front has risen like a sphinx from the ashes in the form of the national front," proclaimed Fischer. "At the present time in France, Belgium, Holland, Norway, *Yugoslavia* and Czechoslovakia . . . people of all possible parties, religions and world-views have joined in a great national front of peoples against the Fascist oppressors and the native quislings."[37]

Here it might be noted that the inclusion of Yugoslavia in this list of primarily West European countries helps to explain Dimitrov's well-known exhortations to Tito during 1942 to give his movement a multiparty character devoid of antimonarchist innuendoes.[38] For in the same issue of the Comintern journal there was a perceptible broadening of the social and political scope of the various national fronts—in contrast to earlier allusions to the leading role of the proletariat. In an article on France, Thorez commented that the French National Front was open to royalists as well as socialists.[39] By early 1943 he had added former members of the Fascist

---

33. Quoted in Milorad M. Drachkovitch, "The Comintern and the Insurrectional Activity of the Communist Party of Yugoslavia in 1941–1942," in *The Comintern: Historical Highlights,* ed. Milorad M. Drachkovitch and Branko Lazitch (New York: Praeger, 1966), 184–213 at 192.

34. Cited by A. Rossi [Angelo Tasca], *A Communist Party in Action* (New Haven: Yale University Press, 1949), 154–55 and 283.

35. Ercoli, "Fashistskaia Italiia nakanune bankrotstva," *KI,* nos. 1–2 (1942; to press March 13, 1942): 25–37 at 33–36.

36. S. Bogdanskaia, "Polskii narod v borbe protiv gitlerovskikh okkupantov," *KI,* no. 12 (1941; to press January 24, 1942):42–47 at 47.

37. E. Fischer, "Ot narodnogo fronta k obshchenatsionalnomu frontu," *KI,* nos. 8–9 (1942; to press October 12, 1942):26–30 at 30; my emphasis.

38. Moše Pijade, *La favola sull'aiuto sovietico all'insurrezione dei popoli della Jugoslavia* (Belgrade: n.p., 1950), 5 and 12.

39. M. Thorez, "Narodnaia Frantsiia protiv okkupantov i ikh prikhvostnei," *KI,* nos. 8–9 (1942; to press October 12, 1942):16–25 at 20–23.

Croix de Feu to the eligible participants.[40] The composition of the anticipated Italian national front was similarly enlarged. An unsigned piece in
the October 1942 issue stressed the need to include alongside the anti-
Fascist parties and Catholics "all political forces without exception who
protest the continuation of the war," dissident Fascists included.[41]

Togliatti's writings and broadcasts during this period reflected the national front line articulated in the Comintern journal. As he stated in an
April 1943 article, "among the officers of the army and navy, in the ranks
of the Catholic bourgeoisie, *in monarchical circles,* among the indus-
trialists and intelligentsia, *among the Fascist cadres* themselves the
number is growing of those . . . national forces bent upon leading the
country out of the war by the overthrow of Mussolini."[42] This line of
reasoning was repeated time and again in Togliatti's radio dispatches to
Italy over Radio Moscow and over yet another station beaming from Ufa,
Radio *Milano Libertà*.[43] Not only that, it echoed his many letters to the
PCI's Paris leadership in 1935–36. Indeed, the similiarity between his
advice to the Italian party during the popular front era and Moscow's
national front strategy suggests that Togliatti played an influential role in
formulating the latter, at least with regard to its sociopolitical breadth.

Meanwhile, there were veiled references in the seminal October 1942
issue of *Kommunisticheskii Internatsional* to manifestations of sectarianism in the French and Italian parties.[44] More significant with regard
to the PCI is Wolfgang Leonhard's firsthand account of the campaign
against sectarianism at the Comintern school near Ufa. The issue was first
raised in late October 1942 in an unscheduled lecture by a member of the
CPSU Central Committee. According to Leonhard, "from that day on-
wards, every lecture and every seminar contained repeated references to
the greatest of all dangers: 'sectarianism.'"[45] Then, toward the end of
1942, the head of the school announced: "Sectarianism has gone so far in
the Italian group that it has reached a point of serious political shortcom-
ing."[46] He went on to explain that one of the PCI students had asked
whether Italian partisans should eventually hide their weapons from the
Anglo-American liberators. The answer was a resounding no. This incident underscored Moscow's commitment to an interclass alliance strategy
of indeterminant duration in the case of the PCI. Stated somewhat differ-

40. M. Thorez, "Nastuplenie Krasnoi Armii i osvoboditelnaia borba frantsuzskogo naroda,"
KI, nos. 2–3 (1943; to press March 24, 1943):17–26 at 22.
41. "Za antifashistskoe edinstvo italianskogo naroda," *KI*, nos. 8–9 (1942; to press October
12, 1942):88–89 at 89.
42. Ercoli, "Krizis fashistskikh verkhov v Italii," *KI*, no. 4 (1943; to press April 28,
1943):11–20 at 19; my emphasis.
43. Togliatti, *Opere 1935–1944*, vol. 2, passim.
44. "Za antifashistskoe edinstvo italianskogo naroda," *KI*, nos. 8–9 (1942):90.
45. Wolfgang Leonhard, *Child of the Revolution* (Chicago: Henry Regnery Co., 1958), 208.
46. Ibid., 212–13.

ently, it portended the Soviet Union's ready acceptance in early 1944 of Italy's place in an Anglo-American sphere of influence.

Parallel to such innovative trends, however, the Comintern journal also exhorted the Communist parties of Western Europe to secure organizational control within their respective national fronts. The Soviet/Comintern leaders evidently envisaged the national fronts as monolithic grassroots structures rather than genuine political coalitions. A rare directive to this effect appeared in the lead editorial of the August 1942 issue: "The national front, *strongly united organizationally in the popular base and supplemented by agreements among the leaderships of all genuinely anti-Hitler parties and groupings,* will multiply tenfold the strength of the people."[47] In other words, it was to be a tightly knit mass movement that would, in turn, seek to conclude agreements "from above" with other anti-Fascist forces on unity of action in the actual resistance struggle. That the Communists were to play the guiding role in the national front was unstated but self-evident.

The French National Front may be taken as Moscow's prototype. Throughout 1941, it was merely a shadow organization utilized by the PCF as a goad to greater activism in the anti-Nazi Resistance.[48] Not until sometime in 1942 was a decisive organizational drive undertaken. By December 1942, however, Marty had issued a call in the Comintern journal for the "unification of all national forces in the various committees of the national front" which were currently being formed in the factories, on the railroads, in the schools and universities, and so forth.[49] The French National Front ultimately became one of the most important groups in the French underground. Yet according to Alfred Rieber, "its ideology and propaganda were similar to, if not identical with, the Communists', and the command posts in the political and military branches were exclusively in the hands of leading Communists."[50]

Unity of action between the French Communist movement (PCF, French National Front, *Francs-Tireurs et Partisans Français*) and the non-Communist groups was by and large realized in the armed resistance struggle. Nevertheless, the PCF adamantly opposed organizational unity. Only where the opportunity for infiltration assured its predominance did it participate in multiparty committees. But a genuine coalition based on the principle of unanimity, such as developed in Italy, was out of the question. Federation with the seven non-Communist resistance movements in

---

47. "Bit zakhvatchikov," *KI*, no. 7 (1942):6; my emphasis.

48. Rossi, *A Communist Party in Action,* 156–57.

49. André Marty, "Chas Frantsii probil!" *KI*, no. 12 (1942; to press December 12, 1942):9–19 at 14–15.

50. Alfred J. Rieber, *Stalin and the French Communist Party: 1941–1947* (New York: Columbia University Press, 1962), 60.

France was likewise repeatedly rejected since the Communists would have been in a minority of one to seven.[51]

The PCI's Initial Conformity[52]

Until Italy's surrender to the Allies and the flight of the royal family and government from Rome the night of September 8–9, 1943, the PCI cadres operating in France and Italy dutifully tried to implement Moscow's national front strategy.[53] In light of Moscow's prewar criticisms, their compliance was hardly surprising. From early 1940 onward Togliatti's "delegates" in France had bent over backward to follow the Comintern's directives. During the period of the German–Soviet pact they had agitated for an end to the war in the West, branding both sides as "imperialist bandits."[54] Their conformity was equally pronounced after the onset of the German–Russian war.

Immediately after the Nazi invasion of the Soviet Union in June 1941, the PCI called for an armed anti-Fascist resistance struggle. It simultaneously began to rebuild its defunct domestic apparatus. In late July 1941 the first member of the PCI's foreign bureau to return to Italy, Umberto Massola, crossed the Yugoslav-Italian border, reaching Milan about August 1.[55] In July 1942 Massola resumed the clandestine publication of *l'Unità* in northern Italy,[56] albeit on a monthly basis. And in early 1943 the PCI's foreign bureau, all of whose members had by then reentered their homeland, was reconstituted as an "internal," or domestic, center of direction under the guidance of Massola.[57]

For the Italian cadres in Italy the chief source of instructions were the daily programs transmitted over Radio Moscow and Radio *Milano Libertà*, both of which operated under Togliatti's supervision in Ufa.[58] Togliat-

---

51. Ibid., 88–93.

52. Paolo Spriano, in *Storia del Partito comunista italiano* 4:92–115, devoted a chapter to the efforts of the PCI cadres in Italy and France to implement the national front policy in 1942; he did not, however, suggest any linkage between these efforts and the Comintern's general line for Western Europe. While he did occasionally note the similarity between Togliatti's position and that of the PCI cadres (ibid., 100, 106, and 114–15), he remarked that from the autumn of 1941 "there were no further public positions taken by the international organ [Comintern] as such"; ibid., 119.

53. Two key PCI sources for the years 1939–43 (as well as 1943–45) are *Il comunismo italiano nella seconda guerra mondiale: Relazione e documenti presentati dalla direzione del partito al V Congresso del Partito comunista italiano* (Rome: Editori Riuniti, 1963) and Giorgio Amendola, *Lettere a Milano: Ricordi e documenti 1939–1945* (Rome: Editori Riuniti, 1973), 3–167.

54. "Lottiamo per la pace! Resti l'Italia fuori della guerra!" *SO* [NYC] 14, no. 1 (March 15, 1940):3–7; *Il comunismo italiano*, doc. 5:127–33, and doc. 6:133–40.

55. Massola, *Memorie*, 113–17.

56. Spriano, *Storia del Partito comunista italiano* 4:100, see also 67–69.

57. Amendola, *Storia del Partito comunista italiano, 1921–1943*, 492 and 516–18.

58. Ibid., 477–78, 488–89, and 514; and Togliatti, *Opere 1935–1944* 1:clv.

ti himself delivered a number of regular commentaries over both stations.[59] Although one-sided, this channel of communications proved rather effective. By the autumn of 1942 Massola was able to begin publishing material from the broadcasts in *l'Unità* for the benefit of those militants with no access to powerful shortwave radios.[60] As for the members of the foreign bureau in Marseilles, they were presumably able to benefit from the PCF's sporadic two-way radio contacts with the Comintern–Soviet authorities,[61] at least until the German occupation of southern France in late 1942.

The Italian Communists' objective during this period, as stated in a party document of November 1942, was to push for the *"rupture of the alliance with Germany and the overthrow of the Fascist dictatorship before the inevitable Hitlerite defeat and by means of a popular insurrection."*[62] To this end the PCI undertook to promote partisan warfare against the Mussolini regime. Its first step was to announce the formation of partisan units that were in fact nonexistent. In early 1942 Togliatti reported in the Comintern journal[63] and over Radio Moscow[64] that Italian partisans were operating in Venezia Giulia. The following summer Massola's network in Italy began to do likewise, declaring that partisan bands had appeared not only in the Yugoslav-Italian border area but also in the vicinity of Rome.[65] Aside from some Italian involvement with the Yugoslavian partisans, however, these were merely fabricated reports designed as a goad to action. The PCI admitted as much some two decades later.[66]

After the transformation of the foreign bureau into an internal center in early 1943, such agitational maneuvers were superseded by formal orders to create partisan groups. According to the later testimony of Luigi Longo, "the Yugoslavian example" was profoundly influential "in the drafting of these first instructions for the partisan struggle."[67] The actual creation of guerrilla units did not occur until the following autumn. Nevertheless, the PCI clearly sought to comply with the Comintern's order to promote armed resistance based on the Yugoslavian pattern.

59. Ibid., vol. 2, passim.

60. Ibid. 1:clvi.

61. Boffa, *Storia dell'Unione Sovietica* 2:175.

62. "Marsiglia 1942: Discussione tra PCI e 'Giustizia e libertà,'" *Rinascita* 22, no. 12 (March 20, 1965):17–21 at 20.

63. Ercoli, "Fashistskaia Italiia nakanune bankrotstva," *KI*, nos. 1–2 (1942):35–36.

64. Mario Correnti [Togliatti], *Discorsi agli italiani* (Moscow, 1943), 154.

65. "Sull'esempio di partigiani Jugoslavi sorgono i partigiani in Italia," *l'Unità* 19, no. 3 (September 5, 1942):2.

66. "Marsiglia 1942," *Rinascita* 22, no. 12 (March 20, 1965):21, n. 9; cf. Spriano, *Storia del Partito comunista italiano* 4:107.

67. "Longo, Parri, Pajetta: La Resistenza difficile—Coloqui tra i protagonisti," *Rinascita* 22, no. 27 (July 3, 1965):19–23 at 20.

Likewise in line with the directives of the Comintern, the Italian party started to campaign in the autumn of 1942 for the creation of an Italian national front open to all sociopolitical elements opposed to nazism. As its foreign bureau proclaimed in a November 1942 document, drafted in the course of negotiations with the democratic leftist movement, *Giustizia e Libertà* (GL), "Italian anti-Fascism ought to unite in a vast *national front* of struggle with . . . the Catholic opposition, the *monarchist opposition* and the *Fascist opposition.*"[68] The resistance appeals disseminated (if not signed) by the PCI thereafter included references to catholics, Liberals, and dissident Fascists as well as democrats, republicans, and anti-Fascists.[69] By March 1943 monarchists were also explicitly mentioned.[70]

Even more important, in early June 1943 Professor Concetto Marchesi, a Communist spokesman and noted Latinist from the University of Padua, met secretly in Rome with a Liberal senator with access to the court. The gist of his message was that the Communists were willing to collaborate with King Vittorio Emanuele in a move to oust Mussolini and were even prepared to participate in a democratic government invested by the monarch.[71] Marchesi expressed a similar view several weeks later in Milan at two exploratory meetings with representatives of the anti-Fascist parties that were ultimately to form the CLN. In opposition to the traditionally republican parties, he proposed that the so-called institutional question, that is, the decision as to whether Italy should remain a monarchy or become a republic, be postponed until the end of the war.[72] At the second of these meetings Marchesi presented the PCI's political intentions in such a moderate light that the Christian Democratic delegate was prompted to remark: "In that case we Christian Democrats are farther to the left than the Communists."[73]

The PCI activists in France attempted from the beginning to enlist the support of the PSI and other Italian center-left groups in the anticipated national front. Yet the Communists' concrete organizational proposals reflected the Comintern's directives. As a case in point, the above-cited November 1942 document of the foreign bureau in Marseilles included the following statement: "When we support the formation of this vast national front of struggle we think—without excluding the possibility of contacts from above—above all of uniting everywhere, in an organized way, in the factories and barracks, on ships and in offices, in villages and

68. "Marsiglia 1942," *Rinascita* 22, no. 12 (March 20, 1965):20; my emphasis.
69. *Il comunismo italiano,* doc. 13:166–71 at 169; and doc. 16:177–78.
70. Ibid., doc. 18:182–85 at 185.
71. Amendola, *Storia del Partito comunista italiano, 1921–1943,* 546–48.
72. Franco Catalano, *Storia del CLNAI* (Bari: Editori Laterza, 1956), 20–21; cf. Amendola, *Storia del Partito comunista italiano, 1921–1943,* 549–50.
73. Quoted in Lelio Basso, "Il rapporto tra rivoluzione democratica e rivoluzione socialista nella Resistenza," *Critica marxista* 3, no. 4 (July–August 1965):11–20 at 14.

in schools, all Italians . . . of whatever political opinion, anti-Fascists or Fascists of opposition, who want to act to save Italy."[74] The parallels here with *Kommunisticheskii Internatsional's* organizational guidelines and the PCF's actual conduct suggest considerable coordination among Moscow, the PCF, and the Italian cadres in southern France.

The PCI foreign bureau along with some members of the PSI leadership (Nenni and Giuseppe Saragat) and the GL movement had in fact agreed in September 1941 to create a Committee of Action for the Union of the Italian People.[75] Soon, however, the local Communist organizers sought to manipulate this nascent interparty committee. In the autumn of 1942 they disseminated two appeals signed in its name. The first, dated September 1942, not only summoned all Italians to form grassroots committees of action but also implied that such committees already existed: "In every center of work, of thought, of life a Committee of Action is springing up through your effort."[76] The second appeal closed with the slogan, "Long live the National Front of Action for peace, independence and liberty!"[77] All the same, throughout the greater part of 1942 the committees of action and the Italian national front existed largely on paper, similar to the Italian partisan bands of that time.[78] It therefore appears that by spreading reports of sham resistance committees the PCI cadres hoped to stimulate "popular demand" for an Italian national front.

By the same token, the national front committees that actually did take shape in late 1942 were rather spurious. According to the party leadership's report to the Fifth PCI Congress after the war, a first such committee "composed of representatives of the Socialist, Communist, Christian Democratic and Action parties" was formed and began to function in Turin in October–November 1942.[79] Similar bodies were purportedly created in Milan and Rome shortly thereafter. Yet according to an independent Italian scholar, the interparty committee in Turin was "little more than symbolic, lacking any kind of effective structure"; and it was called a "National Front Committee" only by the Communists.[80]

In reality most center-left leaders were reluctant to conclude an organizational agreement with the PCI. In November 1942 GL representatives

---

74. "Marsiglia 1942," *Rinascita* 22, no. 12 (March 20, 1965):20. A similar set of guidelines, dated March 20, 1942, was sent by the foreign bureau to militants in Italy; see Spriano, *Storia del Partito comunista italiano* 4:92–93.

75. *Il comunismo italiano,* doc. 11:60–65; cf. Amendola, *Storia del Partito comunista italiano, 1921–1943,* 481–92. At that time Amendola represented the foreign bureau in Marseilles.

76. *Il comunismo italiano,* doc. 13:166–71 at 169.

77. Ibid., doc. 15:175–76.

78. Cf. Spriano, *Storia del Partito Comunista italiano* 4:103.

79. *Il comunismo italiano,* 10.

80. Mario Giovana, "Ricerche sulla storia del C.L.N. Piemontese," *Il movimento di liberazione in Italia* [henceforth cited as *MLI*] nos. 34–35 (January–April 1955), 69–74 at 71. Cf. Spriano, *Storia del Partito comunista italiano* 4:144.

insisted that the prerequisite for "unity of action" was the autonomous development of the various political formations within Italy.[81] Soon thereafter the GL movement merged with other democratic leftist currents to form the Party of Action.[82] As described by a founding member, the Pd'A (whose members were called Actionists) represented a "synthesis" of democracy, liberalism, and socialism.[83] Yet, it was intransigently anti-monarchist and also viewed the Communist Party as its arch competitor, both ideologically and organizationally.[84] On both accounts, it was reluctant to enter into an alliance with the PCI. The Communists, in short, could rely only upon segments of the PSI for close collaboration.

One final effort to form a national front prior to the downfall of Mussolini took place in late June–early July 1943. On two occasions representatives of the major anti-Fascist parties in northern Italy met clandestinely in Milan on the initiative of the Communists. A major obstacle to any meeting of minds, however, was the PCI's readiness to cooperate with the House of Savoy. The proposal by the Communist representative, Marchesi, to table the institutional question until after the war has already been mentioned. The only tangible result of these meetings was thus the creation of a Committee of Oppositions to serve as a liaison among the various parties.[85]

Shortly thereafter, on July 25, 1943, Mussolini was deposed by a palace coup instigated largely by dissident Fascists and officers. The ensuing period between July 25 and September 8, the so-called 45 days, was one of political vacillation on the part of Mussolini's successor, Pietro Badoglio.[86] The Rome–Berlin Axis was declared intact ("The war continues," announced Badoglio). Yet cautious steps were taken to arrange an armistice with the Allies. The ban on anti-Fascist parties and newspapers remained in effect. Yet the Fascist Party was dissolved on July 27, and political prisoners were released during the month of August. At the same time, the Committee of Oppositions—although strictly speaking still illegal—organized itself on a more regular basis and transferred its operations from Milan to Rome. Ivanoe Bonomi, a right-of-center pre-Fascist premier, assumed the leadership of this group. Yet Badoglio refused to

81. "Marsiglia 1942," *Rinascita* 22, no. 12 (March 20, 1965):18.

82. For a concise history of the Pd'A, see Carlo Ludovico Ragghianti, *Disegno della liberazione italiana* (Pisa: Nistri-Lischi Editori, 1954), app. 2:273–353.

83. Giuliano Pischel, *Che cosa è il Partito d'Azione* (Milan: Antonio Tarantola Editore, 1945), 213–14.

84. This is clear from the letters exchanged between Pd'A leaders during 1943–45, collected in *Una lotta nel suo corso*, ed. Sandro Contini Bonacossi and Licia Ragghianti Collobi (Venice: Neri Pozza Editore, 1954); henceforth this volume will be cited as *Una lotta nel suo corso*.

85. *Il comunismo italiano*, 27; cf. Catalano, *Storia del CLNAI*, 18–22.

86. For a general account of the overthrow of Mussolini and the 45 days, see Charles Delzell, *Mussolini's Enemies: The Italian Anti-Fascist Resistance* (Princeton: Princeton University Press, 1966), 223–58.

keep its representatives informed on the course of armistice negotiations or to instruct them on the measures to be taken after Italy's rupture with Germany.[87]

On the other hand, the anti-Fascist parties were able to regroup under the conditions of semilegality in effect during the 45 days. In this respect the PCI, like all other parties, faced tasks of considerable magnitude. As Longo pointed out in 1965, "we had to overcome rapidly a perceptible disintegration (despite our much vaunted organization) and to extend and organize our contacts."[88] The Communist cadres had to rebuild their ties with the party's domestic base, which had grown to about 5,000 activists before July 25 and multiplied tenfold during the remaining summer weeks. The 2,000 or so Communist political prisoners who were released beginning August 18, 1943, also had to be absorbed into the party's new organizational structure.[89] To be sure, ranking PCI leaders who had been in prison or confinement were now able to resume their previous roles. But their political views were often at odds with the current national front strategy. Such was the case with regard to the 500 or so Communists confined on Ventotene. This group, led by Secchia, Mauro Scoccimarro, and several others, had pressed for the expulsion of Terracini not only because of his opposition to the German–Soviet pact but also because of his subsequent support for PCI cooperation with all anti-Fascist forces, including monarchists, in a post-Fascist democratic transitional stage.[90]

In other words, a number of those arrested a decade or so earlier clung to the sectarian orientation that had prevailed from 1929 through 1933 as well as before 1926. They interpreted the national front line through orthodox lenses, viewing unity of action with middle-class groups as a maneuver to shorten the anticipated post-Fascist democratic interlude and expedite the creation of a dictatorship of the proletariat.[91] The same was true of many rank-and-file Communists who, passive since the early 1930s or before, now resumed an active role at the party base.[92]

All the same, a temporary leadership body called the *Direzione* was established by a meeting of PCI notables in Rome on August 29–30 and placed under the de facto supervision of Scoccimarro. It was composed of the six members of the internal center (Massola, Roasio, Novella, Giovanni Roveda, Negarville, and Amendola) plus four members of the

87. The relations between Badoglio and the anti-Fascist Committee of Oppositions in Rome are described in Ivanoe Bonomi, *Diario di un anno: 2 giugno 1943–10 giugno 1944* (Italy: Garzanti, 1947), 41–94.

88. "Longo, Parri, Pajetta: La Resistenza difficile," *Rinascita* 22, no. 27 (July 3, 1965):20.

89. Ibid.; see also Amendola, *Storia del Partito comunista italiano, 1921–1943*, 578–80 and 590–99.

90. Coletti, *Il governo di Ventotene*, 95–96.

91. Cf. Amendola, *Storia del Partito comunista italiano, 1921–1943*, 522–27.

92. Spriano, *Storia del Partito comunista italiano* 4:87–88.

PCI leadership cell from Ventotene (Scoccimarro, Secchia, Longo, and Girolamo Li Causi). And it was divided into two groups, one based in Rome and the other in Milan. While Scoccimarro remained in Rome, Longo soon took over the Milan office with Secchia as his deputy.[93]

Meanwhile, the PCI continued its efforts to form a national front with the PSI and the Pd'A. A unity of action pact with the PSI was concluded on August 4, 1943.[94] The Socialist Party, much smaller and weaker even than the PCI and Pd'A of that time, was eager to consolidate its ties with the Communists.[95] This remained the case even after its merger on August 22, 1943, with two other socialist groups to form the Italian Socialist Party of Proletarian Unity (PSIUP).[96] Communist negotations with the Pd'A were more difficult. Nevertheless, shortly before the September 8 debacle, a compromise was reached in Rome. The PCI agreed to adopt an unequivocal antimonarchist position, while the Pd'A accepted in principle the Communist formula for a national front organization comprising not only interparty committees but also all mass organizations at the grassroots level. A declaration to this effect was approved by the PCI, the PSI, and the Pd'A.[97] Only one critical point remained unsettled: the structure of the so-called Central Committee of the National Front to which the tripartite declaration repeatedly referred. This entire arrangement soon fell by the wayside, however, with the creation of the far more broadly based Italian Committee of National Liberation.

The PCI and the CLN: Organizational Unity and Republican Intransigence

On September 8, 1943, General Eisenhower announced to the world that Italy had surrendered unconditionally to the Allies. The royal government's subsequent flight from Rome during the early hours of September 9 and its failure to take any measures whatsoever for the defense of the capital against German retaliation evoked the disdain and fury of even the most moderate and promonarchist anti-Fascists. As a result the Committee of Oppositions, which had hitherto met on an informal basis, transformed itself that very day into the Committee of National Liberation.[98] There are, unfortunately, no records of the discussions that led to this decision.

93. Amendola, *Storia del Partito comunista italiano, 1921–1943*, 595–98; cf. *Il comunismo italiano*, 38.

94. *Il comunismo italiano*, doc. 2:122.

95. Oreste Lizzadri, *Il regno di Badoglio* (Milan: Edizioni Avanti, 1963), 29ff.

96. Ibid., 106–7.

97. *Il comunismo italiano*, doc. 28:195–97; cf. Ragghianti, *Disegno della liberazione italiano*, 34–40.

98. *Il comunismo italiano*, doc. 30:198.

But the rapidity with which it was made indicates that it was a spontaneous and unanimous act.[99] Faced with the desertion of the official government and the immediate occupation of north-central Italy by German troops, the Committee of Oppositions was left with no choice but to assume the leadership of the anti-Nazi Resistance and to issue a call to arms on the side of the Allies.[100]

The day-to-day course of the Resistance is beyond our scope. Suffice it to say that the PCI provided the major impetus for the formation of urban groups whose chief task was sabotage.[101] Its agitators were also primarily responsible for the rash of strikes that broke out in the northern industrial cities during November and December 1943.[102] These, in turn, inspired the CLN-organized and eminently successful general strike that swept northern Italy during the first week of March 1944.[103] Finally, the Communists constituted the largest single contingent of armed partisans. Already in the fall of 1943 their units, according to the Pd'A leader, Leo Valiani, were among the most "numerous and pugnacious."[104] By the summer of 1944 the Communist detachments, known as the Garibaldi Brigades, represented more than 50 percent of the 50,000 or so guerrillas then mobilized.[105] And in the closing months of the war, when the total number of combatants reached upwards of 100,000 men,[106] approximately 40 percent were *Garibaldini*.[107] In short, the PCI cadres complied with Moscow's basic directive to foment sabotage, strikes, and armed resistance in the Nazi rear.

In contrast, the pluralistic structure of the CLN differed sharply from the monistic national front envisaged by the Comintern. The Soviet directive to form a unitary grassroots network apparently remained in force even after the dissolution of the International.[108] All the same, PCI spokesmen evidently raised no objections to the principle of party parity and the rule of unanimity that were soon to become hallmarks of the Italian CLN. Moreover, in Togliatti's radio broadcasts and articles there was no hint of criticism with regard to the organizational character of the CLN.[109]

The precise structure of the CLN was the subject of much discussion

99. Cf. Bonomi, *Diario di un anno,* 100.
100. Ibid., 101; *Il comunismo italiano,* doc. 31:198; and doc. 33:199–201.
101. Catalano, *Storia del CLNAI,* 88.
102. Ibid., 96.
103. Ibid., 140–41.
104. See his *Tutte le strade conducono a Roma* (Florence: La Nouva Italia, 1947), 121–22.
105. Parri to La Malfa, July 24, 1944, *Una lotta nel suo corso,* 231.
106. Delzell, *Mussolini's Enemies,* 296.
107. Valiani, *Tutte le strade conducono a Roma,* 330.
108. Cf. Amendola, *Storia del Partito comunista italiano, 1921–1943,* 592 and 596.
109. Togliatti, *Opere 1935–1944* 2:487–515, passim.

until the end of September 1943.[110] Here again the relevant debates are not available. Nevertheless, the views of the center-right parties, the Liberals, Labor Democrats, and Christian Democrats, plainly prevailed over those of the left, the Communists, Socialists, and Actionists. In the first place, the promonarchist Bonomi remained the president and spokesman of the CLN.[111] In the second place, its very name, intentionally patterned after the Gaullist *Comité Français de la Liberation Nationale,* represented a defeat for the left.[112] This was particularly true in the case of the Communists, for whom the term ''national front'' had acquired a seemingly liturgical connotation. There is no better evidence of the term's hold over the Communist mentality than the fact that many militants—including Togliatti during his first months back in Italy—continued to refer to the CLN movement as the national front in private correspondence and party meetings.

Third and most important, since the political parties that made up the CLNs in Rome and elsewhere were only presumptively representative of Italian public opinion, they held power jointly and majority rule was precluded. In the words of Scoccimarro, PCI representative on the Rome committee, ''the decisions of the CLN always had to be taken unanimously and hence each of its members had a kind of veto right.''[113] According to Communists and Actionists alike, the rule of unanimity was not always observed in northern Italy.[114] However, decisions of importance were apparently made only on this basis. Indeed, even in factory CLNs on which the Liberal representative was simultaneously the manager or owner, unanimity prevailed.[115]

The CLN originated and was formally based in Rome. However, as the Resistance gathered momentum in Italy's industrial and mountainous northern region, the CLN's center of gravity—in terms of authority and activity—soon shifted to Milan. And in late January 1944 the Milan CLN, which had hitherto assumed de facto responsibility for the northern region, was officially designated the Committee of National Liberation for Upper Italy (CLNAI). The CLNAI was composed of representatives from the five anti-Fascist parties present in the north—the PCI, PSIUP, Pd'A, DC, and PLI—and was presided over by the independent financier, Al-

110. Ragghianti, *Disegno della liberazione italiano,* 40.
111. The question of his suitability or replacement was evidently not even raised; ibid., 42–43.
112. Ibid., 81; cf. Amendola, *Lettere a Milano,* 162.
113. Mauro Scoccimarro, ''L'appello del PCI nel settembre 1943,'' *Rinascita* 20, no. 47 (November 30, 1963):22–25 at 24; cf. Ragghianti, *Disegno della liberazione italiana,* 40–41.
114. Ibid., 41. Cf. Amendola, *Lettere a Milano,* 230–41 and 250–59, esp. 256.
115. ''Amendola, Basso, Pajetta: Unità e socialismo—Colloqui tra i protagonisti,'' *Rinascita* 22, no. 29 (July 17, 1965):15–19 at 16.

fredo Pizzoni.[116] The Communist delegates were Dozza and Li Causi, with Emilio Sereni replacing Li Causi in the spring of 1945. Although Longo was the top PCI figure in Milan, he was otherwise occupied with the direction of the Garibaldi Brigades. The PCI delegates to the Rome CLN were Scoccimarro and Amendola, with Negarville replacing Amendola in May 1944. And in southern Italy the Communists were represented by Velio Spano and Eugenio Reale until Togliatti's return in March 1944.[117]

In addition, a network of interparty military committees developed during the winter of 1943–44 with nuclei in Milan, Rome, and Florence. In the vital Milanese Military Committee the Actionist leader, Ferruccio Parri, was generally recognized as *primus inter pares*. However, the Garibaldi Brigades remained under the autonomous command of Longo, with Secchia as political commissar, until the late spring of 1944.[118] And during the early months of the armed Resistance there was considerable competition between Communist units and those formed by other parties. This is well documented in the letters of the northern Actionist leaders (especially those based in Florence). According to them, the Communists agreed only reluctantly to the formation of interparty military committees, and they obstructed for some time the effective coordination of partisan operations.[119] They snatched Allied airborne "drops" of military supplies destined for other units.[120] They purloined radio equipment intended for the Florentine CLN by convincing the agents entrusted with its delivery that the CLN was inefficient and suspect.[121] There were even cases of outright theft of arms from non-Communist partisans,[122] who were on one occasion compelled as a result to surrender to the Fascists.[123]

Yet despite these military frictions, political unity within the CLN was preserved throughout this period. Even the bitterly anti-Communist Actionist, Carlo Ragghianti, admits that the Tuscan CLN functioned regularly with the cooperation of its Communist delegates.[124]

Communist cooperation in the CLN network was indeed the official line of the PCI. After proclaiming that "the National Front has been formed in the Committee of National Liberation," a PCI declaration of

116. Marcello Cirenei, "Il primo Comitato di Liberazione Alta Italia," *Mondo operaio* 9, no. 2 (February 1956):109–11; Renato Carli-Ballola, *Storia della Resistenza* (Milan: Edizioni Avanti, 1957), 109.

117. Luigi Longo, *I centri dirigenti del PCI nella Resistenza* (Rome: Editori Riuniti, 1973), 35–36.

118. Ibid., 38.

119. Ragghianti to Bauer and La Malfa, April 27, 1944, *Una lotta nel suo corso,* 142; Ragghianti to Calace, May 19, 1944, ibid., 206–7.

120. Valiani, *Tutte le strade conducono a Roma,* 198.

121. Ragghianti to Parri, June 2, 1944, *Una lotta nel suo corso,* 218–19.

122. Ragghianti to Bauer, November 26, 1943, ibid., 9.

123. Ragghianti to Bauer and La Malfa, April 27, 1944, ibid., 142.

124. Ragghianti to Valiani, February 27, 1944, ibid., 46.

September 1943 enjoined all Communists to support the authority and unity of the CLN.[125] The document also stressed the need for solidarity among the leftist parties within the CLN.[126] However, in light of the unanimity rule, this admittedly ambiguous stance was hardly subversive. Moreover, the PCI's commitment to the CLN movement was backed by none other than Secchia in the December 1943 issue of *La Nostra Lotta* (a Communist journal published in northern Italy from October 1943 until liberation). Despite his sectarian tendencies, he affirmed that it "would be an error of infantile extremism and a sign of political immaturity and incomprehension to anticipate or want *today* a schism in the CLN that would reduce it to the leftist parties alone."[127]

In addition, the PCI cadres in Italy diverged from the Soviet line and from Togliatti as well in their attitude toward the Badoglio government. They had been prepared in the spring of 1943 to cooperate with any establishment circles to overthrow Mussolini. Even after the coup they had been, in the words of Bonomi, "reasonable, pliant, disposed to make use of all possibilities," including those offered by temporary collaboration with Badoglio and the king.[128] In late August, however, the PCI gave in to the Pd'A's demand for a rigid republican stance. And from September 9, 1943, until the return of Togliatti in March 1944, despite some internal dissension at the outset, the Communists joined with the other anti-Fascist parties in calling for the resignation of Premier Badoglio and the formation of "a government of the CLN" free of royal investiture.

To be sure, both the PCI leaders in Italy and Togliatti in Russia demanded the abdication of the king and the convening of a constitutional assembly after the war to determine the ultimate institutional shape of Italy. Nevertheless, Togliatti continued to urge by radio that the Italian resistance forces cooperate with Badoglio in the common struggle against the German occupation.[129] Although there is some evidence that Moscow opposed the circumspect dealings the opposition had with Mussolini's successors during the 45 days,[130] after the armistice PCI commentators over Soviet radio, including both Grieco and Togliatti, called upon all Italian anti-Fascists to "rally around the Badoglio government."[131]

---

125. *Il comunismo italiano*, doc. 37:205–16 at 209.

126. Ibid., 212.

127. Pietro Secchia, "Politica da seguire—Errori da evitare," *La Nostra Lotta: Organo del Partito Comunista Italiano* 1, no. 5 (December 1943):12–14 at 13; my emphasis. Henceforth this journal will be cited as *LNL*.

128. Bonomi, *Diario di un anno*, 48–49.

129. See the broadcasts over Radio *Milano Libertà* dated September 23, October 10 and 16, and November 5, 1943, in *Opere 1935–1944*, by Togliatti, 2:487–99.

130. Ibid., 472–79, esp. 477; cf. Amendola, *Storia del Partito comunista italiano, 1921–1943*, 592–94.

131. Amendola attributed the above-quoted phrase specifically to Ruggero Grieco in his *Lettere a Milano*, 205.

Yet even the conservative anti-Fascist leaders turned against Badoglio as a result of his conduct at the time of the armistice. Although the CLN agreed from its inception to defer the final decision regarding the House of Savoy to a postwar constitutional assembly, it rejected any collaboration with Badoglio, let alone Vittorio Emanuele. And it demanded the right to form an "extraordinary government" endowed with "all the constitutional powers of the State" until the institutional question was resolved. This position was first set forth in an October 16, 1943, declaration of the Rome CLN.[132] Its substance was reiterated in subsequent documents throughout the fall and winter of 1943–44.

From the start the position of the PCI center in Rome was identical to the one expressed in the CLN declaration of October 16, 1943. It refused to collaborate with the king or Badoglio and called for a government composed of the anti-Fascist parties. As Scoccimarro had already stated at a CLN meeting on September 28, 1943, "it is not possible to unite the Italians around the king and Badoglio; they must therefore step aside in order to permit the unity of the Italians." He went on to warn that "if *the English* insist on championing the king and Badoglio, they will provoke a schism in Italy. . . . There is no possibility of compromises with the Badoglio government."[133]

On this issue there was, as suggested above, some dissension among the PCI cadres. Scoccimarro and Amendola, based in Rome, were intransigent in their refusal to accord any legitimacy to Badoglio.[134] Longo, on the other hand, pleaded from Milan for a more flexible approach, one in which priority would be given to the armed struggle against the Germans and Mussolini's new puppet state, the Republic of Salò. He insisted that the comrades in Milan were as opposed as those in Rome to a government headed by Badoglio, all the while anticipating an eventual need to compromise, to include some supporters of Badoglio in a future CLN government.[135] Secchia agreed with Longo.[136]

PCI Cleavages over Togliatti's Authority

Where Longo and Secchia most diverged from Amendola and Scoccimarro, however, was on the question of whether Togliatti was empowered to issue directives to them from Moscow. This difference

132. *Il comunismo italiano*, doc. 34:201–2.

133. Quoted from a copy of the minutes of the meeting in Ragghianti, *Disegno della liberazione italiana*, 45; my emphasis.

134. Amendola, *Lettere a Milano*, 179–82, 188–93, and 216–17. For Scoccimarro's views, see his letter of October 5 in Longo, *I centri dirigenti*, 56–61.

135. Ibid., 47–55 and 66–77.

136. Ibid., 78–85.

surfaced during the course of a discussion of whether the Milan or Rome party center should have primary authority. According to Longo, in a letter of October 18, the most important argument in favor of the center in the capital was that "with the liberation of Rome you can have the advice of our elders: of Ded (G. Dimitrov) and Ercoli, especially, who is the chief of our party."[137] In other words, the Rome group could establish direct communications with Moscow. Meanwhile, he said, the two domestic PCI centers could use the broadcasts of Radio *Milano Libertà* as a vehicle of political coordination.[138] This led Amendola to retort on November 9 that, with all due regard for Ercoli's authority, he (and Grieco) did not have sufficient information on what was actually going on in Italy.[139]

At a meeting of the Rome leadership on November 4, 1943, Amendola was even more blunt, maintaining that Togliatti had no right to give the PCI orders from abroad: "In my opinion the transmissions from Moscow cannot constitute for us directives that we are obliged to follow. . . . They aren't directives, first, because the seat of the Communist International is no longer in Moscow. . . . Secondly, the leadership of our party isn't in Moscow, Comrade Ercoli who is the chief of our party is in Moscow. But he isn't today in a position to exercise this function."[140] Scoccimarro, in a letter written to the Milan center toward the end of November, made it clear that he agreed with Amendola. The broadcasts of Togliatti and Grieco, he asserted, "made so as to appear like directives given to the party, were absolutely inopportune, and it is to be hoped that they are not repeated."[141]

The question of Togliatti's authority, which arose almost inadvertently during the debate over the approach to take toward Badoglio, soon superseded all other points of disagreement. Most members of the acting *Direzione*, moreover, were drawn into the controversy. The polemics escalated as a result of two opposing resolutions. The first, passed by the Rome center at its November 4 meeting, declared that "the political line indicated by E. and G." was no longer in force, that the call to unite around Badoglio was unworkable and, by implication, ill-conceived.[142] The second, proposed by Massola and approved by the Milan center in early December, expressed "its faith and devotion to Comrade Ercoli" and its hope that Togliatti would "reenter Italy as soon as possible and resume his post as immediate leader of the party."[143]

137. Ibid., 76.
138. Ibid., 77.
139. Amendola, *Lettere a Milano,* 205.
140. Ibid., 214–15.
141. Longo, *I centri dirigenti,* 149–55 at 153.
142. Ibid., 145–48.
143. Ibid., 221.

But the controversy was even more complex than suggested above. We can actually distinguish three different groupings: the autonomists, Amendola and Scoccimarro; the Togliatti loyalists, Longo and Secchia; and the Stalinists, Massola and Roasio, relative newcomers to the PCI leadership appointed by Togliatti to run the Paris foreign bureau in the winter of 1940. They all agreed that Togliatti was head of the party. Where they differed was on the appropriateness of his giving orders from Moscow and on the ideological culpability of those who rejected such orders. The autonomists were the forerunners of Titoism, Maoism, Eurocommunism. They believed that party policy should be shaped in accord with local conditions. The Stalinists were prototypical: the gist of Roasio's argument was that the party line should emanate from Togliatti precisely because he was in Moscow and had the confidence of the "leaders of the CI [sic]"; and those who objected were political renegades.[144] Longo and Secchia were simply being loyal to Togliatti and the Soviet Union at one and the same time.[145]

To complicate matters still further, there was little correlation between the different attitudes toward Togliatti (and the related issue of Badoglio) and strategic preferences. Scoccimarro and Amendola, for example, were unbending toward Badoglio and hence reserved toward Togliatti—but for quite different reasons. Scoccimarro, as shown by his treatment of Terracini on Ventotene, opposed cooperation with monarchists and former Fascists for sectarian reasons. What he sought was an entente among left-wing parties committed to a postwar socialist transformation. Apparently he hoped the CLN could be used for this purpose and therefore supported the temporary unity of all parties in that body. But as he disclosed in an early October 1943 letter to the Milan center, what he had in mind was a "popular front" type of democracy, a government embracing the three parties of the left.[146] Amendola, in contrast, favored "a government of the CLN because only this government will be able . . . to create a democratic state."[147]

A similar divergence between Secchia and Longo was to develop in later years. Secchia was edged out of the party leadership by 1956 for sectarian intransigence on organizational matters and relations with Moscow, while Longo's political evolution paralleled that of Togliatti. Both became innovators in the Western Communist context. As for Massola and Roasio, they soon disappeared from the top echelons of the PCI.

144. See Roasio's letter of January 2, 1944, in ibid., 278–86; cf. Massola's letter of December 8, 1943, in ibid., 180–82.
145. For their alignment with Togliatti, see Longo's letter of December 6, 1943, in ibid., 159–79 at 168–71; and Secchia's letter of December 10, 1943, in ibid., 183–214 at 207–8.
146. Ibid., 57.
147. Amendola, *Lettere a Milano*, 202.

The timing and circumstances of an individual's involvement in party affairs was thus more important than strategic preferences in explaining the divergences that developed among the PCI leaders in late 1943. Scoccimarro's prewar militancy ended with his arrest in late 1926,[148] prior to the Stalinization of the Comintern. And although Amendola joined the party only in 1929, he was—aside from a five-year term in confinement—assigned largely to clandestine work in Italy, far from the reach of Stalin's henchmen and often even his own party superiors.[149] The independent bent of these men was thus comprehensible. By way of contrast, the personal alignment of Longo and Secchia with Togliatti—despite their many policy disagreements—had been demonstrated during the PCI's traumas of 1929–31. Secchia's backing of Togliatti at the crucial August 1929 meeting of the PCI politburo and Longo's apparent disinclination to replace Togliatti as PCI head were evidence of their sense of loyalty to him.

Roasio, in contrast, was representative of the very small group of PCI cadres who were trained in the Soviet Union in the 1930s and thoroughly bolshevized.[150] His association with the PCI's Paris leadership had been extremely limited until his cooptation into Berti's reorganization committee in the turbulent summer of 1938. As for Massola, he began to appear at party meetings in March 1937 and became de facto head of the PCI's internal center in late 1941. Yet he was in that capacity orthodox and compliant to the core, flaunting his status as Togliatti's "delegate" and displaying a high-handed manner toward the growing band of domestic comrades which often provoked friction and resentment.[151]

What this all added up to was a remarkably heterogeneous leadership. And Togliatti, when he finally did return to Italy in late March 1944, dealt with the situation in his typical conciliatory fashion. Not only did he incorporate all of these groups into the *Direzione* named after his return to Italy and confirmed at the Fifth PCI Congress in December 1945;[152] he also appointed Di Vittorio to the new *Direzione* and declared null and void the organizational sanctions taken against dissidents such as Terracini.[153] Meanwhile, few PCI cadres in this early post-Fascist period remained untouched by the CLN experience. Obliged to negotiate and compromise as equals with the delegates of other parties spanning a wide political

148. Spriano, *Storia del Partito comunista italiano* 2:64.

149. Giorgio Amendola, *Una scelta di vita* (Milan: Rizzoli Editore, 1976), 258–65.

150. For Roasio's disclosures in this regard, see his above-cited letter in Longo, *I centri dirigenti*, 285.

151. See Amendola's comments based on his personal dealings with Massola in his *Storia del Partito comunista italiano, 1921–1943*, 516–18 and 592; cf. Spriano, *Storia del Partito comunista italiano* 4:94.

152. For the composition of the *Direzione*, see *l'Unità*, January 9, 1946, 1.

153. See Longo's introduction to his *I centri dirigenti*, 13.

spectrum, most Communist functionaires, whether they liked it or not, were exposed to the workings of the democratic process.

Togliatti's prestige, already high among those PCI members with whom he had worked in the past, was surely enhanced by his conciliatory handling of the contentiousness that pervaded the party's upper reaches in 1943. This heightened authority enabled him, in turn, to carry out the *svolta* of Salerno on April 1, 1944. In a word, Togliatti announced his party's willingness to participate in a cabinet headed by Badoglio or anyone else, regardless of whether the king first withdrew from public life.[154] This shift was all the more staggering in that at the end of 1943 Togliatti had come around to a position close to that of the PCI's Rome center, implying in *Pravda* and over Radio *Milano Libertà* the need for a CLN government independent of both the Badoglio circle and the king.[155] He presumably did so at that time in response to the more complete information on the Italian scene that he was able to receive from the liberated south.

By mid-winter 1944, however, Italy had become entangled in the Allies' sparring over the postwar political shape of Europe. As will be discussed in chapter 6, Stalin's interest in a division of Europe along the lines of Allied spheres of military responsibility led him to extend diplomatic recognition to the Badoglio government in mid-March 1944. Under these circumstances Togliatti concluded—undoubtedly in consultation with the Soviet leaders—that the most effective way to advance the domestic interests and status of the PCI was to give in for the time being to the conservative, pro-Badoglio leanings of the Anglo-American occupation authorities. Despite the recriminations the *svolta* provoked among CLN leaders, the Anglo-Americans, and the PCI cadres themselves, the end result was the formation on April 21, 1944, of a cabinet of all six anti-Fascist parties headed by Badoglio and invested by the king.

We know very little about Togliatti's thinking from mid-1940 through March 1944—in contrast to the abundance of material available on the views of the PCI leaders in Italy. To be sure, the parallels between the Comintern's wartime line of Communist unity with all imaginable forces opposed to Hitler and Togliatti's exhortations to the PCI in the mid-1930s to exploit cleavages even among Fascist cadres suggest his close involvement in the formulation of Moscow's national front strategy. His supervision of the foreign broadcasts from Ufa points in the same direction. At the same time, his ability to make concrete policy decisions for the PCI

154. See the report of Togliatti's April 1 press conference in *The Times* [London], April 3, 1944, 4.
155. Togliatti, *Opere 1935–1944* 1:clxvi; and ibid. 2:347–55.

was limited by his heavy day-to-day administrative responsibilities and his lack of firsthand information on what was really going on in Italy.

On balance, it seems that Togliatti's most important accomplishment during this period was his success in securing his own place in Moscow's plans for the postwar era. For one thing is clear: during the formative stage of the PCI's domestic center of direction in 1943–44, Togliatti was an outsider. Throughout the 1930s he had stood out as the only major European Communist leader who owed his position not to Stalin but to his authority among his own comrades. In the mid-1940s, however, his personal situation was quite the reverse. In a word, it was thanks to Stalin that he returned to Italy as leader of the Italian Communists' *partito nuovo*.

PART THREE

THE *PARTITO NUOVO* IN
THE POSTWAR ERA

I n June 1946 the Italian people voted to repudiate the House of Savoy by a 54 to 46 percent margin while also electing delegates to a constitutional assembly that was to give institutional shape to the new Italian Republic. During the three years between the fall of Mussolini and this first postwar election, the Italian Communist Party underwent a dramatic transformation. From a clandestine sect numbering fewer than 2,500 active members in the mid-1930s and some 5,000 members all told in mid-1943, it mushroomed into a mass-based party boasting over 1.7 million fresh recruits. If one considers that well over 1 million of these newcomers enrolled in the PCI only after liberation, indeed, during the last eight months of 1945, the growth rate is even more spectacular.

Several circumstances help to explain this rapid increase in PCI membership. Communist parties throughout Western Europe benefited from the wartime surge in Soviet prestige brought about by the heroism of the Red Army and Stalin's prominence as one of the "Big Three" Allied leaders. The ethos of social reformism that permeated the Resistance movements in Italy, France, and elsewhere on the Continent also lent an aura of respectability to the Western Communists, as did their own central, often preeminent, role in the anti-Nazi partisan fighting.

The PCI, however, enjoyed several special advantages. First of all, its anti-Fascist credentials were—compared to the other *Italian* political parties—unparalleled, both in the number of members imprisoned under Mussolini and the tenacity with which it sought over the years to foment domestic opposition to the Fascist regime. It was thus in a position to project a public image of martyrdom. Second, unlike the PCF, it was an equal partner in the Italian CLN from its inception in September 1943,

well before becoming a member of the national government the following
April. Third, its drawing power was enhanced by the open admissions
policy championed by Togliatti upon his return to Naples in late March
1944.

The political profile of the *partito nuovo* is discussed at length in
chapter 6. Suffice it here to say that the PCI's new mass base was afflicted
with considerable political schizophrenia. On the one hand, the rank and
file willingly engaged in electoral politics. The PCI's emergence as a mass
organization under conditions of anti-Fascist mobilization, Communist
participation in the Council of Ministers (the cabinet), and the Togliatti
leadership's receptivity to a post-Fascist democratic stage engendered
positive attitudes toward the democratic process in general. All the while,
the rapid pace of party growth precluded systematic indoctrination in
Soviet-style Marxism-Leninism. There were but fleeting allusions to Soviet theoretical positions and the cult of Stalin in the PCI press during the
immediate post-Fascist years. On the other hand, with the onset of the
Cold War pro-Sovietism of an emotional, dogmatic sort became the public
philosophy of the PCI. East-West polarization at the international level,
combined with United States support for Christian Democratic hegemony
within Italy, led the Italian Communist leaders actively to cultivate anti-
Americanism and its mirror image, pro-Sovietism. As party membership
continued to grow into the early 1950s, these twin sentiments seemed to
become a substitute for doctrinal discourse at the mass level.

American postwar animosity toward the PCI surely contributed to this
public philosophy. The depth of official opposition in the United States
was graphically illustrated in a top-secret telegram from the then director
of the Policy Planning Staff, George F. Kennan, to Secretary of State
George C. Marshall on the eve of the April 1948 Italian parliamentary
elections—in which the Communists and left-wing Socialists together
won only 31 percent of the total vote. "I question," cabled Kennan,
"whether it would not be preferable for Italian Government to outlaw
Communist Party . . . before elections. Communists would presumably
reply with civil war. . . . This would admittedly result in much violence
and probably a military division of Italy; but we are getting close to the
deadline and I think it might be preferable *to a bloodless election victory*,
unopposed by ourselves." [1] The point here is not to disparage Kennan but
to convey some sense of how Cold War hysteria caused even the most
astute American statesmen to exaggerate the danger of a Communist
takeover in Western Europe. Kennan's recommendation was rejected.
Still, the United States government went to great lengths to fan anticom-

---

1. *Western Europe*, vol. 3 of *Foreign Relations of the United States 1948* (Washington, D.C.:
Government Printing Office, 1974), 848–49; my emphasis.

munism, instigating an Italian-American letter-writing campaign to rela-
tives in Italy and threatening to withhold economic aid should a leftist
government be elected.[2]

Such conduct had a critical impact on the PCI, leaders and base alike.
In a nutshell, they had every reason to think that the advance of their
domestic political fortunes was contingent on the reduction of American
influence on the Continent. For the old-guard cadres from the Fascist era,
moreover, such anti-Americanism was not simply the result of spontaneous anger or political calculation. It also stemmed from their doctrinaire Bolshevik disdain for democracy. The new recruits may have been
ambivalent toward democratic politics, hoping for a one-shot electoral
leap to socialism. But the attitude of the older cadres was often manipulative in a traditional sectarian vein.

The views of the party elite, on the other hand, were more heterogeneous and complex. They had experienced two diverse paths of development during the long years of fascism: imprisonment or exile. Those in
the first category were closer to the old-guard cadres in outlook. Those
who returned from exile were, in contrast, more attuned to Togliatti's
expectation of a post-Fascist democratic stage, an expectation fortified by
the Comintern's popular front line and wartime Resistance policy. Not
only that, but they had a mixed view of the Soviet Union. Their adulation
of the early 1920s had been tempered by their tribulations at the hands of
the Stalinists in the late 1920s and late 1930s.

As we shall see, the influence of Togliatti and his colleagues from
exile, including Longo, was predominant in shaping the *partito nuovo*.
Yet their political perspectives were by no means clearly defined, regarding either the duration of the anticipated democratic transitional stage or
the contours of the socialist society to which it was ultimately to lead.
During the postwar decades (Togliatti headed the party till 1964, Longo
till 1972), their conceptions on both scores were vitally affected by developments in Italy, the Soviet Union, and the Communist world. At the
same time, the very success of the PCI compared to its prewar travails—
its size, steady growth in electoral strength, and expanding participation
in local government—had the effect of blunting, among the older elite,
the perceived need to articulate an Italian path to socialism.

Like most West European Communist parties, the PCI emerged from
the wartime Resistance with its national roots strengthened and its international identity attenuated—by force of circumstances if not always conviction. The advent of the Cold War quickly reversed this process. While
the United States used its political and economic leverage to promote the
domestic ostracism of the Western Communists, the Soviet Union created

2. Ibid., 816–90.

the Communist Information Bureau (Cominform) in September 1947 to reinforce the primacy of international Communist ties over national loyalties. Meanwhile, as during the 1930s, the touchstone of a West European Communist party's rectitude in Moscow's eyes remained not its commitment to revolutionary transformation but its unqualified support for the foreign policy and ideological credentials of the Soviet Union.

Nevertheless, over the longer haul the postwar international Cummunist environment changed fundamentally from what it had been during the Comintern era. Despite the Kremlin's recurring efforts to impose control and uniformity, national self-assertion and diversity became ever more pronounced. Stalin's move to create East European satellite regimes triggered the Soviet-Yugoslav split in June 1948. Khrushchev's post-1956 hopes for attaining Soviet bloc cohesion through economic and military interdependence were dashed by Chinese and Romanian demands for sovereign independence. The "general laws" for the construction of socialism (formulated after the Hungarian Revolution and widely propagated after the 1968 invasion of Czechoslovakia) were flatly rejected by West European Communist innovators. And the CPSU's attempt to regain a modicum of ideological authority over Communists not under its direct control through a pan-European Communist summit in East Berlin in June 1976 was foiled by an autonomist coalition of Yugoslavian, Romanian, Italian, Spanish, and French Communist parties.

If the international Communist movement was characterized by constant turbulence and change, the domestic political environment in which the PCI operated for almost three decades was one of the striking stability and continuity. The 1948 conquest by the Christian Democratic Party (DC) of an absolute majority of seats in the Chamber of Deputies (with 48.5 percent of the popular vote) led to its entrenchment in the bureaucratic infrastructure of the postwar Italian Republic. The DC's courtship of the "hand of Washington," which long predated Premier Alcide De Gasperi's January 1947 visit to Washington,[3] paid off handsomely in political backing and economic aid by the United States. Years after the DC's decline from majority to plurality status, moreover, it could still count on its minor coalition partners to the right and left to ensure the continuing exclusion of the PCI from the national government. Notwithstanding the Communists' gradual advance from 18.9 percent of the popular vote in 1946 to 27.2 percent in 1972, they remained on the periphery of Italian national politics. Their isolation only increased when their long-

3. Particularly informative in this regard is the chapter by Ennio Di Nolfo, "The United States and the PCI: The Years of Policy Formation, 1942–1946," in *The Italian Communist Party: Yesterday, Today, and Tomorrow,* ed. Simon Serfaty and Lawrence Gray (Westport, Conn.: Greenwood, 1980), 37–58. See also Simon Serfaty, "The United States and PCI: The Year of Decision," in ibid., 59–74.

time ally, the PSI, joined forces with the DC in a series of center-left coalition ministries beginning in 1963.

Given the immobilism of the domestic Italian political scene until the mid-1970s, the PCI elite's chief outlet for policy innovation and impact lay in the international Communist arena. Its domestic political platform remained relatively unchanged during the first three post-Fascist decades: an alliance strategy across class and religious lines to achieve structural reforms conducive to an open-ended democratic transition to socialism. In the international Communist movement, on the other hand, the Italian Communists—under the successive leaderships of Togliatti, Longo, and (from 1972) Enrico Berlinguer—took advantage of the ongoing flux to propose initiatives aimed at resisting the imposition of Soviet norms and enhancing each Communist party's independence. The PCI's post-Stalin challenge to Soviet centralism and search for transnational allies among like-minded European Communist parties form the focal point of chapter 7. Here let us only note that these efforts contributed to the party's conquest of 34.4 percent of the popular vote in the Italian parliamentary contest of 1976.

CHAPTER **6**

The Post-Fascist Democratic
Transition: The PCI
between East and West

s World War II drew to a close Italy began the post-Fascist transition to democracy anticipated (if feared) by Togliatti and others in the PCI leadership some fifteen years earlier. The Anglo-American occupation of Italy precluded any other alternative. The Communists had no choice but to accept an open-ended democratic transitional stage and the postponement of the prospect of achieving socialism into the uncertain future. What was at stake was not whether Italy would become socialist or democratic but to what extent the new Italian polity would be animated by the urge for democratic renewal rather than by fear of communism. With the escalation of Cold War tensions between the United States and the Soviet Union in 1946–47, anticommunism won out inside Italy. It became the dominant ethos of the newly formed Italian Christian Democratic Party, enabling the latter's centrist leaders to appeal to former middle-class supporters of fascism as well as to Catholic workers and progressives.[1] In 1944, however, such a denouement was not widely expected, largely because of the wartime alliance between Britain, the Soviet Union, and the United States. Still, Togliatti's foremost goal upon his return to Italy in March 1944 was to prevent political polarization. Above all he hoped to forestall a schism among the three mass parties of the left and center—the PCI, the PSI, and the DC. He thus took pains to project a

1. For an overview, see Antonio Gambino, *Storia del dopoguerra. Dalla Liberazione al potere Dc* (Bari: Laterza, 1975).

184

public image of the PCI as a democratic party geared to the defense of the Italian nation.

Togliatti's awareness that Italy was situated in an Anglo-American sphere of influence was only one of several reasons for such prudence. The years of Fascist repression had also imbued a number of the PCI's cadres with a yearning for legitimacy, for acceptance into the mainstream of Italian political life. As Togliatti put it in an editorial in *Rinascita* in the autumn of 1944, those who had "survived the harsh and heroic tests of clandestine work, of the Special Tribunal, of the prisons, of the islands of confinement, of exile, of the Spanish war," felt above all "the need to be liberated . . . from verbal extremism and from the impotence of maximalism."[2] To be sure, some of the old guard took an instrumental view of the party's newly found moderation. For them participation in the democratic process was simply a way of maneuvering the PCI into a position to subvert the democratic order. Yet such *doppiezza,* as this attitude was called, did not detract from their eager involvement in electoral politics.

For Togliatti himself, moreover, the PCI's democratic comportment was more than just the dictate of *Realpolitik.* The major lesson he drew from the Fascist experience was that the middle classes had to be won over to democracy before there could be any thought of attracting them to socialism. Gone were his illusions of the mid-1920s that the advocacy of democratic goals, or even a brief democratic interlude, might unleash a revolutionary chain reaction that would quickly lead to socialism. By 1935 his "Lessons on Fascism" revealed how aware he had become of the broad popular base of support for Mussolini's regime. And if in the mid-1930s he was alarmed by the extent of Fascist influence over the middle classes and workers, in the mid-1940s he was bent upon eliminating the possibility of a resurgence of such influence. In short, the thrust of Togliatti's postwar alliance strategy was anti-Fascist, not anticapitalist.

We may surmise that there was yet another motive for stressing the democratic and patriotic credentials of the PCI, a motive shared by Togliatti with the inner core of the PCI elite from the 1930s. Because of the repeated browbeatings they had suffered from the Stalinists, these men were even more concerned than would normally be expected to build the PCI into a mass party, to create a strong national base of support. In this way they would be able to clear their record of the charges of ineffectuality that had so often been leveled against them in the past. They doubtless also hoped to make their party less dependent on Moscow and hence less vulnerable to the whims and outbursts of Stalin's spokesmen. It

2. "Partito nuovo," *Rinascita* 1, no. 4 (October–December 1944):1–2 at 1.

seems hardly accidental that three of the men most directly involved in trying to extend the PCI's presence throughout Italian society after World War II were among the individuals most sharply criticized in 1938: Ruggero Grieco, Giuseppe Di Vittorio, and Giuseppe Dozza. In the immediate postwar years Togliatti was joined by Longo and Secchia in the top leadership of the party. The task of policy implementation, however, devolved *inter alia* upon Grieco as head of the PCI's land reform campaign in the *mezzogiorno* (southern Italy); Di Vittorio as head of the General Confederation of Italian Labor (CGIL); and Dozza as the long-time mayor of the Communist stronghold, Bologna. Meanwhile, their chief detractor of 1938, Giuseppe Berti, was relegated to the post of head of the Soviet-Italian Friendship Society. And Stalinists such as Antonio Roasio and Umberto Massola were soon removed from the inner circles of the PCI leadership.[3]

At the same time, one must guard against viewing the PCI's policies of the mid-1940s in isolation from the then current Soviet perspectives on trends in Europe. Three characteristics stand out in this regard. The first was Moscow's encouragement of nationalism and patriotism as integral parts of its national front directives. Support for such sentiments was indeed a central theme of the Soviet Union's own domestic wartime propaganda. The second was the uncertainty that apparently existed among the highest circles of the Soviet leadership regarding the prospects and paths of socialist transformation, especially in Western Europe.[4] As might be expected, Stalin made no public pronouncements on this subject. But his private remarks suggested perplexity and ambivalence. On the one hand, he spoke to Milovan Djilas of each great power imposing its own system in the areas occupied by its army.[5] But in conversations with English Labour leaders and others (including Djilas), he also contemplated a "British," or electoral, path to socialism,[6] plainly impressed by the mid-1945 victory of Clement Atlee over Churchill. These latter comments, moreover, were reminiscent of a letter sent by Stalin, Molotov, and Klement Voroshilov a decade earlier to Spanish Socialist premier,

---

3. Massola was removed from the PCI *Direzione*—although he remained a member of the Central Committee—between the party's Fifth and Sixth congresses; see *l'Unità*, January 11 and 13, 1948, page 1 each day.

4. Cf. Giuseppe Boffa, *Storia dell'Unione Sovietica*, 2 vols. (Milan: Arnoldo Mondadori Editore, 1979), 2:343–44.

5. Milovan Djilas, *Conversations with Stalin* (New York: Harcourt, Brace and World, 1962), 114.

6. Karel Kaplan, "Il piano di Stalin," *Panorama* [Milan] 15, no. 575 (April 26, 1977):169–89 at 174–77; for background information on Kaplan's documentation, see Mario Margiocco, "Segretissimo dall'Est," in ibid., 164–69.

Largo Caballero, in which they raised the possibility of a "parliamentary path" of revolutionary development in republican Spain.[7]

The third facet of the Soviet Union's position was its public support for a post-Fascist transitional stage in Europe, East and West, that would be national in form and democratic in theory if not in fact. The talk of "new paths" to socialism and the revival of the slogans of "people's democracy" and "democracy of a new type" by every Communist leader in Eastern Europe pointed to a coordinated policy. Political developments in Poland and Romania revealed, of course, that Stalin viewed such a democratic transitional stage in areas of vital Soviet interest as but a ploy even in the short run. All the same, there was a brief period of genuine democracy in Soviet-occupied Hungary, when the Communists won a mere 17 percent of the popular vote in December 1945.

What remains unclear is the genesis of this transitional stage policy. Everything we know about Stalin's temperament suggests that he was utterly hostile to the democratic strains in the Western Marxist tradition. During 1936 and again during 1945–46—the two times he broached the idea of a parliamentary path to socialism—Stalin was above all preoccupied with securing the national interests of the Soviet Union (i.e., avoidance of war in the mid-1930s, hegemony over Eastern Europe a decade later) and consolidating his own grip on all levers of domestic power. It is likely, therefore, that insofar as he attended to the doctrinal aspects of the international Communist movement, he was influenced by such individuals as Dimitrov and Togliatti, on the one hand, and Andrei Zhdanov on the other.

The imprint of the two Comintern secretaries, Dimitrov and Togliatti, on Stalin's policy toward Spain was clear. The Soviet leader's expression of support for a parliamentary path to socialism in December 1936 was a natural corollary of their formulations earlier that year of "people's democracy" and "new democracy" as anti-Fascist, progressive variants of bourgeois democracy that could ease the way to socialism. The extension of Dimitrov's stay in the Soviet Union for over a year after the liberation of Bulgaria[8] strongly suggests his contribution to the evolving Soviet line on Eastern Europe. Togliatti's departure from the Soviet Union in late February 1944 ruled out involvement in policy making with regard to that region. But, as will be argued below, he surely participated in the shaping of Soviet initiatives toward post-Fascist Italy and perhaps Western Europe in general.

---

7. For excerpts from the December 1936 letter, see Spriano, *I comunisti europei e Stalin* (Turin: Giulio Einaudi editore, 1983), 19.

8. Boffa, *Storia dell'Unione Sovietica* 2:343.

As for Zhdanov, Stalin's heir apparent and a key figure in CPSU relations with foreign Communist parties in 1946–47, the findings of Werner G. Hahn indicate that he can be classified as neither a sectarian nor an innovator; rather, he was an ideological revivalist. At home he pushed for the reimposition of doctrinal norms in culture, party work, and social organization. But he remained tolerant of diverse viewpoints in the natural sciences and philosophy.[9] As the Cold War developed he shifted from support for domestic consumerism and East–West cooperation[10] to the two-camp imagery and anti-Americanism with which his name became identified after the creation of the Cominform in September 1947. Nevertheless, his elastic orthodoxy in domestic matters was consistent with the mid-1940s search for new and different paths to socialism abroad. Only as Zhdanov's influence declined from early 1948 onward was doctrine transformed into dogma and concern with the ideological shape of social transformation superseded by a system of Soviet imperial controls over Eastern Europe. Zhdanov's role as overseer of the international Communist movement was thereupon assumed by Mikhail Suslov and Pavel Yudin, among others.[11] Meanwhile, extreme chauvinism and dogmatism came to dominate all areas of Soviet academic inquiry, most notoriously biology. And Zhdanov himself was out of favor when he died on August 31, 1948.[12]

It was during the period of Zhdanov's ascendancy that CPSU analysts in the academic community began to explore the prospect of a democratic transitional stage on the path to socialism. Such a major figure as Eugene S. Varga, director of the prestigious Soviet Institute of the World Economy and World Politics, argued—however cautiously—that the conquest of socialism might even come about by using rather than destroying the institutions of the bourgeois state. In his controversial book, *Changes in the Economy of Capitalism as a Result of the Second World War,* which was written during 1945–46 and published in September 1946, Varga anticipated both the temporary stabilization of capitalism and, under the stimulus of mass pressure, the possibility of some degree of welfare-oriented state planning at one and the same time. Varga's line of reasoning clearly harmonized with West European Communist policies. If the collapse of European capitalism was not imminent, a frontal attack against it through radical demands and insurrectionary activity would be futile. Furthermore, if government regulation of the capitalist economy in the public interest was possible, the West European Communist parties would

9. Werner G. Hahn, *Postwar Soviet Politics: The Fall of Zhdanov and the Defeat of Moderation, 1946–53* (Ithaca, N.Y.: Cornell University Press, 1982), chaps. 1 and 2.
10. Ibid., 20–25.
11. On the political ascendancy of Suslov and Yudin, see ibid., 77, 94, and 100–112.
12. Ibid., chap. 3.

do well to advance this cause from within their respective governments. They might thus be able to convert the bourgeois state into a "democracy of a new type" that would, as Varga suggested, bring about the peaceful transformation of capitalism into socialism.[13]

In short, the PCI elite's urge to distance itself from Moscow in terms of actual policies and power relationships (if not ideological alignment) was not inconsistent with Soviet perspectives on the European Communist movement in the mid-1940s.

On the other hand, the Italian party leaders also had to contend with pervasive pro-Sovietism among the cadres and recruits of the *partito nuovo*. Among the activists dating from the 1920s, most—whether because of clandestinity or confinement—had not known firsthand either the popular front initiatives or the Stalinist vituperation experienced by their exiled leaders. Their militant pro-Sovietism of the early Bolshevik era thus remained untarnished. Meanwhile, many members of the burgeoning PCI rank and file were captivated by the myth of Soviet prowess spawned by the popular image of the Soviet Union as all but single-handedly resisting the Nazi war machine for most of World War II.[14] As a result, new members as well as veteran cadres became active participants in Italy's transition to democracy while remaining sentimental enthusiasts of an idealized view of Soviet socialism.

Here it bears mentioning that the character of the PCI in the mid-1940s differed substantially from that of the French Communist Party. The PCF's success during the popular front years not only spared its leaders the vagaries of Stalinist recrimination but also led to the formation of a large body of working-class cadres drilled in democratic centralism and steeped in the 1930s' brand of Soviet Marxism-Leninism.[15] The French party leadership thus had the will and the apparatus to shape its expanded postwar base in the Stalinist mold. As Thorez reported to the PCF's June 1945 congress, the party rolls had grown from 340,000 in late 1937 to over 900,000 at the war's end.[16] This represented a sharp contrast with the PCI, whose membership had leaped from a mere 5,000 or so in mid-1943 to over 1,700,000 in December 1945. The PCF had, in other words, an

13. This interpretation owes much to the discussion of Varga in Jerry F. Hough's "The Consolidation of the Stalin Orthodoxy," in *The Impact of World War II on the Soviet Union*, ed. Susan J. Linz (Totowa, N.J.: Rowman & Allanheld, 1985).

14. Longo himself wrote to Togliatti in early 1945 that the Soviet Union's widespread influence was responsible for "an increase in the prestige and authority of our comrades"; Luigi Longo, *I centri dirigenti del PCI nella Resistenza* (Rome: Editori Riuniti, 1974), 486.

15. Cf. Irwin M. Wall, *French Communism in the Era of Stalin: The Quest for Unity and Integration, 1945–1962* (Westport, Conn.: Greenwood, 1983), 11–13 and 18–19.

16. For his speech to the congress, see Maurice Thorez, *Une politique de grandeur française* (Paris: Éditions sociales, 1945), 352.

abundance of seasoned cadres to inculcate doctrinal pro-Sovietism and orthodox *ouvrièrisme* in its new recruits. In the case of the PCI, however, the pro-Sovietism of the base was initially a more emotional and spontaneous phenomenon that found only a faint reflection in the official party line and media.

All this was to change with the massive intervention of the United States in domestic Italian affairs and the relegation of the PCI to the periphery of national politics in 1947 and 1948. At that point the PCI leaders themselves began to foster a cult of Soviet superiority in the party press and in their formal statements. In doing so they vented their profound frustration over the political dead-end in which they found themselves. They likewise acquired a surrogate ideological matrix for their doctrinally untutored rank and file. But, on the negative side, they created a potentially explosive contradiction between their private awareness of the flaws of Stalinism and their public depiction of the Soviet Union's perfection. This discrepancy was to engender an all but untenable situation for the PCI elite during the destalinization crisis of 1956. For at that time the contrast between the perceptions of past Soviet reality held by the leaders and those held by the led was to prove too great to be bridged by fiat from above. As will be argued in chapter 7, the departures from Soviet orthodoxy advanced by Togliatti in June 1956 thus proved to be politically premature.

This chapter undertakes a review of the generally known circumstances of Togliatti's *svolta* of Salerno and subsequent policy of national unity. It then analyzes the complex character of the *partito nuovo*, the new mass-based PCI. The third section briefly explores the reverberations of the Soviet–American confrontation and the Cominform era upon the PCI.

Togliatti, the *Svolta* of Salerno, and the Policy of National Unity

Togliatti's *svolta* of Salerno, as his late March 1944 pronouncement that his party would cooperate with the Badoglio government became known, signified two fundamental directives. The first was that the PCI should enter the mainstream of Italian political life, engaging in a policy of interclass collaboration in the interests of national unity and democratic renewal. The second pertained to the nature of the *partito nuovo* itself. The masses flocking to the Communist banner were to become the ward heelers of a huge electoral machine rather than antisystem rebels calling for a new social order. The vision of a future socialist transformation might sustain them, but revolutionary rhetoric was discouraged. Neither criticism nor propaganda but participation in the emerging structures of a democratic Italy was the order of the day.

The Svolta *and Soviet Foreign Policy*

On March 27, 1944, Togliatti returned to Italy after almost two decades in exile with orders for the PCI to shed its antimonarchist intransigence and accept office in any Italian government. This *svolta* was not only in accord with Togliatti's own political preferences, but it also fit Stalin's larger strategy for the division of Europe into a Soviet and Western sphere of influence. Indeed, the PCI's shift was plainly synchronized with the PCF's decision to accede to Charles de Gaulle's terms for participation in the French provisional government in Algiers.

A brief review of the international setting will underscore the role of the *svolta* in Moscow's overall European policy. On March 13, 1944, the Soviet Union granted formal recognition to the royal government of King Vittorio Emanuele. On April 1 Togliatti, barely back from Moscow, announced in a press conference the PCI's readiness to participate in a cabinet headed by Badoglio or anyone else, even if it were invested by the king.[17] About this same time the PCF also engineered a *volte-face*. Unlike the PCI's hitherto hostile attitude toward Badoglio, the PCF had supported General de Gaulle. In fact it held one-fourth of the seats in the Consultative Assembly the general had established in Algiers in November 1943. On the other hand, the PCF had refused to join his provisional government (formerly the French Committee of National Liberation) unless permitted to select its own cabinet posts as well as the individuals who would occupy them. This de Gaulle consistently refused to allow. Then suddenly, in a letter to the general dated March 24, 1944, the PCF Central Committee backed down.[18] And during the first week of April the French Communists accepted the relatively minor posts of commissar of air and commissar of state under de Gaulle.[19]

A Soviet emissary, Alexander Bogomolov, apparently served as the intermediary between Moscow and both the French and Italian Communist parties at this juncture. Bogomolov had been the Soviet ambassador to the Allied governments-in-exile in London during the first half of the war and representative to the Free French (and the PCF) in Algiers during the autumn and early winter of 1943–44.[20] He then succeeded Andrei Vyshinsky as Soviet representative to the Allied Advisory Council for Italy. In early January 1944 a senior member of the Italian Foreign Ministry had suggested the establishment of diplomatic relations to Vyshinsky,

17. *The Times* [London], April 3, 1944, 4.
18. Luigi Cortesi, "Palmiro Togliatti, la 'svolta di Salerno' e l'eredità gramsciana," *Belfagor* 30, no. 1 (January 31, 1975):1–44 at 5–6.
19. Alfred J. Rieber, *Stalin and the French Communist Party: 1941–1947* (New York: Columbia University Press, 1962), 55–59.
20. *Sovetsko-frantsuzskie otnosheniia vo vremia velikoi otechestvennoi voiny, 1941–1945: dokumenty i materialy* (Moscow, 1959), doc. 10:50–51; doc. 91:192–95; and doc. 119:231.

stressing the boost to "Soviet influence in Italy" which would come from such a step. Only on March 4, however, did Bogomolov inform Badoglio of the Soviet Union's readiness to proceed with diplomatic recognition.[21] Thereafter, sometime between March 12 and March 19 the PCI leaders in the south were informed of the approaching change in the party's line.[22] Since Togliatti had not yet arrived, Bogomolov must have been the source of this information. In view of the ease of communications between Naples and Algiers, we may assume that he also remained in close contact with the French Communists during this period.

It seems that the simultaneous shifts in PCF and PCI policy, coming as they did on the heels of the Soviet Union's recognition of Italy, signaled Stalin's acceptance of a political division of Europe along the lines of Allied spheres of military responsibility. This decision, in turn, was very possibly precipitated by Churchill's speech of February 22, 1944, before the House of Commons in which he gave his unqualified support to the Italian government of Badoglio and King Vittorio Emanuele. Not coincidentally, in this same address the British prime minister also, and for the first time, publicly took Moscow's side on the question of the postwar Soviet–Polish frontier.[23]

Neither Stalin nor Churchill is known to have been reluctant to apportion the body politic of Europe according to *raison d'état*. The Soviet–German secret protocols of 1939 and 1940 bluntly delineated the respective "spheres of influence" of the Soviet Union and the Third Reich. By the same token, it was Churchill who in October 1944 calculated the destiny of Southeastern Europe in terms of percentages.[24] More to the point at hand, during the talks among the Big Three at Teheran in late November 1943 Stalin had spelled out Soviet demands for a two-hundred-mile westward extension of the Soviet Union's pre-1939 frontier with Poland, while Churchill had flatly rejected the idea of Soviet involvement in Western Europe.[25] Roosevelt had held aloof, for domestic political reasons, from any concrete agreement regarding Poland's frontiers and continued to do so during the early weeks of 1944.[26] Meanwhile some

---

21. Mario Toscano, *Pagine di storia diplomatica contemporanea*, 2 vols. (Milan: Giuffrè Editore, 1963), 2:324–27 and 333–39.

22. Velio Spano participated in an anti-Badoglio rally in Naples on March 12. The morning of March 20 he confided to the Socialist leader, Oreste Lizzadri, that the PCI was about to shift its line; see Lizzadri's *Il regno di Badoglio* (Milan: Edizioni Avanti, 1963), 159.

23. *Parliamentary Debates* (Commons), vol. 397 (1943–44), cols. 679–701; cf. Herbert Feis, *Churchill Roosevelt Stalin: The War They Waged and the Peace They Sought* (Princeton: Princeton University Press, 1957), 297.

24. Ibid., 447–50; cf. the more recent findings of Daniel Yergin in *Shattered Peace: The Origins of the National Security State* (Boston: Houghton Mifflin, 1977).

25. Feis, *Churchill Roosevelt Stalin*, 271–72 and 284–87.

26. Ibid., 284–85 and 295.

American official circles remained resolutely opposed to the royal Italian government, despite pressure from influential sectors of the Italian–American community.[27] In January 1944 an American economic mission to Italy, headed by Adlai Stevenson, reported that Badoglio and the king commanded "little respect or support" among the Italian people. And just prior to Churchill's February 22 speech, Washington assented to proposals advanced by the recently formed executive junta of the member parties of the southern CLN for the abdication of the king.[28]

In short, Churchill's speech may well have represented an implicit offer of a deal with Stalin which would circumvent the Americans: to wit, Soviet acceptance of Churchill's position regarding Italy in exchange for open British support for the Soviet Union's absorption of a two-hundred-mile-wide chunk of Polish territory. Diplomatic recognition of the royal government of Italy on March 13, 1944, along with the policy reversals of the Italian and French Communist parties, constituted Stalin's reply.

It may, of course, be argued that the Anglo-American furor over Russia's unilateral recognition of Italy hardly bespoke any tacit or behind-the-scenes arrangement.[29] Yet it is likely that the meaning of the Soviet diplomatic move was misconstrued by the British and Americans. Soviet spokesmen had from the summer of 1943 been agitating for some involvement in, or at least greater information on, decisions regarding France and Italy. Moscow had already recognized de Gaulle's Committee of National Liberation on August 26, 1943, refraining from doing so *before* then solely as a result of Churchill's intervention.[30] Stalin repeatedly complained that Moscow was ill-informed on the Anglo-American armistice negotiations with Badoglio. The upshot was the formation in November 1943 of the Allied Advisory Council for Italy; but the council had consultative powers only and was clearly subordinate to the Anglo-American Allied Control Commission.[31]

Vojtech Mastny has persuasively argued that until mid-1944 Stalin did not perceive even his own sphere of influence in Poland as a watertight, exclusively Soviet-oriented domain.[32] Viewed from this perspective, the Soviet leader had no reason to consider France and Italy as impermeable

27. Di Nolfo, "The United States and the PCI: The Years of Policy Formation, 1942–1946," in *The Italian Communist Party: Yesterday, Today, and Tomorrow,* ed. Simon Serfaty and Lawrence Gray (Westport, Conn.: Greenwood, 1980), 37–58.
28. Norman Kogan, *Italy and the Allies* (Cambridge, Mass.: Harvard University Press, 1956), 56–57.
29. Feis, *Churchill Roosevelt Stalin,* 327–28.
30. Rieber, *Stalin and the French Communist Party,* 42–44.
31. Feis, *Churchill Roosevelt Stalin,* 170–74 and 182–87.
32. Vojtech Mastny, *Russia's Road to the Cold War* (New York: Columbia University Press, 1979), 167–82.

Anglo-American bastions. All the same, just as Stalin never wavered in his intent to achieve Soviet predominance in Eastern Europe, he was prepared to acknowledge Anglo-American predominance in Western Europe. His diplomatic overtures toward Italy and other Western powers were simply designed to secure a legitimate Soviet presence in those areas—to enhance the Soviet Union's international prestige, if you will (as well as to accommodate Churchill). This is suggested not only by the subsequent cooperative conduct of the PCI and PCF in their respective coalition governments but also by the fact that Moscow, in response to British and American protests, agreed in early April 1944 to reduce its relations with Italy from de jure to de facto recognition.[33]

The timing of Togliatti's departure from Moscow lends support to the supposition that Churchill's February 22, 1944, speech spurred Soviet policymakers into spelling out these limited intentions toward Italy, France, and, by implication, other West European countries. Sometime during the autumn of 1943 the PCI leader requested permission from Badoglio to return to Italy. Around the turn of the new year permission was granted,[34] and in January 1944 the British and American governments indicated that they had no objections to this step.[35] Yet Togliatti himself stated in 1961 that he did not leave the Soviet Union until "late February 1944."[36] It may thus be surmised that his departure was delayed until Moscow's policy toward Italy was finalized; and this occurred only after Churchill's February 22 speech.

We have no hard information on Togliatti's role in the formulation of the Soviet Union's March 1944 initiatives, and he himself denied in 1951 that he even knew of the Soviet move to recognize Italy until his arrival in Algiers.[37] However, the timing of the denial suggests that it was linked to the PCI's efforts to refute charges of subservience to Moscow during the height of the Cold War. In actuality, it is improbable that he was not involved in shaping a policy in which he was to play so central a part. Indeed, there are those who speculate that Togliatti himself pressed for the entire *svolta*—including Soviet diplomatic recognition.[38]

33. Kogan, *Italy and the Allies,* 59.

34. Agostino Degli Espinosa, *Il regno del Sud: 8 settembre 1943–4 giugno 1944* (Rome: Migliaresi Editore, 1946), 264; cf. Toscano, *Pagine di storia diplomatica contemporanea* 2:322.

35. Cordell Hull, *The Memoirs of Cordell Hull,* 2 vols. (New York: Macmillan, 1948), 2:1553.

36. Palmiro Togliatti, "Diversità e unità nel movimento operaio e comunista internazionale," *Rinascita* 18, no. 12 (December 1961):909–16 at 912. Spriano states that Togliatti left Moscow February 18, 1944, but the sources he cites (Cerreti, *Con Togliatti e Thorez,* 284; Ferrara and Ferrara, *Conversando con Togliatti,* 311) do not bear this out; the Ferraras, in fact, give the date of departure as February 26 or so. Cf. Paolo Spriano, *La Resistenza, Togliatti e il partito nuovo,* vol. 5 of *Storia del Partito comunista italiano* (Turin: Giulio Einaudi editore, 1975), 282–83.

37. Spriano, ibid., 283, n. 4.

38. See, for example, Cortesi, "Palmiro Togliatti," *Belfagor* 30, no. 1 (January 31, 1975):2–7; and C. Pinzani, "Togliatti e l'Unione Sovietica," *Rinascita* 32, no. 15 (April 11, 1975).

Whatever its precise origins, once the decision on the *svolta* had been made, its implementation had to await Togliatti's circuitous journey home via the Middle East and Algiers. There was little other alternative to this delay in view of the altercations over the Badoglio issue which had troubled the domestic PCI leadership, and the commitment of many cadres to the CLN's intransigence on this score. Hence it was only after Togliatti's return to Naples and briefing before the PCI National Council on March 30–31—at which the new policy was approved[39]—that the *svolta* was publicly announced.

Despite the consternation of the other CLN members over the PCI's initiative, the step led to the formation on April 24 of a cabinet of all six anti-Fascist parties headed by Badoglio and invested by the king. Following the liberation of Rome and the controversial transfer of royal authority to Crown Prince Umberto on June 5, 1944, Togliatti reportedly fought for the inclusion of Badoglio in a revamped cabinet embracing representatives of the Rome CLN.[40] It seems hardly coincidental that this was also the express wish of Churchill.[41] The other anti-Fascist leaders, however, insisted on excluding Badoglio. And he was succeeded as premier by Ivanoe Bonomi, chairman of the Rome CLN.

On balance, it would appear that Togliatti was trying to maneuver his party into a position of influence by pandering to Churchill and coming to terms with Badoglio. Whatever his concrete role in devising overall Soviet policy toward Italy, his own aim was clear. As he stated at a meeting of the CLN's executive junta on April 18, he wished above all to bring the PCI into "a position of equality with any other party."[42]

The distribution of posts within the subsequent Italian wartime ministries indicates that Togliatti's wish was fulfilled. In the cabinet named by Badoglio on April 21, 1944, and installed three days later, five ministers without portfolio were designated, corresponding to the five major CLN parties, with Togliatti occupying the PCI post. The minister of agriculture and forests was also a Communist, Fausto Gullo.[43] In the first Bonomi cabinet, named on June 9, 1944, Togliatti and Gullo were reassigned to their previous positions.[44] In a second Bonomi cabinet formed in December 1944, Togliatti became one of two vice-premiers, sharing this honor with a Christian Democrat. Gullo retained the agriculture portfolio.

39. *Il comunismo italiano nella seconda guerra mondiale* (Rome: Editori Riuniti, 1963), doc. 42:224–27.

40. Kogan, *Italy and the Allies,* 77; cf. Pietro Badoglio, *L'Italia nella seconda guerra mondiale: Memorie e documenti* (Verona: Arnoldo Mondadori Editore, 1946), 218–19.

41. Hull, *Memoirs* 2:1564.

42. "La Giunta esecutiva dei partiti antifascisti nel Sud (gennaio–aprile 1944): Verbali," *Il movimento di liberazione in Italia,* nos. 28–29 (January–March 1954):41–121 at 114.

43. *Allied Control Commission Weekly Bulletin* 1, no. 3 (April 22, 1944):1.

44. Ibid. 1, no. 10 (June 10, 1944):1.

A Communist economist, Antonio Pesenti, became minister of finance, while Scoccimarro was named head of the newly created Ministry of Occupied Territories.[45] And in the first postwar cabinet, headed by Actionist leader Ferruccio Parri, Togliatti became minister of justice and Scoccimarro minister of finance.[46]

Domestic Policy Implications

Togliatti was to lead his party in a policy of national solidarity for the next three years. From the vantage point of what was transpiring during this time in Eastern Europe, where Communist parties everywhere were maneuvering for exclusive power, the PCI leaders bent over backward not to offend their moderate coalition partners.

Togliatti initially justified this line by citing the need for a united Resistance struggle against the Nazi occupation forces. This motif was soon joined and then replaced by warnings of a Fascist resurgence and appeals to close ranks against the most reactionary circles of Italian society.[47] The contentious institutional question and the future political structure of Italy were to be decided by popular consultation: a referendum and a constitutional assembly. Meanwhile, the PCI cemented its ties with the Italian Socialists, reviving the mid-1930s call for the eventual fusion of the two working-class parties. And it also cultivated high-level contacts and agreements with the Christian Democrats. It thus assured itself a place in the coalition ministries headed by Alcide De Gasperi which governed Italy from December 1945 until May 1947. All the while, Togliatti exhorted party members to avoid sterile criticism and to participate constructively in the tasks of economic recovery and democratic renewal.[48]

The public policies that flowed from this general orientation have been analyzed by others and need only be briefly touched on here.[49] By way of introduction, the PCI's approach to discrete issues was usually characterized by a willingness to compromise, to sacrifice its stated preferences in order to achieve a consensus in cabinet deliberations or in the Constitutional Assembly elected in June 1946. The party's position on the Lateran

45. Ibid. 1, no. 36 (December 10, 1944):1.
46. Ibid. 2, no. 12 (June 23, 1945):1.
47. Palmiro Togliatti, *Politica Comunista (Discorsi dall'aprile 1944 al'agosto 1945)* (Rome: Società Editrice l'Unità, 1945), passim.
48. Ibid., 18–19, 96, 172–76.
49. See, for example, Giorgio Galli, *Storia del Partito comunista italiano* (Milan: Schwarz Editore, 1958), 235–93; Donald Sassoon, *The Strategy of the Italian Communist Party* (New York: St. Martin's, 1981), 8–97; and Lawrence Gray, "From Gramsci to Togliatti: The *Partito Nuovo* and the Mass Basis of Italian Communism," in *The Italian Communist Party*, ed. Serfaty and Gray, 21–35.

Pacts of 1929 illustrates this well. Communist spokesmen repeatedly called for a revision of the concordat, for an agreement that would regulate relations between the Vatican and the Italian church but also disestablish Catholicism as the state religion of Italy. They expounded on the dangers of a "reborn mass anti-clericalism" that the continuation of the privileged position of the church would generate.[50] Yet when push came to shove in March 1947, the PCI joined with the Christian Democrats in supporting the incorporation of the existing concordat into the Constitution of the new republic (Article 7).[51] On this controversial question it broke with the lay parties of both center and left, its Socialist allies included. In doing so it plainly hoped to blunt the anti-Communist crusade launched by Pope Pius XII with his November 1946 battle cry, "either for Christ or against Christ." The vote, coming as it did when pressure was mounting to exclude the PCI from the government, bespoke the intensity with which the party hoped to avoid such a denouement. The fundamental aim of the vote, however, was to reduce political polarization between Communists and Catholics, and thus to enhance the electoral appeal of the Communists.

Togliatti reversed himself in a similar fashion on the issue of amnesty for former Fascists. In his speeches of 1944 and 1945 he urged the punishment of those responsible for Italy's two decades of tyranny, echoing one of the stipulations for a "new democracy" he propounded in his 1936 essay on Spain. Yet as minister of justice under De Gasperi, he went along with the other party leaders in drafting a law to pardon former Fascist cadres not implicated in actual crimes.[52] This move recalled the PCI's discredited 1936 appeal for national reconciliation rather than the blanket anti-Fascist prescriptions associated with the Spanish Civil War and the Italian Resistance. But by this very token it underscored Togliatti's concern with winning over former Fascists to the postwar democratic order.

The PCI's stand on economic issues reflected the same kind of ambiguity. On the one hand, the party's stated purpose was to work toward a more equitable distribution of wealth, a "progressive democracy" in which farmers would own the land they tilled, workers would receive a just wage, and the power of the "plutocrats," the "great economic oligarchies," would be curbed. On the other hand, the Communist leaders were also attuned to the requirements of postwar economic reconstruction.

50. "Totalitarismo?" (lead editorial), *Rinascita* 3, nos. 11–12 (November–December 1946):289–91.
51. "Sui rapporti tra la Chiesa e lo Stato," Session 75, March 25, 1947, in *Discorsi alla Costituente*, by Palmiro Togliatti (Rome: Editori Riuniti, 1973), 41–56.
52. Gambino, *Storia del dopoguerra*, 19–22.

As Togliatti made clear to a party economic conference in August 1945, the PCI must develop constructive solutions to combat inflation and raise productivity. Polemicizing against sectarian approaches, he deplored the notion of "the worse, the better," debunked as "utopian" the idea of a national economic plan at that time, and expressed reservations toward even limited nationalization.[53] He was backed up on this score by Di Vittorio, head of the unified CGIL from its creation in June 1944. As Di Vittorio flatly declared in early 1946, protection of the interests of laborers must be reconciled with the "need to increase production and improve quality, to revive vital productive firms and force the development of the general economy," notwithstanding the "harsh sacrifices" this would require of the working masses.[54]

The party's position on land reform was less equivocal: uncultivated agricultural property in the Po Valley and the impoverished south should be given to landless peasants. The Communists organized and agitated widely in behalf of this goal.[55] Still, Togliatti repeatedly stressed the PCI's support for the interests of middle-class farmers as well as landless peasants.[56] And the head of the party's section on agricultural affairs from 1947 until his death in 1955 was Grieco, Togliatti's long-time ally in the struggle for flexible and realistic transitional strategies.[57] Even as the PCI intensified its mobilization of the countryside, Grieco spoke of eliminating all "precapitalist" obstructions to the development of agricultural productivity and of forming land reform committees representative of "all the population" for the purpose, *inter alia,* of resolving "contrasts that can emerge among diverse categories of peasants."[58]

Turning to purely political questions, the PCI leadership's attitude toward the local CLNs during the last months of the war underscored its preference for conventional electoral (and parliamentary) politics over militant grassroots democracy. In a word, the party endorsed the depoliticization of the CLN structure. This became clear during a head-on clash with the Pd'A over the future of the CLN network in northern Italy. In August 1944 Premier Bonomi had authorized the CLNAI to coordinate all political and military activities in occupied Italy in the name of the

53. Togliatti, *Poitica Comunista,* 327–43.
54. Giuseppe Di Vittorio, "Il movimento sindacale nella società democratica italiana," *Rinascita* 3, no. 4 (April 1946):71–73 at 72.
55. The key work on this subject is Sidney G. Tarrow's *Peasant Communism in Southern Italy* (New Haven: Yale University Press, 1967).
56. A case in point was his speech of September 24, 1946, "Ceto medio e Emilia Rossa," *Critica marxista* 2, nos. 4–5 (July–October 1964):130–58.
57. "Prefazione di Giorgio Amendola" in *Scritti scelti,* by Ruggero Grieco, 2 vols. (Rome: Editori Riuniti, 1966), 1:lviii and lxvi.
58. Ruggero Grieco, "Prospettive della riforma agraria," *Rinascita* 4, nos. 11–12 (November–December 1947):324–27.

Rome government.[59] On November 20, 1944, the Pd'A circulated an open letter proposing that the CLNAI transform itself instead into the legal government of northern Italy until after the expulsion of all German forces.[60] The Actionists were also ready to relinquish the CLN unanimity rule in favor of democratically elected local governments in liberated areas.[61] Plainly they wished to exploit the revolutionary spirit pervading the northern Resistance movement.

The PCI, in a reply dated November 26, 1944, stressed that it too opposed the unanimity rule in principle,[62] a position Togliatti reiterated several weeks later in a *l'Unità* interview.[63] Yet on the crucial issue of the powers of the CLNAI, the *Direzione* cautioned: "It is important to reaffirm with particular insistence . . . our decisive desire to avoid any manifestation which might, even formally, undermine the principle of unity and national discipline."[64] It was more openly negative in a declaration of January 7, 1945, asserting that after liberation the CLNs should serve only as "auxiliary organs" of the central government.[65] In late May 1945, in the wake of the CLN-organized insurrections that swept the northern Italian cities prior to the victorious Allied advance, Togliatti publicly rejected the Pd'A's proposal for a national assembly of delegates from the local CLNs.[66] And on July 3, 1945, the PCI *Direzione* enjoined the Italian workers to bear in mind that any further steps toward the renewal of Italy "must be accomplished by means of the democratic path of the Constitutional Assembly." It thereupon exhorted Communists to devote all their energy to the forthcoming election campaign for that body.[67]

However, the Liberals and Christian Democrats, correctly betting on the rapid dissipation of the spirit of Resistance radicalism, managed to delay both the election to the Constitutional Assembly and the referendum on the House of Savoy until June 2, 1946. Meanwhile the Parri government floundered and finally fell in November 1945. This led to the formation the following month of the first cabinet of Alcide De Gasperi. The five major CLN parties (the Democratic Labor Party had by then ceased to

---

59. Franco Catalano, *Storia del CLNAI* (Bari: Editori Laterza, 1956), 218.

60. "Lettera aperta del Partito d'Azione a tutti i partiti aderenti al Comitato di Liberazione Nazionale," text reprinted in *Critica marxista* 3, no. 2 (March–April 1965):48–58 at 53.

61. Ibid., passim.

62. "Lettera aperta del Partito Comunista Italiano ai Partiti e alle organizzazioni di massa aderenti al CLNAI," *LNL* 2, no. 21–22 (December 15, 1944):7–12.

63. "Gli insegnamenti della crisi," *l'Unità*, December 12, 1944, 1.

64. "Lettera aperta," *LNL* 2, nos. 21–22 (December 15, 1944):11.

65. "Risoluzione della Direzione del PCI," *l'Unità*, January 7, 1945, 1.

66. Leo Valiani, *L'avvento di De Gasperi: Tre anni di politica italiana* (Turin: Francesco de Silva, 1949), 14–16.

67. *Il comunismo italiano*, doc. 73:338–43 at 340.

exist) continued to hold portfolios on the basis of parity. But as the 1946 elections were to prove, neither the Liberals nor the Actionists had any mass appeal. Of the popular vote, 18.9 percent went to the PCI, 20.7 percent to the Socialists, and 35.2 percent to the Christian Democrats, with the balance split among the half-dozen or so smaller parties. The brief era of tripartite government thus began with the left and center in uneasy equilibrium.

The Political Profile of the *Partito Nuovo*

On December 29, 1945, the Fifth PCI Congress convened in Rome. Eighteen hundred delegates representing a membership of more than 1.75 million assembled to hear Togliatti's formal affirmation of the moderate line described above. To what extent did the new party base comprehend that line? To what degree did the old-guard cadres—veterans of clandestinity, persecution, and the partisan war in northern Italy—share the views of the PCI elite? Was the new *Direzione* itself united? We have seen the cleavages that developed among the domestic party leaders in late 1943 over the postion to take toward Badoglio and the even more searing issue of Togliatti's authority when in Moscow. Did similar differences emerge after the *svolta* of Salerno? Not only that, but was Togliatti's subsequent policy of national unity viewed as a realistic program or simply as a ploy? Should electoral politics not be accompanied by grassroots militancy? Did the PCI not intend to use its anticipated electoral gains to push for a left-wing government and eventual Communist domination along the lines of a "people's democracy" Soviet-style? Or, alternatively, were its goals already then widely perceived within the party as more limited? In short, did "progressive democracy," the term Togliatti used instead of "people's democracy" or even "new democracy" after his return to Italy, carry the connotation of a real transitional stage during which the proletariat would cooperate with middle-class democrats until such time as the latter embraced socialism?

In answering these questions one is on firmer ground when speaking of the party leadership and even the rank and file of the *partito nuovo* than when trying to fathom the outlook of the old-guard cadres. The convictions of the PCI elite can be gleaned from archival sources as well as from the particular slant they gave to agitprop materials destined for the party at large. In this latter category belong, *inter alia,* Togliatti's public speeches as well as the articles that appeared in *Rinascita,* the journal he edited beginning in June 1944. As Longo commented in a letter to Togliatti in early February 1945, both *Rinascita* and "all the speeches of Ercoli" enormously aided the northern party center in "deepening the study of our line and clarifying it to all the comrades."[68] The political attitudes of the new members can be deduced from the timing and circumstances of their admission into the PCI; for, the vast majority joined only after the PCI's entry into the government and Togliatti's articulation of the party's moderate program and electoral orientation. The mentality of the long-time militants remains more elusive, however, partly because whatever doubts they had regarding Togliatti's ballot box approach were offset by an ingrained sense of party discipline.

The Party Elite: Unity in Diversity

With regard to the *svolta,* the reaction of the provisional *Direzione* established in late August 1943 was one of general acceptance. One of the *svolta's* most ardent supporters in inner party councils turned out to be Amendola. He and Scoccimarro, it may be recalled, had been outspoken opponents of any compromise whatsoever with Badoglio and the king in late 1943. His attitude thus underscored the changes that had since occurred in the political climate of the anti-Fascist underground. Even before Amendola had any inkling of the *svolta,* he began to press for some modification of the republican intransigence that was by late winter 1944 beginning to tear apart the Rome CLN. As the Liberals and Christian Democrats, along with CLN president Bonomi, gave signs of responding to overtures from the Badoglio government for a political agreement that would not impugn the constitutional powers of the House of Savoy, the Socialists and Actionists reacted with threats to boycott the CLN.[69] Amendola pleaded for an accommodation that would preserve the unity of the anti-Fascist parties while also contributing to a united war effort against the Germans. As he bluntly stated at a meeting of the PCI's Rome center on March 11, 1944, the enhanced domestic and international standing of Badoglio made acceptance of "the two principles of constitutional continuity . . . and cohabitation with the institution of the monarchy" the prerequisites for the immediate formation of a government representing the CLN.[70] And such a government was essential for the effective conduct of the anti-Nazi Resistance struggle.

Amendola thus eagerly accepted the political breakthrough augured by the *svolta* of Salerno when news of it first reached Rome about the first of April. Time and again he referred to the new policy of cooperation with Badoglio as the proper application of the party's "national front" line, thereby accurately (if ironically, in view of his fall 1943 opposition to

68. Longo, *I centri dirigenti,* 469.
69. Giorgio Amendola, *Lettere a Milano: Ricordi e documenti 1939–1945* (Rome: Editori Riuniti, 1974), 282–89.
70. Ibid., 286.

taking orders from Moscow) identifying it with the Comintern's wartime directives. Not only that; he also insisted on a self-critical recantation of the PCI's post-September 1943 position, readily admitting his own errors on this score.[71]

In other words, the eventuality that Longo and Secchia had anticipated in their polemics with the PCI leaders in Rome during the autumn of 1943, namely, the strengthening of the Badoglio forces and the consequent need to compromise with them, had come to pass. Accordingly, the party center in Milan passed a resolution endorsing the *svolta* on April 17 at a meeting attended by two delegates from Rome, Scoccimarro and Negarville. The resolution was said to be unanimous.[72] In fact, however, Scoccimarro opposed the new line at sessions of the party's Rome center on April 3 and 27 and presumably in Milan as well. His explicit objections were procedural: the absence of consultation with the core domestic leadership and the image this projected of PCI subordination to Soviet interests.[73] But his refusal to heed Amendola's pleas for more flexibility just prior to the *svolta* indicated that his reservations were also substantive.[74]

It was probably out of deference to Scoccimarro's views as well as their own undiminished aversion to Badoglio and the king that the drafters of the Milan resolution took care to point out that the *svolta* should in no way be taken "as a disavowal of the political line followed till now, [or] as a tacit acknowledgement of its substantive erroneousness."[75] Rather, circumstances had simply changed. In the same vein, Longo and Secchia later took Amendola to task for informing Togliatti of Scoccimarro's opposition and recommending self-criticism.[76] In short, the reaction of the PCI's northern leaders to the *svolta* was one of compliance rooted in realism but executed with dignity.

As the PCI's ranks and public stature grew, the recriminations surrounding the *svolta* faded. This is not to say that all members had the same understanding of what the new line entailed. During the heat of the controversy over the *svolta*, Amendola charged that the Milan center was fostering grassroots mobilization to achieve exclusive Communist power.[77] In his later reminiscences, he recalled that after his reassignment to Milan in May 1944, "the Yugoslavian example was a recurring subject of discussion among us."[78] And he singled out Gian Carlo Pajetta as one who

71. Ibid., 301–5 and 311–23.
72. Text in Longo, *I centri dirigenti*, 413–16.
73. Amendola, *Lettere a Milano*, 312.
74. Ibid., 303 and 313.
75. Longo, *I centri dirigenti*, 415.
76. Amendola, *Lettere a Milano*, 323 and 327; cf. Longo, *I centri dirigenti*, 427.
77. Amendola, *Lettere a Milano*, 303–18.
78. Ibid., 340–41.

favored such an approach.[79] Scoccimarro had early on admitted that he looked to a popular front style government. Secchia, for his part, appeared to waver between Communist hegemony and the popular front option, arguing in December 1943 that the PCI should make every effort to secure "the most important posts" in a future CLN government (for example, the ministries of war and interior) and explicitly citing the Yugoslavian experience in this context.[80] Amendola, in contrast, spoke of supporting "parliamentary democracy" and "progressive democracy" at one and the same time, calling the first the precondition for the second.[81]

It was this last view that won out in the mid-1940s. PCI press references to a proletarian-led "people's democracy" had been prevalent in late 1943. The keynote was sounded in a September manifesto published in both the Roman and northern editions of *l'Unità*. The democracy to which the Italian Communists aspired, it proclaimed, was "a *people's democracy* which . . . has in the working class its vanguard and its most secure defense. In the new democracy *the proletariat will constitute the principal moving force.*"[82] Secchia reiterated in a December 1943 article in *La nostra lotta* that the working class should win sufficient influence among the Italian people "to become the leading force in an effective *people's democracy.*"[83] By mid-1944, however, this radical tone gave way to talk of a "progressive democracy" dedicated to the interests of the middle classes as well as the workers and the peasants.

Soon all the major PCI spokesmen began to voice variations on the same theme. Togliatti noted the political rectitude of Pajetta in a letter of December 9, 1944, to Longo.[84] Pajetta himself wrote of propagating "the slogan, progressive democracy,"[85] even though—judging by his reflections years later on the failure to use the CLNs and the PCI's government role to press for democratization of the state bureaucracies[86]—he apparently continued to have reservations regarding the early postwar line. Scoccimarro consistently maintained that his party was for the time being working for democracy, not socialism,[87] all the while justifying this line

79. Ibid., 344.

80. Longo, *I centri dirigenti*, 275–77.

81. Amendola, *Lettere a Milano*, 318–19 and 344.

82. *Il comunismo italiano*, doc. 37:214; my emphasis.

83. Pietro Secchia, "Politica da seguire," *LNL* 1, no. 5 (December 1943):12–13; my emphasis.

84. Longo, *I centri dirigenti*, 456.

85. Ibid., 451.

86. Gian Carlo Pajetta, "Dalla liberazione alla repubblica. Le scelte del PCI fino al passaggio all'opposizione," in *Problemi di storia del Partito comunista italiano*, ed. Paolo Spriano et. al. (Rome: Editori Riuniti, 1973), 85–103 at 98–100.

87. Longo, *I centri dirigente*, 351.

as fully consistent with "Marxist-Leninist doctrine."[88] And Secchia immersed himself in organizational details and supervision.[89]

As for the partisan war in northern Italy, an interparty agreement was reached on June 9, 1944, for the creation of a unified military command that would be organized on the same principles of party parity and unanimity as the CLNAI.[90] Joint responsibility for military operations was assumed by Parri and Longo, with the career officer General Raffaelo Cadorno serving as military adviser. In early November 1944 Cadorno was appointed supreme commander while Parri and Longo were designated as vice-commanders,[91] an arrangement that aroused considerable apprehension among all concerned.[92] Nevertheless, from June 1944 onward Longo and Parri worked together in harmony. As Parri wrote to the Actionist leader Ugo La Malfa in July 1944, "our relations with the Communists have much improved. . . . Collaboration is being effected without friction and oscillation; at the center I find them flexible and reasonable."[93] He added that unification was being achieved more slowly in the outlying regions. But by September even this situation had improved.[94]

The PCI leadership's approach to its goal of fusion with the Socialists reveals another dimension of its readiness to compromise. As Longo proposed in a revealing March 26, 1945, letter to Togliatti, the Socialists should be granted parity in leadership posts and decision making in the anticipated unification process so as to assure them that the numerically and organizationally superior PCI was not out "to cheat them." Even more noteworthy was Longo's recommendation that the organizational structure, name, and international ties of the projected new party be left to the decisions of a unity congress, "decisions we will accept whatever they may be."[95]

A number of reasons may be suggested for the party elite's backing of the Togliatti line. First of all, there was no cause not to do so. For several years his policy gave every sign of enhancing the clout of the PCI. Not until the electoral defeat of 1948 did a manifest dichotomy develop be-

---

88. See his speech to the Second National Council of the PCI in April 1945, "Dottrina marxista e politica comunista," *Rinascita* 2, nos. 5–6 (May–June 1945):135–38. In this address Scoccimarro used the terms "people's democracy," "new democracy," and "progressive democracy" interchangeably.

89. Amendola, *Lettere a Milano,* 348.

90. Ibid., 341–42.

91. Catalano, *Storia del CLNAI,* 163–66 and 230–31.

92. Longo, *I centri dirigenti,* 472–78.

93. Parri to La Malfa, July 24, 1944, *Una lotta nel suo corso,* ed. Sandro Contini Bonacossi and Licia Ragghianti Collobi (Venice: Neri Pozza Editore, 1954), 231.

94. Cf. Valiani to comrades in Florence and Rome, September 7, 1944, ibid., 233.

95. Longo, *I centri dirigenti,* 489–91.

tween the observance of democratic procedures and the goal of left-wing hegemony.

Furthermore, Togliatti himself acted in such a way as to rally the party leadership behind him. The conciliatory tendencies he had displayed in the past returned to the fore steeled by time. He rejected out of hand Amendola's call for self-criticism of the PCI's pre-*svolta* republican intransigence.[96] He quickly moved to readmit dissidents such as Terracini and Ravera into the party and eventually the leadership.[97] And at the end of the war he declared a general amnesty for all those placed under a cloud of suspicion by the accusations and recriminations of the late 1930s.[98] Only Berti was excluded from absolution.

At the same time, Togliatti's conduct can be attributed in part to circumstances. Not trial by fire in the Resistance underground but the backing of Moscow accounted for his designation as general secretary. Little wonder that he sought to conciliate divergences and assuage hurt feelings. He needed to firm up his local support if he were to have any leverage vis-à-vis the Soviets. Beyond that, seasoned leaders were in short supply and great demand, given the organizational tasks confronting the PCI. Ongoing bickering would only detract from party building. In addition, Togliatti must have been both appreciative and a bit awestruck at the transformation of the party wrought by the domestic cadres prior to his return to Italy. He was, in short, in no mood to chastise anyone for past or present deviations.

The acceptance of Togliatti's directives by the party leaders may also be explained by the respect he enjoyed among his comrades. As Secchia argued during the winter 1943–44 polemics between Rome and Milan, the obligation to acknowledge Ercoli's authority did not derive from his formal position as PCI secretary (the position he regained in Moscow in the summer of 1940) but rather "from the undisputed gifts and qualities that made him *capo* of our Party."[99]

It should be noted, finally, that despite the divergences among the PCI's wartime leaders inside Italy, their frame of political reference was overwhelmingly domestic. Only rarely did they refer to the Soviet Union in their private correspondence and discussions, and then usually when speaking about international affairs. (The late 1943 polemics over Togliatti's authority were obviously an exception.) Longo made a few passing references to the publication of CPSU materials (for example, Stalin's

---

96. Ibid., 427; Amendola, *Lettere a Milano*, 323.

97. Longo, *I centri dirigenti*, 470 and 503; see also Spriano, *Storia del Partito comunista italiano* 5:380–83.

98. Amendola, *Lettere a Milano*, 338.

99. Longo, *I centri dirigenti*, 308.

Short History) and the celebration of benchmarks in Soviet history (the anniversary of the founding of the Red Army).[100] But he and the rest were preoccupied above all with internal Italian developments, almost to the exclusion of perceptible concern with the international Communist movement.

The composition of the *Direzione* officially appointed after the Fifth PCI Congress reflected this orientation. Besides General Secretary Togliatti, Deputy General Secretary Longo, and their wives (Rita Montagnana and Teresa Noce), the twenty-two member body included only seven other persons who had spent an extended period of time in the Soviet Union: Terracini, Scoccimarro, Secchia, Pajetta, Grieco, Roasio, and Edoardo D'Onofrio.[101] The Russian sojourns of the first three dated back to the 1920s. Pajetta spent his twenty-first year (1931–32) in Moscow as PCI representative to the Communist Youth International, returning to Italy in early 1933 to face arrest and ten years in Fascist prisons.[102] Grieco and Longo were party delegates to the ECCI in the early 1930s but more as a disciplinary gesture, Grieco because of his alignment with Togliatti in 1929 and Longo because of the failure of the organizational *svolta* of 1930. Only Roasio, as mentioned in chapter 5, seems to have received systematic training in the Comintern's schools for cadres in the mid-1930s, while D'Onofrio worked with Togliatti and Grieco during their wartime broadcasting stint in Moscow and Ufa.[103]

In other words, the political attitudes of the ranking Italian Communists, however sectarian in some cases, were by and large *not* the product of Stalinist regimentation. And the tribulations of the late 1930s gave several of them (for example, Di Vittorio and Grieco) grounds for distrust and resentment toward the Soviet authorities.

Togliatti's Nebulous Vision of Italy's Path to Socialism

As for Togliatti's own political goals, there is reason to believe that they differed from those of Stalin and his protégés in Eastern Europe. He would naturally have welcomed a left-wing electoral majority in the June 1946 elections to the Constitutional Assembly, not to mention the parliamentary elections of April 1948. But there is little indication that he

---

100. Ibid., 470 and 479.

101. The remaining eleven members and candidate members of the *Direzione* were Amendola, Colombi, Di Vittorio, Li Causi, Massola, Negarville, Novella, Roveda, Sereni, Spano, and Giuliano Pajetta; "Gli organi dirigenti del Partito," *La politica dei comunisti dal quinto al sesto congresso: risoluzioni e documenti* (Rome: La Stampa Moderna, 1948), 330.

102. Pajetta, *Il ragazzo rosso,* 128–29.

103. Spriano, *Storia del Partito comunista italiano* 4:117–18.

wished to build a future socialist Italy on the Soviet model. Indeed, a January 1945 *Rinascita* editorial (presumably written by Togliatti) remarked that Lenin "would have been the first to laugh" at such an idea.[104] According to Ernst Fischer, Ercoli had at one point in Moscow confided to him his conviction that socialism in Europe must have a more democratic face than in Stalin's Russia.[105] Fischer's recollections gain credibility from the dismay Togliatti expressed to Comintern headquarters over the absence of genuine democracy in republican Spain in 1937–38.[106] His simultaneous recommendations that the Spanish Communist leaders be given autonomy from Comintern supervision suggested, moreover, that he himself would expect to enjoy independence under similar circumstances.[107]

During the *svolta* of Salerno, moreover, Togliatti postulated the transitional goal of a "progressive democracy," occasionally also speaking of a "new democracy"—the term he had used with regard to Spain—but referring not at all to "people's democracy," the slogan soon to become current in Eastern Europe.[108] He plainly wanted to draw a distinction between the Italian setting and the Soviet sphere. To be sure, in many respects the rhetoric associated with each of these terms was the same: a multiparty system, security for the middle classes, respect for the rights of all except former Fascists, and so on.[109] Yet the reality behind the rhetoric differed markedly. Togliatti's counterparts in Eastern Europe, surrounded as they were by overwhelming Soviet power, were bent upon securing Communist hegemony from the start, the differences between a Gomulka and a Rakosi notwithstanding. Small wonder that they made a point of publicly disclaiming the relevance of the Soviet path.[110]

Still, "progressive democracy" had the ring of a campaign slogan rather than a concrete program and was in fact rarely mentioned from mid-1945 through 1947. In actuality, it appears that Togliatti did not really have a coherent political program in mind for any time frame beyond the short term. He once intimated in public that it would have been nice if circumstances had permitted the PCI to do what Tito had done, that

104. "Lenin," *Rinascita* 2, no. 1 (January 1945): 1–2 at 2.

105. Ernst Fischer, "Un debito di gratitudine," *Il Contemporaneo*, no. 8 (August 1965); supplement to *Rinascita* 22, no. 34 (August 28, 1965):9–10 at 10.

106. See chap. 4, 123.

107. See chap. 4, 144.

108. See his speeches of April 11 and July 9, 1944, as well as early June 1945 in *Politica Comunista*, by Togliatti, 45–47, 88–89, and 304–8 respectively; also, "Partito nuovo," *Rinascita* 1, no. 4 (October–December 1944):2.

109. Cf. Adriano Guerra, *Gli anni del Cominform* (Milan: Gabriele Mazzotta editore, 1977), 62–66.

110. Ibid.; see also Zbigniew Brzezinski, *The Soviet Bloc*, 2d rev. and enlarged ed. (Cambridge, Mass.: Harvard University Press, 1967), 22–32.

is (as Togliatti described it), come to power with the mandate of locally based CLNs.[111] He made these remarks, however, to a National Council of cadres on April 7, 1945, just prior to the urban insurrections that accompanied the Allies' final liberation of northern Italy later that same month. He may thus have wanted to show empathy with the revolutionary impulses of the northern militants. But, as he made abundantly clear, circumstances in Italy were *not* the same as those in Yugoslavia. Rather, they resembled more the situation in Greece where radical demands by left-wing forces had recently led to civil conflict and devastating defeat by conservative circles backed by the Anglo-Americans.[112] More indicative of Togliatti's innermost thoughts was probably the following off-the-record comment he made to the first organizational conference of the party's Naples Federation, or branch, in June 1944: *"We don't know how, concretely, the problems of the social revolution will be posed in Italy. . . . The forms of struggle for the realization of socialism will differ from those that have existed until now. But we know one thing: we have a guide, and this guide is Marxist doctrine.*[113]

Togliatti's failure to mention Leninist doctrine was not accidental. In contrast to his East European analogues and above all to French Communist leader, Maurice Thorez, he omitted references to Marxism-Leninism in his formal addresses until 1947.[114] A similar void was characteristic of many of the theoretical essays appearing in Togliatti's monthly journal, *Rinascita*, during the mid-1940s. Articles devoted to Marxism abounded; but they were usually written from a historical and West European vantage point. The few treatises that appeared on Lenin justified the PCI's current line with reference to his (tactical) support for democracy and national liberation.[115] Or they extolled his revolutionary accomplishments in general.[116] But nowhere did they acclaim Lenin's organizational principle of democratic centralism. Indeed, *Rinascita* carried excerpts from Negarville's speech to the Fifth PCI Congress in which, urging Communist–Socialist fusion, he remarked that he "would not be scandalized if a united party of the Italian laborers did *not* take democratic centralism as its organizational principle."[117] (Negarville, it might be noted, was not only

---

111. Togliatti, *Politica Comunista,* 239 and 258.

112. Ibid., 248–50 and 263.

113. See Togliatti's previously unpublished speech, "Ai comunisti napoletani (giugno 1944)," *Rinascita* 28, no. 5 (January 29, 1971):21–22; my emphasis.

114. For Thorez's references to "Marxism-Leninism," see his speech to the Tenth PCF Congress of June 1945 in Thorez, *Une politique de grandeur française,* 353 and 357–58.

115. See, for example, the two articles by Vincenzo La Rocca, "Il marxismo e la nostra lotta per la democrazia," *Rinascita* 1, no. 2 (July 1944):7–9, and "Lenin e le guerre di liberazione nazionale," *Rinascita* 2, nos. 5–6 (May–June 1945):132–34.

116. "Lenin," *Rinascita* 2, no. 1 (January 1945):1–2.

117. Celeste Negarville, "L'unità organica della classe operaia," *Rinascita* 3, nos. 1–2 (January–February 1946):7–10 at 8; my emphasis.

a member of the party's new *Direzione* but had also been associated with its mid-1930s Paris center.)

Meanwhile, Togliatti's many speeches from the spring of 1944 through the spring of 1947 resounded with affirmations of the national character of the Italian working class, its role in the *Risorgimento* and thereafter, rather than adulation of the Soviet Union. Often they contained little in the way of pro-Sovietism except for praise of the Soviet Union's war effort[118] or occasional allusions to Stalin as one among several contributors to Communist praxis.[119] Glorification of the original Bolshevik victory and the more recent exploits of the Red Army rather than the Soviet system per se was the central theme even of an autumn 1944 address devoted to the anniversary of the October Revolution.[120] To be sure, in his opening report to the Fifth PCI Congress, Togliatti devoted about one page out of fifty to the egalitarian and "evangelical" (in the sense of charitable) virtues of contemporary Soviet society.[121] On the other hand, he made no mention whatsoever of Marxism-Leninism, democratic centralism, or Lenin himself, again unlike Thorez who extolled all three in his comparable report to the June 1945 congress of the PCF.[122]

On January 10, 1947, Togliatti delivered a major speech to a national party conference on organizational matters that represented both a synthesis of the above themes and a departure from them.[123] With regard to the latter, he stressed the need to raise the "ideological level" of the PCI cadres. "Without a doctrine of the vanguard, a party of the vanguard doesn't exist," he admonished. "In our party these truths have been a bit forgotten."[124] In this context he broached the need to study not just "Marxism" but also "Leninism." And in March 1947 *Rinascita* began to carry a supplementary "Guide to the Study of Marxism" which, while still concentrating on the European Marxist tradition (including Gramsci), contained materials by Lenin and Stalin as well. This new attentiveness to theoretical rigor may be ascribed to several causes: the doctrinal illiteracy of the *partito nuovo,* for one; the influence of Zhdanov, for another.

In early 1947 Zhdanov was at the peak of his power.[125] Given his campaign for a return to ideological concerns in Soviet domestic life (after the relative laxity of the war years), we may assume that he urged ideolog-

---

118. Togliatti, *Politica Comunista,* 8–9, 16, 44–45, 59, 229, and 256.

119. Ibid., 21, 45, and 257.

120. Ibid., 213–16.

121. See text, "Rinnovare l'Italia," in *Critica marxista* 2, nos. 4–5 (July–October 1964):77–129 at 118.

122. Thorez, *Une politique de grandeur française,* 353–65.

123. Text, "La nostra lotta per la democrazia e per il socialismo," in *Critica marxista* 2, nos. 4–5 (July–October 1964):159–99.

124. Ibid., 191.

125. Hahn, *Postwar Soviet Politics,* 61.

ical revivalism upon foreign Communists as well. There is no evidence of any personal link between Togliatti and Zhdanov. The latter was party chief of Leningrad during the German siege of that city and returned to Moscow only in mid-1944, after Togliatti's departure for Italy.[126] However, the simultaneous allusions to "new paths" to socialism voiced not just by Togliatti but by Communist leaders throughout Europe in 1946–47 bespoke coordination by Zhdanov.

All the same, it must be emphasized that in his January 1947 speech Togliatti was speaking of theoretical rigor, *not* regimentation. His call to study "Marxism, Leninism" (still not "Marxism-Leninism") was couched in an appeal for a "collective" search by "old" and "new" cadres for "our path, the Italian path, the path that is dictated by the particularities . . . of our country," to democratic reforms and socialism. He insisted, for example, on a differentiated analysis of what victory by the Yugoslavian Liberation Front as "a mass organism" had meant in Yugoslavia and what a victory by the CLNs as "a movement founded on a federation of parties" would have meant in Italy. And he urged the Italian cadres to study more deeply not just the history of Italy and the international Communist movement but also the contribution of "democratic Italy" to the Spanish Civil War.[127]

The last allusion in particular set Togliatti's position apart from the by then commonplace East European Communist affirmations of the distinctiveness of their people's democracies from the Bolshevik model. For, as we have seen, in his 1936 essay on Spain Togliatti had set forth a strategy of interclass cooperation. And in his reports from Spain to Comintern headquarters in 1937–38 he had recommended that such a strategy be autonomously implemented.

Meanwhile, in *Rinascita* the focus on West European Marxist writers so evident by 1946 was accompanied by the publication of the first commentary and excerpts from Gramsci's *Prison Notebooks*.[128] Both phenomena were logical corollaries of Togliatti's overriding emphasis on the national identity of the PCI. A plethora of pieces in *Rinascita* played up this theme. At the same time, the journal played down links with the Soviet Union. Party spokesmen defended Soviet foreign policy positions in their ever more frequent discussions of international developments after 1945. But attention to the internal politics of the Soviet Union and the emerging people's democracies of Eastern Europe was minimal in 1946 and largely confined to the reprinting of speeches and articles from Soviet bloc

126. Ibid., 26–27.

127. "La nostra lotta per la democrazia e per il socialismo," *Critica marxista* 2, nos. 4–5 (July–October 1964):192–93.

128. Felice Platone, ed., "L'eredità letteraria di Gramsci: Relazione sui quaderni del carcere," *Rinascita* 3, no. 4 (April 1946):81–90.

The PCI between East and West

sources in 1947.[129] The cult of pro-Sovietism was conspicuous by its absence from *Rinascita* during this period.

There were a few exceptions to this pattern. One was an article on Stalin in the very first issue of *Rinascita* published in mid-1944. Written by Montagnana, it extolled the virtues of the Soviet *vozhd* (boss) in terms reminiscent of the late 1930s (and late 1940s).[130] Montagnana, who had not yet returned from his wartime exile in Mexico, may have been trying to work his way back into the inner circles of the party. If so, his gambit failed; for while he became editor of *l'Unità* in July 1946,[131] he did not hold that position for long and was never reappointed to the PCI Politburo (*Direzione*). Another exception was a piece by none other than Negarville effusively praising not only Stalin but the Soviet Union and Marxism-Leninism as well.[132] However, it appeared immediately after the publication of his heretical comment on democratic centralism. It thus may have been an early and still isolated case of what had once been—and would all too soon again become—a common occurrence: Soviet-inspired self-criticism. Still, for the time being PCI spokesmen continued by and large to disregard, not glorify, Soviet reality.

In short, during the mid-1940s the public image of the PCI bore the imprint of Togliatti's political profile. Togliatti was intent upon carving out political space for the PCI despite the Anglo-American presence in Italy. This led him to compromise with moderate forces, to seek allies among lay and Catholic progressives, and to downplay Leninist principles and pro-Soviet affinities that might alienate both groups. The concrete realities of the Italian situation were his point of departure even if the discovery of a viable strategy of socialist transformation remained his ultimate goal. Such an approach was dictated by practical politics. But it also seemed to flow from Togliatti's realization during the Fascist era that the left in Italy needed centrist, middle-class support to survive, let alone to work its will.

The party elite rallied around Togliatti for all the reasons we have already noted. True, such unity was to some extent deceptive. In contrast

129. In September 1946 *Rinascita* began to carry a new column entitled "The international Communist movement," with articles appearing on Yugoslavia in September, Poland in October, and the PCF in November–December. By 1947, in addition, the reprinting of a speech or article by a Soviet bloc leader or publicist became the rule in each issue. However, this did not yet imply a uniformity of views. See, for example, the piece by Eugene Varga, "Cosa è la democrazia di nuovo tipo," *Rinascita* 4, no. 6 (June 1947):141–46.

130. Mario Montagnana, "Il Maresciallo Giuseppe Stalin," *Rinascita* 1, no. 1 (June 1944):11–13.

131. "Alcune questioni di inquadramento e di organizzazione," *La politica dei comunisti dal quinto al sesto congresso*, 84.

132. Celeste Negarville, "L'ultimo discorso di Stalin," *Rinascita* 3, no. 3 (March 1946):36–37.

211

to France where the prewar Communist Politburo had, as Thorez boasted in 1945, reemerged all but intact,[133] the PCI's new *Direzione* embraced at least three currents: veterans from the Paris center of the 1930s; activists responsible for the party's clandestine work from 1939 through 1943; and long-time political prisoners released only in mid-1943 (Arturo Colombi, Li Causi, Roveda, Pajetta, Scoccimarro, Secchia, and Terracini). Some members of the last two groups tended to be sectarian in a traditional Bolshevik manner. On the other hand, precious few had been Stalinized in the full sense of the term. Eleven of the twenty-two members of the *Direzione* were, like Togliatti, from middle-class and/or intellectual backgrounds.[134] And all were united by the shared perception of having overcome fascism.

The New Recruits versus the Old Cadres

As for the PCI's rank and file, we may assume that the overwhelming majority of the new recruits agreed with Togliatti's moderate policies and observance of legality. Indeed, the prestige accruing to the Communists from their role in government probably accounted for a good deal of the surge in membership. A bandwagon effect had been added to the PCI's already solid drawing cards of wartime admiration for the Soviet Union and the urge for radical change that permeated Italy's northern cities and industrial centers. Party membership statistics support this line of reasoning. It was only as Italy was gradually liberated by the Anglo-American forces and the PCI became a major partner in successive coalition cabinets that party rolls began to mushroom. As late as March 1945, for example, Longo estimated that there were just 100,000 PCI members in occupied northern Italy.[135] In the central and southern regions there were already 310,000 members at the end of the war.[136] And by the time of the Fifth Congress at the close of 1945, total membership had quadrupled, climbing to over 1,750,000. As Togliatti remarked in his opening speech to the congress, "those registered in our party exceed today by a long shot the predictions we were able to make several months ago, at the time of the liberation of the north."[137]

When speaking of the mass base of the *partito nuovo,* moreover, one must bear in mind the PCI's unprecedented open admissions policy. Ac-

---

133. Thorez, *Une politique de grandeur française,* 353.
134. For their classification by occupation or social origin, see "Elenco dei membri del Comitato Centrale del Partito," *La politica dei comunisti dal quinto al sesto congresso,* 325–30.
135. Longo, *I centri dirigenti,* 482.
136. Alessandro Natta, "La Resistenza e la formazione del 'partito nuovo,'" in *Problemi di storia del Partito comunista italiano,* 57–83 at 57.
137. "Rinnovare l'Italia," in *Critica marxista* 2, nos. 4–5 (July–October 1964): 126.

cording to the statutes approved at the Fifth Congress, "all honest laborers of either sex who have reached the age of 18 years, regardless of race, *religious faith or philosophical convictions,*" were welcomed into the Communist Party's ranks.[138] Political screening and systematic indoctrination were precluded by the enormity of the immediate organizational tasks confronting the party. To quote from Longo's March 1945 letter to Togliatti, cited earlier, the PCI base in northern Italy displayed "all the deficiencies inherent in the rapid growth of the party and the insufficient work of political and theoretical education it has been able to do. Along side a minority of old cadres, . . . there is the large mass of comrades and new cadres animated in general by great fighting spirit but not very firm in their political orientation."[139] Such problems were the same, he surmised, as those facing Ercoli in liberated Italy.

In point of fact, soon after his return Togliatti ordered the decentralization of the admissions process to the local sections. The crush of new applicants virtually necessitated such a break with the traditional procedure of evaluating each individual candidate at the federation level.[140] Togliatti's departure from orthodox Leninist criteria for party membership could also have hardly been more blatant. In his first major speech on April 11, 1944, he admonished the Naples cadres to accept all comers as long as they were "good and honest" anti-Fascists.[141] Six months later he approved the acceptance into the party of workers who had been Fascists out of necessity, such as railroad employees.[142] And in April 1945 he bluntly stated that "we are not making adherence to Marxist ideology a condition for entry into the party."[143] Once again, this approach stood in stark contrast to that of PCF leader Thorez who, at the French Communists' mid-1945 congress, spoke of the need for the "Marxist-Leninist formation of the party's new adherents."[144]

The creation of a powerful electoral machine rather than doctrinal orthodoxy was plainly Togliatti's paramount concern. As he declared in his speech to the Fifth Congress, the PCI's main organizational objective was the creation "prior to the Constitutional Assembly" of a Communist section in every village and neighborhood.[145] In view of the circumstances of their entry into the party, there is no reason to suppose that the new recruits thought otherwise. Some were initially caught up in a kind of

138. *Statuto del Partito Comunista Italiano (Approvato dal V Congresso Nazionale del PCI)* (Rome, 1946), 5-6; my emphasis.
139. Longo, *I centri dirigenti,* 483.
140. Natta, "La Resistenza," in *Problemi di storia del Partito comunista italiano,* 65.
141. Togliatti, *Politica Comunista,* 51.
142. Ibid., 205.
143. Ibid., 253.
144. Thorez, *Une politique de grandeur française,* 357.
145. "Rinnovare l'Italia," in *Critica marxista* 2, nos. 4-5 (July–October 1964):126.

"primitive political messianism," as Togliatti himself put it, in that they identified the coming of socialism with a one-shot victory at the polls.[146] But after the June 1946 elections this simplistic view of the electoral process began to give way to recognition of the need to garner votes over the longer term.

The old-guard cadres from the 1920s, in contrast, were often imbued with the doctrinaire Bolshevik disdain for democratic principles as well as the militant pro-Sovietism characteristic of the early Comintern years. During the 1930s many of them had either withdrawn from active politics or—as had happened to leaders like Scoccimarro and Secchia—endured arrest and imprisonment by the Fascists. The sectarianism of the old-guard cadres had thus not been tempered by the popular front experience. Nor had their reflexive loyalty to the fatherland of socialism been shaken by direct exposure to the heavy-handed methods of the Stalinists, as was the case for so many of their own leaders in exile. Instead their Bolshevik matrix remained intact, reinforced by the Red Army's heroism and Stalin's international stature. The presence of scattered circles of more recent militants, often middle-class intellectuals drawn to the PCI during the mid-1930s,[147] did not alter this overall profile.

We know from data furnished by Longo[148] and Secchia[149] that the bulk of Resistance cadres and partisan leaders were "old comrades." Less clear is the extent of their opposition to the post-*svolta* line. After Amendola's transfer to the PCI's northern center in May 1944, he found considerable evidence of maximalism and sectarianism "of the 1919 sort" during inspection tours of Emilia-Romagna and the Veneto. One local leader wanted to build up the PCI's armed detachments for the party's political battles ahead;[150] others spoke of the "immediate" consignment of land to "farmhands and sharecroppers";[151] and so on. In his reports to the party center in Milan, Amendola stressed the need to inculcate in the local cadres the real meaning of "Ercoli's" directives.[152] In December 1944 Togliatti himself, in a widely publicized letter, exhorted Longo to "seriously react in the party against any tendency which might still exist to consider our policy of unity as a game."[153] On balance, perhaps the most one can say is that the prewar militants' reluctance to cooperate with

---

146. "La nostra lotta per la democrazia e per il socialismo," ibid., 160.

147. Sergio Bertelli, *Il gruppo: La formazione del gruppo dirigente del PCI, 1936–1948* (Milan: Rizzoli Editore, 1980), 29–32.

148. Longo, *I centri dirigenti*, 485.

149. For Secchia's statistics, see Sassoon, *The Strategy of the Italian Communist Party*, 40, n. 14.

150. Amendola, *Lettere a Milano*, 441.

151. Ibid., 398.

152. Ibid., 361, 398, and 432.

153. Longo, *I centri dirigenti*, 455.

other political forces in the partisan battles, urban insurrections, and post-war administrative arrangements was counterbalanced by two additional strains in the Bolshevik tradition: party discipline and deference to the Comintern.[154] Regardless of the actual political preferences of the old guard, these latter traits worked to the advantage of Togliatti qua party head and erstwhile secretary of the Communist International. Meanwhile, with the end of the war came an influx of new, more malleable cadres and grassroots activists.

In short, as the *partito nuovo* entered the Cold War era it constituted a fairly heterogeneous body. Leadership, cadres, and base alike were united not so much by Leninist-style discipline or a shared vision of the future as by the expectation of coming electoral victories. Such anticipation, in turn, stemmed from the extraordinarily rapid expansion in the PCI's membership and *presenza* in Italian society. This pragmatic—as opposed to theoretical—wave-of-the-future mentality was doubtless reinforced by the perception of Communist gains in Eastern Europe, even though the actual political dynamics of developments in that region were never discussed in the party's media.

To be sure, the PCI's failure to surpass the Socialists in the June 1946 election to the Constitutional Assembly alerted the leadership to the need to devise organizational and doctrinal guidelines that could sustain both the cadres and the base over the longer haul. But from the public and internal party documents of the period, one senses a search for innovative rather than doctrinaire solutions to this problem. Togliatti's speech to the January 1947 national conference was a case in point. So, too, was the *Direzione* resolution on the results of the June 1946 election. It stressed the need to combat—yet again—the "verbal extremism" and "opportunist passivity" of some and to raise the "ideological level," "political discipline," and "Bolshevik formation" of all.[155] Still, it made no references to Marxism-Leninism, let alone democratic centralism, and emphasized the need to develop mechanisms for reaching out to the rural and urban middle classes, intellectuals, and women.[156]

There was, however, one new theme of extraordinary importance in the *Direzione* document: it castigated the party's "grave weaknesses" in rebutting attacks against the Soviet Union during the electoral campaign. Instead of "timid defenses" of the Soviet Union, the document admonished, Communists should have extolled its contribution to the defeat of nazism and its magnificent successes in "suppressing for always, on one-

154. Amendola noted the presence of both traits among northern PCI cadres on the eve of the April 1945 insurrections in *Lettere a Milano*, 533 and 549.
155. Text in *La politica dei comunisti dal quinto al sesto congresso*, 66–83 at 80.
156. Ibid., passim.

sixth of the globe, the exploitation of man by man.''[157] This line of criticism was surprising on two accounts. Most significant, it revealed that the *partito nuovo*, in its inception, *was not nearly so pro-Soviet as has often been portrayed.*[158] But the reproach also ran counter to the low profile accorded Soviet domestic developments in Togliatti's speeches and in *Rinascita*, which suggests that the criticism emanated from Moscow. Whatever the case, the exaltation of Soviet reality was a theme the PCI media would increasingly emphasize, both for the party's own purposes and to ensure CPSU support.

The Cold War and *Cominformismo* Italian-style

Volumes have been written on the impact of the Cold War on European politics and the Communist movement. The division of the Continent into two hostile blocs was accompanied by the exclusion of the PCI and PCF from their respective national governments in May 1947 and the brutal imposition of Soviet controls and Stalinist conceptions of sociopolitical order on Eastern Europe. In the Soviet bloc the glimmers of ideological vitality that had appeared in the mid-1940s were quickly snuffed out as CPSU ideologues embraced Great Russian chauvinism and sterile dogmatism. In the Soviet party apparatus ultrasectarians such as Mikhail Suslov and Pavel Yudin became the watchdogs of domestic orthodoxy and foreign Communist conformity, functions performed by Zhdanov until his political eclipse and death in mid-1948. The Cominform and its biweekly newssheet, edited by Yudin, became the forum for the anathema of the independent Titoists and the dissemination of Stalinist dogma to the rest of the Communist world. And an intricate system of covert controls backed up by military power enabled Moscow to transform the new Communist party-states of Eastern Europe into compliant satellites, to press the people's democracies, in theory and in practice, into the single mold of the Soviet dictatorship of the proletariat.[159]

During this dark age of late Stalinism, the Italian and French Communists—much like the Maoists on the other side of the globe—were confronted with the dilemma of a single alternative. The Western Communists were stigmatized by the United States and its allies as subversives out to undermine their constitutional orders; the Chinese Communists were rebuffed in their overtures to American diplomatic personnel on the eve of

---

157. Ibid., 69.
158. See, for example, Gambino, *Storia del dopoguerra,* 159–61.
159. The classic work on this subject is by Brzezinski, *The Soviet Bloc.*

their victory over the Kuomintang.[160] In a word, Communist parties beyond the boundaries of the new Soviet empire had little choice but to align themselves with Moscow.

Under these circumstances it seems more fruitful to explore the ways in which the PCI parted from the pack than to document the manifold ways in which it conformed to what became known as *Cominformismo*. From 1948 through 1953 the Italian party's conduct was idiosyncratic in three important ways. In the first place, the ideological void that characterized the *partito nuovo* was filled with the doctrine of anti-Americanism and pro-Sovietism rather than Soviet-style Marxism-Leninism. In the second place, the PCI's alignment with the CPSU in international affairs was accompanied by ongoing observance of the democratic rules of the game and relative policy moderation at home. Lastly, the conciliatory propensities of the party elite became more pronounced than ever before (or since!) in PCI history. This was all the more remarkable in light of the purges that engulfed the PCF Politburo as well as the East European Communist regimes.

To say that the doctrinal matrix of the *partito nuovo* was the dual creed of anti-Americanism and pro-Sovietism is not to deny the Marxist beliefs of the PCI elite and its new intellectual recruits or the Bolshevik roots of the "ten thousand expert cadres from the clandestine struggle against fascism" who formed the backbone of the party apparatus.[161] Moreover, after mid-1947 commentaries couched in an orthodox Marxist-Leninist vein became ever more prominent in *Rinascita* and, we may assume, in the manuals of the party schools. All the same, the two-camp mentality of the Cold War became the PCI's public philosophy as projected in the proceedings of party congresses and in the pages of *l'Unità*. In this context it should be noted that the pervasive American support for the emerging Christian Democratic establishment in Italy played a role similar to that of the Wall Street Crash of 1929: both served as powerful inducements to unswerving PCI alignment with the Soviet Union. If the Wall Street Crash bolstered the Comintern's 1928–29 prognosis of capitalist instability and revolutionary upheaval, official intervention by the United States in behalf of anti-Communist forces in Italy vindicated the Cominform's allegations regarding the implacable hostility and global ambitions of American imperialism.[162]

---

160. Seymour Topping, *Journey between Two Chinas* (New York: Harper and Row, 1972), 82–87; and "49 Cables Show Chou Made Secret Overture to U.S. on China Aid," *The Washington Post,* August 13, 1978, A32.

161. Giorgio Amendola, "Il PCI all'opposizione. La lotta contro lo scelbismo," in *Problemi di storia del Partito comunista italiano,* 105–29 at 112.

162. For details of United States involvement in Italian politics during this period, see the chapters by Ennio di Nolfo and Simon Serfaty in *The Italian Communist Party,* ed. Serfaty and

Nowhere does the PCI's public philosophy of anti-Americanism and pro-Sovietism come more clearly to the fore than in Togliatti's keynote addresses to the Sixth and Seventh Congresses of the party in January 1948 and April 1951. Already in July 1947 he had expressed alarm over the aggressiveness and imperial ambitions of the United States, drawing the grim conclusion that democracies "of a new type" could be formed only "in countries where the armies of the Soviet Union have assured political stability."[163] But that speech was addressed to the Central Committee—mostly old-guard cadres, many of whom had questioned the party's moderate line all along—and was never made public. It was instead Togliatti's report to the Sixth PCI Congress on January 5, 1948, which heralded the new line of unremitting hostility to what he called American encroachments on Italian sovereignty and vital public interests.[164] The Soviet delegates to the Sixth Congress were, not coincidentally, Cominform overseer Yudin and one Vagan G. Grigorian,[165] by many accounts then head of the Foreign Commission (later International Department) of the CPSU Secretariat.[166]

Still, at the 1948 congress the thrust of Togliatti's remarks was anti-Americanism, not pro-Sovietism. And he continued to proclaim both his support for "progressive democracy" as a "general strategic plan" and his opposition to "maximalism and verbal extremism." It was only at the Seventh PCI Congress in April 1951 that Togliatti gave equal time to the cult of pro-Sovietism and the denunciation of United States imperialism—while omitting any allusion to an "Italian path" to socialism.[167] Meanwhile, shortly before the 1951 conclave Velio Spano pointedly criticized the PCI's silence on the Soviet Union in its propaganda of the mid-1940s.[168] Even a nonconformist like Terracini, whose opposition to the 1939 Hitler–Stalin pact had led to his temporary expulsion and who had again been formally rebuked in late 1947 for equating the foreign policies of "the imperialist aggressors" and the Soviet Union,[169] espoused the party's new public philosophy. On the eve of the Seventh

---

Gray, 37–74; the relevant documents in *Western Europe*, vol. 3 of *Foreign Relations of the United States*, U.S. Department of State, 1947 and 1948; R. Faenza and M. Fini, *Gli americani in Italia* (Milan, 1976), 298–304; and Joseph G. LaPalombara, *The Italian Labor Movement: Problems and Prospects* (Ithaca, N.Y.: Cornell University Press, 1957), 57.

163. For extensive quotations from the text, see Spriano, *I comunisti europei e Stalin*, 274–77.

164. Text in *l'Unità*, January 6, 1948, 1–4.

165. Both were identified in *l'Unità* as professors from Moscow State University; ibid., 1.

166. Hahn, *Postwar Soviet Politics*, 107; and Jerry F. Hough, "Soviet Policymaking toward Foreign Communists," *Studies in Comparative Communism* 15, no. 3 (Autumn 1982):167–83 at 170–71.

167. Text in *l'Unità*, April 4, 1951, 1, 3–5.

168. Ibid., February 28, 1951, 3.

169. "Questione dell'intervista del compagno Terracini," *La politica dei comunisti dal quinto al sesto congresso*, 311.

Congress he flatly declared that in the event of an East–West war he would favor a Soviet victory.[170]

The canons of Marx, Lenin, and Stalin nevertheless continued to receive scant attention in Togliatti's reports to the 1948 and 1951 congresses. As earlier, his conduct in this regard differed markedly from that of Thorez, whose address to the Twelfth PCF Congress in April 1950 extolled more obsequiously than ever before Soviet-style "Marxism-Leninism" and "democratic centralism."[171]

With regard to the second PCI particularity, Donald Sassoon has amply documented the disparity between the party's Cold War rhetoric and its domestic public policy during these years.[172] The many militant demonstrations against the Marshall Plan and NATO notwithstanding, Grieco sought to mobilize the *mezzogiorno* across class lines in order to win advantages for both landless peasants and small landholders and shopkeepers. Di Vittorio as head of the CGIL campaigned for economic reforms that would improve productivity and employment and thus benefit a far broader sector of Italian society than organized labor. Communist members of Parliament cooperated more often than not in the passage of legislation essential to the normal functioning of the state.[173] In the jargon of the bygone Comintern era, the PCI set out to form multiple united fronts "from below" in order to win "partial" economic and political improvements. From the perspective of the party's own historical experience, it sought to use all available legal possibilities to shore up (and, it was hoped, extend) its presence in a polity dominated by the Christian Democrats and polarized by intense hostility and distrust.

The leadership's reaction to an assassination attempt on Togliatti's life in July 1948 demonstrated beyond doubt its overriding commitment to restraint. Within a few hours PCI activists in northern Italy had launched a spontaneous and paralyzing general strike. Yet, as Secchia recalled years later, from the very first moment he and Longo were in agreement on the need "to control the movement, not to break with legality."[174]

In a sense the *partito nuovo* began to mirror the psychological and structural characteristics of Italian Catholicism rather than the political culture of Soviet Leninism. For one thing, the PCI's lowest territorial

170. *L'Unità*, March 28, 1951, 3.

171. Maurice Thorez, *La lutte pour l'indépendance nationale et pour la paix: XII Congrés National du Parti Communiste Français* (Paris, 1950), 81–95.

172. Sassoon, *The Strategy of the Italian Communist Party*, 73–83.

173. Donald L. M. Blackmer, "Continuity and Change in Postwar Italian Communism," in *Communism in Italy and France*, ed. Blackmer and Sidney Tarrow (Princeton: Princeton University Press, 1975), 21–68 at 48.

174. Quoted in Sassoon, *The Strategy of the Italian Communist Party*, 65–66; cf. "Archivio Pietro Secchia, 1945–1973," in *Annali Feltrinelli* 19 (Milan: Feltrinelli Editore, 1979), "Promemoria autobiografico," 135–256 at 214–18.

units, its neighborhood sections, soon assumed the same comprehensive role as the church in the everyday lives of their members. The neighborhood organizations of the Communist Party and the parishes of the Catholic church fulfilled similar social, cultural, and political functions, all the more so because of the close personal ties between Christian Democratic politicians and clergy at the local level.[175] Even though the number of Soviet-type Communist cells (usually geared to the workplace) grew more rapidly than sections in the late 1940s,[176] the latter became the more influential organizational bodies.[177] Meanwhile, for PCI militants the ageless dichotomy between the things of God and the things of Caesar took on a temporal cast. Rank-and-file Communists participated constructively, if reluctantly, in a system dominated by the Christian Democratic establishment, all the while dreaming of the heaven on earth which the PCI media and their own sentiments equated with Stalin's Russia.

Above all, the PCI deviated from the pan-European Communist norm in regard to the stability of its top leadership. The *Direzione* named in January 1946 after the Fifth Congress remained virtually intact until the post-Stalin era. Massola was demoted to Central Committee membership in 1948, and his successor, Giuseppe Rossi, died shortly thereafter.[178] Otherwise the only change in 1948 was the removal of Pajetta's brother from candidate membership in the *Direzione* and his replacement by the head of the Communist youth movement, an educated young man of middle-class background by the name of Enrico Berlinguer. After the 1951 congress there was one further change. Dozza was admitted to candidate membership, while Grieco was promoted to full membership. At a time when other European Communist parties were enduring purges reminiscent of the late 1930s, these two targets of Stalinist vituperation in 1938 were at last fully rehabilitated.

The contrast between developments in the Italian and French Communist parties could not have been more striking. For in 1952 two historic leaders of the PCF were denounced for treason to the party: André Marty, former Comintern secretary and political commissar of the International Brigades in Spain; and Charles Tillon, leader of the Communist combatants in the French Resistance. Publicly they were accused of factionalism and national deviationism. The real reason for their purge was more likely personal rivalries among Stalin's loyalists in the PCF Politburo, who made Marty and Tillon the scapegoats for whatever deficiencies the

175. For details see the valuable study by David I. Kertzer, *Comrades and Christians: Religion and Political Struggle in Communist Italy* (Cambridge: Cambridge University Press, 1980).

176. See the statistics in *l'Unità*, April 1, 1951, 3.

177. Cf. Giuseppe Are, "Il PCI come organismo politico," in *Il PCI allo specchio*, ed. Renato Mieli (Milan: Rizzoli Editore, 1983), 7–47 at 29.

178. For the members of the *Direzione* named after the Sixth and Seventh Congresses, see *l'Unità*, January 13, 1948, 1, and April 10, 1951, 1.

French party suffered in Moscow's eyes.[179] The only difference between the purge of the PCF and the ones that wracked the East European Communist parties during these years was that the victims of the latter faced imprisonment or execution as well as disgrace.

The Italian Communists' "opportunism of conciliation" was particularly notable because of the many parallels that otherwise existed between Soviet–PCI relations in the late 1940s and in the late 1920s. As we shall see, the criticism of the Italians at the founding meeting of the Cominform in September 1947 recalled the Stalinists' treatment of Togliatti, Grieco, Di Vittorio, and others at the Tenth Plenum of the ECCI in July 1929. In late 1947, moreover, Secchia conveyed negative views of his party to the Soviet leaders, much as he and Longo had raised objections to the Togliatti–Grieco line when in Moscow in 1927–28. And in 1951 Stalin personally urged Togliatti to take over the leadership of the Cominform, just as the German Stalinists had conspired to transfer Ercoli from the PCI Politburo to the WEB of the Comintern in early 1928.

One of the initial objectives of the Cominform, according to Eugenio Reale's firsthand account of its first meeting, was to denounce the postwar strategy of the PCI and the PCF.[180] Reflecting the surge in Cold War tensions during 1947, the two West European parties were admonished to follow a policy of obstructionism rather than cooperation on the local scene, to do everything possible to block the consolidation of the Atlantic Alliance. As in 1929, the Italian party was castigated for toeing the very line Moscow had previously condoned. Similarly, the attack was spearheaded by non-Russians, in this case the Yugoslavs. Edvard Kardelj criticized the PCI for its wartime acceptance of party parity in the CLNs, for not trying to seize power at the close of the war, for failing to secure key ministries in the Italian government, for excessive observance of parliamentary rules, and for eschewing the "two-camp" line.[181] He added, pointedly: "The errors of the PCI are greater than those of the PCF."[182] As for the PCI's response, Longo reportedly reacted "with dignity and with a certain pride" in contrast to the obsequiousness of the French delegate, Jacques Duclos.[183] According to Vladimir Dedijer, Longo rebutted the Yugoslavian delegation's criticism of the PCI's mid-1940s alliance strategy by bluntly stating that the party had acted on Soviet instructions.[184] Togliatti himself refused to attend the meeting,

179. Wall, *French Communism in the Era of Stalin*, 144–47.

180. Eugenio Reale, *Nascita del Cominform* (Verona: Arnoldo Mondadori Editore, 1958), passim.

181. Ibid., 116–22.

182. Ibid., 120.

183. Ibid., 47.

184. Vladimir Dedijer, *Tito* (New York: Simon and Schuster, 1953), 305.

pleading reasons of health,[185] and he urged Thorez to do likewise.[186] Precisely because of his past experience in the International, Togliatti must have sensed that he would once again be subjected to public reproach.

Soon thereafter, in December 1947, Secchia went to the Soviet Union to report on developments in Italy. He presented his views first to Zhdanov in person and then in writing, for later discussion with Stalin, Molotov, Grigorian, and Lavrenti Beria as well as Zhdanov.[187] For the most part his views coincided with those of Togliatti and the *Direzione*. He did not question, for example, the goal of "progressive democracy" or the party's alliance policy and electoral strategy. Where he diverged from his own leadership was over the issue of mass mobilization. Secchia argued that the PCI should exert greater pressure "from below" (and should have done so from the end of the war), placing more emphasis upon grassroots militancy than parliamentary activity. Indicative of the relative moderation that still held sway in Moscow, his Soviet interlocutors objected that the kind of mass mobilization proposed by Secchia would lead to insurrection and defeat.[188] Nevertheless, in February 1948 he was promoted to deputy general secretary of his party—a position he shared with Longo until January 1955—with the approval, if not at the behest, of Stalin.

During the winter of 1950–51 a direct clash occurred between Togliatti and Stalin. Giorgio Bocca reconstructed the details of this incident on the basis of interviews with Secchia, Longo, and others directly involved,[189] and Secchia also recounted it in his memoirs.[190] Briefly stated, while Togliatti was in Moscow recuperating from an auto accident, Stalin repeatedly proposed that he become head of the Cominform and reside henceforth in Prague or the Soviet Union. Such a move, Stalin argued, would enhance both the Cominform's prestige and Togliatti's security. Togliatti strenuously objected. Stalin thereupon summoned Secchia and Longo to Moscow to apprise them of his wishes. Again Togliatti refused. Once back in Rome, Secchia formally conveyed Stalin's proposal to the PCI *Direzione*, recommending that it be accepted despite Togliatti's objections. (Plainly, for Secchia, compliance with Soviet *diktat* now took precedence over loyalty to Togliatti.) The overwhelming majority of the

185. Reale, *Nascita del Cominform*, 16–17.
186. Wall, *French Communism in the Era of Stalin*, 60.
187. Text in "Archivio Pietro Secchia," *Annali Feltrinelli* 19, "Relazione sulla situazione italiana presentata a Mosca nel dicembre del 1947," 611–27; for Secchia's reflections on this episode, see "Archivio Pietro Secchia," *Annali Feltrinelli* 19, "I Diari," 257–608 at 425–27.
188. Ibid., 426.
189. Giorgio Bocca, *Palmiro Togliatti* (Bari: Editori Laterza, 1973), 543–57.
190. "Archivio Pietro Secchia," *Annali Feltrinelli* 19, "Promemoria autobiografico," 229–32.

leadership went along with the recommendation, with only Longo and Pajetta abstaining and Longo's former wife and Terracini voting no.[191] At that point Secchia and Colombi traveled to the Soviet Union to inform Togliatti of the *Direzione*'s decision. Confronted with his unbounded fury and indignation, the two emissaries agreed to request that Togliatti return to Italy for the Seventh PCI Congress before assuming the Cominform post. Stalin reluctantly agreed, only to give his Italian visitors the cold shoulder thereafter. Togliatti returned to Italy in late February 1951. At the Seventh Congress he was reelected general secretary. And—again in contrast to Thorez, who stayed in the Soviet Union ostensibly for reasons of health from December 1950 through March 1953[192]—the Italian leader never again returned to Moscow during Stalin's lifetime.

How is one to explain this bizarre episode? Stalin's intentions seem clear. By transferring Togliatti to the Cominform, he would get rid of the one surviving independent-minded European Communist leader. Throughout Eastern Europe Stalin was placing in power individuals who had for the most part spent years in Soviet exile. Lacking any local constituency, they were wholly subservient to his will. Plainly he calculated that by depriving Togliatti of the authority that emanated from the *partito nuovo* he could break him as well. The Italian leader, uprooted from his domestic base of support, would become as psychologically dependent on Stalin as the new cohort of East European Communist secretaries.

We may likewise surmise the reasons for Togliatti's objections. After virtually masterminding the creation of the *partito nuovo*, he had no intention of leaving it to head an organization he well knew was a hollow shell, a facade for the imposition of Soviet *diktat*. He said as much to his private secretary, Luigi Amadesi.[193] Equally important was Togliatti's long-ingrained preference for working within his own party. As he burst out in anger to Secchia, "You who knew how I have always been against staying abroad in the headquarters of international organs ought not to have voted in favor of such a decision."[194] His similar reaction to the attempt to transfer him from the PCI Politburo to the WEB of the Comintern in 1928 is striking.

Less easy to explain is the conduct of the PCI *Direzione*. Were its members misled by Secchia with regard to the depth of Togliatti's opposition to Stalin's scheme? Were they cowed by the intensity of Cold War hostilities and their own domestic isolation into heeding Stalin's wishes more readily than would have otherwise been the case? Had their memo-

---

191. Bocca, *Palmiro Togliatti*, 550.
192. Wall, *French Communism in the Era of Stalin*, 135.
193. Bocca, *Palmiro Togliatti*, 546.
194. "Archivio Pietro Secchia," *Annali Feltrinelli* 19, "Promemoria autobiografico," 231.

ries of earlier clashes with Moscow receded in the wake of the more recent setbacks wrought by the American-backed Christian Democratic establishment? There is probably some truth to all these suppositions.

What is most important, however, is that in the end Togliatti's influence over the *Direzione* proved greater than Stalin's. Once he returned to Italy to plead his case in person, the issue was resolved in his favor. The authority he enjoyed among his comrades derived, in part, from the conciliatory approach he had taken toward internal party differences over the years. The loyalty of his associates may also have been reinforced by their perception, however clouded, of the dissension and purges then afflicting the other European Communist parties. At the same time, the very strength of the *partito nuovo* helps explain Togliatti's successful defiance of Stalin. The party continued to grow during the Cominform years—in members, cadres, and organizational development. The official statistics may have been inflated. But with upwards of two million members and the apparatus and revenues that flowed therefrom, the PCI elite was—in the final analysis—able to control its own affairs.

CHAPTER 7

The Post-Stalin Challenge
to Soviet Centralism

The death of Stalin in March 1953 opened up a new era for the PCI, as for all other members of the international Communist movement. Togliatti took advantage of the ferment triggered by Khrushchev's denunciation of Stalin at the Twentieth CPSU Congress to voice certain ideas about the structure and role of the Communist world that he had probably been contemplating for some time. These ideas were initially set forth in his widely publicized interview in the Italian journal, *Nuovi argomenti,* in June 1956. They included the suggestion that Communist parties were just one among several forces in the global march toward socialism, a notion inherent in the PCI's later support for socialist pluralism. They also included the affirmation of autonomy as the basic organizational norm of the world Communist movement, a norm that could however lead to voluntary ententes among like-minded Communist parties. In advancing these notions Togliatti plainly sought to make the Communist world safe for the Italian path to socialism, a path that would lead to a form of socialism different from the type prevailing in the Soviet bloc.

From 1956 onward the aura of *doppiezza* that had hung over the PCI, the suspicion that the Italian Communists wanted to use electoral institutions in order to subvert the democratic order, began to dissipate. But there was another sense in which *doppiezza* continued to characterize the PCI's outlook. Here I am referring to the double standard by which the Italian Communists judged political life in the East and in the West. Violations of legality and restrictions on civil rights that would be consid-

A small part of this chapter is reprinted by permission of the publisher from *The European Left; Italy, France, and Spain,* ed. William E. Griffith (Lexington, Mass.: Lexington Books, D.C. Heath and Company, copyright 1979, D. C. Heath and Company).

ered intolerable in their own country were usually passed over in silence by PCI publicists when they occurred in the Soviet bloc.

The persistence of the PCI policy makers' application of a double standard to Communist and capitalist polities was partly a result of their great expectations regarding an improvement in the quality of Soviet life under Khrushchev. The dismantling of *Gulag,* the promise of consumer welfare, the upward social mobility of the working class all compared favorably, if viewed through the rose-tinted glasses of Italian Communist militants, to the socioeconomic inequalities that continued to plague Italy despite the ''economic miracle'' of the 1950s and 1960s, with its surge in GNP growth rates and middle-class well-being. It was only after the suppression of the Czechoslovakian liberalization process by Soviet armed forces in 1968 that the PCI elite as a whole began to acknowledge the universal value of ''bourgeois'' civil liberties and political competition, even under socialism.

The task of the analyst of Soviet–PCI relations becomes considerably easier for the years after 1956 than earlier, partly because of the greater openness of Italian Communist publications but primarily because of the excellent works already written in this field. Foremost among them is Donald L. M. Blackmer's indispensable study of the 1956–64 period, *Unity in Diversity: Italian Communism and the Communist World.* In scope and depth there is nothing comparable in Italian or English to Blackmer's volume. For the PCI's domestic policies during this same time frame, Donald Sassoon's *The Strategy of the Italian Communist Party* is likewise very useful. The many articles and monographs that have also contributed to an understanding of the post-1956 era are too numerous to cite here but are mentioned throughout the footnotes of the next three chapters.

I begin this chapter with a discussion of what the Italian Communists themselves so aptly call ''the unforgettable 1956.'' A brief overview then follows of the pressures and constraints involved in the PCI policy makers' search for a viable Italian path to socialism. The concluding section focuses on the most innovative area of Italian Communist policy during the years 1956–76: namely, its strategy of building transnational coalitions within the larger international Communist movement for the purpose of defending autonomy in general and the *via italiana* in particular.

Throughout this chapter there is a recurring theme that underlies my analysis, if only implicitly. This concerns, on the one hand, the question of why the PCI elite did not move more quickly to implement its proposals regarding the international Communist movement and to define its own vision of socialism. On the other hand, it concerns the question of why, during the remainder of Togliatti's lifetime especially, the PCI leadership was so cautious in criticizing the repressive nature of Soviet socialism and in standing up to the CPSU's continuing obsession with imposing its political and organizational norms on the Communist world. From the vantage point of the student of the Communist movement, the PCI was— even during the 1956–68 period—in the forefront of innovation compared to other Western Communist parties. The student of comparative European politics, in contrast, is prone to ask why the PCI did not emulate the more rapid pace of evolution undertaken by the German Social Democratic Party (SDP) from the 1950s onward. This chapter seeks to shed some light on these queries.

"The Unforgettable 1956"

The year 1956 brought unprecedented upheaval in the Communist world. It began with Khrushchev's "secret speech" against Stalin at the Twentieth Congress of the CPSU in late February, saw mounting ferment in Poland during the summer and early fall, and culminated in the Red Army's suppression of the Hungarian Revolution in early November. These benchmarks, taken together, constituted the first of the major post-Stalin crises that were to wrack the international Communist movement and radically transform it by the 1970s and 1980s. The crisis of 1956 also gave rise to the last Soviet–PCI confrontation in which Togliatti was to play the leading role. If the PCI's reaction to destalinization in Moscow and unrest in Eastern Europe marked the party as an innovative force among Western Communists, it also bore the unmistakable imprint of Togliatti's political mentality and style. In a word, the PCI's conduct during that time of troubles displayed the same mix of innovation and conformity which had characterized Togliatti's relationship with Moscow over three decades and which was, indeed, an integral feature of his *partito nuovo*.

Togliatti's Initiatives: The Organizational Focus

Togliatti's response to Stalin's death and posthumous denigration took a primarily organizational turn, both within the PCI and in the international Communist movement at large. With regard to his own party, he re-emphasized the early postwar character of the *partito nuovo* as a mass movement and downplayed the cadre network set in place by Secchia in the late 1940s. This ultimately led to the removal of Secchia as organizational overseer and deputy general secretary of the PCI. With regard to the global Communist context, he went beyond the principle of autonomy to which even Khrushchev had begun to pay lip service and proposed the complex and fertile concept of polycentrism. Togliatti also provoked the public ire of Moscow by echoing the (post-1948) Titoist notion of the bureaucratic degeneration of the Soviet system. It was, however, the challenge to Soviet centralism inherent in the idea of polycentrism—the several meanings of which will be discussed below—that was to have the most enduring impact on Soviet–PCI relations.

Togliatti's showdown with Secchia came well before the Twentieth CPSU Congress. Secchia, it will be recalled, was promoted to co-deputy general secretary—a post Longo had occupied since the Fifth Congress— in February 1948. In that capacity he not only actively supported Stalin's abortive effort to transfer Togliatti to Cominform headquarters, but he also pushed for the creation of a centralized apparatus of cadres capable of regimenting the party at the grassroots level. This was to be done by organizing all rank-and-file members into "groups of ten," each directed by a member of the cadre network.[1] It was Secchia, too, who represented the PCI in mid-July 1953 at a series of secret meetings in Moscow attended by the Cominform members, the Chinese, and Khrushchev, Malenkov, and Molotov. The CPSU triumvirate had summoned their foreign comrades to the Soviet Union to inform them of the purge of Beria and the impending campaign against Stalin and his "personality cult."[2] Togliatti, in turn, took advantage of this news to reduce Secchia's authority back home.

The steps in this process need only be briefly mentioned here. In the autumn of 1953 Edoardo D'Onofrio, who had worked with Grieco in Paris in the mid-1930s and was part of Togliatti's broadcasting team during the war, published a two-part article in *Rinascita* in which he blamed Secchia in barely disguised terms for the party's excessive centralization and bureaucratization.[3] As D'Onofrio put it, certain "leading Communist cadres" who had spent the 1930s and early wartime years "in jail, in confinement, in complete clandestinity" had brought to the PCI "too rigid a conception of life and organization" and "a personal and oppressive method of leadership."[4] Secchia was unable to fight back because of a scandal surrounding his private secretary, Giulio Seniga. Seniga absconded with party funds in mid-1954 and thereafter engaged in anti-Communist exposés based on materials acquired through his close

1. See, for example, Secchia's speech to the Seventh PCI Congress in *l'Unità*, April 6, 1951, 1 and 4.

2. Secchia's notes on these meetings are reprinted in Giulio Seniga, *Togliatti e Stalin,* 3d ed. (Milan: Sugar Editore, 1978), 53–68; cf. "Archivio Pietro Secchia," *Annali Feltrinelli* 19 (Milan: Feltrinelli Editore, 1979), "I Diari," 239–40.

3. Edoardo D'Onofrio, "Il problema della direzione collettive nel P.C. dell' U.S.," and "Il problema della direzione collegiale nel P.C.I.," *Rinascita* 10, nos. 10–11 (October and November 1953):566–68 and 628–32, respectively.

4. Ibid., 629.

association with Secchia.[5] Under suspicion himself because of the trust he had placed in Seniga, Secchia felt obliged to toe rather than combat the emerging Togliatti line.[6] In due course, therefore, he was demoted from the post of co-deputy general secretary (at the Fourth Conference of the PCI in January 1955), deprived of his organizational duties,[7] and eventually assigned to direct the party in Lombardy.[8] Meanwhile, there was a wholesale removal of Secchia's appointees among the secretaries of the PCI's provincial federations.

By early 1956, in other words, Togliatti's position as party head was considerably stronger than it had been five years earlier when the *Direzione* had, for a time, backed Stalin's proposal to shift him to the Cominform. He was thus able to put his personal stamp on the PCI's reaction to destalinization.

As was the case throughout the European Communist movement, Togliatti's initial reaction to Khrushchev's anti-Stalin speech was one of public reserve. He, along with Thorez and other foreign Communist leaders attending the Twentieth Congress, had been shown a copy of the "secret speech" with the understanding they would not divulge its contents.[9] Accordingly, at a meeting of the PCI Central Committee some two and one-half weeks later, Togliatti confined his remarks to the formal proceedings of the CPSU conclave. Notwithstanding his reticence on Stalin, however, he applauded Khrushchev's receptivity to different paths to socialism. He welcomed the promise of economic reform and consumerism in the Soviet Union. And, just as in April 1954 he had echoed Malenkov's thesis that nuclear war would mean "the destruction of human civilization,"[10] he hailed Khrushchev's pronouncements on peaceful coexistence and the noninevitability of war.[11] At a meeting of the PCI National Council in early April, after news of the secret speech had leaked to the West, Togliatti stuck to his policy of silence on Stalin, much to the chagrin of some of his colleagues in the *Direzione* (Amendola and Pajetta, among others).[12] Only in his closing speech did he touch on the Stalin issue. But even then he voiced ritualistic words of praise for the late Soviet leader.

5. Seniga, *Togliatti e Stalin,* passim.

6. For Secchia's version of these events, see "Archivio Pietro Secchia," *Annali Feltrinelli* 19, "Promemoria autobiografico," 245, and "I Diari," 259–64 and 410–17.

7. See introduction to ibid., 108–20.

8. Ibid., 416, n. 17.

9. Gian Carlo Pajetta, *Le crisi che ho vissuto: Budapest Praga Varsavia* (Rome: Editori Riuniti, 1982), 58.

10. Palmiro Togliatti, "Per un accordo fra comunisti e cattolici per salvare la civiltà umana," *l'Unità,* April 13, 1954, 1.

11. Text in Palmiro Togliatti, *Problemi del movimento operaio internazionale, 1956–1961* (Rome: Editori Riuniti, 1962), 27–72.

12. Pajetta, *Le crisi che ho vissuto,* 59–62.

It was only after the publication of the secret speech by the United States Department of State on June 4 that Togliatti broke with the pack. At that time he gave his interview to the Italian periodical, *Nuovi argomenti,* in which for the first time he directly addressed the Stalin question. Other Western Communist leaders—most notably Thorez—tried to downplay Stalin's culpability by pointing to extenuating historical circumstances (capitalist encirclement and hostility).[13] Togliatti likewise took a historical view of Stalin's errors but in a way that magnified them. The gist of his argument was that it was not enough to denounce *what* Stalin had done; it was also necessary to explain *why* he had been able to get away with it. And the hypothesis he offered was that Stalin's arrogation of power had led to the partial "degeneration" of the Soviet system, thereby making possible the abnormalities associated with his rule. His specific words to this effect, quoted so often, bear repeating. "Stalin's errors," Togliatti speculated, were the result of "the progressive imposition of personal power . . . and, as a consequence, the accumulation of phenomena of bureaucratization, of violation of legality, of stagnation and also, partially, of degeneration, at different points of the social organism"[14] At the same time, the Italian leader also spelled out the coresponsibility of Stalin's present detractors in the Kremlin for what had transpired. The implication was that further reflection and rectification were required on their part if the effects of the personality cult were to be fully overcome.

Togliatti's unwillingness to attribute the Stalinist system solely to Stalin the man may be explained, in part, by his intellectualism. His mode of political analysis had always been marked by attentiveness to historical nuances and avoidance of sweeping generalizations. Viewed from another angle, he well knew that the "personality cult" was not a sufficient explanation for the brutality of Stalinism. For the PCI itself had fostered a cult of Stalin—and Togliatti!—without committing "errors" of the sort disclosed by Khrushchev. In the Italian context adulation of Stalin had served not as a rationale for totalitarian excesses but as a symbol of the PCI's pro-Sovietism and as a source of psychological support for Italian militants during the worst years of Cold War ostracism. Indeed, the tens of thousands of semieducated workers and peasants who rallied to the PCI had, *unlike their counterparts in the Soviet bloc,* precious little inkling of the terrorism and mass deprivation imposed by Stalin. Reports of such tyranny were simply chalked up to bourgeois slander. They were thus bewildered rather than relieved by the denunciation of his crimes. All the

13. François Fejtö, *The French Communist Party and the Crisis of International Communism* (Cambridge, Mass.: MIT Press, 1967), 63–69.

14. "L'intervista a 'Nuovi argomenti,'" in *Problemi del movimento operaio internazionale,* 85–117 at 89.

more reason, then, for Togliatti's attempt to place the Stalin phenomenon in a broader sociological and historical perspective. These considerations aside, his own association (and sometimes cooperation) with Stalin's henchmen from the late 1920s onward surely persuaded him that Stalin alone was not responsible for all the horrors identified with his name.

Togliatti was, however, preoccupied above all with the nature of organizational ties among the members of the international Communist movement. The question of systemic degeneration under Stalin was a matter for the Soviet comrades to pursue. Recommendations regarding interparty relations were, in contrast, clearly a prerogative of the leader of the world's largest nonruling Communist party. Togliatti approached this issue from two vantage points: criticism of the past and proposals for the future. He touched on both in the *Nuovi argomenti* interview but developed his ideas more fully in his subsequent report to the PCI Central Committee on June 24, 1956.

With regard to the past, Togliatti deplored the Comintern's sectarianism of 1928–31 as well as Manuilsky's public attack on the PCI from the podium of a CPSU congress in 1939. More important, he sought to disabuse his own comrades of the mistaken image of the Comintern as a monolithic organization wholly subordinate to Moscow. "It is a lie," he stated flatly, "that there was only a group that gave orders and non-Russian Communists who obeyed. . . . In the Communist International there were great debates for years and years."[15] He thus paved the way for an eventual discussion of his own role as an opponent of the sectarian line as well as a Comintern secretary during the popular front years. In a related vein, he also disclosed his opposition to Stalin's January 1951 proposal to transfer him from the PCI leadership to Cominform headquarters—along with his doubts regarding the establishment of the Cominform in the first place.[16]

Togliatti's proposals for the future focused on the decentralization of the world Communist movement. He devised the fecund term "polycentrism" to describe the diversity that was beginning to characterize the global march toward socialism. In organizational terms, polycentrism had the connotation of multiple ententes of geopolitically kindred Communist parties. Togliatti himself never suggested regional Communist organizations as such, but he did speak of "diverse points or centers of *orientation and development*."[17] All the while, he placed primary emphasis on bilateral relations among autonomous Communist parties. His stress on bilateralism represented less of a threat to Soviet ideological authority. Nev-

15. "La via italiana al socialismo" (report delivered June 24, 1956, to the PCI Central Committee), in *Problemi del movimento operaio internazionale*, by Togliatti, 121–69 at 143.
16. Ibid., 144–45.
17. Ibid., 136; my emphasis.

ertheless, it was the idea of autonomous regional groupings that received the widest currency among Western publicists and Communist circles alike and that was to have an enduring impact on PCI political discourse.

In addition to its regional implications, Togliatti also spoke of polycentrism in the sense of multiple transnational trends toward socialism, variously emanating from the Communist, social-democratic, and progressive Third World movements. Here the crux of Togliatti's innovation and implicit challenge to Moscow was the denial of the need for Communists to play the leading role in the construction of socialism. "There are countries where we wish to start socialism without the Communists being the leading party," he remarked in the *Nuovi argomenti* interview.[18] "We can find," he elaborated in his subsequent Central Committee report, "a drive toward socialism . . . also in countries where the Communist parties not only don't participate in power but at times are not even large forces."[19] Such a situation, he continued, could pertain as readily in an advanced capitalist country as in a newly independent Third World state.[20] The idea that Communists might play a secondary or even negligible role in building socialism was un-Leninist, indeed pluralist, in import. And it would all too soon be countered by the CPSU's promulgation of "general laws" of socialist construction, foremost among them being the leading role of the Communist party.

Togliatti's organizational initiatives of June 1956 probably stemmed from a number of converging influences. For one thing, quite a few colleagues in the *Direzione* were eager for a change in the PCI's relationship with Moscow. Terracini, Pajetta, and Amendola all used the Stalin issue even earlier than Togliatti, that is, in March–April 1956, to press for greater party independence.[21] Negarville joined Pajetta in staunchly backing the Togliatti line during an informational trip to the Soviet Union in late June.[22] Di Vittorio repeatedly went his own way during the following months, defending the worker-rebels of Poznań and Budapest against Soviet-inspired charges of CIA provocation,[23] denouncing the forcible collectivization of agriculture as "pure stupidity,"[24] and rejecting the "transmission belt" concept of PCI relations with the CGIL.[25] Longo's moves to distance the PCI from the CPSU when he succeeded Togliatti as party head would suggest that he, too, was aligned

18. "L'intervista a 'Nuovi argomenti,'" 116.

19. "La via italiana al socialismo," 134.

20. Ibid., 135.

21. Donald L. M. Blackmer, *Unity in Diversity: Italian Communism and the Communist World* (Cambridge, Mass.: MIT Press, 1968), 38–40; cf. Pajetta, *Le crisi che ho vissuto,* 59–62.

22. Ibid., 65.

23. Blackmer, *Unity in Diversity,* 69 and 88.

24. Quoted in Donald Sassoon, *The Strategy of the Italian Communist Party* (New York: St. Martin's, 1981), 173.

25. Ibid., 207, n. 43.

with the innovators in 1956. (Grieco, had he not died in July 1955, would surely have been so.)

Two reasons may account for this readiness to strike out on their own, an attitude that contrasted sharply with the conformity and defensiveness of the French Communist leadership.[26] The first was the Italian innovators' memory of earlier humiliation in the name of Stalinist orthodoxy—an experience the once imprisoned Terracini, for example, had shared with the exile group in Paris. This presumably made them more receptive to Khrushchev's charges against Stalin than might otherwise have been the case. The second was the organizational style of the top PCI leadership group. Through the worst years of late Stalinism the *Direzione* remained intact, despite the diversity of its members' backgrounds and outlooks. Even Secchia was still a member (albeit not in good standing). When the destalinization crisis broke, the more innovative among the PCI elite thus had the sense of security needed to encourage and back Togliatti's assertiveness.

The PCI's contacts with the PCF during the spring of 1956 may, in addition, have helped shape Togliatti's conception of a special relationship among Communist parties with geopolitical affinities. In late March Thorez met Togliatti informally during a family Easter trip to Italy. According to the memoirs of their go-between, Giulio Cerreti, their talks were inconclusive, even discordant, particularly on the Stalin question.[27] All the same, the following May formal PCI–PCF talks were held in San Remo. The participants were Pajetta, Negarville, Spano, and, on the French side, Jacques Duclos, Étienne Fajon, and Raymond Guyot. The meeting was kept secret: such bilateral contacts, forbidden by Stalin in his last years, were still very much the exception. But the results were promising.[28] Tentative agreement was reached on a draft document dealing with issues of mutual interest to West European Communists, on the exchange of representatives between the PCI and PCF central committees and daily newspapers, and on an exchange of opinions with other Western parties at the PCF Congress scheduled for mid-July. It later turned out that the British Communist Party even proposed that the Western Communists attending the French congress issue a statement in common. At San Remo the French and Italian delegations examined, finally, the possibility of publishing a joint journal.[29] In short, there was the prospect of a regional entente of the kind anticipated in Togliatti's public statements of June 1956.

26. Cf. Irwin M. Wall, *French Communism in the Era of Stalin* (Westport, Conn.: Greenwood, 1983), 203–19.
27. Giulio Cerreti, *Con Togliatti e Thorez* (Milan: Feltrinelli Editore, 1973), 319–23.
28. Pajetta, *Le crisi che ho vissuto*, 76–79.
29. Ibid.

If the PCI–PCF contacts pointed to the regional meaning of polycentrism, Togliatti's meeting with Tito in Belgrade in late May 1956 surely had an impact on his discussion of polycentrism in the strategic sense of diverse global trends toward socialism. For that concept, if not the term itself, had provided the ideological underpinning for Yugoslavian sponsorship of the nonaligned movement. As the *Programme of the League of Yugoslav Communists* was to spell out in 1958, "The conception that the Communist parties have a monopoly over every aspect of the movement of society towards socialism, and that socialism can only find its representatives in them and move forward through them, is theoretically wrong and in practice very harmful."[30] The renunciation of ideological exclusivism championed by the Titoists from the early 1950s onward in the international arena offered an enticing theoretical framework for the articulation—in the PCI's domestic environment—of a democratic path to socialism.

The first step in the reestablishment of relations between the PCI and the Yugoslavian Communists followed shortly on the heels of Khrushchev's penitent trip to Belgrade in May 1955. That autumn Pajetta and Alfredo Reichlin stopped in Belgrade en route to and from an anniversary celebration in Albania. This gave Pajetta an opportunity to meet with Vlaho Vlahović, an old Comintern associate of Togliatti, at Yugoslavian party headquarters.[31] Formal party ties were resumed when Togliatti met with Tito in May 1956, using that occasion to endorse the international significance of Yugoslavia's autonomous path to socialism.

Subsequently many other Western Communist parties, including the PCF in 1957, began a rapprochement with Belgrade. But the PCI initiative represented a breakthrough both because of its timing and because of the depth of genuine hostility that had divided the two parties. Other Western Communists joined in Stalin's excommunication of Tito out of discipline. The Italians, in contrast, welcomed the Soviet–Yugoslav schism for their own particular reasons. Tensions between the PCI and the Titoists had developed as early as the wartime Resistance. At that time disagreements over the respective roles and authority of the two parties in the contested territory of Venezia Giulia[32] were accompanied by Yugoslavian criticism of the Italian Communists for not creating a national front on the Titoist pattern, "a front of mass organizations gathered around the party."[33] The

---

30. *The Programme of the League of Yugoslav Communists* (Belgrade: Edition Jugoslavija, 1958), 43–72; see 62 for the above quotation.

31. Pajetta, *Le crisi che ho vissuto*, 43–46.

32. Luigi Longo, *I centri dirigenti del PCI nella Resistenza* (Rome: Editori Riuniti, 1974), 469–70 and 481; and Mario Pacor, *Confine orientale: Questione nazionale e Resistenza nel Friuli-Venezia Giulia* (Milan: Feltrinelli Editore, 1964), 272–89.

33. Amendola refers to this Yugoslav wartime criticism in "Amendola, Basso, Pajetta: Unità e socialismo," *Rinascita* 22, no. 29 (July 17, 1965):15–19 at 17.

resulting resentment was compounded by Yugoslavia's postwar claims to Trieste.[34] It was further exacerbated by the tirades launched against the PCI by Edvard Kardelj and Milovan Djilas at the founding meeting of the Cominform in September 1947. Reports that Togliatti drafted the 1948 Cominform resolution against Yugoslavia, while not backed up by documentary evidence, are accordingly quite plausible.[35] But by the same token, the very intensity of these early PCI–Yugoslav animosities underscored the bold character of Togliatti's move toward reconciliation in 1956. It was also a measure of his commitment to the autonomy principle that the Yugoslavian experience symbolized.

The Limits to Innovation, the Pressures for Conformity

If May–June 1956 was a time of innovation for the PCI, the second half of the year was a time of alignment with the CPSU on a number of key issues.[36] The most notable case was the Italian party's approval of the Red Army's crackdown in Hungary in November 1956. Togliatti also modified his earlier positions on systemic "degeneration" under Stalin and on polycentrism. And the validity of democratic centralism was hailed by Togliatti and Longo in a manner unprecedented in the postwar era at the Eighth PCI Congress in December—and for months thereafter. Still, the very openness of debate at the Eighth Congress pointed to the "national particularities" of democratic centralism Italian-style. Togliatti's June 1956 initiatives, moreover, were only qualified, not reversed. And even on the searing question of the Hungarian Revolution the Italian party's assessment diverged in some respects from that of the Soviet leadership. In other words, if there were limits to the PCI's divergences from Moscow in 1956, there were also limits to its compliance with Soviet desiderata. Nevertheless, given the Italian Communist leadership's later condemnation of the Soviet invasion of Czechoslovakia in 1968 and its polycentric approach to international Communist affairs in the 1970s, the question of interest to us here is not just the extent of its conformity in 1956 but why it chose to conform at all.

With regard to his June 1956 initiatives, Togliatti persisted in criticizing the Soviet policy makers for their deficient analysis of the causes of Stalin's "mistaken political directions," his "errors that were so grave as to amount to crime."[37] He also continued to propose multilateral ex-

34. On this issue Togliatti tried to straddle the fence in the mid-1940s by claiming Trieste for Italy but opposing Western plans for setting up a "free territory" of Trieste.

35. Cf. Giorgio Bocca, *Palmiro Togliatti* (Bari: Editori Laterza, 1973), 504.

36. Cf. Blackmer, *Unity in Diversity*, 68–98.

37. See Togliatti's report to the Eighth PCI Congress in *VIII Congresso del partito comunista italiano: Atti e risoluzioni* (Rome: Editori Riuniti, 1957), 32.

changes of opinion among Communist parties operating in similar environments, even suggesting the inclusion of socialist and democratic representatives in such gatherings.[38] Both these views were expressed at the Eighth PCI Congress in December 1956 and echoed in its final resolution.[39] All the same, after June 1956 Togliatti no longer alluded to the "degeneration" of the Soviet system. He refused indeed to use the term "Stalinism" because it implied that the Soviet system itself was flawed.[40] At the Eighth Congress, moreover, he rejected polycentrism as an organizational concept. "A system of multiple groups and centers was thought of," he said, "but even this form of organization seemed incompatible with the full autonomy of each party and likely to saddle one or another of them with excessive responsibilities."[41]

Togliatti's reconsideration of his original position on polycentrism was probably the result of the reservations voiced by other Communist leaderships. In July, for example, Pajetta and Spano met with Fajon in Paris to follow up on the proposals discussed in the secret San Remo talks the previous May. The French party, however, now opposed any multilateral meeting or statement on the part of West European Communists at the forthcoming PCF Congress. It reneged as well on the idea of publishing a journal with the PCI.[42] Fajon, who—like Pajetta—had visited Moscow in late June,[43] may have got some inkling of Soviet displeasure over such measures, but there is no firm evidence for this. In fact, in early April 1956 Khrushchev had told the new Yugoslavian ambassador to the Soviet Union, Veljko Micunović, that "the [West] Europeans should act by themselves, they have no need for Russian advice," and he had taken a hands-off approach to the Easter 1956 meeting between Thorez and Togliatti.[44] It seems likely, therefore, that the PCF leadership backed off from moves toward a regional entente because of its own conservative equivocation following the dissemination of Khrushchev's "secret speech" in June.[45]

Mao opposed Communist regionalism as well, commenting to a PCI journalist in September 1956 that "there can be no polycentrism that does not break the unity of the workers' movement."[46] Doubts regarding re-

38. Ibid., 40–41.
39. For the final resolution, see ibid., 880 and 882.
40. Ibid., 44.
41. Ibid., 39–40.
42. Pajetta, *Le crisi che ho vissuto*, 78–79.
43. Fejtö, *The French Communist Party and the Crisis of International Communism*, 68.
44. Reported by Silvano Goruppi, "Quando Krusciov sconfisse Molotov: Le memorie dell'ex ambasciatore jugoslavo a Mosca," *l'Unità*, January 13, 1978, 3.
45. Fejtö, *The French Communist Party*, 64–72.
46. Quoted in Blackmer, *Unity in Diversity*, 67.

gional Communist ties were also expressed by the Poles,[47] but on quite different grounds. The new Gomulka regime feared a resurgence of *Cominformismo*. And indeed, Khrushchev had in his above-mentioned conversation with the Yugoslavian ambassador insisted that "for the countries of the 'lager' a new organization is indispensable." That Moscow would dominate such an organization was spelled out in a Soviet circular sent to the ruling Communist parties the following summer. As the document baldly stated, the CPSU "considers that it remains the directing party among all the Communist organizations of the world."[48] Yet the idea of a "directing party" ran directly counter to the cardinal organizational principle advanced by Togliatti in June 1956, namely, the absolute independence of every Communist party. For all these reasons, then, Togliatti watered down his mid-1956 remarks by calling for multilateral *dialogue* in place of regional links.

Togliatti also ceased to speak of the partial "degeneration" of the Soviet system. Here, however, his retreat was in response to direct Soviet pressure. As Molotov brusquely put it to Pajetta in late June 1956: "No, this we cannot accept."[49] Shortly thereafter Molotov's view found its way into an authoritative CPSU Central Committee resolution on the destalinization crisis (published in *Pravda* on July 2, 1956). "One cannot agree with the question raised by Comrade Togliatti as to whether Soviet society has not reached 'certain forms of degeneration,'" the resolution admonished. "There are no grounds whatever for this question."[50]

Such blunt Soviet criticism of a Communist leader was by far the exception rather than the rule in the liberalized atmosphere of 1956. Yet this only begs the question of why Togliatti felt compelled to heed Moscow's rebuke. He plainly had not changed his mind on the subject. For he continued to press in more subtle language for a full investigation into the origins of Stalin's misdeeds. Nor is it plausible to suppose that he dropped the degeneration theme out of a sense of discipline. He remained adamantly opposed to the concept of a leading party or state even after the CPSU attack. Rather, he seems to have feared that continued public denunciation by Moscow would undermine his authority vis-à-vis the *partito nuovo*.

Retrospective PCI analyses of "the unforgettable 1956" point to a fundamental divergence in the reactions of party intellectuals, on the one hand, and unskilled working-class and peasant militants, on the other, to

47. Luciano Gruppi, *Togliatti e la via italiana al socialismo* (Rome: Editori Riuniti, 1976), 182.
48. Quoted in Blackmer, *Unity in Diversity*, 79.
49. Pajetta, *Le crisi che ho vissuto*, 68.
50. Quoted in Blackmer, *Unity in Diversity*, 71.

237

the crisis of destalinization. For many younger intellectuals Khrushchev's exposé of Stalin gave rise to intense ideological soul-searching.[51] In contrast, the mass base of the *partito nuovo* was, to a large extent, either indifferent to the issue or unwilling to relinquish its idealized image of Soviet reality. Attentive students of this period such as Blackmer and Sassoon paint a similar picture.[52] There is no way of empirically verifying the proposition that most Communist workers and peasants were apathetic about or opposed to destalinization. Survey research was not done at the time; and the protagonists were not likely to leave a written record of their views. But the logic of the situation suggests this was the case.

The members of the *partito nuovo* had little knowledge and even less sense of complicity in the Stalinist purges of the 1930s, to which Khrushchev devoted so much attention in the "secret speech." More important, they had not personally experienced what Stalinization meant for the common man in Eastern Europe. The PCI base had been led to believe by their own leaders that the Soviet camp was a land of milk and honey for the working class. Even those who were aware of the repression and persecution exercised in the name of the proletariat could argue that, under Khrushchev, the ills of the past were being rectified. This signified neither sectarianism nor duplicity on their part but rather the strength of their Communist faith in a country where faith was still an integral part of political culture and where, to boot, the gap between the living standards of the disadvantaged and the better-off was growing perceptibly wider with the onset of the Italian "economic miracle."

It was the party leadership that was guilty of duplicity for imbuing the *partito nuovo* with a public philosophy of reflexive pro-Sovietism. Now, in 1956, it was feeling the boomerang effect of this facile solution to the dilemmas posed by *Cominformismo* and Cold War ostracism. For the average Communist stalwart, Togliatti's discourses on polycentrism and Soviet socialism were probably irrelevant. But for the PCI leader to provoke the public anger of the CPSU was quite another matter: the militants of the *partito nuovo* could not conceive of their political dreams coming true independently of the Soviet Union. In short, Togliatti backed down from systemic criticism of the Soviet regime for fear of bringing upon himself further CPSU criticism and hence the wrath of his own party base. The bottom line in this whole calculus was that in the mid-1950s workers, cottage laborers, and farmhands constituted about two-thirds of

51. Pajetta, *Le crisi che ho vissuto,* 103–4; cf. Pietro Ingrao, "Il XX Congresso del PCUS e l'VIII Congresso del PCI," in *Problemi di storia del Partito comunista italiano,* ed. Paolo Spriano et al. (Rome: Editori Riuniti, 1973), 131–68 at 161–62.

52. Blackmer, *Unity in Diversity,* 36–37, 41–46, 77–78, 87–91, and 95; cf. Sassoon, *The Strategy of the Italian Communist Party,* 103 and 197.

the total PCI membership; intellectuals, students, and white-collar employees a mere 3 percent.[53]

The PCI elite's support for Moscow's armed suppression of the Hungarian Revolution seems to have flowed from quite different considerations than those that induced Togliatti to modify his more daring initiatives of June 1956. Reduced to its bare essentials, the assessment expressed by Togliatti and endorsed at the Eighth PCI Congress was that the rebellion was fanned from the start by Hungarian reactionaries and imperialist agents and, if not put down, would have led to a reactionary, even Fascist, restoration.[54] As Togliatti reportedly argued to doubting party intellectuals, "the revolt would not have assumed the dimensions of total subversion if there had not been American meddling in support of the internal reaction."[55] (He had taken a similar position publicly at the time of the Polish workers' uprising in Poznań in late June 1956.)[56]

To be sure, Togliatti repeatedly deplored the failure of Hungary's Communist leaders to undertake urgently needed reforms[57] and regretted the belatedness of the CPSU's statement of October 30, 1956, promising equality and respect for sovereignty in relations with other Communist states.[58] In his report to the Eighth Congress, moreover, his defense of the Soviet invasion came amidst a penetrating indictment of the past "servile imitation of the Soviet model" in the people's democracies, and more muted criticism of the sectarianism and interventionism that had characterized international Communist relations during the Comintern–Cominform years.[59] But the gist of his argument was that one had to choose one side of the barricade or the other: socialism or reaction. The crushing of the Hungarian rebellion was a "painful necessity."[60]

There was a ring of sincerity to the statements of Togliatti and other PCI spokesmen on the Hungarian tragedy. Their support for the Soviet action seemed to spring from conviction rather than external pressure. That conviction, in turn, was rooted in considerations of personal identity, ideological commitment, and a multifaceted sense of political realism.

Togliatti and other *Direzione* members of his generation were, for the most part, not Stalinists; they were, however, Bolsheviks. They were

53. Grant Amyot, *The Italian Communist Party: The Crisis of the Popular Front Strategy* (New York: St. Martin's, 1981), 78.

54. See Togliatti's report in *VIII Congresso*, 36–37; cf. the final Congress resolution in ibid., 881.

55. Quoted in Blackmer, *Unity in Diversity*, 91.

56. Palmiro Togliatti, "La presenza del nemico," *l'Unità*, July 3, 1956; text reprinted in Togliatti, *Problemi del movimento operaio internazionale*, 171–74.

57. Cf. Togliatti's article in the October 1956 issue of *Rinascita*, reprinted in ibid., 203–7.

58. See Togliatti's report to the Eighth Congress in *VIII Congresso*, 36.

59. Ibid., 34–40.

60. The phrase is used in the final Congress resolution; see *VIII Congresso*, 881.

bound to the Soviet Union by their perception of shared principles and a common final goal. As Togliatti declared at the Eighth Congress, it had been Soviet socialist construction that had given "courage and impetus to the entire workers' movement."[61] After enduring the Stalinist years, moreover, one may surmise that it would have been inconceivable for him and others like him to turn against the Soviet Union over Hungary just when Khrushchev's domestic and foreign policy innovations promised a new era for the Communist world.

As for the younger generation of leaders who had entered the PCI in the mid-1940s, their support for the Soviet Union was probably more a derivative of their commitment to revolutionary change at home than of personal identification with the Soviet Union. As the young Enrico Berlinguer argued at the Eighth Congress, it was an illusion to think that capitalist society could be improved or "reformed" simply as a result of economic growth and some "natural evolution of political forces." What was needed was "the struggle for radical structural transformations of society and the struggle for power."[62] Yet given American backing of the Italian Christian Democratic establishment, the upcoming leaders of his age must have realized that it was also an illusion to think that the PCI's struggle for socialism could be successful without Soviet support, at least indirectly through a change in the "correlation of forces" between the United States and the Soviet Union in Europe. Stated somewhat differently, it was in the domestic interest of the PCI to prevent setbacks to Soviet prestige and power in Europe.

The supposition that the younger leaders' approval of the Soviet intervention in Hungary was based on this kind of hard-headed realism gains credence from their treatment of the subject at the Eighth Congress. Berlinguer did not mention it at all. Pietro Ingrao, who entered the *Direzione* at that time, was notably perfunctory on the Hungarian question, concentrating instead on the need to extend the PCI's domestic alliances and dialogue with "the Catholic forces."[63] Only Giorgio Napolitano, among the young speakers who would later rise to first rank, endorsed at some length Togliatti's views on Hungary.[64]

There was another side to such *Realpolitik,* one that could be appreciated by both the older and younger leaders. This had to do with the question of American instigation of the Hungarian revolt. This interpretation, however far-fetched to the detached observer, must have struck the Italian Communists as rather credible after their years of firsthand experience with the "hand of Washington" in domestic Italian politics. Per-

61. Ibid., 43.
62. Text of speech in ibid., 217–23; see 218 for the quotation.
63. Text of speech in ibid., 179–85.
64. Text of speech in ibid., 250–57; see 251–52 on Hungary.

vasive American support for establishment anticommunism in Italy—combined with the Eisenhower administration's rhetoric on "rollback" in Eastern Europe—lent an aura of plausibility to Soviet charges of imperialist subversion in Hungary.

There was, finally, the need to consider the attitudes of the PCI working-class base. On the question of Hungary as well as destalinization, Communist and non-Communist analysts of this period suggest overwhelming alignment with the Soviet Union. Years later survey research would reveal that a third of the Italian Communist middle-ranking cadres favored the Soviet invasion of Czechoslovakia and yet another third considered the Prague Spring "an experiment dangerous to socialism."[65] Small wonder that in 1956, with the party's public philosophy of virulent anti-Americanism and pro-Sovietism still fresh in their minds, they endorsed Soviet military intervention in Hungary. The PCI elite's backing of the CPSU on this issue may have sealed its estrangement from its erstwhile allies in the PSI. But, as the then thirty-eight-year-old Alessandro Natta pondered aloud at the Eighth Congress, if the party leadership had equivocated on Hungary, "wouldn't we perhaps, for fear of losing certain allies, have lost in effect the working class . . . ?"[66]

Such widespread solidarity with Moscow notwithstanding, the events of 1956 sparked debates and doubts throughout the PCI's ranks. Official party statements thus began to laud the organizational principle of democratic centralism to a degree unparalleled since the rise of the *partito nuovo*. At the Fifth PCI Congress at the end of 1945 this Leninist canon had actually been called into question. At the party congresses of 1948 and 1951 Togliatti neglected even to mention it. But it was a centerpiece of discourse at the Eighth Congress. Such public emphasis on democratic centralism was of course a way of curbing dissenting views, especially among students and professionals. Indeed, Togliatti and Longo categorically rejected the right of continued public debate once a majority decision was reached, let alone the formation of permanent minorities (factions) within the party.[67]

All the same, the new insistence on democratic centralism had an innovative facet as well. As Longo stated at the outset of his formal report on the party statutes to be approved at the Eighth Congress, the development of the *partito nuovo* in its early years was "promoted above all from on high, with methods of centralized and often personal direction."[68]

65. For survey data on such dissent, see Kevin Devlin, "The PCI and Its 'Afghans,'" *Radio Free Europe Research*, background report no. 113, April 23, 1981.

66. Text of speech in *VIII Congresso*, 314–20; see 318 in particular.

67. For Togliatti's and Longo's respective views, see ibid., 84 and 561–62; cf. the revised party statutes in ibid., 996–97.

68. Ibid., 552.

This was more than just a veiled denunciation of the centralization Secchia had fostered during the Cominform years; it had the ring of self-criticism on the part of the entire *Direzione*. A bit further in his speech Longo commented that "democratic centralism has had the tendency to be transformed into bureaucratic centralism."[69] What was needed instead, the deputy general secretary stressed, was rank-and-file initiative and participatory decision making at every level of the party structure.

Longo's call for greater internal party democracy cannot be dismissed as mere window dressing. That it was designed to placate Communist dissidents as well as to provide credibility for the PCI's postulation of a "democratic path to socialism" is beyond doubt. On the other hand, the diversity of views voiced at the Eighth Congress was exceptional by Communist standards. It included at one end of the spectrum the preposterous rhetoric of Concetto Marchesi, who compared the Hungarian student and worker rebels to the student and worker supporters of Mussolini.[70] At the opposite end stood the prophetic recommendations of Antonio Giolitti, who cited "*effective* freedom of opinion" within the party, "*unconditional* acceptance of democratic liberties" in the Italian march to socialism, and "full autonomy of *judgment* and action" toward other Communist parties as indispensable for the genuine renewal of the PCI.[71] Giolitti's advice would be followed only some two decades later, and he resigned from the party soon after the Eighth Congress. Meanwhile, between the extremes of Marchesi and Giolitti could be heard what had become the pat pro-Soviet loyalism of Secchia,[72] to the left of the Togliatti–Longo center, as well as the innovative ideas of Terracini to the right. Terracini not only offered a sophisticated explanation for why the PCI should drop the term "dictatorship of the proletariat";[73] he also insisted that there was a legitimate "plurality of interests" among the laboring masses which required "autonomous representation."[74] If Giolitti sounded like a Eurocommunist of the 1970s, Terracini sounded like a 1968 Czechoslovakian reformer.

In addition to countenancing a wide spectrum of opinion at the Eighth Congress, the PCI leadership attempted to use persuasion rather than coercion, "ideological" rather than "organizational" measures (to use the old Comintern language), in its dealings with dissenters from the party line, especially on Hungary. Leaders from Togliatti on down held endless discussions with doubters among students, intellectuals, and simple mili-

69. Ibid., 554.
70. Ibid., 137–43 at 138.
71. Ibid., 229–34 at 233–34; my emphasis.
72. Ibid., 339–46 at 343.
73. Ibid., 414–23 at 417.
74. Ibid., 418–19.

tants.[75] As if to distinguish the PCI's understanding of democratic centralism from that of the CPSU, moreover, Longo explicitly cited the Chinese Communist concepts of the "mass line" and mutual self-criticism in his report on the new party rules.[76] Nowhere did he mention the Soviet example. And to French Communist charges that the PCI had made too many concessions to oppositionists, Togliatti retorted in his Congress report that the Italian party intended to base the unity of its ranks on "reasoned and conscious consent, and not only on obedience."[77] Such a conciliatory approach was perhaps the dictate of necessity in an organization the size of the PCI, which despite the net loss of some 200,000 members as a result of "the unforgettable 1956," still numbered 1.7 million in 1961.[78] Yet Togliatti's words also reflected propensities he had displayed since the 1920s, propensities that had in turn contributed to the size of the *partito nuovo*.

The Search for an Italian Path to Socialism

The debates surrounding the Eighth PCI Congress marked the resumption of the search for an Italian path to socialism that had its tentative beginnings in the mid-1940s and that would by the 1970s lead to a profound divergence in Soviet–PCI perspectives regarding the shape of socialism in the West and the strategy for achieving it. The positing of a democratic, constitutional path to socialist transformation in December 1956 was but the other side of the coin of the reservations expressed that year toward the Stalinist deformities of socialism in the East. Nevertheless, for half a decade or more PCI deliberations focused on the *path* to socialism in Italy rather than on the contours of a future socialist society. This preoccupation with means, not ends, was probably linked both to Togliatti's political mentality and to Khrushchev's reformist policies. Whereas Togliatti's Bolshevik past left him with a perception of shared international Communist goals, Khrushchev's efforts to promote socialist legality and economic vitality in the Soviet Union gave promise of eventual compatibility between the Soviet model of socialism and a future West European one. It was only after Togliatti's death and Khrushchev's ouster, in August and October 1964, respectively, that pressures intensified within the PCI for a more precise formulation of long-term

---

75. See, for example, the accounts in Bocca, *Palmiro Togliatti*, 626–27; Blackmer, *Unity in Diversity*, 77–78; and Pajetta, *Le crisi che ho vissuto*, 105–9. For a dissenting view, see Fabrizio Onofri, *Classe operaia e partito* (Bari: Editori Laterza, 1957), 110–14.

76. *VIII Congresso*, 558 and 564.

77. Ibid., 83.

78. Sassoon, *The Strategy of the Italian Communist Party*, 197.

objectives. These pressures arose, in turn, from the mounting sectarianism of the Brezhnev regime, the continued exclusion of the PCI from power sharing at the national level in Italy, and generational change at all levels of the party, especially by the 1970s.

Despite Togliatti's innovative steps in 1956, there was a conservative cast to his approach to the *via italiana*. For one thing, he clung to doctrinally orthodox terminology. Granted, the tone of his speeches to the Eighth Congress had nothing in common with the schematic two-camp imagery that permeated his reports to the previous two party congresses. Nevertheless, he spoke of the PCI as the "vanguard of the working class"; he upheld the historical necessity of a "dictatorship of the proletariat";[79] he endorsed, if only in passing, "proletarian internationalism," "Marxism-Leninism," and "democratic centralism."[80] He insisted at some length on the urgency of combating not just "maximalist sectarianism" but also "reformist revisionism."[81] And he expounded upon the inherently aggressive nature of imperialism: "One can put a straight-jacket on it," he averred, "but one can't change its nature."[82] Even at the Tenth PCI Congress in December 1962, after Khrushchev had launched his second wave of destalinization at the Twenty-second CPSU Congress in late 1961, Togliatti could not seem to free his mindset from these orthodox formulations. He no longer used the code words mentioned above. But with the important exception of the "dictatorship of the proletariat," he alluded to all of them.

On the other hand, Togliatti also reverted to his mid-1920s conceptual framework of transitional slogans and stages to justify the PCI's domestic strategy. At first he did not do so publicly. In his report to the Eighth Congress he actually denied that the "structural reforms" urged by his party were in any way similar to "what at one time we called transitional demands, that is, slogans to launch at a moment of acute revolutionary crisis."[83] The reason for such skittishness was related, again, to the character of the *partito nuovo*. The post-Fascist generation of PCI activists knew nothing about the controversy over transitional slogans that had bedeviled Togliatti's relations with the Stalinists in the Comintern and his own colleagues, Longo and Secchia, in the second half of the 1920s. Indeed, all they knew about transitional slogans was what they read on the subject in Togliatti's late 1929 recantation in *Lo Stato operaio* of the hotly contested "republican assembly" slogan. For that article was included in

79. Togliatti's report in *VIII Congresso*, 59.
80. Ibid., 39.
81. Ibid., 82.
82. Ibid., 22.
83. Ibid., 51.

a collection of historic party documents published in 1952,[84] the time when the general secretary's standing in inner party circles was weakened by his dispute with Stalin over the directorship of the Cominform.

Such reservations notwithstanding, the draft programmatic declaration presented to the Eighth Congress implicitly endorsed the possibility of advocating transitional objectives even in nonrevolutionary periods.[85] And shortly thereafter Togliatti began openly to speak of the legitimacy of using "slogans of a transitional character" during a democratic transitional stage rather than an "acute revolutionary crisis."[86] Not only that, but at the Tenth PCI Congress in 1962 he revived the transitional slogan he had coined in the mid-1930s, "democracy of a new type";[87] and he spoke of the "governments of the popular front, before the war," as having offered "a new political and social perspective."[88]

The sixty-nine-year-old leader may have become too weary or set in his ways to devise new strategic terms. On the other hand, there were some significant new strategic arguments in Togliatti's 1962 congress report. First of all, he suggested the possibility of using democratic and constitutional means to change gradually the class nature of the existing Italian state structure.[89] In other words, in line with his omission of any reference to the "dictatorship of the proletariat," he tacitly challenged the Leninist dictum that the bourgeois state must be destroyed, not reformed. Second, he flatly declared that to focus on winning "51 percent" of the vote was illusory because "a dominant bourgeois class can always manage to prevent such a conquest."[90] All the same, unlike Berlinguer's use of this latter argument a decade later to justify an accommodation with Christian Democracy, Togliatti put it in the context of support for the PCI's struggle for more extended grassroots alliances and forms of "control from below," of "direct democracy." Furthermore, while the party campaigned intensively for transitional goals in the form of "structural reforms," its spokesmen remained notably vague on just why these partial improvements should galvanize the masses for more radical action. This whole pattern of "transitional" thinking, moreover, only begged the question: Transition to what? and when?

---

84. See chap. 3, n. 78.

85. See Ingrao's commentary in "Il XX Congresso," *Problemi di storia del Partito comunista italiano,* 164–65; cf. the PCI program in *VIII Congresso,* 909.

86. See his speech to the 1957 Moscow conference of Communist and workers' parties in *Problemi del movimento operaio internazionale,* 253–67 at 261–63.

87. See his report in *X Congresso del partito comunista italiano: Atti e risoluzioni* (Rome: Editori Riuniti, 1963), 27–82 at 52 and 64.

88. Ibid., 70.

89. Ibid., 70–71.

90. Ibid., 71.

Meanwhile, the Italian parliamentary elections of April 1963 lent urgency to these queries. The PCI's share of the vote for the Chamber of Deputies rose two and a half percentage points (from 22.7 to 25.3), whereas the DC's share dropped four percentage points (from 42.4 to 38.3), leading to incremental gains for small parties on the right and center left. Yet the PCI's entry into government at the national level was blocked as firmly as ever by the ensuing center-left coalition cabinets that included, for the first time since 1948, the PSI and were headed, until 1968, by Aldo Moro. The Communist policy makers' concern over this turn of events was aggravated by the gradual decline of the party's membership in absolute terms (from over 2.0 million in 1954 to a low of about 1.5 million in 1968) and as a percentage of factory workers (down from 23.5 percent in 1954 to 12.3 percent in 1962).[91] Although Italy's much touted "economic miracle" did not adversely affect the PCI's *electoral* appeal, the prospect of perpetual political isolation seemed to be eroding the party's ability to recruit new members.

An impatient search for a political strategy to overcome this stalemate thus developed among party cadres and intellectuals. That search was influenced by two circumstances: the post-Togliatti succession and the revival of interest in Gramsci's writings that had been under way since the late 1950s. Togliatti's death in late August 1964 added an element of competitiveness and innovation to the various elaborations upon the *via italiana* that began to emerge from 1963 onward. At the same time, the officially encouraged attention to Gramsci's works shaped the terms of that discourse. PCI strategists were henceforth preoccupied not with how the "proletariat" might establish its "dictatorship" but with how a "new historic bloc" might win "hegemony" over the existing Italian state.

The two major groupings involved in this quest were led by Amendola and Pietro Ingrao, a former editor of *l'Unità* who had been promoted to the PCI *Direzione* in December 1956 at the age of thirty-one. Among the protégés of Amendola was Giorgio Napolitano, head of the Naples Federation and *Direzione* member since 1962. One of Ingrao's closest partisans was Alfredo Reichlin, named Apulian regional secretary in 1962 and elevated to the *Direzione* in 1966. Both Napolitano and Reichlin were the same age as Ingrao. The divergences between these two *correnti* have often been depicted as a right-left dichotomy, but this has validity only with regard to the *pace* of social transformation. In other respects they were both innovators, with the Amendola group being more concerned with coalition building across class lines among parties to the left of center and the *ingraoiani* being more intent upon mobilizing working-class support across religious lines.

---

91. Sassoon, *The Strategy of the Italian Communist Party,* 203.

Amendola apparently anticipated the failure of the center-left experiment. He therefore continued to support the strategy of building a new historic bloc of workers and progressive members of the middle class disenchanted by the Moro cabinets. He went so far, indeed, as to recommend in November 1964 the merger of all socialist-oriented Italian parties, including the PCI, into a ''new single party of the left'' which would no longer be based on Marxism-Leninism alone.[92] Plainly Amendola aimed at undermining the PSI's entente with the DC. But the method he proposed for doing so marked him as a pragmatic innovator in the European reformist tradition.

Ingrao, in contrast, was alarmed at the prospect of center-left success. This he sought to avoid by mobilizing the urban and rural laborers dislocated by economic modernization. The exclusive pursuit of political alliances with the lay democratic left would, he feared, only reinforce the tendencies toward capitalist stabilization. The PCI should instead create a new historic bloc at the grassroots level of society by appealing to Catholic as well as Communist workers, and to the unorganized and marginalized migrants from the *mezzogiorno* as well as to unionized workers.[93] If Amendola was a pragmatic innovator, Ingrao was a mobilizational innovator.

Ingrao likewise argued that the party should adopt a more open organizational structure. The decision-making process should become more accessible to participation and more visible, or transparent, in the sense of policy disagreements being spelled out at all levels of the party.[94] Finally, since the *ingraoiani* sought to mobilize for socialism in the near term, they urged the PCI to be more critical toward the flaws of existing socialism in the Soviet Union.

Where the views of the Amendola and Ingrao wings converged was in their pluralist conception of a future socialist society: power would not be held solely by the Communists because the working class would not be represented just by the PCI; the *alternation* of parties in government would thus be legitimate in a Marxist framework.[95] The idea of political pluralism under socialism was in the air even if it was not yet incorporated into formal party documents.

The iconoclastic organizational proposals of both Amendola and Ingrao were rebuffed by their peers in the PCI hierarchy. Amendola's suggestion of Communist–Socialist fusion—a throwback to the mid-1940s hopes for

92. Giorgio Amendola, ''Ipotesi sulla riunificazione,'' *Rinascita* 21, no. 47 (November 28, 1964):8–9.

93. For a concise portrayal of Ingrao's views, see Amyot, *The Italian Communist Party,* 57–67.

94. Cf. Sassoon, *The Strategy of the Italian Communist Party,* 201.

95. Ibid., 169–71.

left-wing unity—appeared far-fetched in the face of PSI–DC collaboration in the mid-1960s. Ingrao's suggestion of putting the theory of democratic centralism into practice, of encouraging open and publicized debates over policy at all levels of the party, fell on deaf ears when it came to the bulk of the cadres of the *partito nuovo*. Coming to political age as they did during the Cold War and *Cominformismo,* they had had little experience with authentic internal party dialogue.

Longo, on the other hand, clearly intended to play the role of loyal heir to the Togliatti tradition of conciliation toward policy disagreements within his own party and the Communist movement at large. His decision to publish the celebrated memorandum Togliatti penned for Khrushchev just hours before his fatal stroke (and about which more will be said in a moment) testified to that. He therefore did not discourage the coexistence of the Amendola and Ingrao groups as long as they did not assume an exclusive and public character, as long as they did not become factions.

Ingrao's mobilizational approach to party strategy received, however, a temporary setback as a result of the spontaneous grassroots protest movements that engulfed Italy along with the rest of Western Europe in the late 1960s. It was vindicated by the sweep of radical labor strikes and student upheavals. But it was also discredited by their excesses. The young PCI intellectuals who rallied to the banner of the new dissident Communist journal, *Il Manifesto,* endorsed not simply participatory decision making but outright factionalism. Moreover, they called for revolution not tomorrow but today. They also did not stop at castigating the Soviet system's flaws but took the side of Peking against Moscow in the Sino-Soviet conflict. In the end Ingrao himself kept his distance from the *Manifesto* rebels, and their leaders were expelled from the PCI for engaging in open factionalism in the autumn of 1969.[96]

There was in the *Manifesto* affair an overarching political consideration. Togliatti's successors, as we shall discuss in the next section, had by then had a head-on confrontation with Moscow over the Soviet invasion of Czechoslovakia. They thus felt the need to define the outer limits of permissible dissent within their own party lest the centrifugal forces get out of hand, lest the anti-Soviet *Manifesto* intellectuals provoke a counter-*corrente* among the pro-Soviet traditionalists at the PCI base. Factionalism was unacceptable not only on doctrinal grounds but in light of the debilitating impact of such organized *correnti*. Alessandro Natta, since 1966 a member of the *Direzione,* went to the heart of the matter in his major report to the PCI Central Committee meeting summoned in October 1969 to deal with the *Manifesto* group. To tolerate their chal-

---

96. For details, see Amyot, *The Italian Communist Party,* 170–93.

lenge, he declared, "would risk profoundly injuring the unity of the Party."[97]

If the pace of change advocated by the PCI's mobilizational innovators was too rapid in the Italian context, the coalitional principle of the pragmatic innovators was too restrictive. Whereas the first could only exacerbate the right-wing terrorism and neo-Fascist revivalism that surfaced on the eve of the 1970s, the second seemed likely to perpetuate the domestic political isolation of the Italian party. The upshot was Enrico Berlinguer's formulation of the *compromesso storico*. The character of this strategic innovation will be explored in chapter 8. Suffice it here to say that it combined the overtures to Catholicism advocated by the *ingraoiani* with the accommodation to parliamentary politics advocated by Amendola.

While questions of domestic strategy were paramount in the eyes of PCI policy makers during this period, their evolving vision of socialism was to have a far more direct impact on the Soviet–PCI relationship. For the concept of a pluralist form of socialism that they articulated with ever greater specificity, especially after 1968, ran directly counter to the CPSU's insistence on "the leading role" of the Communist party in building a socialist society.

As we have already seen, in June 1956 Togliatti suggested a worldwide process of socialist development in which the various national components could be led wholly, partly, or not at all by Communists. In other words, Communist hegemony was not the prerequisite for initiating socialist construction. Inherent in this vision of shared authority in the march to socialism were at least the rudiments of a theoretical justification for socialist pluralism. But Togliatti's most important contribution to the programmatic idea of socialist pluralism was the private memorandum he wrote for Khrushchev while vacationing at Yalta in August 1964. Although he focused on international Communist issues, above all the mounting Sino-Soviet conflict, he also enjoined his Soviet comrades to overcome "the regime of restrictions and suppression of democratic and personal freedom introduced by Stalin." He went on to say that it was "for us difficult to explain" the "slowness and resistance" encountered in returning to Leninist norms, in establishing "a wide liberty of expression and debate on culture, art and also on politics."[98] What this signified in a nutshell was an implicit defense of democratic values under socialism *everywhere*.

It remained for Longo to spell out the logic of his predecessor's posi-

97. Complete text of the October 1969 Central Committee debate is in *La questione del "Manifesto": Democrazia e unità nel PCI* (Rome: Editori Riuniti, 1969); see 21 for Natta's remark.

98. Text of Togliatti's memorandum in *Sino-Soviet Relations, 1964–1965*, by William E. Griffith (Cambridge, Mass.: MIT Press, 1967), 373–83 at 383.

tion. In his report to the Twelfth PCI Congress in February 1969, with the image of the Czechoslovakian reform movement still vividly in mind, Longo explicitly called for socialist pluralism in Italy. He spoke of a form of socialism in which "a plurality of parties and social organizations" would be "engaged in a free and democratic dialectic of contrasting positions, something qualitatively different from the experiences known till now."[99] Thereafter the goal of political pluralism under socialism appeared with growing frequency in party documents. As Longo's successor, Berlinguer, put it in his report to the Thirteenth PCI Congress in 1972, the party's endorsement of "political and intellectual pluralism" (*pluralismo politico e ideale*) was valid not only for the present but also during "the construction of socialism in our country."[100]

The Political Resolution of the Thirteenth Congress defined the PCI's perception of the relationship among leftist parties more precisely than ever before. According to the document, Communists, socialists, and "advanced democratic" (Catholic) political forces should retain full autonomy and compete among one another for the acceptance of their respective viewpoints. In the words of the resolution, "Unity is built through a constant confrontation of programs and ideas that don't presume to eliminate the differences that exist. . . . It is through this confrontation that one may reach convergences, agreements, . . . which tend to reveal *a line expressing the hegemony of the working class.* Such a line has nothing to do with party exclusivism or integration but, on the contrary, is open to a plurality of forces or contributions."[101] Gone, in short, was the presumption of exclusive Communist authority to speak for—and thereby dominate—the working class.

That the PCI was calling for a measure of genuine competition rather than a form of sterile frontism on the postwar East European pattern was further underscored in a major article by Berlinguer published in October 1972 in *Rinascita*. To strengthen the PCI's denial of any ulterior intention of absorbing or emasculating its allies, he took the dramatic step of denouncing the party's 1945 proposal for fusion with the Italian Socialists as an outright "error" and the joint PCI–PSI electoral list of 1948 as "perhaps also mistaken."[102]

The most serious Soviet–PCI divergences prior to the second half of the 1970s, however, had to do with the structure of the international Communist movement. In the early 1960s the Italian party resumed the process of

99. See Longo's report in *XII Congresso del partito comunista italiano: Atti e risoluzioni* (Rome: Editori Riuniti, 1969), 27–83 at 72.

100. See Berlinguer's report in *XIII Congresso del partito comunista italiano: Atti e risoluzioni* (Rome: Editori Riuniti, 1972), 15–66 at 58.

101. "La risoluzione politica," in ibid., 490–501 at 497; my emphasis.

102. Enrico Berlinguer, "La peculiarità socialista," *Rinascita* 29, no. 42 (October 27, 1972):3–4.

transnational coalition building that it had tentatively undertaken in mid-1956. In the final analysis, the challenge to Moscow that this portended was for many years the prime test of the PCI's innovative character.

From Polycentrism to the New Internationalism

By 1976 the organizational implications of Togliatti's June 1956 discussion of polycentrism had become an integral part of PCI doctrine under the rubric of a "new internationalism." From the start the crux of the new internationalism was the insistence on individual Communist party autonomy, on the priority of national party interests over those of the Communist world in general. Beyond that, it signified a search for areas of agreement among Communist parties operating under similar political or geographical conditions. As such it gave rise to the transnational coalitions of Eurocommunists and autonomists that the PCI forged in the pan-European Communist movement during the 1970s. The new internationalism also signified a search for common ground among Communists and other socialist or reformist forces in Western Europe. The PCI's eager overtures to social democratic parties from 1969 onward fit this pattern. On all these accounts the new internationalism ran counter to proletarian internationalism, the CPSU's cherished formula according to which national party interests should be subordinated to the interests of the Communist world—as defined, of course, by Moscow. Nevertheless, it is important to bear in mind that at least through 1976 what the PCI leaders sought from the new internationalism was to change the *structure* of the international Communist movement, not their allegiance to it. They hoped to make the Communist world safe for their evolving *via italiana*.

From 1957 through 1960, however, the PCI's challenge to Soviet centralism remained largely hidden under the facade of what Amendola was later to describe as "fictitious unanimity."[103] The pressures exerted by Moscow (and initially backed by Peking) to reimpose unity on the Communist movement after the East European crises of 1956 had their effect. On the fortieth anniversary of the October Revolution, in November 1957, the CPSU hosted a conference of sixty-four Communist parties in Moscow at which it mustered the support of the overwhelming pro-Soviet majority to force the minority of autonomists, above all Wladyslaw Gomulka and Togliatti, to heel. In his speech to the gathering Togliatti repeated his by then familiar call for the autonomy of each Communist party; he cautioned against creating "new international organisms";[104]

---

103. Blackmer, *Unity in Diversity*, 99–179, passim.
104. See the abridged version of his speech cited in n. 86.

and he insisted that the formula of a *partito-guida* (leading party) in the Communist movement was outdated.[105] But these views were harshly rebutted by Mao and Duclos of the PCF.[106] In the end the twelve ruling party-states (not including Yugoslavia) signed a joint declaration that included two points directly at odds with Togliatti's position: the notion of "general laws" binding upon all countries undergoing socialist construction, and a reference to the socialist camp "headed by the Soviet Union."[107] And when the Italian delegation returned home, the PCI Central Committee endorsed this centralist document.[108] The Italian party's isolation within the Communist world, when added to the sentimental pro-Sovietism of the *partito nuovo,* left its leadership with little choice in the matter.

There was nevertheless one important way in which Togliatti asserted the autonomy of the PCI even during this bleak period of conformity: he called for an objective reconsideration of the history of the international Communist movement, shorn of the fictions of unanimity and infallibility. He likewise encouraged scholarly investigation into the history of Soviet–PCI relations.

We have already referred to Togliatti's June 1956 criticism of the Comintern's sectarian errors and Manuilsky's unwarranted denunciation of the PCI in 1939. At the 1957 Moscow conference he also debunked the Communist Information Bureau on the ground that it "just didn't fulfill its tasks of information. In the years of its existence, we knew almost nothing of the Communist movement in the other countries."[109] When an abridged version of his 1957 speech was published in *Rinascita* two years later, Togliatti accompanied it with a lengthy article on the Comintern in which he deplored the absence of serious historical works on the subject.[110] He then proceeded to discuss the mistaken directions embraced by the International after Lenin's death, for example, the post-1928 "definition of social democracy as social fascism," the delay in perceiving the Fascist danger, the policy of "class against class."[111] He also commented on the inexplicable contradiction between the popular front policy and Stalin's simultaneous purge not just of the CPSU but of the Polish and

105. This was disclosed by Gian Carlo Pajetta in "Togliatti: che cosa ci ha lasciato," a supplement to *l'Unità*, October 14, 1984; see p. 4 of supplement.

106. Ibid.; cf. Bocca, *Palmiro Togliatti*, 630.

107. Zbigniew Brzezinski, *The Soviet Bloc,* 2d rev. and enlarged ed. (Cambridge, Mass.: Harvard University Press, 1967), 298–308.

108. Blackmer, *Unity in Diversity,* 131.

109. Togliatti, *Problemi del movimento operaio internazionale,* 265.

110. "Alcuni problemi della storia dell'Internazionale comunista," *Rinascita* 16, nos. 7–8 (July–August 1959):467–81; reprinted in Togliatti, *Problemi del movimento operaio internazionale,* 299–333. The reference to the absence of historical works is in ibid., 304.

111. Ibid., 323–26.

Yugoslavian Communist leaderships as well.[112] About this time, moreover, he began his own volume on the formation of the Gramsci team in the 1920s (frequently cited in chapter 1), which was published in 1962 and paved the way for the historical works of Paolo Spriano and Ernesto Ragionieri, among others. In his Yalta memorandum, finally, Togliatti alluded with obvious pride to the debate over the origins of Stalinism that was developing "among historians and qualified cadres" of the PCI.[113]

When all is said and done, the impetus Togliatti gave to scholarly reconstructions of PCI, Soviet, and Comintern history had a profound impact on his party's developing political orientation. His concern with historical accuracy inspired a spate of studies which, by the 1970s, provided the intellectual preconditions for an objective assessment of *contemporary* Soviet–PCI relations, not to mention Soviet-style socialism.

Meanwhile, the new internationalism began to take concrete shape in the early 1960s as the old internationalism of Soviet-enforced world Communist unity collapsed in the wake of the Sino-Soviet conflict. At the Tenth PCI Congress, as Sino-Soviet relations worsened, Togliatti reiterated many of the themes he had raised in June 1956. He spoke of the "autonomy of decision of each party" rather than the "existence of impossible international or regional centers" (read Comintern and Cominform).[114] But at the same time, he suggested frequent "bilateral and also multilateral contacts" among Communist parties for the purpose of "precise information, reciprocal understanding, and the exchange of experiences."[115] He repeated these ideas in a more blunt fashion in his Yalta memorandum, written as Khrushchev maneuvered for an international Communist conference aimed at condemning the ultrasectarian Maoists. Togliatti called instead for prior regional meetings, for gatherings of the "different sectors of our movement"—that is, Western Europe, Latin America, the Third World, and the people's democracies—to examine issues of mutual concern.[116] He thereby spelled out more explicitly than ever before the regional connotation of polycentrism. Most significant, Togliatti recommended that his Soviet comrades observe the conciliatory style of discourse that was becoming the PCI's hallmark. He urged that the exchanges with the Chinese be conducted "without verbal exacerbations and without generic condemnations, on concrete themes, in an objective and persuasive manner and always with a certain respect for the adversary."[117] In short, Togliatti laid down the procedural ground rules

112. Ibid., 330.
113. Griffith, *Sino-Soviet Relations*, 382.
114. *X Congresso*, 55.
115. Ibid., 57.
116. Griffith, *Sino-Soviet Relations*, 374–75.
117. Ibid., 374.

for the new internationalism that his successors, Longo and Berlinguer, would pursue both within and beyond the Communist movement.

Nevertheless, the fundamental challenge to Soviet centralism during the 1960s came not from the PCI but from Peking and Prague. Underlying all the sound and fury of the Maoists' ideological polemics against the CPSU was their fear that Khrushchev's push for détente with the West and influence in the Third World portended a reduction in Soviet diplomatic support and military-economic aid to Peking. In the longer run the Chinese Communists would compensate for this loss by normalizing relations with the West. But in the short run Khrushchev's foreign policy initiatives drove the Chinese into a confrontation with the CPSU that resulted in the irreversible fragmentation of the international Communist movement. Meanwhile, if the Maoists gave lie to the solidarity of world communism, the Czechoslovakian reformers' vision of "socialism with a human face" posed a threat to the legitimacy of CPSU domination at home and the reality of Soviet domination over Eastern Europe. And both developments intensified the PCI's defense of autonomy and pursuit of coalition politics in the Communist movement.

Moscow initially tried to combat Chinese influence among other Communist parties by giving an air of legitimacy to the rupture in Sino-Soviet party relations that had occurred by mid-1963. To this end the Soviets proposed an international Communist conference that the Kremlin policy makers hoped would issue a collective denunciation of the Maoist leadership. As Kevin Devlin has masterfully shown, it was largely owing to the opposition of the Italian Communists that this maneuver foundered by the late 1960s.[118] While the PCI championed the Soviet Union's positions on peaceful coexistence and a nonviolent transition to socialism, it categorically rejected the CPSU's method of handling the controversy with the Chinese. In line with Togliatti's injunctions in his Yalta memorandum, his successors appealed for dialogue and tolerance in place of the ideological invective exchanged between the CPSU and the Chinese Communist Party (CCP). They argued, in a word, that the "language of anathema" would only deepen the rift.[119]

The Czechoslovakian drama of 1968 affected the PCI more directly than the Sino-Soviet rupture, but it also presented the Italians with a more complicated set of policy choices. It was one thing to take a conciliatory approach to the political-ideological fight between Moscow and Peking. It was quite another to break with the CPSU over the Soviet-led invasion of

118. Kevin Devlin, "The Challenge of the 'New Internationalism,'" in *The Sino-Soviet Conflict: A Global Perspective,* ed. Herbert J. Ellison (Seattle: University of Washington Press, 1982), 146–71.

119. The phrase is Devlin's.

Czechoslovakia when Alexander Dubček, the hero of the Prague Spring, remained at the helm of his party for months thereafter. At the time, many Western observers viewed Moscow's inability to find immediate replacements for Dubček and his reform-minded colleagues as a setback for the Soviet Union, as evidence of the Brezhnev leadership's political ineptitude. Yet in retrospect the interval between the Warsaw Pact's invasion on August 20, 1968, and the final removal of Dubček in April 1969 proved to be a windfall, however unintended, for the CPSU. For it diffused the initial fury of many West European Communists, leaving the PCI in a much more isolated position than might otherwise have been the case.

There were also other considerations that limited the scope of the PCI's reaction to the invasion of Czechoslovakia. The Brezhnev regime had not yet revealed the full extent of its determination to repress all nonconformist currents in Soviet cultural and political life. (Andrei Sakharov was, for example, still a member of the CPSU.) The massive bloodletting incurred by the war in Vietnam placed the Warsaw Pact's almost bloodless occupation of Czechoslovakia in a relatively benign light. Above all, the pro-Sovietism of the *partito nuovo* had not yet been diluted by the infusion of younger cadres inspired by the social mobilizations of the late 1960s rather than the Cold War antipathies of the 1940s and 1950s.

All this is not to gainsay the substantial backing the PCI gave to the Dubček reformers before the invasion nor the persistence with which the Italian Communists denounced Moscow afterwards. During the months preceding the armed intervention, *Rinascita* devoted extensive coverage to Czechoslovakian innovations in the spheres of cultural freedom, political liberalization, and economic reform. In mid-July 1968 Pajetta and Carlo Galluzzi, then head of the PCI's foreign section, traveled to Moscow with Thorez's successor, Waldeck Rochet, to warn the Soviet leaders that many West European Communist parties were in Prague's corner.[120] Immediately thereafter the PCI *Direzione* affirmed its support for the new course in Czechoslovakia and appealed to other Communist parties to do the same.[121] And once the invasion took place, the PCI Central Committee condemned it in unequivocal terms. As Longo put it to that body on August 27, Czechoslovakia was not Hungary. The Communist Party's unity was intact, the socialist nature of the state was never in question, and the Czechoslovakian leadership had affirmed its allegiance to the Warsaw Treaty Organization (WTO) and Soviet foreign policy. But above all, insisted Longo, the Soviet Union did not have the right under any circumstances to intervene militarily "in the internal life of another Communist

120. Jiri Valenta, *Soviet Intervention in Czechoslovakia, 1968* (Baltimore: Johns Hopkins University Press, 1979), 67–69.
121. Text in *l'Unità*, July 19, 1968, 1.

party or another country.''[122] This last point underscored how far the PCI had come since 1956.

Still, a *Direzione* statement of August 21 expressed its "dissent" over the invasion "in the spirit of the most convinced and firm proletarian internationalism" and only after "confirming once again the profound, fraternal, and genuine ties that unite the Italian Communists to the Soviet Union and the CPSU.''[123]

In other words, the crisis over Czechoslovakia marked the start, not the culmination, of the PCI's emphasis on the new internationalism. The Warsaw Pact occupation of Czechoslovakia, it seems safe to say, made the Italian Communist elite realize that the growth of Soviet military power was not necessarily a good thing. It brought home to them the fact that the Soviet Union's forcible domination of Eastern Europe did enormous damage to the public image of communism in Western Europe. It probably even led some of them to doubt their own political faith. But it did not bring the party leaders to the brink of rupture with Moscow, as the declaration of martial law in Poland would do some thirteen years later, for all the reasons noted above.

The PCI leadership's conduct at the June 1969 Moscow conference of Communist and workers' parties nevertheless differed substantially from what it had been at similar such gatherings in 1957 and 1960. First of all, the Italians—along with other independent-minded parties such as the Romanian one—refused to attend except on the condition that the final resolution be nonbinding on the participants and noncritical of any Communist party whatsoever (the Chinese above all).[124] Second, the PCI was the only major party (among those in attendance) that declined to sign the full conference document. The Italian delegation's leader, Deputy General Secretary Berlinguer, protested that the sections dealing with the Communist movement and socialist system glossed over their problems and divisions.[125] He also questioned the very existence of the "general laws" of socialist development expounded by Soviet ideologues since 1956–57 and posited again in the 1969 document. True to Togliatti's mode of differentiated analysis, he argued that such laws "never exist in a pure state but always and only in particular realities.''[126] Thenceforth the Italian party's public denial of "general laws" developed apace with its support for socialist pluralism.

Furthermore, about this same time the PCI started to devote consider-

122. Text in ibid., August 28, 1968.
123. Text in *Rinascita* 25, no. 33 (August 23, 1968):1.
124. Devlin, "The Challenge of the 'New Internationalism,'" 156.
125. See Berlinguer's speech in *Conferenza internazionale dei partiti comunisti e operai, Mosca 5–17 giugno 1969: Testi e documenti* (Rome: Editori Riuniti, 1969), 492–514.
126. Ibid., 499.

able attention to cooperation with Western socialists as well as Catholic and lay progressives, particularly within the European community. Efforts to launch a dialogue with Northern European social democrats had begun before 1969, the year that PCI representatives first joined the Italian delegation to the then appointive European Parliament. Unofficial contacts with the German SPD were initiated in 1968 and multiplied over the years.[127] By the late 1970s the PCI had established formal links with the British Labour Party as well as socialists in the Scandinavian and Benelux countries.[128] And some nineteen social democratic and labor parties sent delegates to the Fifteenth PCI Congress in early 1979.[129] However, even after Italian Communists entered the European Parliament, the socialists and Communists still commanded only a minority of votes; and the PCF, which entered in 1973, remained basically hostile to closer European integration. The results of the first direct elections to the European Parliament in June 1979 did not alter this fundamental distribution of power among right, center, and left.[130] In other words, for the PCI to have any effective influence in that body, it had to seek allies among centrist as well as leftist delegates—a kind of historic compromise on a European scale.

But the most rewarding international arena for the exercise of PCI influence soon became the *pan-European* Communist movement. It was there that the Italian party developed transnational coalition building into a fine art during the first half of the 1970s. For a start, the Italians entered into a protective relationship with the Spanish Communist Party that in some ways resembled the Sino-Albanian alliance of the 1960s. The PCE had challenged the CPSU on many of the same issues as the Italians, ranging from the Soviet intervention in Czechoslovakia to the nature of socialism in the developed capitalist West. Moscow reacted by attempting to subvert the leadership of the small, clandestine, and hence vulnerable Spanish party.[131] The PCI, in turn, hailed the PCE's expulsion of several pro-Soviet dissidents in 1969–70. It also opened the pages of *Rinascita* to the Spanish Communist leadership.[132] PCI journalists likewise reported

127. Carlo Galluzzi, *La svolta: Gli anni cruciali del Partito comunista italiano* (Milan: Sperling and Kupfer Editori, 1983), 171–85.

128. Heinz Timmermann, "Democratic Socialists, Eurocommunists, and the West," in *The European Left: Italy, France, and Spain*, ed. William E. Griffith (Lexington, Mass.: Lexington Books, 1979):167–201.

129. *Le Monde*, March 31, 1979, 8.

130. Heinz Timmermann, "The Eurocommunists and the West," *Problems of Communism* 28, no. 3 (May–June 1979):31–54.

131. Eusebio Mujal-León, *Communism and Political Change in Spain* (Bloomington: Indiana University Press, 1983), 103–31.

132. For example, "La politica unitaria dei comunisti: Intervista di Santiago Carrillo," *Rinascita* 27, no. 51 (December 25, 1970): 6–7; and Manuel Azcárate, "Un analisi della strategia del Partito comunista spagnuolo," *Rinascita* 29, nos. 47 and 48 (December 1 and 8, 1972): 15–16 and 17–18, respectively.

regularly and favorably upon the PCE's activity, while the Italian party contributed financial support for the conversion of the Spanish party's irregular news weekly, *Mundo Obrero,* into a daily paper.[133] The PCE welcomed and reciprocated this support to the best of its ability. Santiago Carrillo, for example, was the only European Communist general secretary to attend the PCI's March 1975 Congress (which coincided with the congress of the Hungarian Workers' Party); and there he wholeheartedly endorsed Italian Communist policies, including the *compromesso storico.*[134]

The opportunities for coalition building of this sort multiplied during the preparations for the 1976 East Berlin conference of European Communist and workers' parties (otherwise known as the East Berlin, or pan-European Communist, summit). We will examine the Soviet motives for supporting this conference in the next chapter. Suffice it here to say that the East Berlin summit was a direct outgrowth of the Soviet Union's preoccupation with the thirty-five-nation Helsinki Conference on Security and Cooperation in Europe. If in Moscow's eyes the Helsinki agreement was designed to secure the status quo in Eastern Europe, the East Berlin conference was intended to reassure the Western Communist parties that the CPSU opposed the status quo in Western Europe. Détente and class struggle were to be viewed as compatible, at least in theory. For the PCI, on the other hand, the pan-European Communist summit offered an ideal occasion to promote the principles of autonomy and pluralism at one and the same time.

The CPSU agreed to convene the pan-European Communist conference, first suggested by Berlinguer in January 1973,[135] after the start of the Helsinki negotiations. The Helsinki talks, it will be recalled, were conducted according to the consensus principle, partially at Yugoslavian and Romanian insistence. Not coincidentally, the League of Communists of Yugoslavia (LCY) stipulated as conditions for its participation in the East Berlin summit not only the consensus rule but also each participant's right publicly to disclose its position on all matters relating to the conference proceedings. Belgrade's stipulations were announced at preliminary consultations in Warsaw in October 1974 and simultaneously published in the Yugoslavian press,[136] thereby presenting the CPSU with a

133. Disclosed by Santiago Carrillo in his speech to the Fourteenth PCI Congress; *l'Unità,* March 20, 1975, 10.

134. Ibid.; see also Carrillo's interview in *l'Unità,* June 22, 1975, 20.

135. According to Pajetta, Berlinguer first raised the conference idea with Brezhnev in early 1973; see his report in *Rinascita* 31, no. 42 (October 25, 1974):5–6. PCF leader Georges Marchais also ascribed the initiative for the Berlin summit to the PCI in a May 1975 press conference; *L'Humanité,* May 15, 1975, 3.

136. The LCY delegate, Aleksandar Grlickov, announced the Yugoslavian conditions in Moscow on October 17, 1974; they were publicized that same day by the Belgrade press agency, Tanjug.

fait accompli. The Soviet leadership acquiesced, probably anticipating that the cooperation of the Italian, Spanish, and Romanian parties was contingent upon the LCY's presence. Yet the men in Moscow surely understood that decision making by consensus and public disclosure would preclude the imposition of CPSU views, even with majority support, on any document approved at the Berlin conference. Such a procedural approach was, furthermore, an open invitation to the creation of a minority coalition of parties opposed to Soviet positions on autonomist and/or pluralist grounds.

These were the circumstances under which the much publicized Eurocommunist entente of Italian, Spanish, and French Communist parties developed in the mid-1970s. We have already noted the affinities between the PCI and the Spanish party. During the height of the revolutionary crisis in Portugal in the summer of 1975, about which more will be said in chapter 8, Berlinguer and Carrillo signed a joint declaration affirming their electoral and pluralist vision of socialism and thereby distancing themselves from the sectarian Portuguese Communist Party of Alvaro Cunhal.[137] But the development of real significance for the East Berlin summit preparatory process was the PCF's sudden alignment with the PCI and PCE. On November 15, to the surprise of most observers in East and West, French Communist leader Georges Marchais and Berlinguer also signed a common declaration of pluralist and democratic principles that was even more explicit than the joint PCI–PCE statement.[138] From that point onward Moscow was on the defensive in the protracted bargaining that finally resulted in the holding of the pan-European Communist conference in June 1976.

Here a brief digression is in order. At the root of the burgeoning Soviet–PCF controversy was Moscow's barely disguised preference for the status quo in France rather than an electoral victory by the Communist–Socialist Union of the Left, which had been created in 1972. In May 1974 the PCF publicly chided the Soviet Union for its show of support for Valéry Giscard d'Estaing in the midst of his closely contested presidential race with François Mitterrand, the candidate of the Union of the Left. In the autumn of 1975 the French Communists intensified their criticism of Moscow for cultivating harmonious relations with then President Giscard at a time when conditions in France seemed propitious for radical change. On October 13, 1975, the very day Giscard arrived in Moscow on a state visit, the PCF daily *L'Humanité* affirmed the party's intention to pursue its "revolutionary struggle in France . . . against the Giscardian power of

---

137. Text in *The Communist Parties of Italy, France and Spain: Postwar Change and Continuity,* ed. Peter Lange and Maurizio Vannicelli (London: George Allen and Unwin, 1981), 357–58.
138. Text in ibid., 358–60.

the monopolies," Franco-Soviet détente notwithstanding.[139] To top it off, during the final preparatory sessions for the East Berlin summit the PCF submitted a working paper that accused the CPSU of failing to exploit to the full the "general crisis of capitalism" out of "diplomatic" considerations, namely, concern with détente.[140]

In other words, the PCF, by joining the Eurocommunist entente, had hit upon a shrewd way to retaliate against the Soviets for currying the favor of the conservative incumbent in the Élysée. The French party's alignment with the PCI and PCE also enabled it to project a public image of autonomy from Moscow at a time when it was being increasingly challenged in the domestic electoral arena by its Socialist allies. The depth of the PCF leadership's commitment to Eurocommunist principles was, however, highly debatable.

This caveat aside, by 1976 the PCI had counterposed the practice of a new internationalism to the CPSU's abortive effort to impose its formula of proletarian internationalism on the pan-European Communist movement. In mid-February of that year Pajetta, chief Italian delegate to the East Berlin summit preparatory talks, explicitly identified the PCI's promotion of contacts with socialists and Catholics in Western Europe as well as the recent "meetings between the PCI, the Spanish CP, and the PCF" with his party's new internationalism.[141] Shortly thereafter, on February 27, Berlinguer delivered from the podium of the Twenty-fifth CPSU Congress an address that was remarkable for its silence on proletarian internationalism (as well as its candor regarding the PCI's commitment to a "*pluralist* and democratic system" under socialism).[142] And on the eve of his outspoken speech, Berlinguer consulted with Romanian chief Nikolae Ceauşescu and dined with the Yugoslavian representative, Stane Dolanc.[143] The unmistakable message was that the PCI's new internationalism also included coordination with the East European autonomists. The impact of this new internationalism on the East Berlin summit and Soviet–PCI relations in general will be explored in chapter 8.

139. I treat these developments in my chapter, "The Ties That Bind: West European Communism and the Communist States of East Europe," in *The European Left,* ed. Griffith, 203–37 at 217–19.

140. Ronald Tiersky, "French Communism, Eurocommunism, and Soviet Power," in *Eurocommunism and Détente,* ed. Rudolf L. Tökés (New York: New York University Press, 1978), 165–66.

141. "L'Azione internazionale del PCI e la riunione dei comunisti europei," *l'Unità,* February 14, 1976, 13.

142. Text in *l'Unità,* February 28, 1976, 1 and 13; my emphasis. The PCI noted the next day without comment that *Pravda* had substituted the word "multiform" for "pluralist" in its text of Berlinguer's speech; *l'Unità,* February 29, 1976, 14. The Russian text is in *Pravda,* February 28, 1976, 8–9.

143. These meetings were reported in *l'Unità,* February 28, 1976, 13.

PART FOUR

THE SOVIET–PCI RIFT

The PCI's challenge to Soviet centralism that surfaced in the 1960s and gathered momentum during the first half of the 1970s aimed in principle at making the international Communist movement safe for diversity. The Italian Communists may have been concerned primarily with defending their own *via italiana*. But they couched that purpose first in the rhetoric of autonomy and later in the slogan of the "new internationalism," with the latter signifying regional ententes among like-minded Communist parties and other socialist-oriented forces. Only beginning in the mid-1970s did the PCI's conduct suggest an interest in reshaping the Communist world in a pluralist image, in fostering innovation and reducing sectarianism among both ruling and nonruling parties. Yet even then, for reasons examined in chapter 8, the Italian party was careful to combine criticism of Soviet-style socialism with professions of solidarity with the CPSU. Indeed, Berlinguer went to great lengths to observe proper decorum in his relations with the Brezhnev leadership, avoiding anti-Soviet slurs and boycotts such as those indulged in by Carrillo and even, on occasion, by Marchais.

On the eve of the 1980s, however, the PCI began to shift from support for autonomy and pluralism to outright disengagement from the Moscow-aligned Communist movement. Its normalization of relations with the post-Mao Chinese leadership in April 1980 was a benchmark in this process. But it was only after the declaration of marital law in Poland that the Berlinguer group debunked the CPSU's contemporary revolutionary credentials and denied the vanguard role of the international Communist movement as such in the world march toward socialism.

The Brezhnev oligarchy, for its part, displayed considerable forbearance toward the PCI's defiant behavior as long as it did not criticize the Soviet Union's conduct in international affairs. The reason was plain. Moscow had little to anticipate from the pro-American Italian Christian Democratic establishment. Stated somewhat differently, in the land of the Caesars there were precious few Gaullists. As long as the Italian Communists were reasonably supportive of Soviet foreign policy, therefore, the CPSU was prepared to exercise a certain degree of restraint toward their ideological deviationism and even organizational challenges.

On the other hand, as a result of the Soviet Union's military backing of radical Third World liberationism (in Angola, Ethiopia, and Afghanistan), this tenuous equilibrium collapsed. As we shall see in chapter 9, Italian Communist leaders began to suggest that in those areas and elsewhere Moscow was bent upon expanding its military-political sphere of influence rather than advancing the cause of revolution. This charge became explicit after the declaration of martial law in Poland when Berlinguer made his famous statement that the October Revolution had lost its "propulsive force." Whereupon the Soviet leadership responded with invective bordering on anathema. The *strappo,* or "rip," in Soviet–PCI relations had arrived.

In a bizarre twist of fate, however, Mikhail Suslov—the Politburo's chief ideologist and a custodian of international Communist probity since the Cominform era—died of a stroke just when Soviet–PCI ties were approaching the breaking point. At that point Vadim Zagladin, first deputy head of the CPSU Central Committee's International Department and the individual responsible for liaison with the West European Communist parties, adopted a more conciliatory demeanor. He urged that the two parties put aside their differences in order to present a united front against the installation of American intermediate-range nuclear forces (INF) in Europe.

The Soviet–PCI relationship during this period of open rift was conditioned, as always, by what was happening in the Soviet Union and Italy. With regard to the Soviet Union, the stability of the Brezhnev regime had long rested on the twin props of peace and prosperity. Détente with the West and a healthy rate of growth in per capita consumption at home contributed to the system's legitimacy in the eyes of its own citizens. By the start of the 1980s, however, both these props had been undermined. The annual incremental improvements in consumer welfare had all but ceased while Soviet-American tensions threatened to reach Cold War levels. It seems a safe bet that the Brezhnev regime suffered a corresponding decline in popular support. This would help explain the Kremlin's frantic efforts to blunt the impact *within the USSR* of the PCI's challenge to its revolutionary credentials during the winter of 1981–82.

If domestic immobilism characterized the last half-decade of the Brezhnev era, the reverse was true in Italy. There the 1976 parliamentary contest saw a sharp leftward shift in the Italian political landscape: support for the PCI climbed from 27.2 percent (its tally in the general election of 1972) to 34.4 percent of the ballots cast for the Chamber of Deputies, while the DC and parties of the lay center-left held steady. This dramatic change was partly due to the inability in the mid-1970s of the center-left cabinets (headed, as in the 1960s, by Aldo Moro) to cope with the intensifying economic crisis and upsurge in domestic terrorism. It had been heralded by the 1974 referendum on divorce, in which 59.0 percent of the electorate voted in favor of it, and by the 1975 regional elections, in which the PCI first demonstrated its great leap forward in popularity by winning 33.4 percent of the vote in the fifteen mainland regions consulted. And it led to the PCI's participation in Italy's parliamentary majority and to the Berlinguer leadership's demand for a role in the Council of Ministers as well.

Underlying the Communists' participation in the parliamentary majority from mid-1976 through the end of 1978 was their strategy of the *compromesso storico*, which will be discussed shortly. Suffice it here to say that the prospect of the PCI entering the Italian government for the first time since the mid-1940s provoked profound consternation in Washington. At the same time, the Berlinguer leadership's cooperative attitude toward the DC contributed to the wave of radical left-wing terrorism that culminated in the kidnapping and murder of Aldo Moro by the Red Brigades in the spring of 1978. Yet these developments only inclined the PCI toward greater accommodation with the Italian political establishment. What is important for our purposes is that incomprehension among Communist militants over this moderate comportment resulted in the PCI leadership's accommodation with Moscow as well in 1977–78. This is a subject the next chapter elaborates.

Meanwhile, the Communist Party's display of responsibility in Parliament without commensurate power in the Council of Ministers triggered not only dissension in its ranks but also defection at the polls. The 1979 parliamentary contest saw a realignment of Italy's left-of-center forces, with the PCI declining from 34.4 percent to 30.4 percent of the vote for the lower chamber. The election results ultimately led to a revised version of the earlier center-left coalition cabinets in which for the first time since late 1945 the Christian Democrats lost the premiership. That post went in mid-1981 to the leader of the tiny Republican Party, Giovanni Spadolini. Thereafter, in the general election of 1983, the DC experienced a drop even greater than that of the PCI in 1979. The Christian Democrats fell from 38.3 percent (their 1979 tally) to 32.9 percent of the ballots cast for the Chamber of Deputies, while PCI support went down by only half a point, to 29.9 percent. This led to the designation of Bettino Craxi as the first Socialist premier of Italy despite the PSI's command of only 11.4 percent of the total vote in 1983.

From the mid-1970s onward there were also a number of significant changes in the international Communist movement. With the death of Mao in September 1976 and Deng Xiaoping's rise to preeminence in the Chinese Communist leadership, Peking's overtures to the West multiplied. The establishment of diplomatic relations with the United States on January 1, 1979, was the capstone in a process of expanding political and economic ties between the People's Republic of China and the members of NATO. And the more the PCI criticized Soviet foreign policy, the more receptive the Chinese became to a rapprochement with the Italian Communists too.

Equally important developments occurred in Poland. In June 1976 there were clashes in the suburbs of Warsaw between police and workers who were demonstrating against the Gierek regime's abrupt hike in the price of basic foodstuffs. This resulted in growing contacts among discontented workers, dissident intellectuals, and the Polish Catholic hierarchy. From then on disillusionment with the economic policies and promises of the Polish leadership became ever more widespread. The denouement was a wave of strikes, triggered again by price hikes in the early summer of 1980, that culminated in the birth of Solidarity in late August of that year.

Yet another notable development was the PCF's realignment with Moscow after its brief flirtation with Eurocommunism in the mid-1970s. This return to orthodoxy reflected the Marchais leadership's recognition that the French Socialists, under the direction of François Mitterrand, were rapidly overtaking the Communists in popular support. It was apparently predicated upon the hope that a revival of the PCF's traditional pro-Sovietism and *ouvriérisme* might enable it to regain its preponderant position on the French left. Marchais' defense of the Soviet invasion of Afghanistan over Moscow television in January 1980 highlighted this policy reversal. That step, combined with the PCF's electoral decline from 20-odd percent to 15 percent of the popular vote in the spring 1981 French National Assembly elections, marked the effective demise of the Eurocommunist phenomenon. For even though the Spanish Communists continued to pursue the PCI line, their electoral weakness and increasing factionalization made them inconsequential as allies.

The PCI, a still powerful but now fairly isolated force for innovation among West European Communists, thus looked with ever greater interest to expanding its ties with Western socialist and other center-left parties. This, in turn, was yet another reason for disengagement from Moscow and denial of the distinctive character of the international Communist movement.

All the while, the PCI leadership passed as smoothly from Longo to Berlinguer at the Thirteenth PCI Congress in 1972 as it had from Togliatti to Longo in August 1964. At the PCI's 1969 congress, Berlinguer was appointed deputy head of the party. In 1972 he moved into the top position, while Longo was elevated to the new honorific post of party president. As Longo himself described the PCI's way of choosing its leaders on that occasion, "It is an organic, almost physiological, process of development."[1]

Longo's succession to the post of general secretary after Togliatti's death in Yalta on August 21, 1964, did indeed have an "organic" quality about it. It had been agreed upon in principle between Longo and Togliatti, and within the *Direzione*, as soon as Togliatti's health began to deteriorate in early 1964.[2] It was proposed at the meeting of the *Direzione* on August 18, after his stroke;[3] and it was formalized by the PCI's Central Committee on August 26, the day after his funeral. Longo's unqualified alignment with Togliatti had been evident ever since the autumn of 1943. It was symbolized by his decision to publish the Yalta memorandum forthwith should Togliatti not recover from the stroke he suffered on August 13, 1964.[4] And it was underscored by Longo's tenacious observance of the principles and guidelines set forth by Togliatti in his Yalta memorandum. In a psychological sense, Longo may have been making amends for his bitter opposition to "Ercoli" some three and a half decades earlier. But the passage of time had surely also persuaded him of the correctness of Togliatti's views on the PCI and the Communist world at large.

As for Berlinguer, his political biography indicates that he was singled out at an early age for rapid promotion within the party ranks. In 1948, at the age of twenty-five, he entered the *Direzione* as a candidate member representing the Communist youth organization. Two years later he became president of the World Federation of Democratic Youth. He was appointed head of the party school in 1957, entered the national Secretariat in 1958, and became a full member of the *Direzione* and secretary in charge of organization at the Ninth PCI Congress in 1960.[5]

More significant in terms of future Soviet–PCI relations, Berlinguer became a key spokesman for Togliatti's opposition to Soviet attempts to convene a world Communist conference to condemn the Maoists. He first

1. Text in *XIII Congresso del partito comunista italiano*, 209–15 at 214.

2. See the relevant documents in Alessandro Natta, *Le ore di Yalta* (Rome: Editori Riuniti, 1970), 79–81.

3. Ibid., 40.

4. Ibid., 48.

5. For these and other data, see Vittorio Gorresio, *Berlinguer* (Milan: Feltrinelli Editore, 1976), 167–92.

traveled to the Soviet Union to express this view in May 1964,[6] before Togliatti's death; and he returned there in March 1965 as head of the PCI delegation to the CPSU-sponsored "consultative" meeting of nineteen Communist parties at which the PCI's resistance to collective mobilization against Peking won the day.[7] In the meantime, he also went to Moscow with Paolo Bufalini in early November 1964 to convey his party's "perplexity and reservations" over the way Khrushchev had been dismissed from the CPSU leadership.[8] The groundwork was thus laid early on for the independent stance Berlinguer regularly assumed toward the CPSU after his designation as deputy general secretary in February 1969.

6. Natta, *Le ore di Yalta*, 31.

7. William E. Griffith, *Sino-Soviet Relations, 1964–1965* (Cambridge, Mass.: MIT Press, 1967), 83–88.

8. *L'Unità*, November 4, 1964, 1.

CHAPTER 8

Conflict and Conciliation during

the *Compromesso Storico*

A s the PCI's post-Stalin challenge to Soviet centralism gained mo- mentum, the very character of that challenge underwent a subtle transformation. If in the 1960s the Italian Communists were principally concerned with making the international Communist movement safe for their evolving *via italiana,* by the mid-1970s they gave every indication of being interested in seeing the pan-European branch of the Communist world reshaped in a Eurocommunist image. Prior to the open rift with Moscow in late 1981, party spokesmen never admitted to such an aim. Nor did they publicly question their allegiance to the world Communist movement or the appropriateness of special links with the CPSU as the founder of that movement. All the same, there was a proselytizing cast to the PCI's coalition building that preceded the 1976 East Berlin summit, not to mention the ever more explicit criticisms of the Soviet political system that appeared in the Italian Communist press beginning in 1976.

The CPSU, for its part, responded to the ideological challenge posed by socialist pluralism and Eurocommunism with carefully calibrated pol- emics against the Italian party. The Soviet criticisms of the PCI, however, were at first far more veiled and indirect than those that the PCI aimed at Moscow. All things being equal, the Kremlin leaders probably calculated that they had more to lose than the Italians from a public rift. In a word, they feared the blow to their domestic legitimacy and international pres- tige that could result from an open dispute with the largest and most influential nonruling Communist party. This was particularly true in the

A small part of this chapter is reprinted from *ORBIS: A Journal of World Affairs* by permission of the publisher. Copyright 1974, 1976 by The Foreign Policy Research Institute, Philadelphia, PA.

1970s when the People's Republic of China, far from seeking a rapprochement with Moscow as the Mao era drew to a close, tilted ever more toward the West.

On the other hand, as the PCI began its de facto cooperation with Christian Democracy in the second half of 1976, its vulnerability to CPSU charges of opportunist deviationism increased. For what appeared as responsible conduct to many in the non-Communist West smacked of cooptation to the more militant sectors of the PCI's own membership and electoral constituency. To deter CPSU efforts to fan the fires of discontent among the Italian party's rank and file, therefore, Italian Communist publicists muted their criticisms of Soviet socialism in 1977. Berlinguer likewise extolled the enduring character of Soviet–PCI ties and—in contrast to Marchais and Carrillo—took care to observe all due propriety in his public dealings with Moscow. Finally, both to placate the Soviets and to dampen internal party unrest, the PCI leadership reaffirmed the organizational principle of democratic centralism in a manner not heard since the 1960s.

The PCI's ambiguous policy of the *compromesso storico* (historic compromise) was the source of the party's accommodation with the Italian political establishment as well as the malaise of its more militant members. The idea of reaching some form of medium-term agreement with reform-minded Christian Democrats had been adumbrated in the early 1970s in response to the right-wing terrorism and conservative backlash provoked by the "hot autumn" of 1969.[1] The initially defensive character of this strategy was confirmed when Berlinguer formally articulated the *compromesso storico* and indeed gave it its name after the overthrow of President Salvador Allende's *Unidad Popular* government in Chile in September 1973.[2]

According to PCI commentators, *Unidad Popular* had erred in three major ways: its insistence on a government of left-wing parties only; its refusal to deal with the Chilean Christian Democrats; and its concentration on winning 51 percent of the popular vote.[3] With the benefit of hindsight,

---

1. For a sensitive exploration of the pre-1973 roots of the *compromesso storico,* see Stephen Hellman, "The Longest Campaign: Communist Party Strategy and the Elections of 1976," in *Italy at the Polls: The Parliamentary Elections of 1976,* ed. Howard R. Penniman (Washington, D.C.: American Enterprise Institute, 1977), 155–82.

2. Berlinguer first broached the idea of the *compromesso storico* in a series of articles in *Rinascita,* published under the title of "Reflections on Italy after the Events of Chile" in the early autumn of 1973. But he qualified this early discussion with warnings against the dangers of legalistic illusions and "parliamentary cretinism," caveats that had vanished from his official discourses by 1974. The series is reprinted in *Il compromesso storico,* ed. Pietro Valenza (Rome: Newton Compton Editori, 1975), 14–31.

3. For example, Renato Sandri, "Cile: analisi di un'esperienza e di una sconfitta," *Critica marxista* 11, no. 5 (September–October 1973):15–40.

the PCI criticized the Allende regime for failing to anticipate that such policies would lead to domestic polarization, economic destabilization from abroad, and counterrevolution. The military coup in Chile evidently strengthened the Berlinguer leadership's growing conviction that a coalition government of the left in Italy could lead to similar results, given the country's membership in NATO, economic dependence on the European Common Market, and—not least—lingering Fascist heritage.

Broadly conceived, the *compromesso storico* was simply one more step in the PCI's affirmation of an electoral and gradual path to socialism in Italy. Its formulation was historic only in terms of the bluntness with which the party committed itself to the politics of consensus and compromise, especially in its dealings with the DC. Meanwhile, the idea of a single democratic transitional stage between the collapse of fascism and the coming of socialism (Togliatti's "progressive democracy") had long since given way to the notion of a separate (though not clearly defined) stage between the "state-monopoly capitalism" of the postwar era and socialism.

In this latter context the *compromesso storico,* narrowly conceived as a concrete political arrangement, represented a forward strategy: it was to be the penultimate stage in the prolonged democratic transition to socialism—one in which progressive Catholics qua Christian Democrats would join with Communists, socialists, and other lay progressives in carrying to completion the structural reforms about which PCI theorists had so often spoken during the 1960s. But what did this narrower conception of the *compromesso storico* mean in the political here and now? From Berlinguer's formal statements on down to columnists in *l'Unità* the basic premise was the same. Before the *compromesso storico* could be realized, the balance of power within the factionalized Christian Democratic Party (DC) had to shift in favor of the reform wing.[4]

Practical politics soon interrupted abstract theorizing. When national elections were called for June 1976, a year ahead of schedule, Secretariat member Napolitano conceded to the PCI Central Committee that conditions were not yet ripe for the leftward shift within the DC deemed essential for the *compromesso storico.*[5] During the election campaign, therefore, the Communists appealed for the more limited objective of a government of national unity including *all* parties except the monarchists and neo-Fascists on the extreme right. This was not entirely unexpected. At the Fourteenth PCI Congress in March 1975, a number of speakers had

4. For Berlinguer's views on this point, see his reports to the December 1974 PCI Central Committee plenum and the Fourteenth PCI Congress. The former appeared in *l'Unità,* December 11, 1974, 7–14 at 12, the latter in *XIV Congresso del partito comunista italiano: Atti e risoluzioni* (Rome: Editori Riuniti, 1975), 15–76 at 48–51.

5. *L'Unità,* April 14, 1976, 8.

referred to the need for an interim stage, or governing configuration, between the status quo and the *compromesso storico*.[6]

On the eve of the electoral showdown, Berlinguer spelled out the linkage between the party's advocacy of a government of democratic unity and its longer-term goal. As he put it, "our current proposal doesn't contradict the strategy of the 'historic compromise'—that is, of an agreement among the great popular Italian currents, the Communist, the socialist, the Catholic, for a common *long-range* program—but is meant to be something that immediately relates and responds to the urgent necessities of the moment."[7] In other words, what he was suggesting was an emergency government to see Italy through the economic crisis of inflation, trade deficits, and unemployment in the 1970s.

In the wake of the PCI's electoral surge from 27.2 percent of the popular vote for the Chamber of Deputies in 1972 to 34.4 percent in 1976 (while the DC held steady at 38.7 percent), the party continued its appeals for an emergency coalition government. In practice, however, it consented to the creation of a minority, exclusively DC cabinet headed by Giulio Andreotti. PCI abstention (instead of its traditional opposition) on the vote of confidence for the Andreotti government assured the Communists a key role in Parliament, including the presidency of the lower chamber and the chairmanship of seven committees.

This is not the place to elaborate upon the twists and turns of domestic Italian politics between the national elections of June 1976 and June 1979.[8] Suffice it to say that as the PCI moved toward closer cooperation with the Christian Democrats and center-left parties, the narrow meaning of the *compromesso storico* as a strategy for social transformation received less emphasis—in party rhetoric as well as actual practice. Notwithstanding the PCI's repeated demands for entry into a government of national unity, the party also consented to vote *in favor* of a second minority DC cabinet in March 1978, on the eve of Aldo Moro's kidnapping. Moreover, despite the PCI leadership's insistence that austerity measures be linked to concrete social reforms, it supported limitations on wage increases, public spending, and rent control which were designed to remedy Italy's economic ills but which also impinged directly on the material interests of the working class.[9]

6. See, for example, Paolo Bufalini's speech in *XIV Congresso del partito comunista italiano*, 244.

7. *L'Unità*, May 14, 1976, 10; my emphasis.

8. For an excellent concise analysis, see Sidney Tarrow, "Historic Compromise or Bourgeois Majority? Eurocommunism in Italy 1976–79," in *National Communism in Western Europe: A Third Way for Socialism?*, ed. Howard Machin (London: Methuen, 1983), 124–53. A detailed account may be found in the collection edited by Howard R. Penniman, *Italy at the Polls, 1979* (Washington, D.C.: American Enterprise Institute, 1981).

9. For the PCI's economic policies during this period, see Michael J. Sodaro, "The Italian Communists and the Politics of Austerity," *Studies in Comparative Communism* 13, nos. 2–3 (Summer–Autumn 1980):220–49.

As we have already observed, these moderate policies provoked internal party tensions that were to affect in important ways the PCI's relationship with the CPSU. In a word, the Berlinguer leadership balanced conciliation toward Christian Democracy at home with conciliation toward Moscow in the hope of assuaging discontent among Italian Communist militants. But before proceeding to a discussion of what we might call the dialectics of Soviet–PCI relations in the second half of the 1970s, we must take a look at the view from Moscow toward the West European Communist movement in general as well as the PCI.

The View from Moscow

The Soviet attitude toward communism in Western Europe during the 1970s was ambivalent if not downright contradictory. On the one hand, the Brezhnev oligarchy was wary of revolutionary activism during the first half of the decade on the ground that it might disrupt East–West détente. Moscow's restraint toward the prospect of a Communist–Socialist electoral victory in France and a Communist seizure of power in Portugal testified to this. On the other hand, the Kremlin leadership also feared the more innovative, albeit less militant, ideas of the Italian and Spanish Communist parties, ideas that could undermine CPSU legitimacy at home and hegemony in Eastern Europe. Yet despite the Politburo's reservations toward both sectarians and innovators among the Western Communists, it still felt the need to project a public image of pan-European Communist solidarity. This was clear from the concessions it made during the preparations for the June 1976 pan-European Communist summit in East Berlin.

Soviet Perspectives on Revolution in the West

During the Khrushchev and early Brezhnev eras the view from Moscow regarding revolution in the West was essentially the same. Khrushchev's doctrinal innovations at the Twentieth CPSU Congress included acknowledgment of the possibility of a peaceful parliamentary transition to socialism in one or another capitalist country. This position was consistent with his pronouncements on the legitimacy of different paths to socialism in Eastern Europe. Yet given Western Europe's economic strength and political cohesion at the time, it is unlikely that Khrushchev anticipated *any* form of revolutionary transformation in that region in the foreseeable future. Rather, his interest in reducing tensions with the Atlantic Alliance required that he temper the traditional image of the Soviet Union as the fountainhead of violent revolution.

The very ambiguity of the peaceful transition doctrine suggests that it was intended to advance Soviet foreign policy interests rather than the cause of revolution in the West. In 1956 Khrushchev cited the developments in Czechoslovakia during 1948 as an example of a peaceful socialist revolution. Several years later Kuusinen, a leading theorist under Khrushchev, designated "democracy of a new type" as the path to socialism in Western Europe.[10] Although this term had been coined by Togliatti in 1936 and reiterated by him in 1962 in contexts that suggested a genuine democratic transition,[11] it had also been used interchangeably with "people's democracy" to describe the East European systems in the late 1940s. CPSU ideologues insisted, moreover, on the observance even in the West of "general laws" of socialist construction that included the leading role of the Communist Party and a state-run economy. Such equivocal formulations were not likely to enhance the electoral appeal of the West European Communists. In other words, the doctrine of a peaceful parliamentary transition to socialism seemed little more than a rationalization for Moscow's benign neglect of revolution in the capitalist countries with which it sought to normalize state-to-state relations.

This situation did not change substantially even after the widespread leftist surge in Western Europe that began in the late 1960s. Soviet policy makers continued to be preoccupied with improving political and economic relations with the Western powers and remained indifferent toward the prospects for political change, especially in Latin Europe.[12] The Kremlin's conspicuous cultivation of the powers that be in the Élysée during the French national elections of 1973 and 1974 was one of the more glaring manifestations of this attitude. Far more serious was the Soviet leadership's consuming interest in the successful conclusion of the Conference on Security and Cooperation in Europe (Helsinki) even as signs of European radicalization multiplied (growing electoral support for the French Union of the Left, the massive Italian vote in favor of divorce in May 1974, mounting revolutionary extremism in Portugal).

The impact of revolutionary developments in Chile was of a different order, at least among some CPSU functionaries responsible for ideological matters. There was immediate interest in the *Unidad Popular* electoral victory of 1970 and its implications for radical change elsewhere in the West. This was evidenced by the infusion of administrative support and personnel into the moribund Institute of the International Workers' Movement of the Soviet Academy of Sciences in early 1971.[13] Yet, a number of commentators in Soviet international affairs journals soon began to equate the expected socialist transition in Chile with what had transpired

10. Otto Kuusinen, *Fundamentals of Marxism-Leninism* (Moscow, 1959).

11. See chap. 7, 245.

12. Joan Barth Urban, "Contemporary Soviet Perspectives on Revolution in the West," *Orbis* 19, no. 4 (Winter 1976):1359–1402.

13. Ibid., 1360.

in the postwar people's democracies of Eastern Europe.[14] Apparently Soviet ideologues feared the attractiveness of the Allende administration's pluralist rhetoric just as they had feared the contagiousness of the 1968 Czechoslovakian reform movement. Indeed, the more sectarian guardians of Soviet orthodoxy may well have been relieved when the military coup against the *Unidad Popular* government enabled them to focus their attention on where Allende had gone wrong, on the "lessons of Chile." For several establishment analysts seized the opportunity to deplore *Unidad Popular's* failure to dominate the media, infiltrate the military, and—most significant—destroy the old "bourgeois" state structures of Chile.[15] Written *prior* to the collapse of the Portuguese dictatorship in late April 1974, their words read like a prescription for the Portuguese Communist Party's abortive attempt to manipulate its way into power during 1975.

In short, there was a real discrepancy between the conservatism of Moscow's state relations with the West and the radical rhetoric used by some CPSU publicists to depict the shape of eventual revolutionary change in the capitalist world.

In 1974–75 the Soviet leadership made an attempt to reconcile these divergent orientations. Alexander Sobolev, head of the Institute of Marxism-Leninism's Department of International Communist Affairs and editor-in-chief of the new journal of the Institute of the International Workers' Movement, endorsed the idea of a democratic transitional stage on the path to socialism (Soviet-style) in the West.[16] Although such flexibility contrasted sharply with the sectarian "lessons of Chile" propounded just a short while earlier, it was not a new phenomenon in Soviet doctrine. We need only recall the popular front line of the 1930s as well as the discussions in Soviet circles of a democratic transitional stage after World War II. Not for many years, however, had such authoritative and widespread attention been paid to the idea of observing democratic principles during a transitional period between capitalism and socialism.

The intent of the more moderate CPSU ideologues such as Sobolev was clear. By calling for an intermediate democratic stage, they supported a revolutionary perspective that would seemingly be compatible with both

14. Joan Barth Urban, "Socialist Pluralism in Soviet and Italian Communist Perspective: The Chilean Catalyst," *Orbis* 18, no. 2 (Summer 1974):482–509 at 495–502.

15. See, for example, A. I. Sobolev, "Revoliutsiia i kontrrevoliutsiia: opyt Chili i problemy klassovoi borby," *Rabochii klass i sovremennyi mir*, no. 2 (March–April 1974):3–22 at 12–22; M. F. Kudachkin, "Opyt borby Kompartii Chili za edinstvo levykh sil i revoliutsionnye preobrazovaniia," *Voprosy istorii KPSS*, no. 5 (May 1974):48–60; and Boris Ponomarev, "The World Situation and the Revolutionary Process," *World Marxist Review* 17, no. 6 (June 1974):3–15. Ponomarev's article is but a pale reflection of the first two.

16. A. I. Sobolev, "Voprosy strategii i taktiki klassovoi borby na nyneshnem etape obshchego krizisa kapitalizma," *Rabochii klass i sovremennyi mir*, no. 1 (January–February 1975):3–20 at 15–16; cf. Urban, "Contemporary Soviet Perspectives," 1374–75.

East–West détente and Communist gains in Latin Europe. Such a strategy would provide an outlet for the activist zeal of the Portuguese, French, and Italian Communists without constituting a direct challenge to their respective systems of government. At a time of Soviet concern with winning legitimacy for the postwar division of Europe through the Helsinki talks (which drew to a successful close only on August 1, 1975), this was hardly an unimportant consideration.

As we observed in the previous chapter, the CPSU leadership also made compromises of an organizational nature when it agreed in October 1974 to a pan-European Communist conference. The reasons for its concessions in this regard are not difficult to fathom. By the second half of 1974 the domestic standing of all the Latin European parties was on the upswing: the Portuguese Communists because of their close ties with the military leaders of the April 1974 revolution; the Spanish Communists because of the fluidity of the political situation in Spain in anticipation of the post-Franco era; the PCF because of the growing electoral clout of the Union of the Left; and the PCI because of the overwhelming victory of the anti-clerical forces in the May 1974 referendum on divorce. The growing economic cum energy crisis also gave the Western Communists a feeling of ideological vindication. By way of contrast, Moscow's preoccupation with East–West détente and the protracted Helsinki talks placed the CPSU on the ideological defensive. Indeed, by 1972–73 the Spanish party had begun to accuse the Soviet Union of favoring the status quo in Western Europe, and it was soon to become public knowledge that these sentiments were shared by the French Communists. The Kremlin thus looked to the East Berlin summit as a means of restoring its ideological credibility and political authority among its Western comrades.[17]

Indirect support for this interpretation is to be found in the apologetic tone of Boris Ponomarev (head of the CPSU's International Department) at the October 1974 consultative meeting in Warsaw that set the procedural ground rules for the East Berlin summit. In a word, Ponomarev conceded that during the 1960s Moscow may have slighted the interests of class struggle in the West because of the overriding necessity (as he put it) of ending the Cold War.[18] The implication was that the CPSU was now prepared to rectify that imbalance.

Because of the procedural rule of consensus agreed upon at the Warsaw meeting, the twenty-month-long preparations for the East Berlin conference turned out to be a political can of worms for Moscow. In the end the PCI and its autonomist allies won the day in the formulation of the

---

17. I develop this argument at greater length in "The Ties That Bind," in *The European Left: Italy, France, and Spain,* ed. William E. Griffith (Lexington, Mass.: Lexington Books, 1979), 211–14.

18. Text in *Pravda,* October 18, 1974, 4.

final document approved in late June 1976 by the twenty-eight-odd participants. Gone was any reference to the CPSU's "general laws." Proletarian internationalism met with the same fate as the "general laws": total silence. The document appealed instead for "internationalist solidarity," a term that harked back to the Socialist International rather than the Comintern. More significant, as later events were to show, the Berlin statement declared that one Communist party's criticism of another was not tantamount to anticommunism.[19] What this meant in plain English was that Western Communist criticism of Soviet domestic repression was not tantamount to "anti-Sovietism," as Moscow had previously maintained. At the same time, the speeches to the conference itself testified to the actual diversity that characterized the pan-European Communist movement by mid-1976. Berlinguer, Marchais, and Carrillo pointed out the flaws in "existing socialism" just as the pro-Soviet loyalists took pains to paper them over. And the remarks of all of them were published verbatim in the East German Communist party daily, *Neues Deutschland* (only to be censored in *Pravda*).

What, then, did the Soviet decision makers expect to gain from this pluralist spectacle? First of all, failure to hold the East Berlin summit after the fanfare that had surrounded its preparations would have reflected poorly on the CPSU's claim to global ideological authority. Second, through the Soviet media's tested methods of censorship, distortion, and outright falsification, the extent not just of European Communist diversity but of nonruling Communist criticism of the Soviet Union's model of socialism was concealed from the Soviet people. Instead, *Pravda*'s commentaries on the East Berlin summit lauded it as a vindication of "proletarian internationalism," the "general laws," and the growing unity of the international Communist movement. Third, the Kremlin probably calculated that convening the conference on June 29–30, 1976 (the actual date was set only *after* the PCI's sizable gains in Italy's parliamentary elections of June 20–21),[20] would enable the Soviet Union to derive some propaganda advantage vis-à-vis official Western circles from the forward momentum the Eurocommunists seemed to be enjoying. The very holding of the conference, finally, signaled to the West that the unity of the European Communist movement still outweighed its diversity.

All the same, the CPSU concessions that made the East Berlin summit possible were slow in coming and grudging to the end. Soviet ambivalence toward developments in Portugal certainly complicated the process of reaching an agreement on the conference document. No sooner did CPSU spokesmen start expounding upon the virtues of a democratic tran-

19. English text in *New Times* [Moscow], no. 28 (July 1976):17–32.

20. James P. McGregor, "The 1976 European Communist Parties Conference," *Studies in Comparative Communism* 11, no. 4 (Winter 1978):339–60 at 341–42.

sitional stage in early 1975 than the radicalization of the Portuguese scene gave a hollow ring to their words. Indeed, the Soviet media began to speak with at least two voices.

Throughout the spring and summer of 1975 commentaries in the specialized journals and also in *Pravda* reiterated Sobolev's winter 1975 endorsement of a democratic transitional stage.[21] Even in the issue of the CPSU's theoretical journal, *Kommunist,* that was sent to press on July 21, the height of the summer crisis in Portugal, Ponomarev stressed the importance of "*intermediate stages and transitional forms* on the path to socialism" in the capitalist world.[22] By the same token, from March through June 1975 *Pravda* often portrayed Portuguese society as passing through a "transitional period defined . . . as the path to socialism in a multi-party framework."[23]

On the other hand, during this same time frame *Pravda*'s dispatches from Lisbon reported with open praise or barely concealed partiality (i.e., by citing Portuguese Communist approval) the controversial maneuvers of the radicals in the powerful Armed Forces Movement (MFA), the group that had engineered the April 1974 military coup in Portugal. Moreover, during the most critical period from mid-July through mid-August 1975, after the withdrawal of the moderate parties from Lisbon's provisional government in protest against the Communist and MFA radicals' violations of democratic procedures, *Pravda*'s on-the-scene reports became even more slanted. News stories emanating both from TASS and the local *Pravda* correspondent began to accuse the Portuguese Socialists and the moderates in the MFA of colluding, first "objectively" and then "subjectively," with "counterrevolution and reaction."[24]

It was in this context that Konstantin Zarodov—editor of the Soviet-sponsored international Communist journal, *Problems of Peace and Socialism*—wrote his widely publicized *Pravda* commentary of August 6, 1975, in which he derided majority rule and insisted on Communist dominance even during the transitional period between capitalism and socialism.[25] Zarodov's article represented a high-level imprimatur for the kind of reportorial militancy noted above. At no point did he actually mention Portugal. However, his attack on Communist "moderates,"

21. See, for example, T. Timofeev, "Znamia revoliutsionnoi borby proletariata," *Kommunist,* no. 6 (April 1975):98–108; and "Kommunisty v borbe protiv fashizm i voinu, za mir, demokratiiu i sotsializm: Doklad tovarishcha B. N. Ponomareva," *Kommunist,* no. 11 (July 1975):11–28.

22. Ibid., 28; my emphasis.

23. *Pravda,* June 22, 1975, 5; cf. Urban, "Contemporary Soviet Perspectives," 1385–86.

24. Ibid., 1389–90.

25. "Leninskaia strategiia i taktika revoliutsionnoi borby," *Pravda,* August 6, 1975, 2–3. Zarodov, taking the Russian Revolution of 1905 as his frame of reference, called for Communist dominance during *democratic* revolutions as the prerequisite for the ultimate victory of socialist revolutions.

"conciliators," and advocates of broad-alliance and electoral policies was not just a rebuke of the Eurocommunists but also a defense of the Portuguese Communist sectarians.

What this underscored was that the Soviet attitude toward the revolution in Portugal was fraught with ambiguity. On the one hand, considerations of Soviet foreign policy required restraint. The coincidence in timing between the radicalization of Portugal and the final preparations for the Helsinki summit, the capstone of Brezhnev's diplomatic efforts over four years, explains the CPSU's initial efforts to place Portuguese developments within the gradualist framework of a democratic transitional stage. On the other hand, given the ideological matrix of the Soviet regime, it could hardly afford to turn its back on a revolution in progress. The Soviet masses may well have been more concerned with peace and prosperity than doctrinal vindication; indeed, one could argue that Brezhnev's tenacious insistence on the Helsinki summit was partially aimed at buttressing the Soviet regime's *domestic* image as the most active great-power proponent of peace. But among CPSU functionaries steeped in dogma since political adolescence, there must have been at least a residual commitment to the revolutionary precepts of Marxism-Leninism. This would explain the sectarians' preoccupation with the "lessons of Chile." More to the point, it would suggest support among party stalwarts for a Communist takeover in Portugal.

The CPSU leadership coped with these contradictory pressures by combining reportorial militancy with editorial restraint in *Pravda, Kommunist,* and other party media. At no point did Moscow authoritatively endorse the Portuguese Communist Party's transparent power grab. It was prepared to accept a fait accompli, as evidenced by the tenor of Pravda's local coverage. It was not prepared to endanger détente by inciting a Communist takeover. Nor was it ready to risk an open break with Western Communist moderates such as the PCI, as will be amply discussed in the remainder of this chapter.

CPSU caution and ambiguity toward Portugal were counterbalanced by the Kremlin's decision sometime in late August or early September 1975 to give decisive backing to the pro-Soviet Popular Movement for the Liberation of Angola (MPLA), including both military equipment and logistical support for the Cuban troops soon to arrive en masse in Angola.[26] On September 17, 1975, moreover, Brezhnev granted a personal audience to Zarodov, an event headlined on the front page of *Pravda.*[27] The ostensible occasion for this honor was to congratulate Zarodov for his

26. For careful documentation of this specific time frame, see Jiri Valenta, "Soviet Decision-Making on the Intervention in Angola," in *Communism in Africa,* ed. David E. Albright (Bloomington: Indiana University Press, 1980), 93–117 at 102.

27. "Beseda u tovarishcha L. I. Brezhneva," *Pravda,* September 18, 1975.

accomplishments as editor of *Problems of Peace and Socialism*. But the meeting, coming as it did just after the Portuguese Communists had been edged out of their commanding position in Lisbon, yet before public knowledge of the CPSU's decision on Angola, was obviously meant to bolster Communist sectarians at home and abroad. It was probably also intended as a rebuff to the PCI and PCF leaderships for their heated objections to Zarodov's August 6 piece in *Pravda*.

Meanwhile, divergences among CPSU analysts continued to appear in the Soviet theoretical and foreign affairs journals. While articles endorsing variations on the theme of a democratic transitional stage in the West carried the bylines of such prominent figures as Vadim Zagladin, Ponomarev's deputy, more intransigent views also appeared.

A case in point was a commentary by Stepan Salychev in the late November 1975 issue of *Kommunist*. By way of background, in the early 1970s Salychev had argued in *Kommunist* and other journals that mass pressures in the West for radical economic and political change were unleashing a revolutionary process that would lead inexorably to socialism.[28] This prompted establishment publicist Yuri Krasin, in a review of a book by Salychev on the interwar history of the French Socialist Party, to pointedly criticize him for treating "transitional forms of power" inadequately, especially with reference to their contemporary significance. Krasin also implied that Salychev, by underplaying the Comintern's opposition in the early 1930s to "intermediate" democratic tasks, was guilty of the same error.[29] Thereafter Salychev faded from public view for several years.

When he resurfaced in late 1975 Salychev lambasted "parliamentary prejudices" above all. He insisted that the elimination of bourgeois-democratic institutions, including the separation of powers, and their replacement by a "democracy of a new type" (plainly of the East European variety) was the precondition for revolutionary victory.[30] He said not a word on the question of a democratic transitional stage but stressed instead the primacy of grassroots mass mobilization over parliamentary activity. In other words, his essay amounted to an implicit defense of what the Portuguese Communists had tried to do and a refutation of the mid-November 1975 PCI–PCF communiqué upholding bourgeois-democratic liberties, political pluralism, and an independent judiciary even under socialism.

28. S. Salychev, "Ob osobennostiakh sovremennoi klassovoi borby v stranakh kapitala," *Kommunist*, no. 6 (April 1973):71–85 at 76–80.

29. Yu. Krasin, "Sotsialisty Frantsii: uroki istorii," *Mirovaia ekonomika i mezhdunarodnye otnosheniia*, no. 4 (April 1974):143–46.

30. S. Salychev, "Revoliutsiia i demokratiia," *Kommunist*, no. 17 (November 1975):114–24. Thereafter Salychev's articles appeared with some regularity. See, for example, his favorable review of a book published in 1980 by Konstantin Zarodov in *Pravda*, September 18, 1980, 2.

CPSU spokesmen flatly denied the existence of substantive differences among Soviet analysts on these question.[31] By way of contrast, an unsigned *l'Unità* article of December 9, 1975, entitled "Debate in the USSR on Democracy and Revolution," contrasted the simplistic orthodoxy of the Salychev piece with a more nuanced article by Zagladin which welcomed "the search for new paths, forms, and methods of struggle." At the same time, the PCI commentator also rebuked Zagladin for his allusions to some Western comrades' "ambiguous maneuvers" and "compromises that can lead to the loss of revolutionary identity" (an obvious slur against the *compromesso storico*). For the Italian Communists it was a matter of principle, retorted *l'Unità*, that there could be no advance toward socialism without the "consistent development of democracy which is expressed politically in the plurality of protagonists and in the real acquisition of consensus" by the working class and its vanguard.[32]

Implicit in this brief PCI commentary were the three basic approaches to revolutionary strategy around which a pan-European Communist debate would revolve for the rest of the decade: the CPSU sectarians' express support for manipulation of the majority by a militant minority and for the destruction of the bourgeois state; the CPSU moderates' acquiescence to a democratic transitional stage within the framework of existing political institutions; and the PCI's endorsement of bourgeois-democratic liberties and institutions, including electoral competition, even during the stage of socialist transformation.

The CPSU Response to the PCI Challenge

The doctrinal pronouncements and divergences of Soviet ideologues notwithstanding, when all is said and done the Kremlin did not seek revolution in the West. The rise of revolutionary movements in the Third World in the second half of the 1970s provided an outlet for the radical sectarian impulse still apparent among sectors of the CPSU establishment. But what the Brezhnev oligarchy did seek from the West European Communist parties was unqualified backing of Soviet foreign policy, on the one hand, and recognition of Moscow's ideological credentials as the vanguard of world revolution on the other.

Until the end of the 1970s the PCI was in substantial agreement with the Kremlin's version of détente: a relaxation of tensions and an increase in economic ties with the Western powers combined with active support for radical Third World liberationism. The Italian party's acquiescence to Italy's membership in NATO, formally announced by Berlinguer during

31. Boris Vesnin, "Anti-Communist Strategems and Realities of the Communist Movement," *New Times*, no. 50 (December 1975):18–19.
32. "Dibattito in URSS su democrazia e rivoluzione," *l'Unità*, December 9, 1975, 12.

the winter of 1974–75, was portrayed as a contribution to stable East–West relations rather than as a divergence from the Soviet Union.[33] Furthermore, the *compromesso storico,* inasmuch as it signified an accommodation with the pro-Western Italian political establishment, was fully compatible with Brezhnev's pursuit of normal state-to-state relations with the NATO powers. In no way did the PCI's conduct jeopardize the improvement of ties between the Soviet Union and the West; nor did the Berlinguer leadership take part in the Spanish and French Communist allegations that the Soviet Union favored the European status quo.

By way of contrast, the PCI's coalition building in defense of socialist pluralism and Communist party autonomy, not to mention its condemnation of the Warsaw Pact invasion of Czechoslovakia, represented an implicit challenge to the CPSU's ideological norms. As long as these moves were aimed primarily at defending the *via italiana,* Moscow responded with veiled or muted polemics. Even when PCI publicists below the level of the top leadership began to criticize various aspects of the Soviet system in the mid-1970s, the CPSU stopped just short of openly accusing the Italian party of ideological deviationism. As we shall see in chapter 9, it was only after the PCI started to attribute key Soviet foreign policy initiatives to superpower expansionism rather than to revolutionary zeal that Moscow reacted with angry and direct polemical rebuttals.

The CPSU's response to the PCI's challenge to its ideological norms during the late 1960s and 1970s was instead to blend *indirect* polemics with periodic bilateral consultations. Broadly stated, the polemics criticized the Italian party's policies, even if obliquely, as erroneous, revisionist, and "objectively" if not willfully anti-Soviet. Plainly, these public reproaches were designed to bring pressure upon the Berlinguer group in two ways. First of all, they enabled Moscow to inform the Italian party's rank-and-file members of the CPSU's alarm over official PCI positions, thereby helping to fan internal opposition to the leadership's line. Survey research has revealed considerable disagreement among PCI cadres over the *compromesso storico* and the party's condemnation of the Soviet invasion of Czechoslovakia.[34] Roughly one-third of those interviewed opposed the adoption of these policies, taking a more traditional and militant approach to domestic alliance strategy and international alignment. The men in the Kremlin evidently hoped that their anti-PCI polemics would galvanize this discontent to the point where it would have an impact on the party's decision makers. At the same time, the Soviets apparently calculated that by carefully modulating the intensity of the

33. See, for example, Berlinguer's reports cited in note 4 to this chapter.
34. For survey data on such dissent, see Kevin Devlin, "The PCI and Its 'Afghans,'" *Radio Free Europe Research,* background report no. 113, April 23, 1981.

polemics they could force the Italian leaders to moderate their behavior in order to avoid even more pointed verbal attacks.

While the CPSU used the threat of polemical escalation as a stick against the PCI, it held out the promise of Soviet–PCI summitry as a carrot to induce accommodations to Moscow's policies. The summits in question involved talks at the highest level, between Berlinguer and Brezhnev, above and beyond the rather frequent contacts between members of the PCI's *Direzione* and the CPSU's International Department. The reasoning behind this Soviet gambit was clear. The CPSU leaders were fully aware that just as the Italian leaders feared the effect of direct Soviet polemics on their party's internal cohesion, they also needed evidence of overall Soviet–PCI amity, of ongoing top-level party links, to mollify traditionalist or pro-Soviet elements within their ranks. This was especially true during 1977–78 when the Italian party's de facto cooperation with the first Andreotti (DC) cabinet and participation in the parliamentary majority of the second gave rise to disorientation and outright dissent among some members and cadres alike.[35]

The ways in which Moscow combined the polemical stick with the carrot of Soviet–PCI conciliation during the later 1970s will be explored in the final section of this chapter. But first a closer look at the CPSU's polemical techniques is in order.

The prime targets of the Soviet diatribes were the PCI's programmatic concepts and organizational formulas. The late 1960s and early 1970s saw a broad-gauged attack on the notion of socialist pluralism. During the mid-1970s the chief butt of Moscow's polemics became Eurocommunism, with its conceptual embodiment of both pluralism and regionalism. By the end of the decade the Soviet ideologues included the PCI's "new internationalism" on its roster of deviations. But while the targets varied, the polemical techniques remained the same. On the one hand, there were gradations in the explicitness with which the CPSU spelled out the object of its attacks. On the other hand, there were gradations in the official character, or weight, of the polemics.

The variations in explicitness included veiled and surrogate polemics. At the lowest end of the scale stood the veiled polemics in which first pluralism, then Eurocommunism, was denounced as an imperialist tool and/or revisionist deviation without being explicitly associated with the PCI. This was Moscow's preferred approach. The surrogate polemics may best be defined with reference to the blistering critique of Carrillo's *"Eurocommunism" and the State* in the Moscow foreign-language news-

35. Ibid. Cf. Peter Lange, "Crisis and Consent, Change and Compromise: Dilemmas of Italian Communism in the 1970s," *West European Politics* [London] 2, no. 3 (October 1979):110–32 at 122–28; see also Sodaro, "The Italian Communists and the Politics of Austerity," passim.

weekly, *New Times*. Just as the Soviet denunciations of Albania some fifteen years earlier were also aimed at her patrons in Peking, so Moscow's attack on the leader of the small Spanish party was likewise intended as a warning to Carrillo's far more powerful Italian Communist allies. We shall turn to the details of this incident in the next section. The *New Times* article was, of course, an example of a direct polemic against the Spanish party. But the PCI, with the exception of occasional Soviet press jibes at the participation of Italian Communists in Western academic symposia dealing with Eurocommunism,[36] escaped such open sallies in the 1970s. As already suggested, the Soviets probably figured that direct attacks on the electorally strong Italian party would lessen the ideological prestige of the CPSU. Thus, while overt castigation of the PCI remained Moscow's ace in the hole, it also represented a double-edged sword.

As we saw in chapter 7, the Soviet-led invasion of Czechoslovakia crushed the pluralist contagion emanating from Prague, only to provoke a concerted effort by PCI policy makers to formulate their own pluralist model of socialism. The June 1969 Moscow conference of Communist parties provided a ready forum for a Soviet riposte. On that occasion Ulbricht and Gomulka, still the party chiefs in East Germany and Poland, were as quick to denounce socialist pluralism as they had been a year earlier to repudiate the Czechoslovakian reformers. Gomulka took the more moderate position, merely voicing skepticism over the feasibility of permitting "opposition parties . . . within the framework of the socialist system" and cautioning those "fraternal parties in developed capitalist countries" who entertained this perspective against recommending it for "Communist parties presently in power."[37] Ulbricht was less circumspect. He flatly denounced "pluralism" as a capitalist manifestation that, if applied to socialism, would "give the class enemy the possibility of acquiring influence."[38]

In the winter of 1971 the Soviet journal *Znamia*, organ of the Union of Soviet Writers, joined battle with a denunciation of pluralism that combined the views of both Ulbricht and Gomulka, adding up to an exceptional exercise in vitriol even by Moscow's standards. The two-part article explicitly identified "pluralism" with right-wing revisionism; revisionism, in turn, was labeled "an *agentura* of imperialism in the revolutionary movement." Significantly, the piece refrained from disclosing that pluralism was in fact supported by some Western Communist parties, above all, the PCI. It did, however, repeat verbatim (but without attribu-

36. See, for example, *"Reaktsiia aktiviziruetsia," Pravda*, October 1, 1977, 5; cf. "Impressioni sbagliate sulle abitudini del PCI," *l'Unità*, December 14, 1977, 19.

37. Text in *Conferenza internazionale dei partiti comunisti e operai, Mosca 5–17 giugno 1969: Testi e documenti* (Rome: Editori Riuniti, 1969), 123–41 at 139.

38. Text in ibid., 286–308 at 290–91.

tion) the relevant paragraph from Gomulka's June 1969 speech in which he advised "fraternal parties" in the West not to propagate their views among ruling Communist parties.[39] As a final jab, the *Znamia* series carried the byline of none other than S. Kovalev, the publicist who first set forth in *Pravda* what later became known as the Brezhnev doctrine of limited sovereignty—the CPSU's pat justification for the Warsaw Pact invasion of Czechoslovakia. The linkage between Moscow's rejection of pluralism and its earlier repudiation of the Dubček reform movement could hardly have been more pointed.

Meanwhile, the Soviet party's uneasiness over the idea of socialist pluralism was exacerbated by the PCE's affirmation of a pluralist program in 1972–73. Then came the CPSU sectarians' reaction to the anti-Allende military coup in Chile. During this period even the relatively moderate establishment ideologue Sobolev denounced advocates of pluralism. As he put it in the March 1974 issue of the CPSU's mass circulation bi-weekly, *Partiinaia zhizn*, those who claimed that there could be "socialist pluralism, i.e., a multitude of models of socialism, a multitude of political principles of socialist society," were "*contemporary revisionists.*"[40] He further noted that the proponents of these ideas denied the existence of any such thing as "general laws for the transition from capitalism to socialism." What he did not spell out was that these were precisely the positions of the PCI.

During the lengthy preparations for the East Berlin summit such veiled attacks against pluralism were replaced by sarcastic innuendoes.[41] In the aftermath of the June 1976 meeting, however, CPSU publicists began to use the same technique of veiled polemics to discredit Eurocommunism.

The opening salvo in this latest polemical joust was launched, not surprisingly, by Zarodov's journal. In the lead article of the December 1976 issue, Bulgarian leader Todor Zhivkov—ever a faithful mouthpiece for Soviet views—baldly equated the new Eurocommunist movement with imperialist subversion. Eurocommunism, he asserted, had become one of the bourgeois propagandists' "*main lines of ideological subversion against proletarian internationalism.*" Its "ideological principles and objectives" included, moreover, the denial of the "general laws and *universally valid aspects of revolutionary experience.*"[42] The allusion to univer-

39. S. M. Kovalev, "Chuzhdaia ideologiia v revoliutsionnom dvizhenii: Zametki o sovremennom revizionizme," *Znamia*, nos. 2 and 3 (February and March 1971):151–70 and 187–99 respectively. For the paragraph from Gomulka's 1969 speech, see the second installment, in ibid., 190.

40. A. Sobolev, "Aktualnye problemy borby protiv pravogo revizionizma," *Partiinaia zhizn*, no. 5 (March 1974), 75–79 at 77.

41. E. Bagramov, "Zhiznennost leninskoi kontseptsii internatsionalizma," *Kommunist*, no. 6 (April 1976):88–99 at 96.

42. Todor Zhivkov, "Year of Peace, Year of Struggle," *World Marxist Review* [English

sal aspects of revolutionary experience suggested that Zhivkov shared Zarodov's sectarian views on the revolutionary process. An unsigned *Kommunist* editorial sent to press on December 20, 1976, took the less contentious tack of linking regional variants of Marxism merely to revisionism, recalling Sobolev's earlier handling of pluralism.[43] The anonymous writer also extolled the "general laws of socialist construction" while remaining silent on the subject of revolutionary strategy.[44] There were, in other words, both extreme and moderate detractors of Eurocommunism.

Turning to the variations in the official weight of Moscow's polemics, negative remarks by members of the CPSU Politburo or Secretariat were by far the most significant, if least frequent. The first jibe of this sort was made by Soviet ideological chief, Mikhail Suslov, on March 17, 1976.[45] In a speech to the Soviet Academy of Sciences, he charged that those foreign Communists who advocated "regional" or "national" versions of Marxism were guilty of opportunism. Voiced during the heat of the controversy over the final document for the East Berlin summit, Suslov plainly aimed this remark at the Eurocommunist entente that had emerged during the course of the conference preparations. A curious aspect of the Suslov attack was that it was included in the initial TASS report of his speech but cut from the *Pravda* text the next day. Presumably this was the Soviet leadership's way of conveying its displeasure to the Western Communists while limiting domestic awareness of such interparty dissension.

A more pointed incident of this type occurred in the fall of 1979. On October 17, 1979, at a domestic ideological conference, Ponomarev announced that the "leaders" of the nonruling parties in the West were "beginning to understand" that Eurocommunism not only "damages the international Communist movement" but also "provokes great discontent *among simple Communist militants at the base*" of the parties themselves.[46] This was the clearest evidence to date of the CPSU's attempt to use internal party dissent to bring pressure to bear on foreign Communist leaders. In actuality, moreover, only the PCF leadership had backed away from its previous support for Eurocommunist precepts, while just a week earlier Carrillo and Berlinguer—after three days of bilateral talks in Madrid—had affirmed their unqualified commitment to them in a joint

---

language version of *Problems of Peace and Socialism*] 19, no. 12 (December 1976):3–15 at 11; my emphasis.

43. "Ideinoe oruzhie kommunistov," *Kommunist*, no. 18 (December 1976):38–46 at 44.
44. Ibid., 41.
45. The TASS version is quoted in *The Washington Post*, March 18, 1976, A22; compare the text in *Pravda*, March 18, 1976, 2.
46. Quoted in Carlo Benedetti, " 'Giallo' a Mosca sul discorso di Ponomariov," *l'Unità*, October 19, 1979, 1 and 18 at 1; my emphasis.

communiqué.[47] Ponomarev was thus in effect exhorting the Spanish and Italian leaders to follow the French example.

Significantly, the Soviet press treated Ponomarev's denunciation of Eurocommunism much the same as Suslov's slur at regionalism three years earlier. While both TASS and Radio Moscow disseminated it *abroad* on October 17, the next day the central newspapers omitted the relevant passages from their otherwise extensive coverage of the conference.[48] Once again the CPSU leadership was evidently seeking to communicate its views to dissidents among the Italian (and Spanish) Communist rank and file while concealing the entire altercation from the Soviet media's domestic audience.

Less explicit but equally significant, the CPSU Central Committee's official greetings to the Fourteenth and Fifteenth PCI congresses, in the early spring of 1975 and 1979 respectively, were distinctly cooler than comparable messages to the French party.[49] Meanwhile, if Politburo rebukes and equivocal Central Committee greetings were the most authoritative forms of CPSU polemics, slurs in the central press were only slightly less so. At the same time, they were far more frequent. Here the most important distinction was whether the source was a CPSU or foreign Communist spokesman. The Soviet diatribes during the 1970s were usually more circumspect; the non-Soviet polemics tended to be more cutting. Zhivkov's December 1976 attack against Eurocommunism in Zarodov's journal was a case in point. And as the campaign against it intensified in the years after 1976, *Pravda* often preferred to cite the leaders of such loyalist parties as the Czechoslovakian and Portuguese to the effect that Eurocommunism was a revisionist and schismatic deviation. For instance, the CPSU daily chose on the eve of talks between Suslov and Pajetta, in September 1977, to publish a blast against Eurocommunism by the leader of the pro-Soviet Greek Communists.[50] In this way, Moscow avoided the stigma of engaging in the more explicit attacks while also conveying the impression of widespread support for its position.

This same division of labor between Soviet and foreign Communist spokesmen could be observed in the CPSU's use of multilateral party meetings to criticize the PCI (and other deviationist parties). The proceedings of the 1969 Moscow conference offer a good example of this technique. Although at that gathering Brezhnev vigorously denounced the Chinese, he was more restrained on the issues then most in dispute with

47. Text in *l'Unità*, October 11, 1979, 17.

48. Benedetti, " 'Giallo' a Mosca," 18.

49. Texts in *Pravda*, October 24, 1974; March 18, 1975; May 9 and March 30, 1979; p. 1 in all issues.

50. Kharilaos Florakis, "Putevodnaia zvezda Oktiabria," *Pravda*, September 1, 1977, 4; cf. "Incontro tra Suslov e G. C. Pajetta a Mosca," *l'Unità*, September 3, 1977, 1.

the PCI. Brezhnev merely underscored the importance of the "general laws" and the "vanguard role" of the Communists, leaving to Gomulka and Ulbricht the task of chastising the Italians—obliquely, to be sure—for their postulation of socialist pluralism.

The CPSU's affirmation of controversial ideological tenets in a sensitive context was the technique most frequently employed by the top Soviet leaders. Instances of Brezhnev's public support for the "general laws" abounded. At the same time, the Soviets also used silence, selective censorship, and outright falsification to convey their disagreement with the more unpalatable views of the PCI, and others. For instance, *Pravda*'s account of the Central Committee plenum at which Berlinguer went to great lengths to explain the meaning of the *compromesso storico* (in December 1974) neglected even to mention the notion.[51] And in February 1975 *Partiinaia zhizn* published an interview with two PCI leaders which quoted them as saying that their party's medium-term goal was an "advanced democracy,"[52] a French Communist slogan never used by the Italians. But recourse to such distortion was not merely polemical in intent. It was also Moscow's way of withholding from its own people the news that a supposedly steadfast member of the international Communist movement was adopting deviationist ideas.

Berlinguer's Retreat from Criticism to Conciliation

The winter of 1976–77 saw a sharp escalation in PCI press criticism of the Soviet system. Then, just as suddenly, the direct polemics against Moscow gave way to a more conciliatory tack. The Italian party switched from berating repression in the Soviet Union to propagating its own vision of socialism whenever possible, to trying to influence Soviet bloc developments by way of example.

PCI disparagement of CPSU sectarianism became commonplace in early 1976, during the final preparations for the East Berlin summit. But it intensified at the end of the year in response to the Kremlin's polemical campaign against Eurocommunism and growing persecution of Soviet human rights activists. The Berlinguer leadership probably had two purposes in mind in sanctioning the more critical commentary. It hoped to encourage reform in the Soviet bloc; and it sought to buttress its domestic image as a democratic force at a time when it was calling for an emergency government of national unity.

51. For the TASS report on Berlinguer's December 10, 1974, speech to the PCI Central Committee, see *Pravda*, December 12, 1974, 4.

52. "Polozhenie v Italii i rabota kommunisticheskoi partii," *Partiinaia zhizn*, no. 3 (February 1975):76–79 at 78.

The retreat from direct anti-Soviet polemics, on the other hand, was related to the PCI leaders' concern over growing dissent in their own ranks. The Berlinguer group evidently feared that too confrontational a posture toward Moscow might provoke the CPSU to respond in kind, to shift from veiled to direct polemics against the PCI. This, in turn, could exacerbate the Italian militants' malaise, their fear that the *compromesso storico* meant capitulation to capitalism. To repeat what has already been suggested, for the Italian Communist policy makers accommodation with Christian Democracy at home required an accommodation with the Soviet Union as well. In early 1977, therefore, the PCI press not only dampened its negative coverage of the Soviet polity; but Berlinguer also rejected the very notion of a rupture with the CPSU and hailed his party's commitment to the cardinal Leninist principle of democratic centralism. At the time such actions heightened official Western suspicions of PCI subservience to Moscow. In retrospect, however, it is clear that Berlinguer's avowal of the enduring character of Soviet–PCI relations was intended to reassure Italian Communist dissidents, while his reaffirmation of democratic centralism was designed to curb them.

A similar pattern of PCI criticism of the Soviet Union, followed by a retreat to a more conciliatory position, occurred in mid-1977 and again in mid-1978. The first of these two dialectical scenarios was triggered by the *New Times* attack against Santiago Carrillo in June 1977. The second was sparked by a combination of intensified Soviet polemics against Western Communist innovators and repression against domestic dissidents. All the while, Berlinguer observed considerable decorum in his personal conduct toward Moscow. Just as he had attended the Twenty-fifth CPSU Congress (boycotted by Marchais and Carrillo) in February 1976, he was also present at the sixtieth anniversary celebration of the October Revolution (boycotted by Marchais and disrupted by Carrillo) in November 1977. He thus displayed the PCI elite's familiar preference for dialogue over confrontation. In mid-1977 and mid-1978, moreover, the Italian party extracted some not inconsequential concessions from the CPSU in exchange for its retreat from criticism to conciliation.

The Flawed Face of "Existing Socialism"

After the invasion of Czechoslovakia, PCI discussions of the domestic Soviet scene took on a more critical tone, especially those that appeared in *Rinascita*.[53] Moscow's official silence at the time of Khrushchev's death in late 1971 also provoked considerable soul-searching among Italian Communists. Historian Giuliano Procacci deplored the CPSU's failure to

53. For example, Maurizio Ferrara, "La democrazia nel potere socialista," *Rinascita* 28, no. 2 (January 8, 1971):5.

follow through on Togliatti's 1956 call for an analysis of the sources of bureaucratic "degeneration" under Stalin and suggested that the PCI therefore take on this task.[54] Others stressed the need for a critical appraisal of the present Soviet "superstructure" in order to understand the reasons for the nondevelopment of socialist democracy.[55]

Only during the first months of 1976, however, did PCI commentators begin to rail against the Soviet system with some regularity. They were probably emboldened to do so by the emergence of the Eurocommunist entente. For during this same period the PCF "discovered" Soviet repression and political prisoners and likewise renounced with much fanfare the slogan of the "dictatorship of the proletariat" at its Twenty-second Congress.

As an example of the PCI's more critical approach, in February 1976— the twentieth anniversary of the Twentieth CPSU Congress—PCI historian and political analyst Giuseppe Boffa expounded in *l'Unità* upon the Soviet Union's failure to complete the process of destalinization. Boffa not only denounced the regime's continuing disregard for the civil rights guaranteed by the Soviet constitution; he also lambasted the very notion of monolithic unity in a society as complex and highly educated as the Soviet one, arguing that "at this point the need for the free expression of ideas, for their open confrontation, for the legitimacy of dissent cannot but make themselves felt with insistence."[56] Soon thereafter Adriano Guerra, head of the Gramsci Institute's Center for the Study and Documentation of Socialist Countries, remarked upon the actual degree of diversity among CPSU publicists. Guerra drew a distinction between two groups—those who spoke in "monolithic and bureaucratic terms from a time past" and those who were more open to new ideas.[57] In the former category he placed Zarodov, among others. In the latter group he included, less persuasively, Zagladin.

Guerra's article appeared in *l'Unità* on February 19. Five days later Brezhnev delivered a report to the Twenty-fifth CPSU Congress that resounded with what Guerra had called "monolithic and bureaucratic terms from a time past." Brezhnev stressed the "general laws" of socialism, "proletarian internationalism," and Soviet support for a new world conference of Communist parties.[58] *L'Unità* correspondent Franco

54. Giuliano Procacci, "Rileggendo l'intervista a 'nuovi argomenti,'" *Rinascita* 28, no. 51 (December 24, 1971):14–15.

55. "Dopo Krusciov: Tavola rotonda di 'Rinascita,'" *Rinascita* 28, no. 50 (December 17, 1971):17–22.

56. See his two-part series, "Il congresso che accusò Stalin" and "La scossa del 'rapporto segreto,'" in *l'Unità*, February 13 and 14, 1976, p. 3 each day. The above quotation appeared on the second day.

57. "Su democrazia e socialismo," *l'Unità*, February 19, 1976, 3.

58. *Pravda*, February 25, 1976, 4.

Fabiani's coverage of the congress bespoke the PCI's reaction. Fabiani reported with barely concealed irony the parrotlike reaction of the other Soviet speakers to Brezhnev's report, especially on proletarian internationalism. He also described the infrequent speeches on cultural problems as "essentially routine and . . . bureaucratic."[59] He noted without comment the various CPSU rebuttals of Western reports on the repression of Soviet dissidents.

When Suslov made his slur against "regional" versions of Marxism in mid-March, l'Unità promptly reported the substance, then Pravda's omission, of his remarks.[60] Some ten days later, on March 28, it carried an extensive refutation by PCI Secretariat member Gianni Cervetti.[61] The bulk of Cervetti's commentary was devoted to a measured reiteration of the Italian party's preferences regarding the nature of socialism and interparty relations. Nevertheless, the fact that he criticized Suslov by name marked a new polemical threshold.

Then came Berlinguer's bombshell of mid-June 1976, a week before the Italian parliamentary elections. In a series of statements (an interview in Corriere della sera, l'Unità's coverage of that interview, and a television press conference),[62] he suggested that Italy's membership in NATO might actually facilitate the realization of the PCI's vision of socialism. Both Moscow and Washington represented obstacles to Communist advances in Italy, he argued—Moscow because of its insistence on setting the ground rules and Washington because of its reflexive opposition to the very idea of socialism. On balance, however, Berlinguer declared that he would prefer to build socialism in the West (behind the protective shield of the Atlantic Alliance): "It is better to be in this area. This guarantees us the kind of socialism that we want, to be precise, socialism in liberty, socialism of a pluralist type."[63] Years later it became known that the CPSU responded to this slap in the face with a scathing letter of protest.[64]

---

59. L'Unità, February 26 and 29, 1976, p. 14 each day.

60. "Un discorso di Suslov all'Accademia delle Scienze dell'URSS" and "La 'Pravda' omette alcuni brani del discorso di Mikhail Suslov," l'Unità, March 18 and 19, 1976, p. 13 each day.

61. Gianni Cervetti, "I comunisti italiani e l'internazionalismo: A proposito di un articolo del compagno Suslov," l'Unità, March 28, 1976, 1 and 21.

62. The Corriere della sera interview is reprinted in full in La politica internazionale dei comunisti italiani, 1975–1976, ed. Antonio Tatò (Rome: Editori Riuniti, 1976), 149–60. For l'Unità's coverage see the June 15, 1976 issue, 1 and 16; the report on the interview included direct quotes of all the critical foreign policy exchanges except Berlinguer's response to query, "In short, the Atlantic Pact could also be a useful shield to build socialism in liberty?": "I prefer that Italy not leave the Atlantic Pact 'also' for this reason, and not only because our exit would upset the international equilibrium. I feel more secure being here, but I see that even here there are serious attempts to limit our autonomy." However, Berlinguer made almost the same point in a television press conference the evening of June 15, the full text of which appeared in l'Unità, June 16, 1976, 1 and 4.

63. Text of Berlinguer's television press conference, ibid., 4.

64. Carlo Rossella, "Non prendiamolo alla lettera," Panorama, March 2, 1981, 36–39 at 39.

That it did not publicly react at the time was quite possibly a result of the Kremlin's calculation that to do so might throw a monkey wrench in the last minute negotiations for the East Berlin summit.

After a summer lull in polemics, the PCI reacted promptly to the campaign against Eurocommunism that Moscow launched in December 1976 with the Zhivkov and *Kommunist* articles described in the previous section. On December 4—in response to Zhivkov's diatribe—the editor of *l'Unità*, Luca Pavolini, ridiculed the very idea of "general laws" as "an historical absurdity." He also dismissed Zhivkov's definition of Eurocommunism as a "clear distortion of reality." Far from being a bourgeois tool, said Pavolini, Eurocommunism was a bourgeois bête noire because it reflected the growing stature of the West European Communist parties.[65] Soon thereafter a front-page article in *l'Unità* gave outspoken encouragement to dissent in the Soviet bloc. The *l'Unità* piece argued that dissent in the socialist countries was but the tip of the iceberg of intellectual malaise; that many intellectuals, while toeing the party line in public, lived lives that were in reality "fantastically, wildly 'separated'" from official life; that this was caused by the regimes' insistence on controlling the "totality of social relationships"; and that the solution was to permit the existing differences and contradictions in socialist society to surface, to go public as it were.[66]

About this time *l'Unità*'s attacks on Soviet–East European restrictions of freedom and civil rights began to assume a systemic and systematic character. They were systemic in that they touched on the roots of the political system, arguing that the dissidence and even the economic problems in that area (for example, in Poland) could be overcome only by some measure of democratization. They were systematic in that repression of dissent was regularly noted and denounced in *l'Unità*. As cases of repression mounted during late 1976 and early 1977, the PCI daily responded with the following pattern of coverage. First it reported the formal charges against the dissidents. It then juxtaposed to the official line, either in its initial report or soon thereafter, the dissidents' views—giving direct quotations as needed in their defense. It concluded by denouncing editorially the official harassment or arrest of opposition leaders.

The prime targets of PCI censure were the Czechoslovakian, Soviet, and Polish regimes—in descending order of intensity. (East Germany's expulsion of balladeer Wolf Biermann in November 1976 was also treated

65. l. pa. [Luca Pavolini], " 'Eurocomunismo' e internazionalismo," *l'Unità*, December 4, 1976, 14.
66. Roberto Romani, "Il 'dissenso' nei paesi socialisti," *l'Unità*, December 29, 1976, 1 and 14.

according to the pattern described above.)[67] In the case of Czechoslovakia, the dissident manifesto "Charter 77" dominated *l'Unità*'s coverage. For some weeks after its initial publication in the West on January 6, 1977, scarcely a day passed without some reference to the affair. The first full-scale—and front-page—*l'Unità* editorial condemning Prague's harassment of the signers of "Charter 77" came on January 12. But already on January 8 a news report decried the Czechoslovakian party daily's description of the signatories as agents of "anti-Communist and Zionist centers."[68] *L'Unità* followed up on its January 12 editorial with the publication of collective and individual protests as well as other editorial commentaries well into February.

As for the Soviet Union, *l'Unità* focused on the cases of Yuri Orlov and Alexander Ginzburg during the winter of 1977. It cited TASS as the source for Moscow's official charges of anti-Sovietism and links to Western espionage.[69] It quoted Orlov and Ginzburg in their own defense prior to their arrests[70] as well as Roy Medvedev and Sakharov in behalf of Orlov and Ginzburg after their arrests.[71] Then on February 6 an unsigned commentary denounced the Soviet regime's use of police measures against dissenters in general and appealed for a resolution of the "political problems" that gave rise to dissent in the first place.[72]

L'Unità's treatment of the dissident issue in Poland differed somewhat. Official Polish denials of police brutality toward workers arrested in the June 1976 riots over price hikes[73] were juxtaposed to statements by the Workers' Defense Committee (KOR) and other groups sympathetic to the demonstrators.[74] However, the PCI daily refrained from editorial comment. This may have reflected the Italian leadership's hope (later proven correct) that the more moderate circles in the Polish party would ultimately prevail in Warsaw's handling of that situation.

The sharpness of the PCI's criticism of socialism Soviet-style may be grasped by comparing it to the PCF's coverage of the same wave of dissidence. The French approach was neither systemic nor systematic; it was selective and rather superficial. First of all, *L'Humanité* dealt only

---

67. "Conferenza stampa a Colonia del cantante Wolf Biermann," *l'Unità*, November 20, 1976, 14.

68. "Il documento 'Carta 77' e una replica del *Rude Pravo*," *l'Unità*, January 8, 1977, 12.

69. "Perquisizioni a Mosca," *l'Unità*, January 5, 1977, 14.

70. Carlo Benedetti, "Lettera di accuse ai 'dissidenti' sulla *Literaturnaia gazeta*," *l'Unità*, February 3, 1977, 12.

71. "La TASS attacca e accusa Ginzburg di legami con lo spionaggio occidentale," *l'Unità*, February 6, 1977, 12.

72. The editorial commentary, in italics, was appended without headline or byline to the running coverage of the arrests; see ibid.

73. *L'Unità*, January 7, 1977, 11.

74. *L'Unità*, January 9, 17, and February 8, 1977, 11, 12, and 12, respectively.

cursorily with developments in the Soviet Union and Poland. With regard to specific cases of dissent there, the paper largely confined itself to reports from official sources or international press services. Only in the case of East Germany's deprivation of Biermann's citizenship did the PCF daily follow *l'Unità*'s pattern of coverage.[75] But most significant, *L'Humanité*'s denunciation of the persecution of the "Charter 77" signers was relatively mild and conspicuously belated. Whereas *l'Unità* denounced the Prague leadership in a front-page editorial on January 12, *L'Humanité* delayed editorial censure until January 25. Whereas the PCI daily closely monitored developments in Prague after the publication of "Charter 77," the PCF daily was sporadic in its coverage. To conclude this brief comparison, during mid-winter of 1977 *L'Humanité* published one article on Soviet bloc dissent every two to three days[76] whereas *l'Unità* published two to three articles on the subject almost every day.

Nevertheless, the PCI maintained normal working contacts with the CPSU even when its media criticisms of what the Soviets like to call real, or existing, socialism were at their zenith. PCI Secretariat member Paolo Bufalini and Antonio Rubbi of the party's foreign section spent the New Year holiday in Moscow, meeting publicly with Chilean leader Luis Corvalan and doubtless also conferring with Soviet officials.[77] Then on January 28, 1977, Cervetti—author of the PCI's unprecedented rebuttal of Suslov the preceding winter and *Direzione* member since October 1976—held talks with Ponomarev on a number of subjects including "the development of relations between the CPSU and the PCI."[78] Two days later, in a January 30 speech to Communist workers in Milan, Berlinguer hailed as immutable three principles: the goal of socialism, democratic centralism, and *the cultivation of international Communist ties*.[79] In an interview over Italian television in early February Berlinguer once again insisted on the preservation of PCI links with the CPSU. He also pointedly disagreed with Carrillo's recently publicized assessment of the Soviet system as nonsocialist.[80]

The PCI leadership's shift to restraint toward Moscow became more conspicuous with the passage of time. During the first days of February 1977 *l'Unità* published a five-part series on life in the Soviet Union that

75. On November 17, *L'Humanité* reported the facts as stated by the German Democratic Republic. On November 19 it described the protest against the GDR's action signed by a dozen or so prominent East German Communist writers and artists. Then on November 22 it published an article by Claude Prevost denouncing the East German regime's action and defending Biermann's right to express his views even if they were at times provocative (p. 3 in all issues).

76. The most notable were those published February 3, 14, and 21, 1977, 7, 5, and 7, respectively.

77. "Caloroso incontro fra Bufalini e Corvalan," *l'Unità*, January 2, 1977, 1.

78. "Incontro tra Cervetti e Ponomariov," *l'Unità*, January 29, 1977, 13.

79. See the report on the speech in *l'Unità*, January 31, 1977, 1 and 4.

80. *L'Unità*, February 11, 1977, 1 and 11, esp. 11.

was judicious and balanced.[81] As a case in point, the introductory article dealt with both the PCI's doubts about and the CPSU's responses on such controversial issues as political dissent and freedom of information. The series was coauthored by a group of six journalists including Boffa and Pavolini, whose earlier critiques of the Soviet system have been noted. About this same time there was a perceptible if gradual decline in the frequency of *l'Unità* reports on dissidence. And when Berlinguer, Marchais, and Carrillo held their celebrated Eurocommunist summit in Madrid on March 2–3, 1977, their joint communiqué omitted the explicit criticism of Soviet-style regimes proposed by Carrillo.[82]

How are we to understand the PCI's sudden conciliation toward Moscow? As already indicated, the basic reason probably lay in the internal Party tensions sparked by the Berlinguer leadership's backing of the Andreotti cabinet and its austerity measures. Open opposition to the latter had already developed at an October 1976 Central Committee meeting when elder statesman Longo, in an action that seemed a throwback to the sectarianism of his youth, voiced concern that the party was sacrificing its goal of social transformation to cosmetic measures that would only reinforce the capitalist economy.[83] Longo was clearly speaking for others lower in rank. To counteract this festering anxiety, Berlinguer sought to underscore the party's commitment to social revolution by reaffirming its allegiance to the CPSU and the world Communist movement. By the same token, he stressed that support for austerity *now* would facilitate radical social change in the future. This indeed was the central theme of his January 30 speech.

But there may have been more involved than first meets the eye. PCI policy makers had been debating the austerity question for several months. Yet this did not deter party publicists from denouncing Soviet and East European repression. The two issues seemed to develop according to separate if parallel momentums. It was only with Berlinguer's January 30 speech that support for austerity was coupled with insistence on international Communist solidarity. And Berlinguer delivered that address two days after the Cervetti–Ponomarev talks devoted to "the development of relations between the CPSU and the PCI." It thus seems likely that Berlinguer's unusual defense of international Communist ties as well as the muting of press attacks against the Soviet bloc regimes were linked to Cervetti's trip to Moscow. What remains unanswered is the nature of that linkage. In a word, was the PCI's sudden conciliatory approach the result of a mutual agreement or a concession made under duress?

81. "Impressioni e giudizi di una delegazione dell'*Unità* di ritorno dall' URSS," *l'Unità*, February 1–5, 1977, p. 3 each day.

82. Eusebio Mujal-León, *Communism and Political Change in Spain* (Bloomington: Indiana University Press, 1983), 127.

83. Text of Longo's speech in *l'Unità*, October 20, 1976, 8.

With regard to the latter supposition, one must ask what pressure the Soviet leaders could actually bring to bear upon their Italian comrades. The threat of public denunciation of the kind soon to be visited upon Carrillo was a measure of last resort if only because the PCI's domestic standing was at an all-time high. Openly to berate Berlinguer might deprive the CPSU of any potential advantage it stood to gain from the Italian party's growing clout. The threat of financial reprisals, such as excluding PCI-owned export-import firms from the lucrative Soviet–Italian trade market, were quite probably made.[84] But Soviet economic pressure had been notoriously ineffective in bringing to heel Communists genuinely dependent on Soviet aid or trade: to wit, the Spanish, Yugoslavian, Chinese, and Albanian parties.

A more likely source of CPSU leverage may have been provided by those PCI militants who were already upset over their leaders' austerity program and the *compromesso storico* in general. Their discontent could be discreetly fostered by Soviet embassy officials and language instructors in Italy, by Intourist personnel and KGB agents dealing with the many Italians visiting the Soviet Union on low-budget tours, and others. Since the autumn of 1976 internal discord had made the Italian party ripe for such meddling.

Whatever the case (and the full story cannot be ascertained at this point), it appears that at the end of January 1977 the PCI and the CPSU reached some sort of accommodation. The Soviets agreed to look the other way as the Italian party held to its pluralist vision of socialism while plying the slippery path of the *compromesso storico*. The Italians agreed to do the same, to attend to their own political garden instead of dwelling on the flaws of "existing socialism." In short, the "opportunism of conciliation" prevailed.

Carrillo as a Surrogate for Berlinguer?

The above modus vivendi was temporarily interrupted in June 1977 by the CPSU's attack on Carrillo in *New Times*, a Moscow foreign affairs weekly aimed at non-Soviet readers. In an anonymous review of his new book, *"Eurocommunism" and the State*, the Soviets accused Carrillo of objectively aiding imperialism.[85] Specifically, it chided the Spaniard for trying to split the Communist movement by favoring regional coordination among Western Communist parties over ties with the Soviet camp. It also

84. For details on the character of Soviet–PCI economic ties, see Claire Sterling and Michael Ledeen, "Italy's Russian Sugar Daddies," *New Republic*, April 3, 1976, 16–21.

85. "Contrary to the Interests of Peace and Socialism in Europe: Concerning the book 'Eurocommunism and the State' by Santiago Carrillo, General Secretary of the Communist Party of Spain," *New Times*, no. 26 (June 1977):9–13.

charged him, rather illogically it would seem, with backing the strengthening of NATO because of his call for a united Western Europe "independent of the USSR and the USA." And it accused him of "conscious anti-Sovietism" for denying that the Soviet Union was a "workers' democracy." To be sure, the *New Times* article maintained that there were two forms of Eurocommunism: the Spanish version and a "left" version, with the latter constituting "the present strategy of the Communist parties of the developed capitalist countries." Yet it also denounced this second type as "erroneous" because there was only "one" scientific socialism.

The Soviet assessment of even the "left" variation of Eurocommunism as "erroneous" was without doubt aimed at the PCI. Some of the concrete charges against Carrillo—for instance, his preoccupation with West European Communist regionalism and benign view of NATO—must be construed as referring to the Italian party as well. We may therefore assume that the *New Times* attack on Carrillo was also a surrogate polemic against Berlinguer and a hint of things to come should Soviet–PCI divergences intensify.

All the same, the CPSU leadership received a delegation of the PCI *Direzione*, led by Pajetta and including Bufalini and Emanuele Macaluso, in Moscow at the end of June 1977. What little we know about their talks comes from *l'Unità*'s coverage of the visit. Its detailed reports of the Italian delegation's daily activities, including specific timetables of meetings with its Soviet hosts, were unprecedented.[86] But even more surprising were the revealing accounts the Italians later gave of what went on during the formal consultations, conducted on the Soviet side by Suslov, Ponomarev, and Zagladin. In the face-to-face exchange, characterized by "extreme frankness," the Russians insisted that the *New Times* article was directed only at Carrillo's book, not at any Communist party as such, while the Italians elaborated upon positions their party had already expressed editorially in *l'Unità*. For one thing, Moscow rather than Carrillo was guilty of splitting the Communist movement by its use of abusive language and veiled inclusion of other parties (read the PCI) in the *New Times* polemic. For another, the Spanish party's call for a Europe "independent of the USSR and USA" differed little from the PCI's call for a Europe "neither anti-Soviet nor anti-American"; and both views would ultimately contribute to the dissolution rather than the strengthening of military blocs.[87]

At the same time, Macaluso's report on what transpired offered a

---

86. See the accounts in *l'Unità*, July 1 and 2, 1977, 14 and 1, respectively.

87. "Le dichiarazioni di Pajetta sui colloqui a Mosca," *l'Unità*, July 4, 1977, 1 and 11; cf. "Un pesante attacco d'una rivista sovietica a Santiago Carrillo," *l'Unità*, June 24, 1977, 14; and "L'eurocomunismo, 'Tempi Nuovi' e noi," *l'Unità*, June 28, 1977, 1.

fascinating glimpse into the CPSU leaders' thought processes.[88] According to him, they were profoundly skeptical about an eventual dissolution of the NATO and WTO pacts. More to the point, they feared that the PCI's programmatic views might have a "destabilizing" effect on the socialist bloc (adding credence to Western speculation that precisely such fear lay at the heart of Moscow's antipathy to Eurocommunism). Macaluso also commented that the Russians were concerned that criticism of their repression of dissent would be exploited by Western forces opposed to détente. The Italians, in contrast, insisted that the defense of human rights, including by implication those of Soviet bloc dissidents, was not only legitimate but should in no way impede the progress of arms control talks. In other words, on the most sticky issue then dividing Moscow and Washington under the new Carter administration, the PCI tilted to the West.

But Pajetta's remarks were perhaps the most suggestive. For he alluded to the many foreign policy issues that were discussed, including current problems in the Mediterranean and African areas that were raised *on the Italian delegation's initiative*.[89] The reference to Africa was tantalizing. It would be almost a year before the PCI would publicly mention (in *l' Unità*) its reservations regarding the militarization of Soviet policy toward Africa. It is entirely likely, however, that the Italian leaders' doubts on this score were made known during the Soviet–PCI negotiations over the Carrillo affair. Why else would the PCI emissaries have instigated a discussion of African problems? What this suggests is that the Italian Communists, faced with the threat of polemical escalation that the Soviet attack on Carrillo signified, responded with a threat of their own: namely, the public broaching of disagreements over some of the most sensitive issues of Soviet foreign policy. The comments of both Macaluso and Pajetta pointed in this direction.

Not surprisingly, therefore, during the Moscow talks the Soviet leaders agreed (according to Macaluso's testimony) to tone down their criticism of Carrillo. And, indeed, shortly thereafter a follow-up *New Times* article declared that the CPSU did not mean to implicate the Spanish Communists as a group *or any other Communist party* in its personal attack on Carrillo.[90] This was clearly a concession to the Italians.

For its part, the PCI responded to the CPSU's retreat on the Carrillo question by once again muting its criticism of Soviet conduct while accentuating the universal appeal of its own vision of socialism. As political activity resumed in the autumn of 1977, PCI spokesmen stressed that the

---

88. "Conversazione con Macaluso: I colloqui a Mosca—Le nostre tesi e quelle sovietiche," *l'Unità*, July 5, 1977, 1 and 14.

89. See n. 87 to this chapter.

90. "Putting the Record Straight," *New Times*, no. 28 (July 1977):16–17.

best contribution Western Communists could make to "the renewal of existing socialist societies" would be the achievement of a pluralist form of socialism at home. Thereafter they would influence developments in the East by force of example, as it were. As Berlinguer put it at the September 1977 national festival of *l'Unità*, the constellation of ideas known as Eurocommunism was inspired not by a limited regional perspective but by a "global historical vision."[91]

Indicative of this return to the tacit compromise of the previous spring was the Soviet publication in late 1977 of an academic-style book on the PCI which described both the historic compromise and the Italian party's accommodation to NATO as understandable adaptations to national conditions.[92] By the same token, Italian Communist officials affirmed in both their utterances and their actions the PCI's commitment to preserving comradely ties with the CPSU.

This conciliatory approach was underscored at the sixtieth anniversay celebration of the October Revolution in November 1977. On that occasion the Soviet leaders not only accorded "equal time" to Berlinguer, they also displayed an unusual degree of cordiality toward him. This was probably because the festivities were unexpectedly marred by still another clash with Carrillo.[93] Russian emissaries had conferred with Carrillo in Madrid in early autumn, assuring him of an opportunity to present his views if only he would attend the Soviet Union's sixtieth anniversary gala. However, for reasons that have not been clarified, he was actually prevented from speaking in the Kremlin. The Soviet leadership pleaded innocence (Carrillo, they claimed, had arrived too late for his speech to be translated into the seventeen languages required for the event)[94] and proceeded to shower their attention upon Berlinguer.

Not only was Berlinguer permitted to give an address in which he stressed the *universal* relevance of the PCI's commitment to democracy; but the next day, despite the influx of delegations from over a hundred countries, Brezhnev, Suslov, and Ponomarev also managed to find time to meet with Berlinguer for fifty minutes "in an atmosphere of cordiality and friendship."[95] In view of the Western media uproar over the CPSU's muzzling of Carrillo, the Soviet leaders' respectful treatment of Berlinguer was a transparent attempt to keep their snub of the Spanish leader from unduly tarnishing the image of international Communist unity

91. *L'Unità*, September 19, 1977, 1, 3, and 4 at 4.

92. Carlo Benedetti, "Uno studioso sovietico sulla 'via italiana,'" *l'Unità*, November 26, 1977, 3.

93. For the best account of this incident, see Eusebio Mujal-León, "The PCE in Spanish Politics," *Problems of Communism* 27, no. 4 (July–August 1978):15–37.

94. Massimo Ghiara, "Incontro tra Breznev e Berlinguer alla fine della seduta al Cremlino," *l'Unità*, November 4, 1977, 1 and 14 at 14.

95. "Il comunicato sul colloquio," ibid., 1.

they had so assiduously tried to project. As for Berlinguer, he graciously went along with their attentiveness, not the least because in the eyes of the dissidents within his own party he stood only to gain from it.

Berlinguer's Tenuous Compromise: The Soviet–PCI Summit of October 1978

The late 1977 facade of Soviet–PCI amity notwithstanding, in early 1978 the Soviets again threw down the gauntlet to their Eurocommunist comrades. The lead editorial of the March 3 issue of *Kommunist* set forth in unusually simplistic and uncompromising terms the most sectarian CPSU prescription for revolution in the capitalist world. Electoral tactics and parliamentary activity should take second place to infiltration of the state bureaucracy, mass media, and military. The threat of force if not its actual use should remain a key weapon in the proletarian arsenal. And under no circumstances should revolutionaries guarantee the survival of the bourgeois political system which, on the contrary, must ultimately be smashed and replaced.[96] A companion piece in the same issue bluntly set forth as "general laws" of the transitional stage injunctions that were identical to the "general laws" of socialist construction.[97]

The tone and thrust of the entire issue recalled the Soviet rhetoric of early 1974—a period of sectarian militancy but seeming revolutionary stasis following the Chilean coup. Yet its consignment to press on March 3, 1978, coincided with the final stages of the Union of the Left's bid for victory in the March 1978 elections to the French National Assembly (to which no reference was made) and the PCI's maneuvers for formal entry into the Italian parliamentary majority (to which there was one allusion).[98]

The intent behind this sectarian offensive remains obscure. Did the Soviet oligarchs, anticipating the defeat of the Union of the Left, mean to lecture the French Communists on where they had gone wrong? Or, in the event of victory, did they wish to chart the path to further success? Then again, was the CPSU's sudden burst of radical rhetoric simply a defensive ploy aimed at those among its own cadres whose expectations of revolution in the West had been unduly aroused by the prospect of PCF and PCI political gains? For whether their Western comrades met with victory or defeat in March 1978, the *Kommunist* message was the same: it didn't really matter. The criteria for genuine revolutionary change were made so stringent they could not conceivably be met under the conditions then current in France or Italy.

---

96. "Revoliutsiia i demokratiia," *Kommunist*, no. 4 (March 1978):3–15.

97. Yu. Poliakov, "Nekotorye problemy istorii perekhodnogo perioda ot kapitalizma k sotsializma," ibid., 53–64.

98. L. Iugov, "Zatiazhnoi krizis," ibid., 82–89.

However one interprets it, the journal's injunctions represented a veiled slap in the face of both the French and Italian Communists. It seems, moreover, hardly accidental that this intransigent rhetoric was accompanied by a mounting CPSU campaign against "anti-Sovietism." Here the object of concern was as much Peking as the nonruling parties of the West. For it was precisely during the first months of 1978 that the pro-Western tilt of the post-Mao leadership became unmistakable, thus triggering Moscow's resumption of the anti-Chinese polemics that had been in abeyance since Mao's death in 1976.[99]

Perhaps anticipating this new wave of Soviet orthodoxy, Boffa used the occasion of the twenty-fifth anniversary of Stalin's death (March 5) for a *l'Unità* commentary that brought to mind his critical thrust of early 1976 rather than his more evenhanded depiction of Soviet society in February 1977. The current Soviet leaders, he argued, had rejected terrorist methods only to remain wedded to the "Stalinist conception" of the party-controlled "monolithic" state.[100] Several weeks later Boffa authored a sympathetic *l'Unità* feature on the life and thought of Nikolai Bukharin.[101] Bukharin had long been a subject of scholarly inquiry by PCI historians. But Boffa's balanced discussion of the Old Bolshevik on the fortieth anniversary of his untimely death represented a breakthrough for the party's daily.

Then came the mid-1978 Soviet trials and sentencing of the three renowned dissidents arrested in early 1977: Yuri Orlov, Anatoly Scharansky, and Alexander Ginzburg. The pattern of *l'Unità*'s coverage of the Orlov trial in May and, even more so, of the Ginzburg and Scharansky trials in July was similar to its treatment of Soviet bloc repression in early 1977. The CPSU version of events was juxtaposed to reports by dissidents and interspersed with PCI denunciations in the form of editorials and statements by the *Direzione*. At the same time, the Italian party expressed its displeasure in yet another way. It signaled its interest in a reconciliation with the Chinese Communist Party at the very time the Peking regime was about to intrude into Moscow's East European preserve. The Soviet Union's fear of hostile encirclement must surely have been exacerbated as CCP leader Hua Guofeng prepared to visit Bucharest and Belgrade in August 1978. Yet *l'Unità* nonetheless proceeded to publish a series of favorable commentaries on life in China during July,[102] to carry extensive coverage of Hua's August tour—including sardonic reports of Moscow's furious

99. Morris Rothenberg, "The Kremlin Looks at China," *Contemporary China* 3, no. 2 (Summer 1979):25–35.

100. "Lo stalinismo," *l'Unità*, March 5, 1978, 1 and 16.

101. "Bucharin, un protagonista," *l'Unità*, March 26, 1978, 3.

102. Emilio Sarzi Amadè, "Il 'profitto' di Sun Yeh-fang: Cosa cambia in Cina dopo la caduta dei 'quattro'," and "Pechino: i segnali della politica estera," *l'Unità*, July 19 and 21, 1978, p. 3 each day.

reaction[103]—and to quote Pajetta in early September to the effect that the PCI leadership had for some time been receptive to a renewal of ties with the Chinese party.[104]

Paradoxically, however, the overtures to Peking were accompanied by conciliatory gestures toward Moscow. At the end of July avowals by PCI officials of enduring ties with the CPSU multiplied.[105] To be sure, the circumstances differed from the preceding year. The Italian Communists were now being challenged by their PSI competitors, led by Bettino Craxi, to prove their democratic credentials by breaking once and for all from Moscow. Such a provocative demand could only be rejected out of hand, if only for reasons of party pride and internal cohesion. At the same time, an upcoming *Direzione* member, Adalberto Minucci, insisted that the Soviet connection was legitimate because of Moscow's support for Third World liberationism, a cause with which many Italian Communists deeply empathized.[106] Nevertheless, the basic message was the same as in early 1977: an open rift with the CPSU was not in the offing.

Berlinguer confirmed this in his address to the annual festival of *l'Unità* in mid-September 1978 by extolling once again his party's unbreakable links to the land of the October Revolution. He also hailed the Soviet Union's support for Third World liberationism, thus echoing Minucci's argument. His conciliatory approach did not, however, include the defense of Soviet-style socialism. On the contrary, he praised the strides PCI historians had made in coming to grips with "existing socialism." Rather, Berlinguer seemed intent upon emphasizing the revolutionary credentials of Italian communism in the eyes of its own militants.[107]

On this latter account he had cause for concern. The returns from scattered local elections in mid-May 1978 indicated a decline in the PCI's electoral support by a magnitude of almost ten percentage points. In June, referendums to abrogate key legislation that *both* the Communists and the Christian Democrats officially backed were defeated but only by a narrow margin, again evidence of eroding support for the PCI. As Secretariat member Napolitano put it in a mid-September interview with *Corriere della sera*, "The Party is ill at ease."[108] Berlinguer thus continued the same delicate balancing act he had begun in early 1977. He tried to

---

103. Emilio Sarzi Amadè, in *l'Unità*, August 17–30, 1978, passim; for his coverage of Moscow's reaction, see esp. *l'Unità*, August 29, 1978, 11.

104. Interview with Pajetta in *l'Unità*, September 9, 1978, 1 and 12.

105. See, for example, the report on a speech by Pajetta to a provincial PCI press festival, in *l'Unità*, July 24, 1978, 1–2; and Adalberto Minucci, "In realtà ci chiedono di scomunicare la storia," *l'Unità*, July 30, 1978, 1 and 14.

106. Ibid.; compare a second Minucci article on the same theme, "Le ragioni di una critica," *Rinascita* 35, no. 29 (July 21, 1978):1–2.

107. Text in *l'Unità*, September 18, 1978, 1 and 3–5.

108. *Corriere della sera*, September 15, 1978, 1–2.

assuage Communist rank-and-file misgivings over the PCI's accommodation with the Christian Democrats by stressing the party's undiminished affinity with the CPSU.

Moscow, for its part, also took a more conciliatory tack, probably because of the hints of a thaw in PCI relations with the Chinese. The late July issue of *Kommunist* included an article that represented a sharp reversal from the ultrasectarian pieces that had appeared in the journal the previous March. Written by Zagladin, its target was almost certainly the PCI. The gist of Zagladin's argument was that an electoral approach to power in the West was acceptable but anti-Soviet criticism was not. Gone were references to "general laws" of any kind, let alone allusions to the need for coercion in the quest for power. He endorsed, at least implicitly, the strategy of a democratic transitional stage, conceding that some advance toward socialism was feasible within the framework of bourgeois legality. The Soviet official qualified these moderate remarks with the warning that socialist gains were "irreversible" (i.e., not subject to an electoral upset).[109] Still, the only point upon which Zagladin really flexed his muscles was on the need for Western Communists to defend "existing socialism." This, he insisted, was not a question of like or dislike but of *Realpolitik*. To the extent that the socialist camp was weakened by "anti-Sovietism," the advance of nonruling Communist parties would also be thwarted.[110]

Furthermore, in mid-September—just a week after Pajetta's disclosure of the PCI's interest in a rapprochement with Peking—the CPSU leaders held out the offer of a summit meeting with Berlinguer.[111] They apparently did so as a means of dissuading him from the normalization idea. Berlinguer, in turn, must have been gratified at the opportunity to stress his party's revolutionary credentials through a Moscow summit precisely because of the growing unrest among PCI members (and voters). The party leadership was in fact prepared to delay the restoration of ties with Peking in exchange for the boost that a Berlinguer–Brezhnev meeting would give to it in the eyes of its militants. All the same, Berlinguer pointedly alluded to the possibility of a rapprochement with the Chinese Communists the day before his departure for the Soviet Union as a means of enhancing his bargaining power.[112]

Both the formal Soviet–PCI communiqué published on October 10 and subsequent developments suggest that a deal was struck. On the one hand, the communiqué condemned antidétente moves by "certain imperialist,

---

109. V. Zagladin, "Istoricheskaia missiia rabochego klassa i sovremennoe rabochee dvizhenie," *Kommunist*, no. 11 (July 1978):67–80 at 72–73.

110. Ibid., 76–77.

111. See Frane Barbieri's report in *la Stampa*, October 15, 1978, 1.

112. "Berlinguer a Mosca dopo i colloqui con Marchais," *l'Unità*, October 7, 1978, 1.

militarist, and reactionary circles,"[113] the term "militarist" meaning the Chinese in the current Soviet lexicon. And Berlinguer conceded in a press conference upon his return to Rome that "for now" the PCI would *not* normalize relations with the Chinese.[114] On the other hand, the communiqué also reiterated a major Soviet concession made at the 1976 East Berlin summit: the legitimacy of disagreements among Communist parties. And in his press conference Berlinguer listed as ongoing areas of Soviet–PCI discord their conceptions of socialism, views on political dissent, and *positions on China.* In short, the Italian leader agreed to postpone, not renounce, a rapprochement with Peking, probably in return for continued Soviet polemical restraint toward the PCI.

The CPSU actually did exhibit such restraint in the aftermath of the Soviet–PCI summit. References to the "general laws" vanished for some time from *Pravda,* although the twin bogies of Eurocommunism and anti-Sovietism continued to be roundly trounced. More significant, it was the PCF rather than the PCI that was singled out for direct attack in the late December 1978 issue of *Kommunist,* ostensibly on account of an unflattering portrayal of the Soviet system coauthored by five French Communists several months earlier.[115] (Their criticisms were no more cutting than those expressed so much more frequently by PCI analysts, but the volume had received the PCF Politburo's imprimatur in its preface.) Meanwhile, at an international Communist ideological conference in Sofia that same month the PCI was included only by implication in the many attacks on Eurocommunism.[116]

In retrospect, autumn 1978 marked the high-water point of the PCI's vulnerability to Soviet pressure. The compromise on China was the price the Italians had to pay for maintaining a public image of Soviet–PCI harmony. And a semblance of harmony was required by the exigencies of internal party politics. But this "correlation of forces" between the Soviet leaders and their Italian comrades was soon to alter decisively. By the last weeks of 1978 PCI policy makers had reached the conclusion that participation in the Italian parliamentary majority without commensurate cabinet status was no longer expedient: the gains in terms of policy results and

---

113. "Sovmestnoe kommiunike o prebyvanii tovarishcha E. Berlinguera v. Sovetskom Soiuze," *Pravda,* October 10, 1978, 1 and 4; my emphasis.

114. 'L'iniziativa internazionale del PCI: Berlinguer a Roma parla del suo viaggio," *l'Unità,* October 12, 1978, 1 and 14.

115. For the official English Version, see E. Ambartsumov, F. Burlatsky, Y. Krasin, and E. Pletnyov, "Against Distortion of the Experience of Real, Existing Socialism," *New Times,* no. 52 (December 1978):18–28.

116. For abridged texts of the conference speeches, see *World Marxist Review* 22, nos. 2–4 (February, March, April 1979):3–27, 3–107, 3–73, respectively.

political clout were negligible and hardly worth the decline in the party's unity.[117]

The PCI thus withdrew its backing from the second Andreotti cabinet in early 1979, precipitating national elections two years ahead of schedule. And when, at the Fifteenth PCI Congress that spring, Berlinguer re-affirmed the policy of the *compromesso storico,* he focused on its broad meaning as a procedural principle permitting competition as well as coop-eration with the Christian Democrats within the framework of a democrat-ic system.[118] Still, his ambiguity on this score combined with the uncer-tain image the party had projected for over two years resulted in defection at the polls. The Communist total fell to 30.4 percent of the votes cast for the Chamber of Deputies in June 1979, a drop of four full percentage points from June 1976. Again the Christian Democrats held steady, with their share of the vote for the lower house declining by a mere four-tenths of 1 percent. The PCI lost ground not to the parties on its right but to those on its left: the Radical Party and the Party of Proletarian Unity.

These electoral losses notwithstanding, the withdrawal of the PCI's parliamentary support for Christian Democratic governments eliminated a key source of rank-and-file discontent. More significant from the vantage point of Soviet–PCI relations, the decision to return to the opposition within Italy strengthened the Italian party's hand in its dealings with Moscow. Stated somewhat differently, its renunciation of concessions to the Italian political establishment liberated it from the need for conces-sions to the CPSU.

---

117. For a superb treatment of the dilemma in which the PCI leadership found itself by late 1978, see Stephen Hellman, "The Italian CP: Stumbling on the Threshold?" *Problems of Communism* 27, 6 (November–December 1978):31–48.

118. The text of Berlinguer's speech is in *l'Unità,* March 31, 1979, 9–16. For his discussion of the *compromesso storico,* see 15.

CHAPTER **9**

The PCI's Challenge to Moscow's Revolutionary Credentials

On the eve of the 1980s conciliation gave way to open confrontation between Moscow and the PCI. As we have seen, Soviet–PCI relations during the 1970s were marked by mutual, if reluctant, efforts at forbearance toward each other's divergent conceptions of socialism, revolutionary strategy, and international Communist organization. With the Soviet invasion of Afghanistan in late December 1979, this delicate equilibrium collapsed. Foreign policy issues became intertwined with political and ideological norms in the mounting verbal combat between the two party leaderships. It quickly became apparent that while the Italian party's compliance with CPSU axioms may have been negotiable in Moscow's eyes, its support for the Soviet Union's foreign policy and revolutionary credentials was not.

The Soviet Union's growing use of military force in the Third World provoked the PCI into an ever more comprehensive challenge to Soviet international conduct, the first subject of this chapter. But as we shall see in the second section, it was the Italian party's unqualified condemnation of martial law in Poland that brought Soviet–PCI relations to the brink of rupture. In an explosive round of polemical exchanges during the winter of 1981–82, the Berlinguer leadership claimed that the Soviet model of socialism had exhausted its creative impulse and that the Soviet Union's foreign policy was, to boot, not everywhere a force for peace and progress. There was, therefore, no longer any reason for special ties to the Moscow-centered Communist world as a movement separate and distinct from other political forces oriented toward socialism. The Kremlin, in turn, launched a personalized polemical offensive against the PCI which mirrored the most sectarian current of establishment thought voiced during the preceding decade.

As will be discussed later in the chapter, both parties backed off rather quickly from a complete break in relations. For the PCI the avoidance of a rupture was as much a matter of principle as its denial thenceforth of any special links with the CPSU. The Soviet leaders, for their part, probably figured that an open split with the PCI would undermine both the Soviet Union's propaganda campaign against NATO's acquisition of intermediate-range nuclear forces (INF) and Brezhnev's spring 1982 overtures to Peking. Meanwhile, the CPSU's scathing polemics of early 1982 were rallying the base of the Italian party to the defense of its leaders. Moscow thus embarked upon a kind of conciliation Soviet-style toward the PCI. CPSU publicists retreated from open name calling to the veiled polemics so characteristic of the 1970s. Vadim Zagladin repeatedly declared Moscow's opposition to a break with the PCI and innocence with regard to any provocative action toward the Italian comrades. All the while, multiple signs pointed in the direction of covert Russian support for pro-Soviet elements within the Italian party.

As for the PCI—leaders, cadres, and base alike—the surge in Soviet–PCI tensions served as a stimulus to the structural reform of the party itself. Much to the surprise of a number of observers, the Italian Communists remained united in the face of the Soviet maneuvers. But many turned out to be united on another point as well, namely, the need to open up the party's decision-making process to the scrutiny and perhaps even the participation of the rank-and-file members. As was to become clear during the preparations and debates of the Sixteenth PCI Congress in early 1983, the party's disengagement from the Soviet orbit sparked a grassroots move to modify the organizational precepts of Leninism. Pietro Ingrao, a spokesman for the Communist "new left" in the 1960s, championed organizational revisions that would permit unprecedented *trasparenza,* or openness, in PCI policy making as well as Central Committee control over the *Direzione.*

Meanwhile, in 1980 the *compromesso storico* was renounced in favor of the so-called *alternativa,* an alliance strategy focused on the small parties of the Italian left and center left rather than on Christian Democracy. It quickly became evident that the meanings attached to the "left alternative" were as varied as those formerly associated with the *compromesso storico.* Yet given the dramatic changes in the Italian political landscape during the first part of the decade, there was little urgency for the PCI to clarify its position. The DC's decline in the June 1983 national elections (down from 38.3 percent of the vote for the Chamber of Deputies in 1979 to 32.9 percent in 1983, while the PCI tally dropped by just half a percentage point to 29.9), followed by the precedent-breaking designation of PSI leader, Bettino Craxi, as premier, led to a situation that would itself take time to clarify. This remained the case at the time of Berlinguer's sudden death from a stroke in June 1984. The PCI Central Committee's choice of Alessandro Natta as Berlinguer's successor was thus suggestive of a holding pattern in anticipation of the further evolution of political trends at home and abroad. For Natta had long been known for his close affinity with the late general secretary's positions rather than for the projection of a distinct policy profile of his own.

Moscow's Use of Military Force: "Bloc Politics" or Revolution?

Until the late 1970s the Italian party's criticism of Soviet international conduct remained fairly restrained and selective. To be sure, the PCI took issue with Moscow's handling of its dispute with Peking and condemned out of hand the invasion of Czechoslovakia as a violation of national sovereignty. But its support for the European Economic Community and its accommodation to Italy's membership in NATO were couched in the terms of an adaptation to national conditions, not a dissent from the Soviet position on these questions. Only in 1978 did foreign policy differences begin to impinge upon Soviet–PCI divergences on international Communist issues. At that time the Italian party's disagreement with certain aspects of Soviet behavior in black Africa verged on a more general criticism: namely, PCI spokesmen began to suggest that Moscow was using military force to expand its own sphere of political influence under the guise of aiding Third World liberationism. Remonstrances on this score were first voiced by international affairs expert Romano Ledda with regard to Africa in late spring 1978. The Soviet Union's December 1979 invasion of Afghanistan (purportedly at the invitation of the local Marxist–Leninist leadership) elicited intimations by Berlinguer himself that the Soviet move was motivated by superpower rivalry rather than revolutionary considerations. The rapid escalation of the Polish crisis soon thereafter led the PCI leadership formally to back Solidarity and to warn the CPSU against military intervention in Poland.

In the spring of 1978 the PCI reversed its initially favorable view of revolutionary developments in Ethiopia because of the campaign by the Addis Ababa regime, now armed with Soviet weapons, to suppress the Eritrean national liberation movement. As tensions escalated in the Ethiopian borderlands in late 1977, Pajetta visited both Addis Ababa and the Somali capital of Mogadishu with the apparent aim of urging Ethiopian restraint toward Eritrea and Somali restraint in the contested Ogaden

Desert region.[1] When such efforts failed, *l'Unità* shifted from support for the Ethiopian position[2] to rather evenhanded coverage of the Ethiopian–Somali border war over the Ogaden and open sympathy for the Eritrean cause. With regard to the latter, it quoted *Agence-France Presse* (AFP) dispatches that described lightly armed Eritrean youth bravely taking on heavy artillery fire and Soviet MIGs.[3] Thereafter, during the first few months of 1978, *Rinascita* published an extraordinary series of letters to the editor detailing the historical and juridical legitimacy of the Eritrean cause and criticizing Pajetta's earlier positive assessment of the Ethiopian regime and the Soviet–Cuban military intervention in its behalf.[4]

Then in mid-May *l'Unità* carried a front-page commentary on the Ethiopian crisis by Romano Ledda, head of the PCI's newly formed Center for the Study of International Politics. Ledda maintained that the twenty-year Eritrean liberation struggle was "just" and that the new Ethiopian leadership should prove that it was "really new" by recognizing the right of the Eritreans to self-government. This was, moreover, a cause to which the "socialist countries" should commit themselves as well by virtue of "their presence in Ethiopia."[5] By implication, therefore, he also reprimanded the Soviets. The following month Ledda returned to the argument in a second front-page *l'Unità* piece. This time he openly questioned overall Soviet military involvement in Africa. Ledda endorsed the initial Cuban move into Angola as a necessary response to South African intervention in that country's civil war. But at the same time he expressed alarm over the extension of the "Cuban presence" to a "Soviet military presence of notable proportions," over the reemergence in the African context of "what seems to us a temptation . . . to make the expansion of the liberation process coincide with the stipulation of political-military alliances and the *conquest of zones of influence.*"[6]

These critical innuendoes were echoed by Pajetta in a report to the PCI Central Committee in mid-November 1979. After noting regretfully the absence of Soviet "political-diplomatic" initiatives in the aftermath of the

1. See Emilio Sarzi Amadè's reports on Pajetta's trip in *l'Unità*, November 24, 25, and 26, 1977, 14, 14, and 1, respectively.

2. See, for example, Amadè's report in *l'Unità*, November 28, 1977, 1 and 12.

3. See the unsigned report in *l'Unità*, December 29, 1977, 14.

4. *Rinascita* 35, no. 1 (January 6, 1978):46; no. 8 (February 24, 1978):31; and no. 10 (March 10, 1978):30–31. See also Gian Carlo Pajetta, "Scegliamo il fronte della trattativa e della pace," *Rinascita* 35, no. 7 (February 17, 1978):7–8.

5. Romano Ledda, "L'Eritrea non è l'Ogaden: La prova di forza etiopica non si giustifica," *l'Unità*, May 18, 1978, 1 and 13.

6. Romano Ledda, "Ma l'Africa non è degli africani?" *l'Unità*, June 7, 1978, 1 and 13; my emphasis. The quoted passages are on page 13 of an article whose general thrust is directed against French intervention in Zaire and Western efforts in general to shore up so-called reactionary and racist regimes in Africa.

Helsinki summit, he deplored the idea that "support for forces engaged in revolutionary transformation could be entrusted to military aid more than to solidarity linked to the political prestige or economic aid of the socialist camp."[7]

Meanwhile, during 1979 two additional foreign policy issues entered the Soviet–PCI dialogue: the Soviet-backed Vietnamese invasion of Cambodia at the turn of the year and the controversy over INF in Europe. The PCI—in contrast to the PCE—initially refrained from passing judgment on the Vietnamese defeat of the Khmer Rouge. Indeed, commentaries in *l'Unità* displayed barely concealed satisfaction at the overthrow of the ultrasectarian Pol Pot regime.[8] After China's retaliatory attack against Vietnam in late February 1979, however, the Italian party joined the PCE in denouncing *both* the Vietnamese move into Cambodia and the Chinese border war with Vietnam as unacceptable violations of the principles of national sovereignty and independence.[9]

There were several reasons for this reappraisal of the Vietnamese action. The Berlinguer leadership still sought a rapprochement with Peking, a goal that it would achieve just one year later (March–April 1980). It would have thus been impolitic to condemn military action on the part of the Chinese Communists while tacitly condoning it on the part of China's Vietnamese adversaries. Viewed somewhat less cynically, the PCI's *volte-face* on the Vietnamese–Cambodian conflict coincided with its withdrawal from the parliamentary majority and return to the political opposition at home. During the first weeks of 1979 the Italian party leaders still felt the need to placate those militants who opposed the *compromesso storico* and who in many cases had also ardently sympathized with Hanoi during the American–Vietnamese War. This constraint had been lifted by the time of the Fifteenth PCI Congress in late March when Berlinguer denounced both Vietnam and China.

The PCI reacted to the INF controversy that erupted in the fall of 1979 by calling for East–West negotiations to determine the actual military-strategic balance in Europe. In other words, it equivocated on whether or not the Soviet replacement of older intermediate-range weapons with the mobile and multiple-warhead SS-20 missiles had tilted that balance in the Soviet Union's favor. Much to the dislike of Western policy makers, the PCI opposed the NATO plan to deploy United States cruise and Pershing II missiles on the Continent and voted against Italy's support for it. But the PCI also declined to accept at face value Brezhnev's October 6, 1979,

7. Text in *l'Unità*, November 15, 1979, 8–9.

8. See the editorial, "Capire," *l'Unità*, January 8, 1979, 1; and the commentary by Romano Ledda, "Il vero senso di questo dramma," *l'Unità*, January 9, 1979, 1.

9. See Berlinguer's March 30, 1979 report to the PCI's Fifteenth Congress, *XV Congresso del partito comunista italiano: Atti e resoluzioni*, 2 vols. (Rome: Editori Riuniti, 1979), 1:27.

assertions in East Berlin that the Soviet Union had in no way altered the strategic balance in Europe. Instead the Italian party formally proposed, in a *Direzione* resolution of October 16, 1979, that a NATO–WTO conference "ascertain the real state of nuclear armaments in Europe," correcting any imbalances that might come to light by means of arms reductions.[10]

While this fence-straddling approach met with skepticism in the West, it provoked a cutting rebuke from Moscow on Eurocommunist deviationism. Previously, only Suslov among the top Soviet leaders had publicly castigated Western Communists for ideological heresy of a "regional" variety. Now, on October 17, 1979—the day after the PCI *Direzione*'s INF resolution—Ponomarev made the remark noted in chapter 8 that the "leaders" of the Western Communist parties were "beginning to understand" that Eurocommunism "provokes great discontent among simple Communist militants at the base." The sequence of timing between the PCI's INF statement and Ponomarev's attack suggests that the Soviet official was threatening to stir up dissent among the Italian Communist rank and file as a way of retaliating against the leadership's equivocation on the INF issue.

In what may have been a veiled riposte, Pajetta insisted in his already mentioned November 1979 report to the PCI Central Committee that the Italian party was free of "any prejudice toward this or that great power" in taking the position it did on the INF issue. This was, of course, the acme of evenhandedness. All the same, he refrained from actually treating Moscow and Washington in a balanced manner. For Pajetta explained the worsening of Soviet–American relations in a manner reminiscent of revisionist interpretations of the Cold War: namely influential circles in the United States were seeking a confrontation with the Soviet Union as an excuse for imposing American economic and political policies on Western Europe; and this, in turn, was leading Moscow to fortify its own "political-military and economic bloc."[11]

In the wake of the Soviet invasion of Afghanistan, however, PCI analyses became notably more evenhanded and less encumbered by ideological arguments. Thus in January 1980 party spokesmen denounced the Soviet Union for its violation of Afghan sovereignty (its "act of aggression," in the words of one commentator),[12] and the United States for its provocative posture toward the Soviet Union (the INF decision and the shelving of SALT II). Above all, PCI officials inveighed against the

---

10. Text in *l'Unità*, October 18, 1979, 1 and 15; as stated on page 1, the resolution was passed at a *Direzione* meeting held on October 16.

11. Text in *l'Unità*, November 15, 1979, 8–9.

12. The phrase is used editorially, in a report on Berlinguer's speech to a meeting of PCI local secretaries, in *l'Unità*, January 27, 1980, 1 and 18.

"logic of confrontation" between the two superpowers that was threatening the world with nuclear disaster.[13] And very shortly thereafter the party leadership undertook the most significant step to date in its disengagement from the Moscow-oriented Communist movement: to wit, the restoration of relations with the Chinese Communist Party in April 1980. Not only that, but when Berlinguer—upon his return from a ceremonial visit to Peking to formalize the reconciliation between the two parties—was asked who most threatened world peace, he replied: "The greatest danger . . . arises from a growing confrontation [*contrapposizione*] between the two supreme powers."[14]

The CPSU's initial reaction to this series of PCI challenges was restrained, involving more in the way of organizational steps than polemical sallies. Berlinguer's normalization of party ties with Peking during his April 1980 trip to China met with a direct, albeit mild, reproach in *New Times*.[15] But on the whole, both *New Times* and *Problems of Peace and Socialism* confined themselves to indirect polemics, that is, attacks on *unnamed* Communists who opposed Soviet conduct in Afghanistan or blamed the deterioration of détente on the logic of superpower confrontation rather than on United States provocation.[16]

By way of contrast, in late April 1980 the CPSU and its once again loyal ally, the PCF, hosted a pan-European Communist "peace" conference in Paris to rally opposition against the NATO decision to install cruise and Pershing II missiles in Europe. The PCI leaders had conveyed their objections to confining a meeting of this type solely to Communist parties during January 1980 talks with Marchais in Rome.[17] Their opposition notwithstanding, invitations to the Paris meeting were issued in "mid-March."[18] The coincidence in timing between this finalization of plans for the Paris conference and the PCI's announcement on March 14 of its intention to normalize relations with Peking hardly seems accidental.[19] Indeed, the CPSU decision to proceed with the "peace" rally may have been intended in part as a rap on the knuckles of the Berlinguer group

13. See ibid.; also text of *Direzione* resolution in *l'Unità*, January 6, 1980, 1 and 15; and Berlinguer's speech on the fifty-ninth PCI anniversary in *l'Unità*, January 21, 1980, 1–2.

14. Berlinguer's press conference in *l'Unità*, April 28, 1980, 1–2.

15. I. Ivanov, "On the Visit of the Italian Communist Party Delegation to Peking," *New Times*, no. 20 (May 1980):10–11.

16. See, for example, "World Communist Solidarity with the Afghan Revolution," *New Times*, no. 3 (January 1980):8–10; and Boris Ponomarev, "Pakt mira i pakt agressii," *Problemy mira i sotsializma*, no. 8 (August 1980):3–10.

17. See Gian Carlo Pajetta's report on the PCI's opposition to the Paris peace rally in *l'Unità*, April 3, 1980, 1 and 21.

18. The "mid-March" date was mentioned by Antonio Rubbi in "L'iniziativa internazionale del PCI," *Rinascita* 37, no. 15 (April 11, 1980):3–4.

19. The PCI's *public* announcement of Berlinguer's forthcoming trip to Peking was made at a Central Committee meeting on March 14, 1980; see *l'Unità*, March 16, 1980, 1 and 20.

for their rapprochement with Peking. Then again, it may also have been related to the Italian party's growing ties with West European socialists, yet another sign of PCI disengagement from Moscow. Some nineteen socialist and labor parties sent delegates to the Fifteenth PCI Congress in the spring of 1979.[20] But a breakthrough in such contacts developed precisely in March 1980 when Berlinguer held long-solicited talks with SPD chairman Willy Brandt and French Socialist leader François Mitterrand.[21]

It is impossible, of course, to establish any concrete linkage between these PCI challenges to the CPSU and the April 1980 Paris gathering of European Communist parties loyal to Moscow. What can be said with certainty, however, is that the very holding of that conference entailed a reversal of the procedural concessions made by the CPSU at the time of the 1976 East Berlin summit. For the 1980 meeting was organized on the basis of orthodox democratic centralism (read Soviet manipulation) rather than consensus. It was, in turn, boycotted not only by the PCI but by nearly half the smaller West European Communist parties and by the ruling Yugoslavian and Romanian parties as well.

Dramatic as the foregoing developments were, they were quickly up-staged by the Polish strike movement that erupted in the summer of 1980. PCI support for the revolutionary changes under way in Poland in 1980–81 was significantly more assertive than its backing of the Dubček reformers in 1968. Then, the Italian Communist leaders—along with their French and Spanish comrades—had confined themselves to bringing behind-the-scenes pressure to bear upon Moscow in an effort to prevent the military suppression of the Prague Spring.[22] Now, in the case of Poland, the Italian Communists not only emphasized the negative aspects of the political system under attack by the emerging independent trade union movement; they also threatened a rupture with the CPSU should the Soviets resort to armed intervention. The PCI thus rejected the quiet diplomacy that had proven so ineffective in deterring the invasion of Czechoslovakia twelve years earlier.

On August 19, 1980, shortly after the outbreak of massive strikes in the Baltic coast shipyards, Alfredo Reichlin, editor of *l'Unità*, blamed the Polish crisis on the "pyramidal and totalitarian" (*totalizzante*) nature of Poland's Soviet-style political structures and called for the development of "democracy and participation" forthwith.[23] Thereafter, the PCI press as

20. *Le Monde*, March 31, 1979, 8.
21. See the reports on the talks in *l'Unità*, March 14 and 25, 1980, 1 and 18, and 1 and 4 respectively.
22. Jiri Valenta, *Soviet Intervention in Czechoslovakia, 1968* (Baltimore: Johns Hopkins University Press, 1979), 67–69.
23. Alfredo Reichlin, "Il nostro invito," *l'Unità*, August 19, 1980, 1; cf. unsigned editorial, "La Polonia è già diversa," *l'Unità*, August 31, 1980, 1.

well as official party statements hailed both the victories of Solidarity and the ascendancy of reformers within the Polish party itself. With regard to the latter, *l'Unità* commentators expressed an unabashed preference for those elements in the Polish establishment who had during the second half of the 1970s urged, with tacit PCI backing, political innovation as the solution to the growing economic crisis.[24] Above all, the PCI argued that the realization of broad participatory reforms—far from abetting anti-socialist forces, as the CPSU so insistently warned—was the only sure way of defeating the opponents of socialism.[25]

Meanwhile, as the threat of a Soviet invasion of Poland mounted in the fall of 1980, with Warsaw Pact maneuvers occurring on all borders, the Italian party made known its categorical opposition to such a move during talks in Rome between Zagladin and Berlinguer on December 9 and 10. The precise contents of what was described by both sides as a "long and frank discussion" were not disclosed.[26] The substance of the Italian position can, however, be inferred from an announcement issued by the PCI *Direzione* on the first day of the talks which declared that "military intervention" in Poland would have "the gravest consequences." The document disclosed, moreover, that this view had been communicated to the socialist countries involved.[27] The PCI's message to the CPSU, according to non-Communist sources, threatened a de facto break in relations between the two parties in the event of a Soviet invasion,[28] a report the PCI neither affirmed nor denied. What the Italians did say publicly in a front-page *l'Unità* editorial of December 10—while the Soviet–PCI talks were still going on—was that even the threat of intervention "already represents an unacceptable limitation of sovereignty."

Still, the CPSU refrained from all but the most mild direct criticisms of the PCI during this period. Only in the winter of 1981, after the Italians' blunt warning to the Soviets to keep their hands off Poland during the December 1980 Zagladin–Berlinguer talks, did the Kremlin shift to polemics and organizational sanctions aimed explicitly at the Italian party. Even then the Soviets seemed to hold out the possibility of compromise.

24. See Franco Fabiani, "Le radici del malessere e il dibattito nel POUP," *l'Unità*, August 19, 1980, 1 and 11; Silvio Trevisani, "Come non furono capiti gli scioperi del 1976," *l'Unità*, August 23, 1980, 13; Giuseppe Boffa, "Lì si narra anche di noi," *l'Unità*, September 2, 1980, 1.

25. See Paolo Bufalini's report on the Polish situation to the PCI Central Committee in *l'Unità*, December 18, 1980, 1 and 7.

26. *L'Unità*, December 11, 1980, 1; *Pravda*, December 11, 1980, 4. Significantly, the Italian delegation included Antonio Rubbi, the official who had represented the PCI in its periodic consultations with the Polish party following the 1976 labor crisis and who had moreover just returned from three days in Warsaw where, as reported by *l'Unità* on December 7, 1980 (page 1), he had a "long and *cordial* discussion" with Polish leaders; my emphasis.

27. "Passi officiali del PCI presso i PC dell'Est," *l'Unità*, December 10, 1980, 1 and 15.

28. *La Repubblica*, December 9, 1980.

In the January 1980 issue of *Voprosy istorii KPSS* one Gennadi (Enrico) Smirnov, a close associate of Ponomarev and former Soviet diplomat in Rome, deplored the PCI's "contradictory search for an 'intermediate' place . . . in a world divided into blocs," and he chided "certain Italian comrades" for avoiding a clear characterization of NATO as "aggressive."[29] Yet he also pointedly disassociated Berlinguer from these reproaches, thereby giving the Italian leader a chance to place himself in Moscow's corner at the forthcoming Twenty-sixth CPSU Congress. However, on February 12 the PCI officially let it be known that Berlinguer would boycott the congress,[30] the first time since Stalin's death that an Italian general secretary would do so.

At this point the Soviets took the offensive, combining organizational moves with ever more explicit polemical attacks. On February 13 the world learned that a CPSU Central Committee letter to the PCI leadership, evidently written after the abortive Soviet–PCI talks the previous December, had been leaked to the Milan newsweekly *Panorama*.[31] The letter, reportedly drafted by Smirnov and Zagladin and approved by Ponomarev and Brezhnev himself,[32] accused the Italian party of objectively supporting "those forces which have in Poland unleashed a veritable offensive against socialism." Other such letters had been sent to the PCI in the past, for example on the occasion of Berlinguer's June 1976 allusion to the protective shield of the Atlantic Alliance.[33] But this was the first one to be made public. On the heels of this leak came the Soviet refusal to permit Pajetta, Berlinguer's representative to the February 1981 CPSU congress, to present the PCI's customary greetings unless he deleted some rather circumspect criticisms of the Soviet intervention in Afghanistan and intimidation of Poland.[34] This Pajetta declined to do. He was thus prevented from addressing the congress, in a replay of the rebuff Carrillo had received in November 1977. (The only difference was that Pajetta went along with the Soviet offer of letting him deliver his uncensored remarks at a minor gathering some blocks from the Kremlin.) Thereafter, for the remainder of 1981, the CPSU's attacks on the PCI

29. G. P. Smirnov, "Italianskaia Kommunisticheskaia Partiia," *Voprosy istorii KPSS*, no. 1 (January 1981):98; cf. *l'Unità*, February 7, 1981, 17, regarding the identity of the author, known as Enrico in Italy.

30. "La delegazione del PCI al Congresso PCUS," *l'Unitá*, February 12, 1981, 1; cf. *la Stampa*, February 10, 1981, 1.

31. "A proposito di un documento pubblicato da 'Panorama'," *l'Unità*, February 14, 1981, 2.

32. Carlo Rossella, "Breznev manda a dire . . . ," *Panorama* [Milan], February 23, 1981, 83 and 85.

33. Carlo Rossella, "Non prendiamolo alla lettera," *Panorama*, March 2, 1981, 39.

34. See the reports of this incident in *The Washington Post*, February 27, 1981, A21; *la Repubblica*, March 1–2, 1981, 3; and *l'Unità*, February 28, 1981, 1. The text of Pajetta's speech appears in *l'Unità*, February 28, 1981, 1 and 18.

moved from the pages of *Voprosy istorii KPSS*, a journal of fairly limited circulation, to the more general forum of *New Times*.[35]

There was, to be sure, one final effort to contain the escalating tensions. During a visit to Moscow on July 29–31, 1981, a PCI delegation composed of Cervetti and Bufalini had occasion to meet with Smirnov at a celebration commemorating Longo's death the previous year and to speak more formally with Ponomarev.[36] According to *l'Unità*'s report on the latter talks (there was no official communiqué), the topics discussed "in an atmosphere of frankness and cordiality" included the international situation, the peace movement, and "questions concerning the relations between the two parties."[37] Since the PCI visit coincided with the Tenth PCE Congress, Eurocommunist as well as foreign policy issues were probably on the agenda. Whatever the case, there could have been precious little meeting of minds. For the day after the meeting with Ponomarev, *Pravda* published a biting critique of Carrillo's "catechism of Eurocommunism" and his attribution of current international tensions to the "bloc politics" of the "great powers."[38] Clearly the Soviet attack was also a surrogate polemic against the Italian party, whose sympathies for Carrillo had been reiterated yet again in *l'Unità*'s extensive coverage of the PCE congress.

The PCI's reply to this and, even more, to the Soviet Union's ongoing intimidation of Poland came in a Central Committee report delivered on October 5, 1981, by Ledda, whose earlier criticism of the militarization of Soviet policy in Africa we have noted. Ledda now flatly declared that the Soviet Union had in recent years followed a policy "of power politics, of consolidation and extension of its own political-military bloc, as the prevailing and most secure instrument of international initiative."[39] At this same Central Committee session Reichlin, whose outspoken denunciation of Soviet-style socialism in Poland has also been noted, was promoted to the PCI Secretariat.[40] The Soviets responded with a *New Times* diatribe against Ledda for his "distorted" views and "totally unfounded accusations." The most nefarious of these, in the words of the author, was that "Moscow is said to be just about as much to blame for the arms race as Washington."[41] The polemical knives of the CPSU publicists appeared a bit rusty. It was nonetheless obvious that Soviet–PCI relations were going from bad to worse.

35. For example, Y. Samoilov, "Strange Position: Concerning an Article in the Italian Journal *Rinascita* about the Events in Poland," *New Times*, no. 26 (June 1981):14–15.

36. "Una strada di Mosca intitolata a Longo," *l'Unità*, July 31, 1981, 11.

37. "Bufalini e Cervetti incontrano Ponomariov," *l'Unità*, August 1, 1981, 1.

38. "Na sezde KPI," *Pravda*, August 1, 1981, 4.

39. Text in *l'Unità*, October 6, 1981, 7.

40. "Il comunicato sugli incarichi di partito decisi dal CC," ibid., 1.

41. E. Fryazin, "The Communists and the Fight for Peace," *New Times*, no. 47 (November 1981):14–15.

Martial Law in Poland: The "Rip" in Soviet–PCI Relations

The Polish regime's imposition of martial law on December 13, 1981, brought Soviet–PCI tensions to a head. The topmost Italian Communist authorities denounced not just the Polish move but also Soviet international conduct across the board. Equally galling to Moscow, we may surmise, the PCI leaders gave a substantive dimension to their hitherto rather vague goal of a *terza via*. The documents of the Fifteenth PCI Congress in 1979 had affirmed that the form of socialism to which the Italian party aspired was neither social democracy nor Soviet-style Communism: it was instead a *terza via* (third way) that would in crucial respects partake of each while improving upon both. Now the *berlingueriani* explicitly proclaimed the need for a West European alternative to the Soviet model of socialism that would serve as an inspiration for—nay, give a propulsive impulse to!—reform in the Soviet bloc and revolution in the Third World.

If the PCI's challenge resembled that of the Spanish party in the mid-1970s, Moscow's reaction can better be compared to its treatment of the Chinese Communists some two decades earlier. The CPSU denounced the Italian Communist leaders in its foremost organs, *Pravda* and *Kommunist*, rather than in lesser journals aimed primarily at a foreign audience. And it proceeded to mobilize an international Communist campaign of collective censure against them. Loyalist Communist parties around the world echoed the Soviet polemics. These non-Soviet attacks were then excerpted in *New Times* (published in an Italian edition since October 1980) and, for a while, in *Pravda* as well. The latest test of pro-Sovietism seemed to have become a given Communist party's readiness to criticize the PCI.

The PCI's first reaction to developments in Warsaw was to issue a *Direzione* declaration the very day that martial law was imposed, condemning it as a "blow" to the "efforts to resolve politically the crisis in Poland."[42] Soon thereafter Berlinguer made a statement on Italian television that was to resonate throughout the PCI's ranks and beyond for the following year. In his words, the Polish military dictatorship demonstrated that "the innovative impulse that had its origin in the October Revolution has been exhausted."[43] The very next issue of *Rinascita* carried articles by Napolitano, Ingrao, and other prominent figures expressing their revulsion at the suppression of the Polish reform movement and their utter disillusionment with the Soviet type of socialism that was responsible for such a denouement.[44]

42. Text in *Socialismo reale e terza via* (Rome: Editori Riuniti, 1982), 233–34.
43. *L'Unità*, December 16, 1981, 1.
44. See Giorgio Napolitano's lead editorial, "Polonia, una vicenda cruciale," and Pietro

These ad hoc views received the imprimatur of the PCI *Direzione* in a resolution published on December 30, 1981. In a categorical yet states-manlike manner, the document attributed the suppression of Solidarity in part to the "persisting dogmatism, conservative positions, [and] inertia" within the Polish party. But it placed equal blame for this turn of events upon the Soviet Union's "pressures, undue interference, and battering political and ideological campaign against the effort at renewal in which an important part of the POUP [Polish Communist Party], Solidarity, and the Church were engaged." At the same time, the resolution delivered a ringing indictment of the Soviet Union's postwar imposition of its model of socialism on Eastern Europe and its repeated crushing of all reform initiatives in that part of the world. And it echoed Berlinguer's earlier assessment by declaring that the phase of socialism initiated by the October Revolution had "exhausted its propulsive force."[45] In effect, the PCI disavowed the revolutionary credentials of the CPSU.

The *Direzione* resolution thereupon enjoined the West European left to take the lead in the worldwide advance toward socialism as well as in the "democratic renewal" of the Communist societies in the Soviet orbit. Perhaps most offensive to Soviet ears, it also asserted that the PCI would seek the same kind of relations with socialist and progressive groups as with Communist parties. In other words, there would be no "particular or privileged ties with anyone." Indeed, the resolution rejected outright "the idea of a homogeneous Communist movement separated from the totality of forces in the international workers' movement."[46] It thus repudiated once and for all the fundamental Leninist demarcation between commu-nism and social democracy. The PCI's disengagement from the Moscow-centered Communist world had moved from the level of practice to principle.

The position of the PCI *Direzione* on Poland was upheld (against the negative vote of Armando Cossutta and two abstentions) at a meeting of the party's Central Committee in mid-January 1982. Moreover, Ber-linguer went even further than the December resolution in his major address on that occasion, baldly equating the Soviet Union's foreign pol-icy with that of the United States. The PCI general secretary underscored what had been implicit in his party's reaction to the Afghan crisis and all but explicit in Ledda's October 1981 Central Committee report: namely, he accused the Soviet Union, like the United States, of engaging in sheer "bloc politics," of seeking the expansion of its own power not just in

---

Ingrao, "In Polonia e altrove c'era e c'è altro da fare," *Rinascita* 38, no. 50 (December 18, 1981):1 and 55, and 3–4, respectively.

45. Text in *l'Unità*, December 30, 1981, 1 and 16 at 16.

46. Ibid., 16.

Eastern Europe or Afghanistan but on a global scale. As Berlinguer put it, "the two great powers [continue to] work for the rigid maintenance of blocs and their logic and, more generally, for the defense and possibly the extension of their mutual areas of influence."[47] He went on to say that the PCI looked beyond bipolarity to the day when an independent Western Europe would play an autonomous role in the international arena and a reunited European workers' movement would become "the epicenter" of a new phase in the world march toward socialism.[48]

The Soviet leadership responded to the PCI's initial condemnation of the military crackdown in Poland with another confidential letter (probably written prior to the *Direzione* resolution) that deplored the falsifications and "violent criticisms" directed by Berlinguer, Napolitano, and Ingrao at both the Polish and Soviet parties.[49] However, the PCI's global indictment of Soviet international conduct, expressed in the *Direzione* document and even more so in Berlinguer's mid-January Central Committee speech, led to a *public* polemical offensive unparalleled in the history of Soviet relations with the West European Communist parties. As Pajetta later disclosed, a CPSU political adviser who came to Rome shortly after the Central Committee session bluntly stated: "You have criticized us and offended us; we will be compelled to criticize you and to offend you."[50]

In a biting riposte in *Pravda* on January 24, 1982,[51] the CPSU called the Berlinguer leadership's equation of Soviet and American foreign policies "truly blasphemous," given the "aggressive, militaristic" nature of imperialism and the "NATO bloc." (In this sense it echoed the June 1977 *New Times* attack on Carrillo for his "monstrous statement" that the Soviet Union was a " 'superpower' . . . [that] pursued great-power objectives.")[52] The *Pravda* diatribe also derisively dismissed the PCI leaders' positive appraisal of some West European "bourgeois" governments (read West Germany) on such issues as arms control and détente. It then went on to extol at some length the glories of "existing socialism," clearly for the benefit of its domestic readers.

Only toward the end did the unsigned *Pravda* editorial broach ideological issues. The gist of its charges was that the PCI leaders had over the years engineered "a gradual departure" from Marxism-Leninism under the guise of cunning "innovations." And they had now "openly come out against world socialism" with their position on Poland. Such conduct,

---

47. Text in *l'Unità*, January 12, 1982, 1, 8, and 9; see 8.
48. Ibid., 9.
49. Text in *l'Unità*, March 17, 1982, 16.
50. Gian Carlo Pajetta, *Le crisi che ho vissuto: Budapest Praga Warsavia* (Rome: Editori Riuniti, 1982), 173.
51. "Vopreki interesam mira i sotsializma," *Pravda*, January 24, 1982, 4.
52. "Contrary to the Interests of Peace and Socialism in Europe," *New Times*, no. 26 (June 1977):12.

the statement concluded, amounted to giving "aid to imperialism, . . . [and] aid to anti-Communism." For all practical purposes the *berlingueri-ani* had thus ceased to be members in good standing of the international Communist movement whose very existence they now questioned.

Kommunist published almost simultaneously an even harsher attack that lambasted many PCI leaders by name (Napolitano, Ingrao, Macaluso, in addition to Berlinguer) for "distorting" Soviet foreign policy, for supporting counterrevolution in Poland, and for "repeating almost word for word the fabrications of Reagan, Weinberger, Haig, Brzezinski and other imperialist politicians" on the Polish question.[53] Meanwhile, the Soviet press refused to publish the PCI documents in question, just as it had declined to air the Chinese side during the Sino-Soviet polemics of the 1960s. Such obstinacy persisted despite the verbatim reprinting of the Soviet attacks in *l'Unità* and *Rinascita* and the PCI's repeated pleas for reciprocity in this regard. Even the few copies of *l'Unità* normally on sale in Moscow's newsstands were unavailable during this period.[54] On the other hand, so-called information assemblies for CPSU cadres were held throughout the Soviet Union at which officials repeated, often with rhetorical embellishments, *Pravda*'s accusations against the Italians.[55]

Late in February *New Times* published the first of two sets of excerpts from loyalist Communist parties' denunciations of the PCI.[56] The substance varied from party to party. Nevertheless, the Italian party's "preposterous" equation of Soviet foreign policy with the superpower politics of NATO and Washington constituted a major focal point. The second installment of the *New Times* series went even further. It noted editorially the identity of views in *l'Unità,* and in the Chinese Communist *People's Daily* "which openly lines up with imperialist forces against the Soviet Union and détente."[57] In early March the appearance in *Pravda* of an article by the American Communist Gus Hall condemning the "Eurocommunist" views of Berlinguer and Carrillo marked yet a further step in the Soviet–PCI rift.[58]

About this same time the CPSU joined the fray once again with a second *Kommunist* article that appeared simultaneously in *New Times.*[59]

53. For the official English version, see "On a Slippery Path: Concerning Recent Statements by the Leadership of the Italian Communist Party," *New Times,* no. 5 (February 1982):18–24.

54. Reported by Franco Pantarelli in " 'Bene compagni italiani.' E il Kgb li arresta," *Paese sera,* May 27, 1982, 4.

55. Reported by Adalberto Minucci, "Guardiamo ai fatti e rileggiamo bene Carlo Marx," *l'Unità,* February 14, 1982, 1 and 16; see 16.

56. "Communist and Workers' Parties on the Position of the Leadership of the ICP," *New Times,* no. 8 (February 1982):18–21.

57. "More Comment on the Position of the Leadership of the ICP," *New Times,* no. 10 (March 1982):18–23 at 23.

58. "Realnyi sotsializm i kommunisty mira," *Pravda,* March 10, 1982, 4.

59. For the official English version, see "Once More Concerning the Position of the Leadership of the ICP," *New Times,* no. 11 (March 1982):18–27.

Its tone differed markedly from the late January diatribes. Like the earlier attacks, it painted Soviet domestic reality and the Soviet Union's contribution to international peace in glowing colors. Yet it avoided allegations of PCI ideological deviationism and collusion with imperialism. Instead it was for the most part a logically coherent refutation of the views of the Italian Communist leaders (in this case Berlinguer and Pajetta), whose misguided notions were corrected, so to speak, with pointed quotations from Longo and Togliatti.

The tract declared, among other things, that the Italian party's "economic program does not open up the perspective of socialism . . . [but] is directed at rationalizing . . . and modernizing Italian state-monopoly capitalism." This left the working class little to do but defend, at best from "more advantageous positions," its daily interests.[60] In a similar vein, it argued that the idea of making Western Europe the "epicenter" of a new phase of socialist advance amounted to "demands that do not go beyond the framework of the bourgeois-democratic system," adding that this was "indeed a strange call 'to nowhere.' "[61] And it concluded with the following cutting appraisal of the *compromesso storico, terza via,* and new internationalism: "The content of these concepts is nebulous, eclectic, ambiguous. In the ranks of the Italian Communist Party itself the interpretations given them vary and futile debates over the real meaning of one or another concept have been going on for years. Why is this so?" The anonymous author answered his own query by dubbing them "arbitrary, speculative, armchair constructions."[62]

The PCI press, contrary to its earlier practice, declined to reprint this piece. The Soviet publicists had finally hit upon a way to strike a responsive chord among Italian Communist militants. The underlying drumbeat of the CPSU tirades of early 1982 had been the distinction they drew between the leadership and the base of the PCI. The attempt to turn the Italian rank and file against the *Direzione* was transparent. Yet it was one thing to accuse the *berlingueriani* of betraying Marxism-Leninism and colluding with the Reagan administration. It was quite another to suggest that they had deflected the PCI from the goal of socialist transformation. For there was a ring of truth to this second line of argument in the eyes of at least some Italian Communists. The March 1982 *Kommunist* article was doubtless all the more persuasive because it evoked the authority of the Italian party's historic leaders, Togliatti and Longo.

The Soviet leadership's angry reaction to the PCI's debunking of its revolutionary credentials is hardly surprising. What does require some explanation is the magnitude of Moscow's retaliation, especially when

60. Ibid., 23.
61. Ibid., 24.
62. Ibid., 27.

compared to the CPSU's earlier treatment of the Spanish Communists and even its relative restraint toward the Italian party in 1980–81. As we have seen, Moscow's polemics against the Spanish party were aimed primarily at a foreign audience, whereas its attacks on the PCI were widely disseminated inside the Soviet Union. This suggested, first of all, that in the Kremlin's view the Italian Communists had begun to represent a potential challenge to the domestic legitimacy of the CPSU. Indicative of such an eventuality was the KGB's reported discovery of a letter addressed to the PCI leadership in the apartment of a Soviet dissident by the name of Pavel Kudiukin. "Thanks to you," it read, "the word 'Communism' is no longer a bogey. It is possible to be Communists and to fight for the liberation of man. . . . We are certain that if your arguments were known, the interest and respect that they merit would be enormously more widespread."[63] Kudiukin and a dozen or so associates were imprisoned in April 1982. Members of the group reportedly had connections with both *samizdat* journals and establishment think tanks (the Institute of World Economics and International Relations, for one) in Moscow.[64]

Another consideration that may have entered into the Soviet decision to launch such an intensive campaign against the PCI was the worsening international atmosphere. Soviet–American détente was in shambles, creating the psychological climate for a return to Cold War tensions. Yet at the same time the possibility of a West European shift "beyond bipolarity" had increased, precisely because of disagreements among Europeans and Americans over East–West issues. From the perspective of early 1982, Mitterrand's electoral landslide in France and Bonn's unprecedented assertivensss toward Washington on the question of economic links with the Soviet Union gave the CPSU some reason to envisage an autonomous Europe maneuvering between Washington and Moscow. And no one knew better than the Soviet leaders how destabilizing such a development might be among the Soviet Union's restive East European clients. The CPSU's solution, in short, was to pursue détente with West European *states* while attempting to resurrect the two-camp mentality of the Cominform era among Western Communist parties.

There is yet another explanation for the intensity of the Soviet Union's offensive against the PCI. By the Kremlin's standards, it had for years displayed a rather remarkable degree of forbearance toward the Italian comrades' wide-ranging political-ideological defiance of the CPSU. The PCI's ringing denunciation of Soviet international behavior must have released a wellspring of pent-up fury and frustration on Moscow's side, with the CPSU sectarians rapidly gaining the upper hand in determining

---

63. Quoted in Franco Pantarelli, "Eurocomunisti alzatevi," *L'Espresso*, March 6, 1983, 39.
64. See Kevin Devlin, "Soviets Praise Togliatti in Order to Attack Berlinguer," *Radio Free Europe Research*, background report no. 81, April 14, 1983.

the Soviet reaction. The April 1980 Paris conference of pro-Soviet Communist parties pointed in this direction. More important, the tenor of the CPSU's late January 1982 anti-PCI diatribes was remarkably similar to the tone struck by the Kovalev, Zarodov, and Zhivkov polemics of the 1970s.

Not only did *Pravda* and *Kommunist* accuse the Italian Communist leaders of aiding imperialism, but the January 24 *Pravda* piece also rebutted the Italians' charge that the Soviet model had outlived its "propulsive impulse" by citing those Third World liberation movements that had aligned themselves with the Soviet Union. "Revolutionary-democratic parties emerging from the national liberation movement" were reaching out toward "scientific socialism," it asserted. Indeed, many had actually "proclaimed Marxism-Leninism the theoretical basis of their activity." The *Pravda* statement conveyed the distinct impression that for the more extreme CPSU ideologues Moscow's expanded ideological constituency in Angola, Ethiopia, and elsewhere in the Third World had reduced its need for pan-European Communist solidarity except with those parties that docilely served the interests of the Soviet state.

The role of Mikhail Suslov in these developments is impossible to establish with any certainty. As the result of "a brief grave illness" (presumably a stroke), he lost consciousness on January 21 and died four days later,[65] that is, immediately after the publication of *Pravda*'s initial tirade of January 24. He was thus apparently still on the job when the Kremlin made the decision to engage in a head-on confrontation with the PCI. Indeed, the issue of *Kommunist* in which the most vitriolic Soviet commentary appeared was sent to press on January 25, 1982, the day of his death. In view of Suslov's decades-long preoccupation with the political and ideological cohesion of the international Communist movement, we may assume that he was cut to the quick by the PCI's rejection of any special or "privileged" ties with that movement. He may, in other words, have instigated the January attacks against the Italian party. If so, his passing would have strengthened the hand of the publicists responsible for the more nuanced and sophisticated *Kommunist* polemic that appeared toward the middle of March.

Conciliation Soviet-style

The many reasons for the CPSU's polemical outburst of early 1982 notwithstanding, the Soviet line soon shifted. The men in the Kremlin may simply have had second thoughts on how to deal with the PCI

---

65. Dusko Doder, "Mikhail Suslov Dies," *The Washington Post*, January 27, 1982, C8.

challenge. Then again, the more moderate policy makers—those who preferred modulated polemics to anathema ("ideological" as opposed to "administrative" measures, to use the Comintern lexicon of yesteryear)—may have regained the upper hand after Suslov's death. In any event, even as the inquisitorial attacks on the Italian party resonated among the loyalist Communist parties and in the pages of *New Times*, Moscow initiated a public relations campaign to affirm its interest in dialogue with the PCI and aversion to any kind of "rupture." Soviet officials soon adopted the conciliatory demeanor usually associated with their Italian comrades, while the CPSU's direct polemics ceased entirely after the second *Kommunist* article in mid-March. All the while, signs of Soviet meddling within the PCI's ranks multiplied. In short, the CPSU policy makers seemed to have hit upon a division of labor, whether by default or intent, whereby the moderates among them played to the gallery while the sectarians maneuvered behind the scenes.

Zagladin, as so often in the past, took the lead in projecting a public image of reasonableness, tolerance of doctrinal differences, and wounded innocence. Already in early February 1982, he plaintively remarked in an interview with the crypto-Communist Roman daily, *Paese sera*, that the Soviets had never contested the PCI's right to choose its own path to socialism; yet now the Italian comrades "tell us we have chosen a mistaken path." He also professed to be "petrified" at seeing that NATO officials and "the Americans" had begun making "propaganda for the PCI." Still, he insisted, there was a "fundamental convergence" between the Soviet and Italian Communists on the question of peace and other basic issues. And he concluded by leaving the door open to dialogue: "We have checked our schedule of meetings in 1982, and we will certainly hold discussions with the Italian comrades."[66]

Shortly thereafter, on February 13, 1982, an editorial in *Pravda* resumed the "dialogue" with the PCI in terms that reflected more the conciliatory tone of Zagladin's *Paese sera* interview than the CPSU's earlier tirades or the loyalist Communist attacks soon to appear in *New Times*. The gist of the article was that the *Kommunist* and *Pravda* philippics of late January were written in self-defense against the PCI's repeated public criticisms of the Soviet Union. They were, to boot, made necessary by the Italian leadership's refusal to reply to the CPSU Central Committee's private letter of late December 1981 (which had reached PCI headquarters on January 2). "The CPSU is not interested in sharpening the polemic," declared the commentator. "Neither will it retreat if a polemic is imposed on it, as was the case in December–January." Gone were the pejorative allegations and jibes at individual PCI leaders; and on only one

66. See the extensive excerpts from the interview in *l'Unità*, February 9, 1982, 2.

322

point did the February 13 piece add to the previous exchanges. The editorialist demanded to know just how it was possible for the PCI to fight for peace when it was disassociating itself from the "decisive peace-loving force of the modern epoch," the Soviet Union, and giving moral-political support to the Chinese leaders as well.[67] This pointed query went to the heart of Moscow's more conciliatory approach: namely, its interest in the rapidly growing West European peace movement.

If the Soviet broadsides of January 1982 were reminiscent of Moscow's anti-Chinese invective of the 1960s, this latest Soviet article could well have been written by Zagladin himself. It displayed his knack for appearing flexible and willing to compromise on a wide range of issues while remaining hard-nosed and intransigent only on those points of vital concern to Moscow at the time of writing. Above all, the February 13 editorial's preoccupation with the "struggle for peace" was suggestive of Zagladin's key role in coordinating Soviet support for the burgeoning European peace movement against American INF deployment in Europe.[68]

Moscow's conciliatory gestures toward the PCI were soon followed by a quite unexpected turn in Soviet foreign policy: conciliatory signals toward Peking. In a widely publicized speech in Tashkent on March 24, 1982, Brezhnev stressed his country's readiness to enter into a dialogue aimed at the normalization of relations with the People's Republic of China. The following May an authoritative commentary in *Pravda* spoke of "a real possibility for improving Soviet-Chinese relations," an optimistic assessment that was borne out by the start of periodic Sino-Soviet talks in October 1982. This initiative went against the grain of the CPSU's established China-watchers, who after two decades had developed a bureaucratic stake in the Sino-Soviet conflict. But Zagladin was known to be receptive to an accommodation with Peking, if only because of his liaison function with the West Europen Communist parties, many of which had started the process of normalizing relations with the Chinese after the PCI's rapprochement with Peking in April 1980.[69] (Suslov, in contrast, may have opposed such steps in light of his role as a leading spokesman for Moscow's position during the bitter Sino-Soviet recriminations of the mid-1960s.)

Here it bears repeating that Moscow halted its direct polemics against the PCI about the very time that Brezhnev gave his March 24, 1982, speech in Tashkent. Plainly the continuation of public tirades against the PCI would not have been conducive to a rapprochement with the Chinese

67. *Pravda*, February 13, 1982, 4.

68. Cf. J. A. Emerson Vermaat, "Moscow Fronts and the European Peace Movement," *Problems of Communism* 31, no. 6 (November–December 1982):43–56.

69. See Gilbert Rozman, "Moscow's China-watchers in the Post-Mao Era: The Response to a Changing China," *China Quarterly*, no. 94 (June 1983):215–41; Rozman refers to Zagladin's views on 236.

party, whose affinities with the Italian Communists the CPSU itself had acknowledged in its earlier polemics. A broader consideration underlying both moves, moreover, was probably the Kremlin's perception of its growing international isolation as Soviet relations with the Reagan administration worsened and détente with Western Europe seemed likewise threatened by the NATO decision regarding INF.

During the next few months Zagladin made several conciliatory overtures to the PCI. In early May he granted an interview to *la Repubblica* in which he reiterated the theme of *Pravda*'s February 13 editorial. "The Soviet party is not interested in continuing the polemic," he insisted, unless the PCI should again provoke it with "attacks against the CPSU, the USSR, or real socialism." More significant, he emphasized Moscow's solidarity with "the battle that the PCI is waging against the installation of the new missiles in Italy," adding that "we consider them our allies in the struggle for peace."[70] And in June Zagladin expressed interest in visiting Bologna to the city's Communist mayor, whom he encountered during an international conference in Sofia celebrating the centenary of Dimitrov's birth.[71]

That trip eventually took place in late October 1982. Zagladin, accompanied by Smirnov, his close adviser on Italian affairs, visited Bologna on October 20–21 and then proceeded to Rome for high-level talks with Pajetta, Minucci, and Rubbi (as well as a protocol call on Berlinguer). During a question-and-answer period in Bologna, Zagladin remarked that Soviet–PCI "discussions are not altercations." He thereupon held out the prospect that "tomorrow . . . at the headquarters of the PCI we will manage to resolve our problems."[72]

Such did not turn out to be the case. While both sides praised the frankness and the wide-ranging nature of the formal discussions held on October 21 and 25, some five hours of talks and two telephone calls to Moscow did not suffice to work out a joint communiqué.[73] As far as one can glean from the press reports of what transpired, the PCI refused to downplay its foreign policy disagreements with Moscow for the sake of presenting a united front against the American missiles. *Pravda* implied that this was the case, that there was a consensus that "collaboration in the struggle against imperialism, for the prevention of war and the halting of the arms race was more important [*vyshe*] than existing disagree-

70. Sandro Viola, "L'intervista a Zagladin," *la Repubblica,* May 8, 1982, 3.

71. "Arriva Zagladin Mosca cerca un nuovo contatto con Berlinguer," *la Repubblica,* July 30, 1982, 2.

72. Jenner Meletti, "Due ore e mezza di botta e risposta con Zagladin," *l'Unità,* October 22, 1982, 3.

73. Personal communication from a high-ranking PCI official close to the talks in an interview on November 26, 1982.

ments.''[74] Not a word to this effect appeared in *l'Unità*'s two accounts of the meetings. While the first alluded to a discussion of international issues,[75] both reports stressed the mode rather than the substance of the talks and affirmed the importance of explaining as clearly as possible each side's respective views, including their points of disagreement.[76] As for *Pravda*'s suggestion of a common Soviet–PCI position on the struggle against imperialism and the arms race, Pajetta pointedly retorted in *l'Unità* that the Italian spokesmen had not only reiterated the PCI's opposition to the Soviet positions on Poland and Afghanistan; they had also emphasized their party's conviction that the struggle for peace "cannot be identified with the diplomatic action of one side or considered as *acritical support for the conduct of Soviet diplomacy.*"[77]

Meanwhile, a public opinion poll taken in the late winter of 1981–82 suggested that pro-Soviet elements among the Italian Communists numbered about 10 percent of the membership,[78] a figure that would be confirmed a year later during the meetings of the party's 108 local federations preceding the Sixteenth PCI Congress in March 1983. It seems likely that one purpose the Soviet sectarians had in mind when they launched the direct polemics against the PCI in January 1982 was to split and weaken the Italian party, to bring upon it the same fate that had befallen the Spanish Communists. In point of fact, the Soviets had encouraged and abetted the fragmentation of the PCE ever since 1969. The emergence in the early 1970s of Moscow-oriented splinter groups was followed a decade later by the factionalization of the Spanish party itself. By 1981 Carrillo confronted internal opposition from at least three distinct groups: traditional working-class militants, pro-Soviet loyalists, and younger intellectuals even more innovative and anti-Soviet than the Carrillo leadership. There is considerable evidence of Soviet and East European organizational and financial aid to the two sectarian factions.[79]

In the case of the Italian party, however, history was not about to repeat itself. The Soviet polemics boomeranged for any number of reasons. For

74. G. Zafesov, "Obmen mneniiami," *Pravda*, October 27, 1982, 4. The only other reference to the Soviet–PCI talks appeared in a short reference to Zagladin's appearance in Bologna; G. Zafesov, "Obmen mneniiami," *Pravda*, October 23, 1982, 4.

75. "Franco colloquio con Pajetta, Minucci, Rubbi," *l'Unità*, October 22, 1982, 3.

76. Ibid.; cf. "Conclusi i colloqui di Zagladin Ieri ha incontrato Berlinguer," *l'Unità*, October 26, 1982, 3.

77. Ugo Baduel, "Pajetta racconta; 'Ecco cosa ci siamo detti con Zagladin,'" *l'Unità*, October 28, 1982, 1 and 20 at 20; my emphasis.

78. See the analysis in Kevin Devlin, "PCI Majority Backs Leadership on Poland, USSR," *Radio Free Europe Research*, background report no. 85, April 6, 1982.

79. Eusebio Mujal-Leòn, "Cataluña, Carrillo, and Eurocommunism," *Problems of Communism* 30, no. 2 (March–April 1981):25–47; cf. his contribution to the symposium, "Soviet Policies and Negotiating Behavior toward Nonruling Communist Parties," *Studies in Comparative Communism* 15, no. 3 (Autumn 1982):236–65.

325

one thing, the younger PCI activists—those in their thirties—had been exposed to criticism of past and present Soviet reality by their own ideological mentors from the time of their entry into the party in the late 1960s or early 1970s. For another, even those activists who had come to political maturity during the Cominform years, when the party's public philosophy of pro-Sovietism/anti-Americanism prevailed, could hardly have been pleased to hear *Kommunist* compare the PCI leaders to members of the Reagan administration.

The Italian party's rebuttals to the Soviet polemics also carried considerable punch. Why, queried *l'Unità*, had the January 24 *Pravda* diatribe sidestepped the entire issue of martial law in Poland?[80] How, asked the PCI daily, could *Pravda*'s February 13 editorial uphold the Soviet Union as the bulwark of world peace when recent Soviet moves had had the effect of actually "exacerbating the international situation and obstructing détente?"[81] And on what grounds, party commentators repeatedly demanded to know, did the Soviet Union refuse to let its citizens read the PCI documents under attack?

Furthermore, *l'Unità*—while partial to the Carrillo leadership—kept its readers well informed about the Spanish party's factionalization as well as about its electoral decline from 10.0 percent in the late 1970s to a mere 3.8 percent of the votes cast in the October 1982 Spanish parliamentary elections. Doubtless even among those PCI members who harbored sympathy for Moscow, many were inclined to keep their own counsel lest their party experience a similar fate.

For many reasons, therefore, CPSU publicists returned to the more modulated polemics of the 1970s, at least in *New Times* and the Soviet mass media. Specialized journals of limited circulation continued to dissect the ideological and political foibles of the PCI in a manner reminiscent of the March 1982 *Kommunist* article, probably in order to nip in the bud any interest in the Italian heresy among CPSU cadres. The May–June 1982 issue of *Rabochii klass i sovremennyi mir,* for example, carried a devastating critique of the *compromesso storico*. It was co-authored by Timur Timofeev, head of the Institute of the International Workers' Movement and probably the CPSU official who had in January 1982 forewarned Pajetta of the coming Soviet polemical onslaught.[82] And it spelled out what the PCI leaders had long known: cooperation with Christian Democracy had led to disorientation and alienation among a number

---

80. "Risposta alla Pravda: Le nostre posizioni scaturiscono dai fatti," *l'Unità*, January 26, 1982, 1 and 16.

81. "Questo non è dialogo," *l'Unità*, February 14, 1982, 1 and 16.

82. This was implied by Pajetta in an interview with Antonio Padellaro in *Corriere della sera*, January 27, 1982, 2.

of Italian Communists.[83] Still, with the exception of attacks on PCI policy by *Italian* militants, published in the form of letters to the editors,[84] direct polemics disappeared from *New Times* and *Pravda*. Even on the eve of Zagladin's October 1982 trip to Italy, Moscow confined itself to its earlier method of indirect criticism. Without mentioning any names, a *Pravda* commentary warned that "slandering" other branches of the Communist movement and promoting contacts with reactionary forces in place of international Communist ties could only undermine the political authority "of a proletarian party."[85]

On the other hand, the muting of the CPSU's polemics was accompanied by indications of Moscow's financial support for publications sponsored by pro-Soviet Italian Communists. The technique of using Italians to criticize Italians had been foreshadowed by sympathetic letters from PCI militants in *Pravda* and *New Times* (the latter, it may be recalled, had appeared in an Italian edition since October 1980). Circumstantial evidence indicates that Moscow also channeled funds into a pro-Soviet Italian journal, *Interstampa,* and acquired substantial influence over the management of the crypto-Communist Roman daily, *Paese sera.*

Interstampa began as a journal of documentation on the countries of "real socialism" in early 1981, about the time of the Twenty-sixth CPSU Congress when Soviet–PCI relations took a turn for the worse. But in February 1982 it was "relaunched" with considerable fanfare by a group of Italians long identified with a pro-Soviet orientation. Its editor was a relatively young PCI member, Roberto Napoleone, but its guiding spirit appeared to be the veteran Communist and octogenarian Ambrogio Donini, who had vaunted his pro-Soviet leanings during the Czechoslovakian crisis of 1968.[86] Groups of *Interstampa* supporters quickly sprang up in a dozen or so cities, and an editorial house, Casa editrice Aurora, run by individuals with ties to the *Interstampa* group, was also formed.[87] In the meantime, *Paese sera,* which had been in tight financial straits for some time, was bought up by an Italian businessman who had been closely involved in export-import trade with the Soviet Union for years and had many personal ties in Moscow.[88]

83. S. Vasiltsov, A. Galkin, T. Timofeev, "Italianskie problemy," *Rabochii klass i sovremennyi mir,* no. 3 (May–June 1982):98–107, esp. 99–102.

84. "Italians on the Position of the ICP Leadership (From Readers' Letters)," *New Times,* no. 14 (April 1982):21–22; cf. the letter of B. Donatelli in *Pravda,* March 22, 1982.

85. I. Mints, "Istoki internatsionalizma: s ideologicheskogo fronta," *Pravda,* October 19, 1982, 4.

86. For details, see Matteo Spina, "Tutti gli uomini di Breznev," *Panorama,* March 1, 1982, 35–38; and Adriano Botta, "Non toccate Lenin. E compagni come prima," *Europeo,* August 30, 1982, 12–13.

87. Ibid.

88. Mario Margiocco, "Contro Berlinguer," *Secolo 19* [Genoa], October 10, 1982.

There is, of course, no hard proof that the Kremlin financed these publications. But the available evidence points to a Soviet connection. For one thing, the PCI authorities undertook organizational sanctions—for the first time in well over a decade—against several persons connected with *Interstampa*. Fausto Sorini, head of the Aurora publishing house, was accused of violating party statutes and suspended for six months.[89] Reportedly he had been involved in "factional activities" such as trips to Warsaw, contacts with East European embassies, and coordination of the circles of sympathizers associated with *Interstampa*, all with the support of "external forces."[90] Then on the eve of Zagladin's formal call on Berlinguer during his October 1982 trip, the journal's editor, Roberto Napoleone, was excluded from the PCI on somewhat specious grounds.[91] By way of contrast, Armando Cossutta, the only member of the *Direzione* to oppose the PCI's position on the CPSU and Poland, carefully kept his distance from the *Interstampa* group. The PCI leadership reciprocated by limiting itself to a reprimand of Cossutta for violating party discipline.[92]

Another case of probable Soviet behind-the-scenes manipulation concerned Franco Pantarelli, the *Paese sera* correspondent who had publicized the pro-PCI letter and leanings of the young Soviet dissidents mentioned earlier in this chapter. For writing a free-lance article on their arrest and forthcoming trial in the newsweekly *l'Espresso* in March 1983, Pantarelli was promptly fired by the new management of *Paese sera*.[93] Yet most of the material in that article, including the verbatim text of the dissidents' letter to the PCI, had been printed a year earlier under Pantarelli's byline in *Paese sera* itself.[94] The management reversed its initial decision to fire him the next day,[95] probably because of the adverse publicity that would have accrued from such overt pandering to Moscow's interests.

89. "Cremona: sospeso il compagno Fausto Sorini," *l'Unità*, July 4, 1982, 5.

90. "Se manca la fiducia nel partito," *l'Unità*, July 27, 1982, 2; cf. "Dopo un processo per 'frazionismo' sospeso a Cremona un dirigente del PCI," *la Repubblica*, July 6, 1982, 2.

91. "L'editore Roberto Napoleone è stato radiato dal PCI," *l'Unità*, October 24, 1982, 6; cf. the analyses by em. ma., "Le 'finezze' dell' editore Napoleone," *l'Unità*, October 26, 1982, 3; and Kevin Devlin, "The Bitter Legacy of Comrade Robotti," *Radio Free Europe Research*, background report no. 231, November 2, 1982.

92. "Documento della Direzione PCI: Sviluppare il dibattito nel rispetto delle regole dello Statuto—Deplorato il comportamento del compagno Armando Cossutta," *l'Unità*, February 10, 1982, 1. Cf. text of Cossutta's speech in Perugia which gave rise to the reprimand; ibid., 18.

93. "Licenziato da 'Paese sera' per un articolo sull'Urss," *la Repubblica*, March 2, 1983, 5.

94. Franco Pantarelli, " 'Bene compagni italiani,' E il Kgb li arresta," *Paese sera*, May 27, 1982, 4.

95. "Pantarelli non verrà licenziato da 'Paese sera,' " *la Repubblica*, March 3, 1983, 12.

The PCI in Search of Itself

As already suggested, the ferocity of the CPSU's polemics against the PCI in early 1982 actually had a unifying impact on the Italian party as a whole vis-à-vis Moscow. Yet the Soviet–PCI *strappo*, or rip in relations, also had the effect of unleashing a passionate debate over the rules governing the decision-making process within the PCI. The Italian Communist elite's rejection of the antidemocratic character of Soviet-style socialism was accompanied, in other words, by a grassroots backlash against the oligarchical structure of the Italian party itself.

Ordinary PCI members plainly had had a bellyful of *svoltas* from above on domestic strategy: Berlinguer's 1973 formulation of the *compromesso storico* in the pages of *Rinascita;* the *Direzione*'s subsequent acquiescence to a government of "national solidarity"; the sudden reversion to the strategy of the "left alternative" in 1980; and, finally, Berlinguer's January 1983 endorsement during a television interview of the eventuality of a left-wing coalition coming to power with a mere 51 percent of the popular vote[96]—a 180-degree reversal from his position in this regard a decade earlier. As Ingrao—for over fifteen years the standard-bearer of greater internal party democracy—put it in a speech to the annual festival of *l'Unità* in September 1982: "We must do away with the system of transmission from above. . . . It is necessary that the comrades understand what alternatives they have and are placed in a position to choose."[97]

With the exception of Cossutta, the PCI leadership stood united from the start on the need to condemn martial law in Poland and to distance the Italian party from the Soviet bloc regimes. On December 22, 1981, the *Direzione* approved the general outline of the party's December 30 resolution on Poland, the final drafting of which was delegated to the Secretariat.[98] In mid-January 1982 the Central Committee backed Berlinguer's global critique of Soviet foreign policy with only Cossutta's dissenting vote and two abstentions. And upon receiving word of *Pravda*'s January 24 attack, Berlinguer, Pajetta, Bufalini, and Reichlin—among others—agreed forthwith that it should be printed the very next day in *l'Unità*, with Bufalini given the task of drafting a rebuttal. The final text of the PCI reply was worked out by Berlinguer, Bufalini, Pajetta, and Natta (at that time the low-keyed coordinator of the Secretariat), with others being

96. Text in *la Repubblica*, January 6, 1983, 5.

97. Quoted in Giampaolo Pansa, "Pietro il sovversivo ha sfidato Berlinguer," *la Repubblica*, March 5, 1983, 3.

98. Miriam Mafai, "Cossutta sempre più isolato Forse il Cremlino prepara la 'scomunica' a Berlinguer," *la Repubblica*, January 2, 1982, 3.

consulted by phone. It was published as an unsigned editorial in *l'Unità* on January 26.[99]

Cossutta, however, strenuously objected to Berlinguer's view that the propulsive force of the October Revolution had been exhausted. Already the previous October he had opposed Ledda's analysis of the Soviet foreign policy line as one of "power politics [and] the consolidation and extension of its own political-military bloc." Instead he had hailed the Soviet Union's positive contribution to Third World liberationism and its cardinal role in the struggle for peace.[100] He elaborated upon these themes many times after the turn of the year, both in the party press and in a book-length essay entitled *Lo Strappo*.[101] But whereas in *l'Unità* Cossutta at least conceded the inappropriateness of the Soviet model for Western Europe, his book read like a throwback to the two-camp imagery and thinking of the late Stalin era. Little wonder he attracted so small a following.

As preparations got under way for the Sixteenth PCI Congress, it soon became clear that the party cadres largely shared the leadership's views on relations with the Soviet Union. The benchmarks in this process of clarification were threefold: a mid-November 1982 Central Committee meeting convened to finalize a programmatic document for the forthcoming national congress; the congresses of the 108 PCI federations at which that Central Committee document was subjected to intense scrutiny and multiple amendments; and the Sixteenth Congress itself. These successive gatherings were all dominated by two themes, the Soviet–PCI *strappo* and the organizational revolution within the party, with the first quickly being superseded by the second.

The Central Committee meeting of November 23–25, 1982, took place less than two weeks after Brezhnev's death. Berlinguer, Pajetta, and Bufalini attended the funeral with due propriety. Nevertheless, the PCI's highest deliberative body incorporated Berlinguer's celebrated thesis on the exhaustion of the Soviet system's "propulsive force" into its formal congress document.[102] An amendment by Cossutta to eliminate this paragraph was overwhelmingly defeated, with only three votes cast in his favor and a handful of abstentions (out of a total of some 200 members of the Central Committee and Central Control Commission).[103] On the other

99. Details disclosed in a.s., "Trentasei ore di passione per decidere insieme la risposta all'anatema," *la Repubblica*, January 26, 1982, 3.

100. Mafai, "Cossutta sempre più isolato," *la Repubblica*, January 2, 1982, 3.

101. Armando Cossutta, *Lo Strapppo: USA, URSS movimento operaio di fronte alla crisi internazionale* (Milan: Arnoldo Mondadori Editore, 1982).

102. Text entitled "La proposta di alternativa per il cambiamento," in *l'Unità*, November 28, 1982, 11–15; see p. 14.

103. Alberto Stabile, "Su alternativa e 'strappo' i comunisti si sono divisi," *la Repubblica*, November 27, 1982, 5.

hand, a passage in the original draft that defined *both* Soviet and American foreign policy as "imperial" met with such strenuous opposition that Berlinguer himself reportedly moved that it be deleted.[104] In the end, the document labeled only the United States as "imperialist." By way of contrast, it noted the Soviet Union's role as a counterweight to United States imperialism. It warned, however, that this role was endangered by Moscow's "power politics" and military extension of its "zones of influence."[105]

The formal amendment process represented a considerable improvement over earlier procedures, as did *l'Unità*'s subsequent publication of Cossutta's dissenting proposals.[106] Still, it was only during the meetings of the 108 party federations that the organizational revolution gathered momentum. During the November Central Committee session Ingrao had proposed an amendment requiring both democratization and openness of debate (*trasparenza*) in the decision-making process at all levels of the party's structure, including the *Direzione*. This amendment, so similar to his recommendations of the mid-1960s, was defeated by five votes.[107] In those federations (about one-half the total) that considered Ingrao's motion, on the other hand, over two-thirds of the delegates voted in his favor.[108] Yet in the case of Cossutta's pro-Soviet amendments, which were raised in all but three of the federations, the upper limit of support (including related proposals) was no more than 15 percent, with only 9 percent voting for or abstaining on his actual motions. Another roughly 15 percent—apparently comprising activists in the peace movement rather than pro-Soviet sympathizers—voted in one form or another for Italy's withdrawal from NATO.[109]

At the Sixteenth PCI Congress itself the issue of Soviet–PCI relations was therefore almost residual. Indeed, Cossutta himself withdrew his amendments although he voted against the final version of the congress document (of some 1,100 delegates, 7 voted no and 9 abstained).[110] To be sure, Cossutta's base of support within the party at large was broader than that reflected on the floor of the congress. As a renowned observer of PCI affairs, Giampaolo Pansa, succinctly explained it, in the party *sections* of Milan—Cossutta's personal stronghold—his position received 30 percent

104. Ibid.
105. "La proposta di alternativa," *l'Unità*, November 28, 1982, 14.
106. Text in *l'Unità*, November 30, 1982, 14.
107. Alberto Stabile, "Requiem per il compromesso il Pci sceglie l'alternativa," *la Repubblica*, November 28–29, 1982, 5.
108. For an excellent analysis of the congresses of the PCI federations, see Fabrizio Coisson e Francesco De Vito, "I post-comunisti," *L'Espresso*, March 6, 1983, 6–13, esp. 12–13.
109. Ibid.
110. Alberto Stabile, "Nel nuovo Comitato centrale più voce alla periferia," *la Repubblica*, March 8, 1983, 11.

of the votes. Yet support for his amendments among section delegates to the Milan Federation Congress was reduced to 16 percent. And of the fifty-two delegates elected there to attend the national congress, only *one* represented his views.[111] In addition, there were currents of covert pro-Sovietism, individuals who preferred not to speak out against the leadership's line either because of the habit of discipline or from fear of harming the party's public image.[112]

All the same, by 1982–83 the PCI leadership no longer had to worry unduly about pro-Soviet loyalties among party activists. This is not to say that the specter of pro-Sovietism had been groundless during the period of PCI–DC collaboration in the 1970s. Doubts over the PCI-backed policies of austerity and public order were real enough among Communist workers and student radicals, as indicated by wildcat strikes and such outbursts as a youth rebellion in the Communist-run city of Bologna in March 1977. Malaise of this kind surely made party militants more susceptible to covert or veiled Soviet insinuations of ideological deviationism among PCI decision makers.

By the start of the 1980s, however, the Berlinguer leadership had carried out an organizational revolution of its own. During the second half of the 1970s it encouraged a substantial generational turnover among functionaries in the PCI federations. By 1976 over 37 percent of the cadres at this level were under thirty years of age and had entered the party only after 1969. (Older activists whom they replaced often assumed local administrative or elective positions, an area of greatly expanded Communist participation after the PCI's dramatic advances in the regional and national elections of 1975–76.) These younger functionaries were also far better educated than their predecessors, with over half having high school or college diplomas.[113]

The composition of the delegates to the PCI's federation congresses in 1979 offers another illustration of this generational turnover. About three-fifths had entered the Communist Party only after 1970, over half were under thirty, almost one-fifth were college educated, and a third had been active in one of the "new left" mobilizational movements of the late 1960s.[114] Most significant for our purposes, an analysis of the political

111. Giampaolo Pansa, "Addio, compagno Cossutta la nave rossa punta ad Ovest," *la Repubblica,* March 6–7, 1983, 5.

112. Cf. the analysis by Alberto Ronchey, "Il compagno è cambiato ma quanto?" *la Repubblica,* March 8, 1983, 10.

113. For relevant data, see Giuseppe Are, *Radiografia di un partito: Il PCI negli anni '70: struttura ed evoluzione* (Milan: Rizzoli Editore, 1980), 221–34; cf. his chapter, "Il PCI come organismo politico," in *Il PCI allo specchio,* ed. Renato Mieli (Milan: Rizzoli Editore, 1983), 38–42.

114. For the survey that produced these data, see *L'identità comunista: I militanti, le strutture, la cultura del Pci,* ed. Aris Accornero, Renato Mannheimer, and Chiara Sebastiani (Rome: Editori Riuniti, 1983).

attitudes of the delegates reveals that those who shared the above characteristics were likely to be more tolerant of unconventional political behavior among their comrades and less responsive to rigid party discipline.[115]

It seems safe to assume that such an independent outlook could lead to sympathy toward unconventional political behavior in the Soviet bloc as well, whether with regard to Solidarity in Poland or human rights dissidents in the Soviet Union and Czechoslovakia. Similarly, the higher educational level of the younger activists also points to the likelihood that they would be attentive to the changing PCI assessment of Soviet-style socialism not simply in the party's mass media but also in its many scholarly works on this subject.

For well over a decade PCI historiography had been making large strides in the direction of objective and archival research on the history of the PCI and its relations with the CPSU. The party's historical quarterly, *Studi storici,* published numerous articles on these and related topics after 1968. For a time attention was focused on the pre-1945 era. For example, Paolo Spriano's five-volume history of the PCI, published between 1967 and 1975, ended with the year 1945. This restricted time frame was, however, questioned by Berlinguer in December 1974. In the same Central Committee speech in which he elucidated the *compromesso storico* and affirmed the PCI's acceptance of NATO, he also praised the achievements of his party's historians as unparalleled in the Communist movement. He then went on to call for a comparable exploration into *postwar* history—especially with regard to the Stalinization of Eastern Europe and its impact upon the PCI.[116]

A Gramsci Institute conference on Soviet history in mid-January 1978 marked a qualitative leap forward in Italian Communist scholarship. On that occasion a number of younger as well as established PCI historians read papers that were notable for their detached and often critical approach to controversial issues: for instance, the Leninist roots of Stalinism, the negative impact of collectivization, the absence of Soviet institutional barriers to the abuse of political power, and so forth.[117] In June the proceedings of the conference were published by the PCI firm, Editori Riuniti.[118] The following month the Gramsci Institute sponsored a similar

115. See the preliminary findings of Sidney Tarrow, Enrico Ercole, and Peter Lange, "Pathways to Partisanship: Social Mobilization, Generational Recruitment and Political Attitudes of Italian Communist Militants," manuscript prepared for presentation to the American Political Science Association annual meeting, Washington, D.C., August 20–September 2, 1984.

116. *L'Unità,* December 11, 1974, 13–14.

117. See the accounts of the conference reports in *l'Unità,* January 14, 15, and 16, 1978, 13, 18, and 12, respectively; compare the analysis in Michael J. Sodaro, "Eurocommunist Views of Soviet History," *Problems of Communism* 29, no. 3 (May–June 1980):65–71.

118. Sergio Bertolissi, ed., *Momenti e problemi della storia dell'URSS* (Rome: Editori Riuniti–Istituto Gramsci, 1978).

symposium on the Prague Spring.[119] Meanwhile Editori Riuniti became a regular outlet for works by dissident or exiled Soviet and East European writers (for example, the Soviet historian Roy Medvedev, the Polish economist Wlodzimierz Brus, and numerous Czechoslovakian and Hungarian émigrés). And in his address to the annual festival of *l'Unità* in September 1978, Berlinguer once again hailed the strides PCI historians had made in coming to grips with "existing socialism."[120]

In other words, the Berlinguer leadership had apparently succeeded in shaping the younger generation of PCI cadres in its own image of receptivity to pluralism and rejection of the monolithic Communist party-state. But it had, at the same time, imbued them with a taste for practicing what their elders preached. The end result was the grassroots movement to modify the PCI's Leninist structures.

The development of real significance at the Sixteenth PCI Congress was thus the landslide vote in favor of an organizational amendment that embraced Ingrao's long-standing call for greater *trasparenza* and internal democracy. It included three provisions with far-reaching implications for the party's decision-making process. First, executive bodies at all levels were now required to give their electors an account of their deliberations, thereby disclosing the pros and cons (as well as the proponents and antagonists) of any given decision. Second, the Central Committee was to resume its statutory role as the key policy-making body between congresses. Third and most important, the divergences that so often appeared within the *Direzione* (as well as lower executive organs) were henceforth to be resolved by the Central Committee (or the respective lower elective bodies).[121]

On the other hand, the widespread agreement on the need for more openness and participation in decision making could not be said to exist with regard to the substance of the key issue facing the party: namely, the precise definition of its strategy of a "left alternative." The policy of an alternative to the DC-dominated center-left coalitions that had governed Italy for most of the previous two decades was subject to as many interpretations as the *compromesso storico* a few years earlier. Not only that, but a similar pattern of divergences reemerged. The mainstream of articulate party opinion seemed to divide along three lines.

The most pragmatic was the one that favored PCI agreements with other political parties on concrete, step-by-step reforms in the political here and

---

119. See the accounts of the conference in *l'Unità*, July 8–10, 1978, 14, 16, and 5, respectively.

120. *L'Unità*, September 18, 1978.

121. *L'Unità*, March 7, 1983, 16; cf. Giovanni Valentini, "Si fa da parte Natta, il numero due," *la Repubblica*, March 6–7, 1983, 4; and Nicola D'Amico, "Sparisce come 'principio' il centralismo democratico," *Corriere della sera*, March 7, 1983, 2.

334

now. This approach underlay the Communists' parliamentary cooperation with Christian Democracy during 1976–1978. Its leading proponents— men such as Napolitano and Reichlin—continued to appeal for interparty cooperation in the early 1980s but with the parties of the lay left, above all the PSI, rather than with the Christian Democrats. While not renouncing the vision of a *terza via* to socialism, they sought a common platform upon which the left could actually achieve an electoral victory in Italy. Regardless of the anticipated alliance partners, they accepted the need for compromise as a matter of principle. As Reichlin put it at the Sixteenth Congress, the call for an alignment between Communists and Socialists required that the PCI become "more open, capable of building new relations between itself and others but also within itself, within its own *loci* of political decision." The PCI's goal of a left alternative, he concluded, was in no sense a "neo-frontist operation" but "an articulation of even intermediate forces [presumably the smaller Republican, Social Democratic, and Radical parties] in which no one demands hegemony."[122]

Equally innovative, it would seem, was the *corrente* that sought to lay the groundwork for interparty cooperation through mass mobilization. While this approach had been integral to the Comintern's popular front and national front strategies, what was new with regard to its recent PCI advocates was their targets of mobilization, namely, the *emarginati* and the *engagés:* the *emarginati* in the sense of the unemployed youth, the unskilled migrants from southern Italy, the pensioners; the *engagés* in the sense of movements rather than organizations—feminists, environmentalists, nuclear freeze militants. Ingrao, of course, had favored such an orientation since the mid-1960s. And after the party's internal dissent and setbacks of the late 1970s, the number of spokesmen for this outlook had grown, coming to include even Berlinguer on the eve of the 1980s.[123] Indeed, as the general secretary put it in his report to the Sixteenth Congress, the PCI's central theoretical point of departure was "a revolutionary process which, while advancing gradually, no longer leaves behind it the exploited, the subordinated, the discriminated, the marginalized, the disinherited *in principle* or by destiny (the 'little,' the 'poor,' the 'weak')."[124]

What separated this latter grouping from the party's left wing, originally inspired by Ingrao, was the purpose behind the mobilizational approach. In the case of the party establishment, the aim was still to promote gradual socioeconomic reform, to use the movements to stimulate some form of

---

122. Text in *l'Unità*, March 4, 1983, 7.

123. See, for example, Berlinguer's speech to the July 1979 PCI Central Committee plenum, following the party's electoral decline in the national parliamentary contest; *l'Unità*, July 4, 1979, 7–9.

124. Text in *l'Unità*, March 3, 1983, 5–9 at 6.

335

accommodation with other political parties. For the PCI radicals, on the other hand, the mobilizational techniques were intended to exert pressure for rapid social transformation. This distinction was, however, blurred by Ingrao's call at the Sixteenth Congress for a program that would galvanize moderates to vote for the left in the next parliamentary elections: "Let us say to the Socialists, to all the forces of the left and of progress, why don't we compete together in ripping away [*strappare*] votes from the DC?"[125]

Berlinguer, in his March 1983 congress report as well as over the previous half-decade or so, had tried to strike a balance between the pragmatic and mobilizational wings of his party. A similar balance appeared to characterize the PCI leadership after the Sixteenth Congress. For example, while Ingrao's prestige had grown immensely, the pivotal position of "coordinator" of the Secretariat was assumed by two men, a long-time functionary, Ugo Pecchioli, and Reichlin, an upcoming leader of the pragmatic innovators—his association with Ingrao in the 1960s notwithstanding.[126] The paramount question, however, was no longer simply the composition of the leadership but the way in which the new party rules would affect the decision-making process. Would the PCI rank and file remain a disciplined cohort imbued with a vision articulated by the party elite? Or would it become a more loosely organized set of opinion groups with a multiply defined reforming ethos? In short, would *trasparenza* lead to *trasformismo?*

During the fifteen months between the Sixteenth PCI Congress and Berlinguer's sudden death of a cerebral hemorrhage on June 11, 1984, Soviet–PCI relations remained in the same tense state that had existed since the late spring of 1982. Neither the rise of Yuri Andropov to the general secretaryship of the CPSU in November 1982 nor Konstantin Chernenko's succession after Andropov's death in February 1984 altered this picture.

At the Sixteenth Congress itself, the exchanges between the Italian leaders and the Soviet delegation, which included Zagladin and was led by *Pravda*'s editor, Viktor Afanasev, were characterized by "a frankness without precedent"—to use Zagladin's own words from a postcongress interview. While he continued to deny the existence of a "rupture," he also rejected out of hand the position reiterated by Berlinguer at the congress that "the USSR has a direct responsibility for the worsening of the international situation."[127] The unusually limited coverage of the

125. Text in *l'Unità*, March 5, 1983, 6.
126. Alberto Stabile, "Berlinguer sceglie due vice," *la Repubblica*, March 16, 1983, 7.
127. Sandro Viola, "Zagladin parla del Pci 'Berlinguer ci tratta male ma non siamo alla rottura," *la Repubblica*, March 9, 1983, 7. Cf. Vera Vegetti, "I sovietici ci dicono: ecco i punti di accordo e quelli di disaccordo," *l'Unità*, March 7, 1983, 3.

Sixteenth Congress in the Soviet press, while nonpolemical in tone, distorted the views of Berlinguer almost beyond recognition. In a nutshell, *Pravda* conveyed the impression that he wholeheartedly supported Soviet foreign policy.[128]

Thereafter the Soviet media followed their 1980–81 pattern of what might best be called semidirect polemics against the PCI. In articles aimed at a domestic audience, Soviet publicists did not attack the Italian party by name. They simply left no room for doubt as to the identity of their target by lambasting such concepts as socialist pluralism, the *terza via,* and the new internationalism. This type of slur appeared most often in journals of limited circulation, for instance *Rabochii klass i sovremennyi mir;* and they tended to be voiced by individuals who had since the early 1970s been identified with an ultrasectarian approach to Western Communist affairs.[129] Another veiled polemical technique was devised by Smirnov. In the March 1983 issue of *Voprosy istorii KPSS* he praised Togliatti's unqualified opposition to NATO, friendship with the Soviet Union, commitment to international class solidarity, and praise of the October Revolution in what was not only a pat simplification of the late leader's views but an obvious rebuke of Berlinguer.[130]

By way of contrast, in early 1984 *New Times* published an "open letter" from the Afghan People's Democratic Party to the PCI which explicitly denounced a *l'Unità* series on Afghanistan as well as Rubbi for his formal endorsement of it. (Rubbi, it may be recalled, was then head of the Italian party's foreign section.) The crux of the "open letter" was that the PCI's assessment of developments in Afghanistan coincided "with the position of Western imperialist quarters."[131]

Pravda meanwhile confined itself to veiled jibes. In January 1984 it welcomed the formation of a splinter "Communist Party of Spain" by sectarian defectors from the mainstream PCE. The CPSU daily approvingly reported the new party's self-depiction as an "integral part" of the international Communist movement, one that was bent upon unmasking "Eurocommunism" and upon placing the blame for current international tensions "entirely" on United States imperialism.[132] A week before Berlinguer's death, moreover, a *Pravda* commentary by Zagladin (on the fifteenth anniversary of the June 1969 Moscow conference) urged the

128. "Na sezde IKP," *Pravda,* March 3, 1983, 4. The only informative and comprehensive article on the congress focused on Cossutta's speech; see *l'Unità,* March 7, 1983, 4.

129. See, for example, I. M. Krivoguz, "Strategiia i taktika kompartii stran razvitogo kapitalizma," *Rabochii klass i sovremennyi mir,* no. 2 (March–April 1984):164–75 at 170–71.

130. G. P. Smirnov, "Palmiro Toliatti—boretz za mir, demokratiiu i sotsializm," *Voprosy istorii KPSS,* no. 3 (March 1983):111–14.

131. Text in *New Times,* no. 4 (January 1984):32.

132. V. Chernyshev and B. Petrov, "Za edinstvo kommunistov," *Pravda,* January 16, 1984, 4.

Communist parties of the world not only to cherish Marxism-Leninism, democratic centralism, and their vanguard role in alliances but also to beware of becoming some kind of "new party" of the old social democratic type.[133] The allusion to the PCI was unmistakable.

The PCI, for its part, assumed a public posture of cool detachment bordering on indifference toward the Soviet Union. All the while, Berlinguer underscored his party's disengagement from the Moscow-aligned Communist movement by spending his summer 1983 holiday in the People's Republic of China. Accompanied by Rubbi on the two-week trip, he spent much of his time conferring with the top Chinese leaders; and he was accompanied on sightseeing trips to Nanking and Shanghai by no less a figure than General Secretary Hu Yaobang.[134]

At the same time, the PCI's tendency toward an evenhanded assessment of the two superpowers which was so much in evidence at the start of the 1980s gave way to more frequent and virulent criticism of Washington than Moscow. Nevertheless, in *l'Unità* commentaries and Berlinguer's speeches, superpower rivalry rather than a global two-camp ideological cleavage remained the key explanation for international tensions, and "Reaganism" rather than imperialism stood out as the chief villain. Berlinguer particularly stressed these themes in a Central Committee report in late November 1983,[135] just after West Germany's decision to accept American Pershing II missiles. And the solution he suggested for easing the East–West stalemate was then more than ever the assertion of greater European autonomy.

Shortly thereafter, in mid-December 1983, Berlinguer embarked upon a personal diplomatic mission to shore up European détente in the face of the imminent INF installation by the United States. He first visited Romania, which had already denounced both the American move and the Soviet reponse of stationing missiles in East Germany and Czechoslovakia. Berlinguer then proceeded to East Berlin where his meeting with Erich Honecker was billed as the first reunion in seven years (since the East Berlin Summit) between two comrades who had known each other well in the early 1950s as activists in the Communist World Federation of Democratic Youth. Press accounts of their six hours of talks carried little by way of substance except for one intriguing detail: Honecker and his visitor spent one and a half hours together without the presence of East Germany's secret service in Berlinguer's quarters. As Honecker was reported to have said to his startled guards, "This is today an extra-ter-

133. V. Zagladin, "Vazhneishii faktor sotsialnogo progressa: O roli i perspektivakh kommunisticheskogo dvizheniia," *Pravda,* June 5, 1984, 14–15 at 15.

134. Kevin Devlin, "Berlinguer's Visit to China Strengthens 'New Internationalism,'" *Radio Free Europe Research,* background report no. 212, September 2, 1983.

135. Text in *l'Unità,* November 26, 1983, 9.

ritorial place; I have been invited to have a drink for old times' sake."[136] We may assume that Berlinguer used that occasion to encourage Honecker's decision to pursue détente between East and West Germany despite the INF controversy. (The subsequent surge in ties between the East and West German governments during the first half of 1984, it may be recalled, elicited Moscow's manifest displeasure, leading finally to the cancellation of a planned precedent-shattering trip by Honecker to Bonn.) The Italian party's European strategy was taking on a new dimension.

One week later Berlinguer went to Belgrade for similar discussions. In addition to the INF issue, the question of a new world Communist conference was also broached. Whereupon both Berlinguer and his Yugoslavian interlocutors announced their sharp opposition to any such idea and their refusal to participate in such a meeting.[137] Meanwhile, in early December 1983 a PCI *Direzione* delegation had traveled to Moscow for talks that were described as a technical exchange of economic views but that reportedly also laid the groundwork for a future meeting between Berlinguer and Andropov, the latter's health permitting. We can only speculate that had those talks taken place, Berlinguer would have expressed the same opinions he did on his East European tour.

Upon Berlinguer's untimely death, political figures across the Italian political spectrum hailed the contribution he had made to Italian democracy and stability. Such had not been the case when Togliatti died twenty years earlier. Then the outpouring of grief was a family affair among Communists. Berlinguer's passing, in contrast, was mourned by many as a loss to the Italian Republic.

Moscow joined in the commemoration, devoting considerable press coverage to Berlinguer's accomplishments and none whatsoever to the Soviet–PCI *strappo*. Mikhail Gorbachev, already viewed as a likely successor to Chernenko, led the CPSU delegation to Berlinguer's funeral. Accompanied by Zagladin, Gorbachev was affable and outgoing with PCI leaders and Italian state officials alike. During the actual ceremony in the huge Piazza San Giovanni, he was overheard to remark: "All of Italy is here."[138] It remained to be seen how the impression of a people in mourning would affect the upcoming Soviet leader's view of Italian communism.

Meanwhile, the task of choosing Berlinguer's successor had already begun. Again the contrast with what had occurred twenty years earlier was striking. Not only was there no deputy general secretary waiting in the wings, but Alessandro Natta, the man eventually chosen, had gone into

136. Ugo Baduel, "Il viaggio di Berlinguer a Est," *l'Unità*, December 15, 1983, 1 and 20.
137. See the report by Ugo Baduel in *l'Unità*, December 24, 1983, 1 and 24.
138. m. f., "Gorbaciov: 'Qui c'è tutta l'Italia,'" *la Repubblica*, June 14, 1984, 4; cf. Alberto Stabile, "Questa volta il Cremlino si è inchinato," ibid.

semiretirement after the Sixteenth PCI Congress. Far from being an "organic" process, a group of elder party statesmen undertook to consult individually the 244 members of the PCI Central Committee and Central Control Commission. A large consensus quickly developed in favor of Natta. However, in line with the procedural innovations of the 1983 congress, there was unprecedented openness regarding the runners-up and the support they commanded.[139] To all appearances, the sixty-six-year-old Natta met with widespread approval only because he had always toed the Berlinguer line and because he was seen as a transitional leader. He himself intimated in his acceptance speech that he would step down from the general secretaryship at the next party congress.[140] In the interim, the cadres of what we might aptly call the *partito nuovo II* could be expected to influence the formation of the leadership that would take command after Craxi, after Reagan, after the Soviet succession had been clarified.

On June 17, 1984—some ten days before the top PCI deliberative bodies elected Natta party chief by a vote of 227 yeas and 11 abstentions, elections were held throughout Italy for the European Parliament. The Christian Democrats' decline by over five percentage points in the June 1983 parliamentary elections had paved the way for Craxi to become Italy's first Socialist premier. Nevertheless, his party had only one-third the popular support enjoyed by the DC and PCI in 1983 (11.4 percent compared to 32.9 percent and 29.9 percent respectively). Under these circumstances, government by a five-party coalition (of Christian Democrats, Socialists, Social Democrats, Republicans, and Liberals) which was dominated by the DC even if headed by Craxi raised the specter of a political stalemate. For the PCI, on the other hand, there was the prospect of eventually recouping its own 1979 electoral losses as voters became disenchanted with establishment immobilism. The results of the elections to the European Parliament pointed in this direction. In contrast to the first direct elections to that body in 1979, when the PCI ran almost seven percentage points behind the DC, in the June 1984 contest the PCI tally jumped to 33.3 percent while the DC dropped to 33.0 percent. For the first time in the history of the Italian Republic, the Communists edged ahead of the Christian Democrats in a nationwide vote. Only time would tell whether this was a sign of homage to the late Berlinguer or of support for the PCI.

139. Giorgio Rossi, "Dietro le quinte del conclave rosso," *la Repubblica,* June 27, 1984, 4; cf. Ugo Pecchioli's speech to the PCI Central Committee regarding the selection procedures, *l'Unità,* June 27, 1984, 3.
140. Text in *l'Unità,* June 27, 1984, 1 and 3.

CONCLUSION

O ne notable conclusion we can draw from the history of the Soviet–PCI relationship is that the stamp Togliatti placed upon the political profile of the PCI elite during the Stalin era goes far in explaining the post-Stalin divergences between the PCI and Moscow. This same finding also sheds light on a central question of comparative Communist studies: namely, the contrast between the Italian and French Communist parties since 1956.[1] If the PCI leaders became radical innovators, the PCF leaders remained for the most part fairly sectarian on issues of alliance strategy, party organization, and relations with Moscow. And these differences are traceable in part to the fact that the PCF under Thorez was fully Stalinized, the PCI under Togliatti only partially so.

It is common to speak of the adaptation of nonruling Communist parties to their national political environments. This approach has only limited explanatory power, however, when it comes to fathoming the post-Stalin contrast between the PCI and the PCF, or between the Spanish and Portuguese Communists for that matter. For the postwar political systems of Italy and France were almost as similar to one another as were those of Spain and Portugal: that is, multiparty parliamentary democracies in the case of the former and traditional authoritarian dictatorships in the case of the latter. Yet in the 1970s it was the Spanish Communists, not the French, who joined the Italians in forging an enduring Eurocommunist entente, while the Portuguese Communists stood out as intransigent sec-

---

1. For two penetrating comparative analyses of the postwar PCI and PCF that focus on "environmental" considerations, see Sidney Tarrow, "Communism in Italy and France: Adaptation and Change," in *Communism in Italy and France,* ed. Blackmer and Tarrow (Princeton: Princeton University Press, 1975), 575–640; and Peter Lange, "The French and Italian Communist Parties: Postwar Strategy and Domestic Society," in *Radicalism in the Contemporary Age,* ed. Seweryn Bialer, 3 vols. (Boulder, Col.: Westview, 1977), 3:159–99.

tarians. This seeming paradox suggests the need for a carefully differentiated analysis of the historical development of any Communist party that had its origins in the Comintern–Stalin era. Such has been the basic premise of this book. And it is with this perspective in mind that I turn to these concluding remarks.

On the eve of Berlinguer's death in June 1984 the PCI's public attitude toward the CPSU was one of cool detachment. The Soviets were only slightly less reserved. True, Zagladin had tried to paper over the *strappo* (the "rip" in relations) caused by the explosive Soviet–PCI recriminations of early 1982. And in December 1983 Berlinguer reportedly sought a meeting with Andropov as part of his transnational diplomacy to save East-West détente in Europe in the face of the American INF installations. But these conciliatory gestures did not prevent Soviet publicists from taking frequent, if esoteric, potshots at the policies of the Italian party. Nor did they deter PCI commentators from coolly dissecting the post-Brezhnev succession in the Soviet Union while their superiors pursued the party's vision of a Europe transcending East–West bipolarity.

The talk of a Berlinguer–Andropov summit nevertheless underscored one of the basic questions surrounding the Soviet–PCI *strappo:* namely, what were the prospects that the rift between the two parties might be overcome? This, in turn, leads us back to the roots of the estrangement.

The PCI's dismay over martial law in Poland was the immediate cause of the CPSU–PCI polemical firestorm in the early winter of 1981–82. Disagreements over Soviet conduct in Eastern Europe had, however, been a major irritant between the two parties ever since the Czechoslovakian crisis of 1968. The sources of the Soviet Union's conduct in its Western borderlands are fairly familiar. East European reform movements, by challenging Soviet hegemony, posed a danger to both the cohesion of the WTO and the legitimacy of CPSU rule at home. Whether the reformers were of the Dubček or Solidarity variety, the men in the Kremlin viewed them as a threat to the national security and domestic stability of the Soviet party-state.

At first glance, *Realpolitik* also suffices to explain the PCI's unqualified condemnation of Soviet domination over its East European clients. For one thing, the Italian Communist policy makers feared, at least from 1968 onward, that Soviet suppression of liberalizing forces in Eastern Europe could lend an aura of legitimacy to American support for conservative opposition to Communist power sharing in Italy. Indeed, the Soviet-backed crackdown on Solidarity by *Polish* security forces must surely have revived the Italian Communist leaders' Cold War specter of a U.S.-backed reactionary coup d'état in Italy. The PCI's high-sounding rhetoric against superpower intervention in European affairs, East and West, thus had a self-serving ring. This was particularly true in view of the United

States military presence in Italy and the multiple ties between American and Italian conservative circles that had existed since the earliest post-Fascist years. The contrast between Italy and France in this regard is striking. For, in addition to de Gaulle's withdrawal from NATO's military structure in 1966, French conservatives were never closely linked to their American counterparts.

At the same time, from the Italian Communist perspective the threat of foreign intervention did not come exclusively from the West. The eventuality of Soviet action against a maverick PCI in power could not be ruled out, certainly not if the long-stated Communist goal of the dissolution of NATO and the Warsaw Pact should actually come to pass. The Red Army's march into Czechoslovakia and the alarm it sparked concerning Soviet intentions toward Yugoslavia brought that message home to the Berlinguer group. And it surely contributed to their decision in the early 1970s to cease calling for Italy's withdrawal from NATO. For without the defensive "shield" of the Atlantic Alliance, a reform-minded Communist government in Italy could be as vulnerable to Soviet military intimidation as was the Dubček regime in Czechoslovakia, especially if Yugoslavia should first succumb to Soviet blandishments or force in the post-Tito era. Here the case of the PCF serves as a counterpoint to illustrate the argument. With France more geopolitically "distant" from the Soviet Union, and with West Germany rather than Yugoslavia occupying the space between France and the Soviet bloc, the PCF could more readily shrug off the Soviet-led invasion of Czechoslovakia and subsequent military maneuvers around Poland.

A final consideration must have also entered into the calculations of the PCI policy makers. It was obvious that the credibility of their party's pluralist rhetoric hinged, in the eyes of many of Italy's voters and foreign allies, on their readiness to denounce repression in the Soviet domain. And without such credibility the Italian Communists could scarcely expect to gain the acquiescence of domestic (and foreign) conservatives essential for entry into government at the national level. Nor would such government participation be acceptable to Rome's NATO partners. For the PCI, unlike the PCF in the cabinet of François Mitterrand, would be a major force in any conceivable coalition arrangement, even a government of national unity including the Christian Democrats.

There is, however, another dimension to the PCI's profile than political expediency: this has to do with conviction. The Italian Communists, as a nonruling party, have plainly sought to change rather than preserve the status quo in their own country. There is thus a fundamental psychological chasm between them and the average East European *apparatchik* that is all too frequently overlooked. To an extent unknown in the Soviet bloc since the immediate postwar years, the PCI cadres' adherence to the Communist movement has been motivated by the dream of social transformation rather than careerism, by the goal of collective betterment rather than personal advancement.[2] What this means in policy terms is that the *partito nuovo* favored a redistribution of wealth; but in addition, survey data suggest that ranking PCI functionaries, at least by the late 1960s, perceived the just society in Italy as one that combined radical economic reforms with participatory democracy and a fair degree of political competition and compromise.[3] As Robert Putnam aptly phrased it, they were becoming "constitutional radicals."[4] Not only that, but an ever increasing number of local cadres after 1968 came to share the party elite's judgment that a pluralist form of socialism was also more appropriate in Eastern Europe. They were, in other words, genuinely supportive of political liberalization in Czechoslovakia and independent trade unions in Poland and not simply fearful of what the suppression of those movements would mean for their own political fortunes.

Where this line of reasoning breaks down is in its failure to explain why the French and Portuguese Communists, for example, did *not* combine their championship of economic reform with concern for democratic values—the PCF's short-lived flirtation with Eurocommunism notwithstanding. For commitment rather than careerism presumably characterized the French and Portuguese militants every bit as much as those of the PCI. Here, of course, we run into the danger of circular reasoning: one could argue on the basis of *Realpolitik* that the French and Portuguese Communists had no need to embrace pluralist norms. They were not close enough to Soviet power, in terms of geopolitical location, to feel threatened by it. Nor were they close enough to national power, in terms of voter appeal, to vie for the support of the democratic center.

The key to the above paradox lies in the fact that after World War II the PCI elite made a conscious choice, unlike their French comrades, to vie for the democratic center. For reasons relating to the character of the *partito nuovo* they created, moreover, they eventually had the prospect of joining the democratic center. An analysis of the political profile of both the pre-1945 Italian Communist elite and the postwar *partito nuovo* is thus essential to an understanding of the PCI's later evolution and confrontation with Moscow. Much of this book has been devoted to just this task.

To sum up what I have written, in late March 1944 Togliatti returned to Italy from wartime exile in Moscow with two objectives in mind. The first

2. For data to this effect derived from a survey of delegates to the 1979 federation congresses of the PCI, see Marcello Fedele, "Il Pci e il suo sociale," in *L'identità comunista: I militanti, le strutture, la cultura del Pci,* ed. Aris Accornero, Renato Mannheimer, and Chiara Sebastiani (Rome: Editori Riuniti, 1983), 369–84.

3. Robert Putnam, "The Italian Communist Politician," in *Communism in Italy and France,* ed. Blackmer and Tarrow, 173–217.

4. Ibid., 211–13.

was to give the PCI a reformist orientation, one that would combine the goal of socioeconomic change with adherence to democratic procedures. The second was to transform his party into a mass political organization through an open admissions policy so broad that not even a commitment to Marxism-Leninism was required for membership. Togliatti was able to impose a policy of democratic reformism on the PCI's domestic ranks for a number of reasons: the inchoate organizational state of the party, the express encouragement (and directives, I surmise) of the Soviet leadership, and his unparalleled prestige as a former Comintern secretary. But what was most important for the future development of the PCI was Togliatti's own commitment to this moderate line. And that derived from a blend of expediency and conviction not dissimilar to the complex of motives undergirding the policies of the Berlinguer leadership three to four decades later.

Togliatti, like Berlinguer, feared the reactionary backlash that a push for socialist revolution might provoke. Initially his concern centered on internal Italian political elements, those that had welcomed the rise of Mussolini and profited from Fascist rule until the bitter reckoning of military defeat in World War II. The potential clout and ruthlessness of domestic reaction was, for Togliatti, the basic lesson to be learned from Italy's Fascist ordeal. It was a lesson reinforced by the Spanish Civil War and magnified by the enormity of the military backing given by Hitler and Mussolini to General Franco's anti-Republican crusade. In the winter of 1944–45, moreover, Togliatti again saw what foreign intervention in support of domestic conservatism could mean as the British army crushed the leftist Greek Resistance movement's bid for control of Athens. The specter of external aid to the traditional Italian establishment became, finally, a reality as the American presence in Italy escalated with the onset of the Cold War.

All of this contributed mightily to Togliatti's formulation of the PCI's postwar policies of backing the creation of a constitutional democracy and extending the Communist presence throughout Italian society by seeking middle-class and Catholic *members* as well as voters. This was a strategy that was rooted in Italy's Fascist experience. And its compelling logic was underscored by the conversion of Luigi Longo, Togliatti's long-time critic on the left, to his views.

Togliatti, like Longo and Berlinguer in later years, did not, however, act from *Realpolitik* alone. He was a convinced Marxist intellectual and Communist militant. Playing by the democratic rules of the game was but the means to the creation of an anticapitalist social order. At the same time, he was hard put to define the precise contours of a future socialist Italy. For, just as the lessons of thirty years of Soviet domination over Eastern Europe were not to be lost on Berlinguer, the lessons of Stalinism had not been lost on Togliatti. His revulsion against the Stalinization of the Comintern has been recounted in Part One. His reservations regarding Stalin's domestic tyranny, while more difficult to document, may be discerned from his passing comments to trusted associates and his yearning for Spanish democracy and PCE autonomy while Comintern adviser in Spain.

All the same, when the chips were down Togliatti's loyalty to the Communist cause outweighed his doubts about Stalinism. In 1928–29 he put up a good fight against the maneuvers of Stalin's henchmen; but in the end he gave in to the Comintern's abrupt turn to the left and engineered the purge of his dissenting comrades rather than face expulsion himself. In the mid-1940s he supported democracy in Italy and sought an autonomous, if nebulous, Italian path to socialism; but as United States political and financial support for anticommunism in Italy grew in tandem with the Cold War, he began to fear that social revolution was possible only in areas occupied by the Red Army. In 1956 he deplored the tenacious sectarianism of the Hungarian Stalinists; but he nonetheless endorsed the Soviet armed suppression of the student-worker rebels in Budapest. Soviet–American rivalry in Europe was still a zero-sum game from his perspective, probably because prior American conduct in Italy led him to believe Moscow's allegations that Washington had instigated the Hungarian uprising. When all is said and done, Togliatti was a complex thinker, astute politician, and well-intentioned man. But, to repeat what I have said before, for him the end justified the means, even in a movement brutalized by Stalin and his successors.

It was essentially this Leninist facet of Togliatti's legacy that his own successors ultimately rejected. But they were able and willing to do so thanks in large part to Togliatti's *non-Leninist* attributes: his reformist and eventual polycentric vision of global trends toward socialism; his concept of a mass party bound together by a political platform rather than an obligatory ideology; and his conciliatory manner of handling political dissent among the PCI elite in the late 1930s and mid-1940s.

We must not lose sight of the fact that Togliatti's *partito nuovo* represented a novel departure from the Leninist tradition. The criterion of Marxist-Leninist orthodoxy went by the board as upwards of one million Italians flocked to the PCI's banner between April and December 1945. The same kind of explosive growth would, to be sure, soon take place in the East European people's democracies. But there the analogy ends. For the Italian Communist leaders did not have the coercive apparatus of the East European Stalinists (or the PCF's numerous Stalinized cadres from the prewar era) to mold their raw recruits into ideological conformists. Nor did they require that new members have working-class credentials.

Indeed, virtually half the PCI's postwar *Direzione* were themselves from the middle class or intelligentsia.

Togliatti's new party was clearly suited to serve as a vast electoral machine penetrating deeply into every corner of Italian society. Still, Thorez was just as preoccupied as Togliatti with garnering votes—and at first much more successful in doing so. The PCF won about 28 percent of the popular vote in 1946, the PCI under 19 percent. Yet the PCF was a thoroughly Leninist organization whose size never approached that of the PCI.

Electoral concerns are therefore not sufficient to explain the unique character of the *partito nuovo*. Togliatti probably also conceived of his open party as a riposte to the prewar humiliations inflicted on himself and his colleagues by Moscow. Its impressive membership was bound to guarantee that the PCI would never again become a butt of public Soviet ridicule on account of ineffectuality. Perhaps more to the point, strength in numbers, and hence in resources, was a precondition for the autonomy Togliatti so desired. But his intentions aside, in the end the unprecedented size, social diversity, and doctrinal slackness of the *partito nuovo* facilitated the emergence of a successor generation of Italian Communists that differed dramatically from most of their European counterparts.

A related circumstance that contributed to the Italian party's future development was the character of its *Direzione* during the postwar Stalin years. This was a time when other Communist leaderships were being rent by internecine clashes, outlandish allegations, expulsions in Western Europe, and show-trials and executions in Eastern Europe. In the PCI, by contrast, conciliation triumphed over purge. From 1944 onward Togliatti sought to blend into a cohesive whole the diverse tendencies among the party's interwar elite: old-guard Bolsheviks who had spent years in Fascist prisons and camps; former Parisian exiles smarting from repeated Moscow-inspired recriminations; and younger cadres tapped to rebuild the domestic network after 1939. Few of these individuals had been fully Stalinized. Yet all joined together to form the executive body of the PCI during the last bitter years of Stalinism, from late 1945 until the dictator's death in 1953. Not until 1954 did Togliatti begin to reshape the composition of the *Direzione* in his own image, and then only by means of quiet demotions and ceremonial promotions, not public denigration. This, then, was the leadership style to which the younger cadres of the *partito nuovo*, men like Berlinguer and Natta, were exposed during their politically formative years in the late 1940s and early 1950s.

If the organizational character of the *Direzione* was conducive to a freer circulation of ideas and thus to innovation in the long run, the public philosophy of anti-Americanism and pro-Sovietism that the Togliatti group inculcated in the *partito nuovo* during the late 1940s was not. This credo served as a convenient surrogate for grassroots ideological uniformity. It was, in addition, readily assimilated at all levels of the party by virtue of the official United States role in the political ostracism of the PCI during those years. But it also obstructed Togliatti's pursuit in 1956 of a polycentric vision of revolutionary strategy and international Communist organization, not to mention his call for investigation into the roots of Stalinism. The reflexive pro-Sovietism of the *partito nuovo,* when added to Moscow's readiness to criticize Togliatti publicly and the PCI leadership's isolation within the European Communist movement, deterred an open challenge to the CPSU's political and ideological rectitude in the immediate wake of the "unforgettable 1956."

During the decade and a half after 1956, however, this situation was to change. In the first place, the PCI policy makers were beset by a number of organizational and conceptual dilemmas. The root of the problem was that there seemed to be little prospect of advancing from the post-Fascist democratic stage they had so willingly endorsed in the mid-1940s to the socialist polity of their dreams. As Italy entered a period of economic growth and consumerism, the party's membership declined—especially among industrial workers—while many of its younger intellectuals were drawn to the radical mobilizational ethos and antibureaucratic tenets of the European new left. To further complicate the picture, the DC–PSI agreement on a center-left coalition formula in the early 1960s circumscribed the PCI's domestic maneuverability just when its electoral appeal was increasing and clerical anticommunism was beginning to recede under Pope John XXIII. Soon thereafter, the conservative Italian backlash against the student-worker mobilizations of 1968–69 rekindled PCI fears of a reactionary threat to democracy. The subsequent military coup against the Allende regime in Chile intensified this kind of anxiety.

These considerations, taken as a whole, finally led Berlinguer to transform Togliatti's transitional brand of reformism into a strategy for building socialism incrementally within the existing Italian political and legal system. Such, in fact, was the enduring meaning of the *compromesso storico* and the Eurocommunist rhetoric that accompanied it.

Well before this occurred, moreover, the PCI launched its challenge to Soviet centralism in the Communist world. It became the champion of autonomy and conciliation, the organizational principles with which Togliatti had so long been identified in inner Communist circles. For precisely in the early 1960s, when the domestic Italian situation all but precluded forward momentum, conditions in the international Communist movement invited this kind of innovative role. Foremost among those conditions was, of course, the outbreak of the Sino-Soviet conflict. Romania's national self-assertion and Khrushchev's renewed search for good relations with Yugoslavia were a few of the related developments. Circumstances were thus ripe both for the creation of an autonomist coalition of Communist parties and for Soviet concessions to such a coalition. Indeed, the CPSU leaders were prepared to bend over backwards to win allies in their rivalry with Peking. By the same token, however, the autonomists were determined to prevent a repetition of what Stalin had done to Tito. Mindful of the pressures for conformity that the Cominform's expulsion of Yugoslavia had unleashed, they opposed Soviet efforts to orchestrate a collective denunciation of Maoism at a world Communist meeting. In all of this the PCI stood out as the most ardent advocate of conciliation, of reasoned dialogue rather than confrontation and anthema, in handling interparty disputes.

The PCI's defense of autonomy and conciliation was grounded in the historical preferences of Togliatti and his associates. But it was plainly also linked to domestic political considerations. Success in projecting a credible image of autonomy, of independence from Moscow, could help the Communists break out of their political isolation. It could enhance their legitimacy at home by counteracting the pervasive center-right charges that they were merely agents of Soviet interests.

On the other hand, the political profile of the by then aging *partito nuovo* ruled out *disengagement* from the Moscow-oriented Communist world. Well after the Warsaw Pact invasion of Czechoslovakia in 1968, a third of the Italian middle-level cadres still endorsed the Soviet Union's conduct in that regard, while another third harbored reservations about the Dubček regime. Autonomy of action combined with loyalty to a joint cause—"unity in diversity" as the PCI put it—was as far as the party leadership could go without disorienting its militants. The PCI's decision to attend the international Communist conference convened by the CPSU in June 1969—after a half decade of interparty wrangling over whether and under what conditions to hold it—should be seen in this light. Berlinguer's presence in Moscow (he was then deputy general secretary) reassured the members of the *partito nuovo* of their party's allegiance to the Communist world despite its condemnation of the Soviet-led invasion of Czechoslovakia.

Disengagement *from* the Moscow-centered Communist movement—not autonomy *within* it—was, however, the course ultimately chosen by Berlinguer. Disengagement was indeed the crux of the PCI's new internationalism. Exactly when Berlinguer settled on that course we do not know. But he must have begun at least to contemplate such an eventuality soon after the Czechoslovakian crisis and his designation as general secretary in 1972.

Several circumstances support this conjecture. The first is that the human corpus of the PCI was radically transformed during the Berlinguer years. The postwar *partito nuovo* gave way to a *partito nuovo II*. By the early 1980s well over 50 percent of all members had joined the party within the past two decades,[5] while at least half the federation cadres had done so *only after 1968*. If there were many reasons for the turnover in members, the turnover in *cadres* could not have occurred without the sanction of the *berlingueriani*. Second, a concerted effort was made to inculcate this *partito nuovo II* with a new view of Soviet–PCI relations. Studies of Soviet and PCI history that approached Western standards of scholarship and objectivity began to proliferate during the first half of the 1970s. The party press started to criticize with regularity the flaws of the contemporary Soviet political and economic system in the mid-1970s. The drawn-out preparations for the June 1976 East Berlin summit provided numerous occasions for authoritative figures like Pajetta to proclaim the PCI leaders' insistence on autonomy, dialogue, and candor in their relations with the CPSU. And at the level of grassroots agitprop, the Lenin posters and Russian *chastushki* (folksy jingles) that dominated neighborhood festivals of *l'Unità* in the early 1970s were replaced by Chinese bric-a-brac and Western rock music toward the end of the decade.

If the PCI's process of disengagement became somewhat erratic during the party's abortive accommodation with the Christian Democratic establishment in 1977–78, it regained momentum after the Soviet Union flexed its military muscles in Afghanistan. At the same time, the very idea of disengagement acquired an aura of ideological legitimacy as a result of the PCI's rapprochement with the post-Mao Chinese leaders in April 1980. The opportunity for disengagement *in principle* was, finally, offered by the declaration of martial law in Poland. This is not to say that similar opportunities were not present in 1968 and 1956 but only that the PCI leaders were, on those occasions, either not inclined (1956) or not yet able (1968) to take advantage of them.

All the while, the alienation of the PCI policy makers from their Soviet counterparts was surely heightened by their realization that Moscow viewed the West European Communist parties much as Lenin had viewed the Bolsheviks: namely, "Better fewer but better." What the CPSU— both the statesmen and the ideologues—wanted from the PCI (as from the French and Spanish Communists) was that it grow in orthodoxy, not in numbers. Given a choice, the Kremlin leaders—if their past conduct was any clue to the future—would prefer to see the Italian Communists remain in the opposition rather than become a coalition partner in the national government of Italy. The PCI's experience of the mid-1960s suggested that the absence of a realistic perspective for sharing power could deprive

5. Enzo Vittorio Trapanese, "Relazione di ricerca," in *Il PCI allo specchio*, ed. Renato Mieli (Milan: Rizzoli Editore, 1983), 48–173 at 120.

the party of the élan needed to attract younger followers. It could also make its ranks more susceptible to the kind of factionalism experienced by the Spanish Communists. From Moscow's viewpoint, both such trends might well increase the Italian party's vulnerability to Soviet manipulation and influence. By way of contrast, enhanced electoral support for the PCI and the attainment of formal governmental responsibility could accelerate its evolution toward reformism at home and Europeanism abroad, if only to allay the fears of Italy's NATO allies and domestic conservatives.

The foregoing discussion of Soviet intentions may be a bit speculative. But it is supported by a large body of circumstantial evidence. The history of CPSU relations with the West European Communists during the 1970s and early 1980s, as during the Comintern era and postwar Stalinism, shows that a nonruling party's support for the foreign policy and ideological credentials of the Soviet state was all that mattered to Moscow. Indeed, the Kremlin's very insistence that socialism in the West conform to the CPSU's "general laws" exposed its basic disinterest in a revolutionary victory. For a revolution supportive of the "general laws" as defined by the Soviets was bound to fail. This was the lesson of the Portuguese drama of 1975. Even the CPSU's most intransigent sectarians must have realized that such a strategy could succeed only in areas of the Third World where discredited social-political orders and radical minorities dependent on Soviet military backing replicated the postwar East European experience.

Meanwhile, as the PCI leaders sought to disengage their party from the Moscow-oriented Communist movement, their evolving European strategy appeared as an alternative to the Soviet connection. In 1969, the year Berlinguer became deputy general secretary, the Italian Communists entered the European Parliament and began informal contacts with the German Social Democrats. By the mid-1970s party foreign affairs spokesmen cited closer ties to European socialists and center leftists as a key objective of their "new internationalism." The PCI leaders' condemnation of superpower "bloc politics," which became ever more insistent after the Soviet invasion of Afghanistan, harmonized with their quest for a *European* identity. This could also be said of Berlinguer's designation of Western Europe as the new epicenter of the global march toward socialism after the military crackdown in Poland. Berlinguer's apparent encouragement of Erich Honecker's spring 1984 rapprochement with Bonn fit the same pattern. Over all, the PCI seemed to be developing the idea of an autonomous Europe that would transcend East–West bipolarity by preserving détente and working out a "third way" to socialism.

The Italian Communists needed the European strategy for much the same reason that Tito needed nonalignment and the Chinese Communists the Third World after their respective breaks with the CPSU. For the sake of ideological coherence, the PCI wished to avoid undue association with the United States as it detached itself from its traditional association with Moscow. Whether its European strategy would improve its domestic electoral appeal, however, would depend on the extent to which young Italians, like their peers elsewhere on the Continent, were shifting from Atlanticism to Europeanism.

Is there, then, any likelihood that the PCI's estrangement from Moscow might be overcome? As of the time of Berlinguer's death, several considerations militated against any substantial change in the relationship between the two parties. With regard to the PCI, the political profile of the *partito nuovo II* reinforced the historically rooted mentality of the party elite. The social composition of the middle-level functionaries had come to resemble that of the traditional leadership circles in that individuals of proletarian and bourgeois intellectual origin were equally represented. More to the point, many of the post-1968 "bureaucrat-intellectuals"[6] among the PCI's cadres had been influenced by the new left mobilizations of the late 1960s. They had been exposed to the antisuperpower bias that had made many new leftists sympathetic to Maoism and hostile to Moscow. This helps explain why the delegates to the PCI's 100-odd federation congresses in early 1983 were overwhelmingly supportive of Berlinguer's position on the Soviet Union. By the same token, the post-1968 recruits had also been influenced by the antibureaucratic ethos of the new left movements. This explains their support for Ingrao's motion on *trasparenza* at those same federation meetings. Yet *trasparenza,* or the disclosure and submission of leadership disagreements to their respective deliberative bodies for resolution, meant among other things to imbue the party as a whole with the PCI elite's historic "opportunism of conciliation." Finally, whereas the party's post-1968 members were drawn to the Communist banner for a variety of reasons, it is a safe bet that only those who shared the Berlinguer group's general outlook enjoyed rapid promotion to the federation offices. All these considerations, in short, augured widespread acceptance by the *partito nuovo II* of the critical view of Soviet-style socialism expounded by the *berlingueriani.*

By way of contrast, as the post-Brezhnev succession process took its tortoiselike course, from Andropov to Chernenko to Gorbachev, precious little was known about the generation of Soviet cadres in their fifties, let alone those in their thirties and forties. There was much speculation regarding the reformist proclivities of Mikhail Gorbachev, himself only fifty-three but already the heir apparent to Chernenko when he attended Berlinguer's funeral. However, even under the best of circumstances—

6. This term (though not the interpretation that follows) is used by Giuseppe Are in "Il PCI come organismo politico," in ibid., 20–21.

that is, that Gorbachev would turn out to be a moderate (if more sophisticated) innovator in the mold of Khrushchev—there was not much likelihood of a change in Soviet policy toward Eastern Europe. History had
shown that the Soviet Union could not manage its client states; neither
could it let them go. It was Khrushchev, after all, who ordered tanks to
Budapest. But the forcible inclusion of Eastern Europe in the Soviet
Empire was a state of affairs the PCI would no longer condone. This was
the intractable obstacle to any real Soviet–PCI rapprochement.

BIBLIOGRAPHICAL ESSAY

The kind of sources used in this study vary substantially, depending on the time frame considered. The book is divided roughly into three periods: the years covered in Parts One and Two, from Togliatti's rise to the PCI leadership in 1926–27 until his return to Italy from exile in early 1944; the era of relative harmony between Moscow and the *partito nuovo* from the end of World War II until the late 1960s (Part Three); and the time of open Soviet–PCI tensions that began with the Warsaw Pact invasion of Czechoslovakia and continued until Berlinguer's death in June 1984 (Part Four).

Up through 1944 archival documentation is largely available for the Italian side of the story and that, in turn, illuminates the Soviet side, too. For the twenty-five years following World War II, much of our knowledge about the PCI and, to a lesser extent, its relations with the CPSU comes from two types of materials. The first consists of the numerous monographs written by English-speaking scholars whose research is based on the Soviet and PCI press, on field work and survey data in the case of Italy, and on the larger body of Western literature on postwar Soviet and Italian politics. The second type comprises memoirs and commentaries by Italian Communists.

For the last fifteen years of the book, the period of the escalating Soviet–PCI rift (1969–84), I relied almost entirely on the CPSU and PCI daily press and political journals. At the same time, my interpretation was facilitated by the surveys of the views and composition of PCI cadres and the studies of domestic Italian politics that proliferated in the 1970s and early 1980s. And I owe my grasp of post-1968 pan-European Communist affairs to scholars whose investigation of other Communist parties and issues paralleled my work on Moscow and the PCI.

From the Rise of Togliatti to the *Svolta* of Salerno

Communist Archives, Documents, and Other Primary Materials

The PCI Archives (*Archivio Partito Comunista*) provided my most important source for the period up until 1939. Photocopies of the originals are in the Gramsci Institute in Rome. By 1982 they were for the most part catalogued and accessible to independent scholars for the years 1921–45.

Beginning in the early 1960s archival materials began to be reprinted on a selective basis in the PCI's political weekly, *Rinascita*. Toward the end of the decade some documents also started appearing in the party's bimonthly journal, *Critica marxista,* and in its quarterly, *Studi storici.* By far the largest published collection from the PCI Archives is in the monumental *Opere* (Works) of Palmiro Togliatti, put out by Editori Riuniti in Rome between 1969 and 1979: *Opere 1921–1925* (1969), *Opere 1926–1929* (1972), *Opere 1929–1935,* two volumes (1973), and *Opere 1935–1944,* two volumes (1979). The volumes covering 1921–35 were edited by Ernesto Ragionieri and those covering 1935–44 were edited by Franco Andreucci and Paolo Spriano. Not only do most of Togliatti's writings and speeches that appear in them come from the archives, but excerpts from PCI meetings, correspondence, and other documents also abound in Ragionieri's and Spriano's lengthy introductions to the *Opere.*

The minutes of Central Committee and Politburo meetings have not been reprinted. Yet they provide the most important information on Soviet–PCI relations. However, the records of some important meetings are missing from the archives, for reasons that are not clear. And after 1938 the PCI's organizational disintegration and the geographical dispersion of its leaders precluded systematic record keeping.

From the overthrow of Mussolini through the *svolta* of Salerno and, indeed, until the end of World War II, the personal papers and correspondence of prominent PCI leaders therefore constitute our basic primary source. Foremost among these are Giorgio Amendola's *Lettere a Milano: Ricordi e documenti 1939–1945* (Rome: Editori Riuniti, 1974) and Luigi Longo's *I centri dirigenti del PCI nella Resistenza* (Rome: Editori Riuniti, 1974). A comparable collection of letters exchanged by leaders of the Pd'A—the Communists' arch collaborators-competitors during the wartime Resistance—is *Una lotta nel suo corso,* edited by Sandro Contini Bonacossi and Licia Ragghianti Collobi (Venice: Neri Pozza Editore, 1954). A large number of these items focus on relations with the PCI.

Similar collections of personal correspondence and papers augment the information in the PCI Archives for the pre-1939 period. The earliest volume of this type is Togliatti's *La formazione del gruppo dirigente del Partito comunista italiano* (Rome: Editori Riuniti, 1962). The most important and comprehensive of such works is Giuseppe Berti's edition of the archives of Angelo Tasca. This appears as the eighth volume of the *Annali* of the Giangiacomo Feltrinelli Institute (Milan: Feltrinelli Editore, 1966), and includes an introductory monograph by Berti entitled "Appunti e ricordi, 1919–1926." A number of useful letters are also available in Jules Humbert-Droz's *Il contrasto tra l'Internazionale e il PCI 1922–28* (Milan: Feltrinelli Editore, 1969).

As for other documentary materials, I made extensive use of the stenographic account of the PCI's June 1928 conference in Basel, Switzerland, *La Seconda Conferenza del Partito Comunista d'Italia (Resoconto stenografico)* (Paris: Edizioni del Partito Comunista d'Italia, June 1928), as well as *Il comunismo italiano nella seconda guerra mondiale: Relazione e documenti presentati dalla direzione del partito al V Congresso del Partito comunista italiano* (Rome: Editori Riuniti, 1963). I did likewise with regard to the Soviet accounts of the Seventh ECCI Plenum, *Puti mirovoi revoliutsii: stenograficheskii otchet* (Moscow, 1927), and the Sixth Comintern Congress, *VI kongress Kominterna: stenograficheskii otchet,* 6 vols. (Moscow, 1929). Even without access to the Comintern archives in Moscow, however, it was possible to establish cases where the official Soviet versions I have cited differed from the original stenographic accounts of the meetings (see, for example, pages 60–61 and 68–69 of chapter 2).

The PCI press during this period is not very important, both because of its sporadic, émigré character and because of the multitude of primary sources available. Note should nonetheless be taken of the party's political monthly, *Lo Stato operaio,* which was published in Paris from 1927 until the signing of the German–Soviet Non-Aggression Pact in 1939. Franco Ferri's two-volume anthology, *Lo Stato operaio, 1927–1939* (Rome: Editori Riuniti, 1964), is valuable, but it does not include any of the self-critical articles that came out after the Comintern–PCI clash of mid-1938. These latter pieces did appear in the 1939 pamphlet, *Unione del popolo italiano per il pane, la pace e la libertà: Documenti e direttive del PCI* (Paris: Edizioni di Cultura Sociale, 1939).

The Comintern press is, on the other hand, essential—if only because of its abundance and the paucity of other Soviet sources. The International's newssheet, published on a more or less weekly basis in the 1920s and 1930s, and its political-theoretical journal, published at first on a biweekly and in the end on a monthly or bimonthly basis, are equally important. I consulted the French and English versions of the former: *La Correspondance Internationale* and *International Press Correspondence* (*Inprecor,* for short). For the latter I invariably used the Russian version, *Kommunisticheskii Internatsional,* because of its authoritative nature and uninterrupted publication. It continued to come out until the dissolution of the Comintern.

Memoirs

Memoirs are by their nature subjective in the selection of and emphasis given to certain details. All the same, they can shed light on the circumstances or motives underlying political conduct. In the closed world of Communist decision making, this kind of information is particularly illuminating. In the first half of the book I benefited from the reminiscences of several former Communists. Among them were Jules Humbert-Droz's *Dix ans de lutte anti-fasciste: 1931–1941* (Neuchatel, Switzerland: Éditions de la Baconnière, 1972), *L'Internazionale comunista tra Lenin e Stalin: Memorie di un protagonista, 1891–1941* (Milan: Feltrinelli Editore, 1974), and *"L'Oeil de Moscou" à Paris* (Paris: Julliard, 1964); Ignazio Silone's much publicized *Uscita di sicurezza* (Rome: Associazione italiana per la libertà della cultura, 1955); and Ernst Fischer's *Ricordi e riflessioni* (Rome: Editori Riuniti, 1973). A number of memoirs by PCI members in good standing also contributed to my understanding of the pre-1945 history of Soviet–PCI relations. They include Camilla Ravera's *Diario di trent'anni, 1913–1943* (Rome: Editori Riuniti, 1973); Umberto Massola's *Memorie 1939–1941* (Rome: Editori Riuniti, 1972); Giulio Cerreti's *Con Togliatti e Thorez* (Milan: Feltrinelli Editore, 1973); and Gian Carlo Pajetta's *Il Ragazzo rosso* (Milan: Arnoldo Mondadori Editore, 1983).

Secondary Accounts

There are no scholarly studies of Soviet–PCI relations for the period from the mid-1920s to the mid-1940s. Treatments of the PCI's pre-1945 history touch perforce on the party's ties with the Comintern but for the most part only in passing after Gramsci's elevation to the leadership in 1924. The most comprehensive history of the PCI from its founding until the end of World War II is Paolo Spriano's masterful *Storia del Partito comunista italiano*, 5 vols. (Turin: Giulio Einaudi Editore, 1967–75). Spriano places the party's development in the broader context of Soviet, European, and Italian interwar and wartime history. However, he skirts or passes over lightly some key issues of Soviet–PCI relations, such as the Togliatti–Longo clash in the late 1920s and the Comintern's wartime national front strategy. The former lapse may be a result of the fact that his volume on the late 1920s appeared in 1969 when Longo was still general secretary and relations with Moscow had only begun to deteriorate. The latter lapse may be related to the fact that Spriano does not use Russian sources. Spriano became a member of the PCI Central Committee in 1972, after the publication of the first three volumes of his *Storia del Partito comunista italiano*.

Ernesto Ragionieri's monograph-length introductions to the first three of the Togliatti *Opere* cited above form in themselves a party history from a more narrow vantage point. With regard to Soviet–PCI relations, his interpretation suffers from some of the same flaws as Spriano's—and for the same reasons. His essays nevertheless provide a perceptive and fairly balanced political biography of Togliatti in the interwar years. Ragionieri was, like Spriano, a PCI member until his untimely death in 1978.

Giorgio Bocca's *Palmiro Togliatti* (Bari: Editori Laterza, 1973) is a more journalistic treatment of Togliatti's life, and Bocca approaches it from a non-Communist perspective. He bases much of his analysis on personal interviews with the party's historic leaders, thereby giving it a lively flavor. All too often, however, he neglects to consult the available primary documentation and thus sometimes raises more questions than he answers.

For the prewar period, among the few notable books in English are Charles F. Delzell's *Mussolini's Enemies: The Italian Anti-Fascist Resistance* (Princeton: Princeton University Press, 1961) and E. H. Carr's *Twilight of the Comintern, 1930–1935* (New York: Pantheon Books, 1982). The sections on the Comintern in Carr's multivolume *A History of Soviet Russia* are, of course, also important. Delzell deals with the PCI from a strictly Italian perspective, however, while Carr treats the Italian party as but a minor actor in the much vaster Communist world.

There is, finally, a large and diversified body of Italian literature on the wartime Resistance movement. The major PCI materials have already been mentioned. For the viewpoint of the Pd'A, I relied heavily on Leo Valiani's *Tutte le strade conducono a Roma* (Florence: La Nuova Italia, 1947) and Carlo Ludovico Ragghianti's *Disegno della liberazione italiana* (Pisa: Nistri-Lischi Editori, 1954). Also useful were the Socialist Oreste Lizzadri's *Il regno di Badoglio* (Milan: Edizioni Avanti, 1963), the centrist Franco Catalano's *Storia del CLNAI* (Bari: Editori Laterza, 1956), and CLN head and, briefly, premier Ivanoe Bonomi's Diario di un anno: 2 giugno 1943-10 giugno 1944 (Italy: Garzanti, 1947).

Moscow and the *Partito Nuovo*

The primary source for the study of Soviet–PCI relations between 1944 and the late 1960s is the PCI press. Italian Communist archival materials for this period are not accessible even to party scholars. In contrast to the Fascist era, however, the PCI's media proliferated after World War II. In 1944 *l'Unità* started daily publication, and Togliatti founded *Rinascita* as the party's theoretical monthly. In 1962 *Rinascita* was transformed into a political weekly, while *Critica marxista* was launched the following year as a bimonthly theoretical journal. Beginning with *VIII congresso del partito comunista italiano: Atti e risoluzioni* (Rome: Editori Riuniti, 1957), the complete stenographic accounts of PCI congresses were published regularly. Meanwhile, anthologies of Togliatti's major speeches and writings came out frequently. Particularly useful volumes of this type were *Politica Comunista (Discorsi dall'aprile 1944 all'agosto 1945)* (Rome: Società Editrice l'Unità, 1945) and *Problemi del movimento operaio internazionale, 1956–1961* (Rome: Editori Riuniti, 1962).

The memoirs and commentaries of PCI participants also continued to be important. Most notable in this regard are the archives of Pietro Secchia, which appeared as volume 19 of the Feltrinelli Institute's *Annali* (Milan: Feltrinelli Editore, 1979). Likewise valuable are Gian Carlo Pajetta's *Le crisi che ho vissuto: Budapest Praga Varsavia* (Rome: Editori Riuniti, 1982) and Carlo Galluzzi's *La svolta: Gli anni cruciali del Partito comunista italiano* (Milan: Sperling and Kupfer Editori, 1983). The collection of essays by leading party personalities in *Problemi di storia del Partito comunista italiano* (Rome: Editori Riuniti, 1973) represents a cross between personal reminiscence and detached analysis, and was a benchmark in the PCI's evolving sense of history.

Secondary accounts in the English language come to the forefront during this period, perhaps because in Italy the "Communist question" still remained too sensitive for dispassionate scholarly treatment. The indispensable work on Soviet–PCI relations from 1956 through 1964 remains Donald L. M. Blackmer's pioneering *Unity in Diversity: Italian Communism and the Communist World* (Cambridge, Mass.: MIT Press, 1968). For my understanding of the PCI in its domestic context the following studies also proved invaluable: Donald Sassoon's *The Strategy of the Italian Communist Party* (New York: St. Martin's, 1981); *Communism in Italy and France,* edited by Donald L. M. Blackmer and Sidney Tarrow (Princeton: Princeton University Press, 1975); Grant Amyot's *The Italian Communist Party: The Crisis of the Popular Front Strategy* (New York: St. Martin's, 1981); and *The Italian Communist Party: Yesterday, Today, and Tomorrow,* edited by Simon Serfaty and Lawrence Gray (Westport, Conn.: Greenwood, 1980). Giorgio Bocca's *Palmiro Togliatti,* cited above, was useful for the postwar period as well as for the pre-1945 years.

The Soviet–PCI Rift

Both the CPSU press and the PCI media provide the primary documentation for the analysis of the Soviet–PCI rift. The Italian Communist sources for the post-1969 period are very similar to those mentioned for the earlier postwar decades. The most important Soviet materials for our purposes are the CPSU daily, *Pravda;* the CPSU political-theoretical journal, *Kommunist; Rabochii klass i sovremennyi mir* (The Working Class and the Contemporary World), the bimonthly periodical of the Institute of the International Workers' Movement attached to the Soviet Academy of Sciences; *Voprosy istorii KPSS* (Questions of CPSU History), published by the CPSU Central Committee's Institute of Marxism-Leninism; *Problems of Peace and Socialism,* the Prague-based but Moscow-orchestrated international Communist monthly founded in 1958 to replace the defunct Cominform organ; and *New Times,* a Soviet foreign affairs weekly disseminated abroad in many languages, including Italian.

The events are too recent to lend themselves to the sort of memoirs available for the earlier periods of this book. On the other hand, by the late 1970s and early 1980s PCI policy makers were rather accessible and outspoken on questions of Soviet–PCI relations.

The character of the secondary accounts used in this section also changed. For one thing, Italian sources became much more important, especially with regard to survey data on the views and sociological make-up of middle-level PCI cadres. Three studies stand out in this regard: one by Marzio Barbagli and Piergiorgio Corbetta in *Il Mulino,* no. 260 (November–December 1978):922–67; Giuseppe Are, *Radiografia di un partito* (Milan: Rizzoli Editore, 1980); and *L'identità comunista: I militanti, le strutture, la cultura del Pci,* edited by Aris Accornero, Renato Mannheimer, and Chiara Sebastiani (Rome: Editori Riuniti, 1983).

For another thing, companion studies to my own were essential for the purpose of comparative analysis. Here Kevin Devlin's regular background reports on world Communist developments, written for Radio Free Europe–Radio Liberty in Munich, are far and away the most valuable source of information and insight. Likewise important are Eusebio Mujal-León's *Communism and Political Change in Spain* (Bloomington: Indiana University Press, 1983); *The European Left: Italy, France, and Spain,* edited by William E. Griffith (Lexington, Mass.: Lexington Books, 1979); and *Eurocommunism and Détente,* edited by Rudolf L. Tökés (New York: New York University Press, 1978). Useful background information on the domestic Italian scene appears in *Italy at the Polls: The Parliamentary Elections of 1976* and *Italy at the Polls, 1979,* edited by Howard R. Penniman (Washington, D.C.: American Enterprise Institute, 1977 and 1981). In citing these works, I do not mean to say that they are the only ones available but that they most influenced my thinking.

INDEX

Index

Index

Index